T0386758

The History and Natural History of
Spices

IAN ANDERSON

The History and Natural History of
Spices

The 5,000-Year
Search for Flavour

The
History
Press

Jacket illustrations
Front: Capsicum from *De historia stirpium commentarii insignes*, illustrated by Albrecht Meyer.
Back: Green peppercorns (author).

First published 2023
Reprinted 2024

The History Press
97 St George's Place, Cheltenham,
Gloucestershire, GL50 3QB
www.thehistorypress.co.uk

British Library Cataloguing in Publication Data.
A catalogue record for this book is available from the British Library.

ISBN 978 1 80399 156 6

Typesetting and origination by The History Press
Printed and bound in Great Britain by TJ Books Limited, Padstow, Cornwall.

Trees for LYfe

Contents

Contents

Introduction

The Allure of Spices and Botanical Origin

The appeal of spices lies in their strong flavours, aromas and colours. In the wild, these factors attract pollinators or defend the plant against predators, but for humans over the last four millennia, or perhaps longer, spices have been sought to add flavour and exoticism to bland and ordinary diets.[1] Many spices are restricted to exotic tropical climates, while others thrive in warm Mediterranean settings; they have all promised the hint of something special and unattainable, or only attainable with great difficulty and expense. In the classical Greek era, spices and herbs were sought after, acquired and studied primarily for their medicinal benefits, and this gradually evolved into the application to cuisine. So highly valued were spices from very early times, the so-called 'Spice Trade' developed, with dynamic networks that spanned South Asia to the Mediterranean from the late centuries BCE.[2] By the first century CE, the demand for spices as seasonings and flavourings in Roman society was huge, and vast sums of money were spent on large fleets importing black pepper from southern India via the Indian Ocean and Red Sea. But it wasn't only pepper they wanted: the kitchens of the upper echelons of Roman society were every bit as sophisticated as modern kitchens in their use of a huge variety of seasonings and condiments.

The nutritional value of spice is modest because of the tiny amounts used for seasoning food, so for millennia the demand for spice has been as a luxury commodity. The practicalities of importing spices from the East were a daunting and dangerous task, whether by sailing ships across the Indian Ocean – a round journey of many months – or by caravan overland along the myriad routings of the Silk Road or other trade routes.

But the continuing demand for spices always outweighed the risks. After the fall of the western Roman Empire, Arab and Byzantine traders ensured the continuing supply of spices to the West. The sources of the more exotic spices like nutmeg, mace and cloves were jealously guarded, and it wasn't until the early sixteenth century that the Portuguese became the first westerners to set foot on the remote Banda Islands, which were the only source of nutmeg. A century later, nutmeg commanded fabulous prices: 10lb of the spice could be bought for less than a penny in Banda and sold in London for £2 10s.[3] Vast fortunes were made by those fortunate to return home from the dangerous journeys, but the trade attracted violent competition between Spanish, Portuguese, Dutch and English, and many lives were lost to weather, shipwreck, war and disease. The search for spices in the fifteenth and sixteenth centuries, allied with political ambition, had led to Columbus' discovery of America (and by chance finding chili in Cuba and Hispaniola), Vasco da Gama's proving of the route to India around the coast of Africa, and Magellan's discovery of the western route to the Spice Islands. All of these incredible achievements had been driven by the huge potential rewards of the strong-flavoured little spices that were so much in demand in Europe.

The Meaning of 'Spice'

There is a need for definition, as spices have meant different things in different periods of history. 'Spice' is not a botanical term, but we can use botanical words to describe them. Today we might reasonably define a spice as the (usually) dried part of a plant used to season or flavour food, typically seeds, fruits, berries, roots, rhizomes, bark, flowers or buds, as opposed to the green leaves and stems. They are often, but not always, strongly aromatic. This is quite a good working definition, but it fails to include substances that have been referred to as spices in earlier times.

The earliest use of spices was for medicines, which then in many cases gradually evolved to culinary use. Black pepper is the best-known example, which became immensely popular for seasoning food from the start of Imperial Rome. Sugar had been used in the kitchen by Europeans since medieval times but only became commonplace in the sixteenth and seventeenth centuries; prior to that it was an exotic luxury spice. The aromatic resins of certain trees from the Middle East have been used as perfumes and as incense since the Bronze Age, and were also regarded as spices. In medieval times, not only did food have to be seasoned, but it also had to look the part, and in many cases this meant adding colour. Yellow was provided by saffron, egg yolk and later turmeric. Alkanet, the roots of a herb in the borage family, was used to add red, as was Red Sanders – an Indian tree that provided a red dye. Pink could come from rose petals and green from a variety of herbs. Turnesole, a plant of the spurge family, was used for purple or blue. (Even black and white were catered for: black by boiling or frying blood, and white from egg whites, crushed almonds and milk.) There was even a peculiar category of spices from animals; musk (from the caudal gland of the musk deer) and ambergris (from the digestive system of the sperm whale) were used both as perfumes and food flavourings.

Notwithstanding medicinal use, the common thing about all of these substances is that they were unassumed luxuries – and they had great value. The search for them was to change the world.

Botanical Classification of Spices

The turbulent world of plant taxonomy needs to be touched on briefly – and we need to do this to understand where spices come from.

The largest group of plants is the Angiosperms, the flowering plants, which first appeared in the Cretaceous period (*c.* 145 to 65 million years ago) and then spread extremely quickly. Most of the plants from which spices are derived, with a couple of exceptions, belong to the Angiosperms. It is certainly very interesting to see how spices group together within that large division (there are a total of 64 Orders and 416 Families of flowering plants in the latest APG IV classification). Table 1 on page 14 shows the broad relationship between ninety-six more or less well-known spice plants. Of the thirty-nine families illustrated, three are of particular interest; the Piperaceae (peppers), Apiaceae (coriander/parsley) and Zingiberaceae (ginger) families each contain many different spices (only the ten most important are shown in the table). While this is of general interest in the context of popular spices, it may not amount to much in the wider sense in that there are likely very large numbers of plant species that might be considered 'spices' that occupy many different taxa. For example, just the Lamiaceae (mint family) contains around 7,000 species including numerous popular herbs and aromatic plants; the Asteraceae have over 30,000 species.

The quandary of which spices to include and which to leave out reaches a head in this chapter. Spices have already been defined, so ostensibly this should be relatively straightforward. But consider the Piperaceae family: it encompasses approximately 3,600 species, 'approximately' because new species are frequently found, others may be disputed, and so on. Furthermore, most of those species occur within the *Piper* genus. Also, should I include obscure species that may be used as a seasoning by an indigenous population dwelling in the rainforest, or restrict the species to the economically important ones? (Answer: I hedged and focused on the most important ones but also included mention of some lesser-known types.) What about species used for traditional medicines (of which there are many)? Many of the well-known spices used today were initially used as medicines by the ancient Greeks and later, before being adapted for use in the kitchen. I've covered both, but with an emphasis on culinary. Some spices have close relatives that are not pungent or aromatic – should they be included? Well, no, not really: I have omitted celeriac (definitely a vegetable), which is a variety of celery (vegetable and herb, and the seeds are a spice) and this has been included. Herbs themselves should also be considered – 'herb' is another imprecise catch-all term generally meaning small, non-woody, aromatic plants with culinary or medicinal uses that die back in the winter. Herbs and herbal remedies are referred to in numerous instances in the book, even though this is not the main focus. How about *Piper methysticum*, the root of which is used to make the well-known stimulant drink 'kava kava' of the Pacific Islands? (It's not strictly a spice, though it does have a certain pungency, but I've included it for its interesting and unusual nature.) Other questions lingered around spices used as food colourings, vegetables such as garlic and mustard (pungent seasonings), pomegranate seeds (a spice in Indian cuisine); all were included. Conversely, chia, flax, quinoa, pine nuts, etc., were excluded as they are neither aromatic nor pungent.

The geographic distribution of native species (i.e. those that have not been introduced through the intervention of humans) is also very interesting, though there is usually significant uncertainty regarding their precise geographic origin. When fifty-five of the better-known spice plants are plotted on a map in their approximate native position, the distribution is complex (Figure 1). But concentrating on two important botanic families only, then two clear geographic groupings appear: one in the Mediterranean–Middle East area, dominated by the Apiaceae, and the other in south and Southeast Asia, dominated by the Zingiberaceae (Figure 2). Latitude appears to be important – one group is largely temperate and the other largely tropical. The distribution of native species is a snapshot of the relatively recent historic past, i.e. a few thousand years BCE and in most cases bears little relation to the distribution in the distant geologic past.

To look further back into that geologic past can at first be somewhat daunting and confusing. There are fossil records of tropical plants now situated in distinctly temperate climates and vice versa, i.e. temperate plant fossils now situated in tropical settings. The key to understanding this state of affairs is the realisation that the continents themselves are not fixed but have moved vast distances across the earth over geologic time by the process of continental drift.

At the start of the Mesozoic era, a little over 250 million years ago, the world was dominated by a single super-continent, named Pangaea. In fact, this continent had already been in existence for about 100 million years at that point in geologic time. Pangaea later split into two large continents, the northern Laurasia and the southern Gondwanaland (see the maps on p. 17).

The Apiaceae family appears to have originated in the Australasia region in the Late Cretaceous, at around 87 Ma.[4] This was after the southern supercontinent Gondwanaland had started breaking up. The Apiaceae spices all belong to the Apioideae subfamily, which seems to have appeared in southern Africa, having made an ancestral jump from Australasia while it was still relatively near. To confuse things even more, the true geographic origins of many commonly known species are only doubtfully known – according to Reduron, this is the case for ajowan, anise, coriander, cumin, dill, fennel and parsley – because they have been used since ancient times, being exchanged, cultivated, etc., and generally moved around, making it impossible to trace them. So-called wild populations may have been plants escaped from cultivation and then naturalised. Could early humans, moving northwards from their origins in East Africa, have helped move these attractive and aromatic fruits with them (by natural ingestion/expulsion)? Possibly, though other animals could also have transported them. So the location of certain prominent native Apiaceae spices, as shown in Figure 2, needs to be taken with a pinch of salt (if you'll pardon the expression). However, in broad terms it seems fair to assess their native region, i.e. not long before the domestication of crops, say 9,000–10,000 BCE, as the Med–Middle East–North

Africa. Today the Apiaceae have a global distribution, but many of the herbaceous genera seem to belong to this region.

With regard to the Zingiberaceae family, we'll take a closer look at the Indian subcontinent, which certainly punches above its weight considering both the large number of spices that thrive there in the present day and the diversity of native species. The ginger family is native to the region, and yet the parent order, Zingiberales, originated in Gondwanaland at around 124 Ma in the Early Cretaceous period.[5] India was part of this southern supercontinent, together with South America, Africa, Antarctica and Australia. Gondwanaland had already started to break up by this time. The Zingiberaceae family split from its close relation the Costaceae at around 105 Ma (the latter became well represented in the Americas), probably before the final break-up of Gondwanaland. The continental fragments were still probably close enough to allow dispersal. India, together with its precious 'cargo' of the ginger family, drifted northwards and finally collided with Asia. The Zingiberaceae became highly diversified and dominant in India and Southeast Asia (53 genera/1,200 species). What about *Aframomum melegueta* (grains of paradise), the ginger family spice that is endemic to West Africa? Well, Africa was also part of Gondwanaland, where the Zingiberaceae originated; however, the genus possibly didn't diversify until the Pleistocene, around 2.7 million years ago, i.e. very recently in geological terms.[6]

The Piperaceae are unusual for different reasons: the approximately 3,600 species referred to earlier mostly occur within just two genera: *Piper* and *Peperomia*. The present distribution is pan-tropical with four main centres of origin: the Neotropics (i.e. the tropical parts of the Americas and Caribbean); Southeast and South Asia; Africa; and the Pacific Islands (Figure 3). Molecular dating suggests a Late Cretaceous age for the origin of the two main genera, though it appears that the current species distribution is a result of much later divergence in the Tertiary.[7] The genus *Piper* appears to have originated in the Neotropics before dispersal to the other areas. Radiation/speciation has occurred in

Table 1 | Taxonomy of Some Well-Known Spice Plants

ORDER	FAMILY	GENUS/SPECIES			
Apiales	Apiaceae	**Cumin** (*Cuminum cyminum*)	**Coriander** (*Coriander sativum*)	**Bishops Weed / Ajowan** (*Trachyspermum ammi*)	**Aniseed** (*Pimpinella anisum*)
	Araliaceae	**Ginseng** (*Panax ginseng*)			
Zingiberales	Zingiberaceae	**Cardamom** (*Eletterria cardamomum*, *Amomum* sp.)	**Ginger** (*Zingiber officinale*)	**Turmeric** (*Curcuma longa*)	**Zedoary** (*Curcuma zedoaria*)
	Marantaceae	**Arrowroot** (*Maranta arundinacea*)			
Piperales	Piperaceae	**Black Pepper** (*Piper nigrum*)	**Cubeb Pepper** (*Piper cubeba*)	**Long Pepper** (*Piper longum*)	**Ashanti Pepp** (*P guineense*)
Solanales	Solanaceae	**Chili** (*Capsicum* sp.★)	**Kutjera** (*Solanum centrale*)	**Wolfberry** (*Lycium barbarum*/ *L. chinense*)	**Lycium** (*Lycium* sp.)
Laurales	Lauraceae	**Cinnamon** (*Cinnamomum verum*, *C. cassia, C. burmanii, C. loureroi*, others)	**Camphor** (*Cinnamomum camphora*)	**Malabathrum** (*Cinnamomum malabathrum, C. tamala*)	**Sassafras** (*Sassafras albidum*)
Myrtales	Myrtaceae	**Cloves** (*Syzygium aromaticum*)	**Aniseed Tree** (*Syzygium anisatum*)	**Indian Bayleaf** (*Syzygium polyanthum*)	**Allspice** (*Pimenta dioica*)
	Combretaceae	**Myrobalan** (*Terminalia* sp.)	**Kakadu Plum** (*Terminalia ferdinandiania*)		
	Lythraceae	**Pomegranate** (*Punica granatum*)			
Fabales	Fabaceae	**Fenugreek** (*Trigonella foenum-graecum*)	**Liquorice** (*Glycyrrhiza glabra*)	**Red Saunders** (*Pterocarpus santolinus*)	**Tamarind** (*Tamarindus ind*)
Asparagales	Amaryllidaceae	**Garlic** (*Allium sativum*)	**Jimbu** (*Allium wallichii*)		
	Iridaceae	**Saffron** (*Crocus sativus*)			
	Orchidaceae	**Vanilla** (*Vanilla planifolia*)			
	Asparagaceae	**Dragon's Blood**★★ (*Dracaena* sp.)		★★ also *Daemonorops* and other genera	
Brassicales	Brassicaceae	**Mustard** (*Brassica nigra, B. juncea, Sinapis alba*)	**Horseradish** (*Armoracia rusticana*)	**Wasabi** (*Eutrema japonicum*)	
	Capparaceae	**Caper** (*Capparis spinosa*)			
Magnoliales	Myristicaceae	**Nutmeg** (*Myristica fragrans*)	**Mace** (*Myristica fragrans*)		

Angiosperms

foetida (‍ula sp.)	Dill (*Anethum graveolens*)	Caraway (*Carum carvi*)	Celery (*Apium graveolens*)	Fennel (*Foeniculum vulgare*)	Parsley (*Petroselinum crispum*)
ngo Ginger (rcuma amada)	Grains of Paradise (*Aframomum melegueta*)	Korarima (*Aframomum corrorima*)	Galangal (*Alpinia* sp., others)	Torch Ginger (*Etlingera elatior*)	Chinese Keys (*Boesenbergier rotunda*)
va Kava (‍per hysticum)	Rough-leaved Pepper (*Piper amalago*)	African Long Pepper (*Piper capense*)	Chui Jhal Pepper (*Piper chaba*)	Spiked Pepper (*Piper aduncum*)	Hoja Santa (*Piper auritum*)

ote there are five domesticated species of *Capsicum*

Angiosperms	Ranunculales	Ranunculaceae	**Nigella** (*Nigella sativa*)			
		Papaveraceae	**Poppy** (*Papaver somniferum*)			
	Sapindales	Rutaceae	**Fagara** (*Zanthoxylum* sp.)	**Sansho Pepper** (*Zanthoxylum piperitum*)	**Black Lime** (*Citrus aurantifolia*)	**Chenpi** (*Citrus reticulata*)
		Anacardiaceae	**Sumac** (*Rhus* sp.)	**Charoli** (*Buchanania lanzan*)	**Amchoor** (*Mangifera* sp.)	**Mastic** (*Pistacia lentiscus*)
		Burseraceae	**Bdellium** (*Commiphora wightii*)	**Myrrh** (*Commiphora* sp.)	**Frankincense** (*Boswellia* sp.)	
	Malpighiales	Clusiaceae	**Kokum** (*Garcinia indica*)	**Malabar Tamarind** (*Garcinia gummi-gutta*)	**Asam Gelugur** (*Garcinia atroviridis*)	
		Euphorbiaceae	**Candlenut** (*Aleurites moluccanus*)	**Njangsa** (*Ricinodendron heudelotii*)		
	Malvales	Malvaceae	**Roselle** (*Hibiscus sabdariffa*)	**Cacao** (*Theobroma cacao*)		
		Bixaceae	**Annatto Seeds** (*Bixa Orellana*)			
	Santalales	Santalaceae	**Sandalwood** (*Santalum album*)	**Desert Quandong** (*Santalum acuminatum*)		
	Lamiales	Pedaliaceae	**Sesame** (*Sesamum indicum*)			
	Austrobaileyales	Schisandraceae	**Star Anise** (*Illicium verum*)			
	Dipsacales	Caprifoliaceae	**Spikenard** (*Nardostachys jatamansi*)			
	Rosales	Roseaceae	**Mahleb** (*Prunus mahaleb*)			
	Asterales	Asteraceae	**Costus** (*Saussurea costus*)			
		Campanulaceae	**Dorají** (*Platycodon grandiflorus*)			
	Ericales	Styracaceae	**Benzoin/Storax** (*Styrax* L.)			
	Boraginales	Boraginaceae	**Alkanet** (*Alkanna tinctoria*)			
	Canellales	Winteraceae	**Dorrigo Pepper** (*Tasmannia stipitata*)			
Gymnosperms	Conifers	Cupressaceae	**Juniper** (*Juniperus* sp.)			
	Ginkgoales	Ginkgoaceae	**Ginkgo** (*Ginkgo biloba*)			

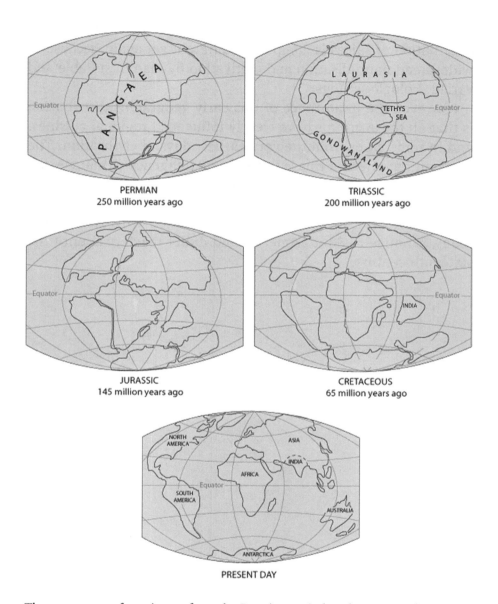

PERMIAN
250 million years ago

TRIASSIC
200 million years ago

JURASSIC
145 million years ago

CRETACEOUS
65 million years ago

PRESENT DAY

The movement of continents from the Permian period to the present day. Note the separation of the Indian subcontinent from Gondwanaland and northwards movement towards Asia, where collision started around 50 million years ago, causing the uplift of the Himalayas.

the Neotropics, Asia and the Pacific, but the species-poor Africa (there are only two native species of *Piper* in the entire continent) appears to be the result of much later introductions. The present distribution of spices is completely different yet again because of widespread naturalisation and cultivation by man in suitable and varied ecologic settings.

However, the importance of this early geographic distribution is that all these groups have clearly influenced regional cuisines, and in some cases from the very earliest days of civilisation. The concomitant effect of this is the extreme pungency of many Asian and Southeast Asian cuisines compared with the milder aromatic cuisines of the Middle East and Mediterranean. *Capsicum* spp. (chili), however, although widely associated with Asian food today, is native to South America and didn't reach Asia until the sixteenth century.

1

Botanists, Physicians and Geographers: The Pioneers

The men who first described plants and spices and the countries they came from often got their geography wrong, as they frequently relied on hearsay and their world was poorly understood. However, when they had direct access to plants, their descriptions were often sophisticated and accurate. The main reason for these studies was to catalogue an array of medicines, as that is how most spices were originally used. These early scientists were often, but not exclusively, Greek and Roman. The geographers themselves were a mixture of theoreticians and adventurers. One thing that unites them all is their enormous level of achievement: many were polymaths and made huge discoveries in differing fields of expertise, while others were specialists and prolific writers; each has become legendary, and justifiably so.

Anonymous Author of Ebers Papyrus

The Ebers Papyrus is an Egyptian hieratic scroll that was written c. 1550 BCE. The papyrus came to light in 1872 when Georg Ebers, a German Egyptologist excavating in the vicinity of Thebes, was approached by a wealthy Egyptian offering the document for sale. It was duly acquired and spirited away to the University of Leipzig, where it still resides. The scroll is a medical text that is mainly devoted to the medicinal treatment of disease, but with some detail given to cosmetics! There is a total of 811 prescriptions written down, some simple, some complex. If that sounds like a lot, the scroll measured 68ft in length by 1ft in width (unfortunately it was cut up into pages at Leipzig to make it easier to study). Many of the prescriptions are, with today's perspective, bizarre. Simple remedies of this category include 'old book cooked in oil', 'the film of dampness which is found on the wood of ships', 'rotted cereals', blood, bile, excrement and urine! Consequently, some of the compounds are interesting (e.g. a worm-cake to treat tapeworm comprising herbs-of-the-field and natron, baked into a cake with cow's bile).[1] Incantations were often part of various treatments.

There are 119 plant remedies, of which around thirty could be deemed herbs or spices, plus many mineral and animal remedies. The more recognisable spices and herbs include acanthus, aloes, balsam, caraway seed, coriander, fennel, juniper berries, peppermint, poppy seeds and saffron.

Many of the remedies described in the papyrus had probably been used for hundreds of years already; despite their strangeness, we can see the start of a pharmacopoeia, which would become much more logical, scientific and effective over the course of the succeeding millennium.

Sushruta (c. Eighth Century BCE)

Sushruta was an Indian physician and surgeon, possibly descended from the legendary sage Vishvamitr.[2] His compendium, the *Sushruta Samhita*, is one of the foundations of Ayurvedic medicine. His specialism was surgery, amazingly advanced for the period, but the book also lists some 700 medicinal plants and their properties. It comprises 186 chapters in six main volumes. Volume 1 Chapter 46 covers food and drink; a long description of grains, meats from wild and domestic animals, fruits, vegetables, etc., is followed by a list of culinary herbs and spices including the relatively well-known sesame, white and red mustard seeds, long pepper, black pepper, ginger, asafoetida, cumin, coriander seed, holy basil, common basil, lemongrass, cassia, sweet basil, brown and black mustard, radish, garlic and onion, as well as more obscure types. Many of these are known to be used in herbal medicines – possibly spreading sneezeweed (*Centipeda minima*), drumstick plant (*Moringa oleifera*), Mullein (a species of *Verbascum*), Himalayan poplar (bark is a useful medicine), gandira (possibly *Coleus forskohlii* Briq., the dried mature roots of which are an aromatic herb), red sanders or pot herb *Cleome gynandra*, purnava (*Boerhaavia diffusa* Linn.), chitrak (the dried root of *Plumbago zeylanica*), and grass pea, *Lathyrus sativus*. The identification of some of the plants named and described in the treatise is not always clear!

In addition to the above, there is a huge list of edible plants, trees, pot herbs, flowers and bulbs, together with descriptions of their taste, digestibility, heating/cooling effect, effect on the Ayurvedic forces (Vayu, Pittam and Kapham) and curative powers.

The book was a huge undertaking and very sophisticated for its era. It has gone through many redactions over its long history. The oldest surviving manuscript may be a palm leaf document that dates to 878 CE, preserved in a library in Nepal.

Valmiki
(no specific dates but within period 500 BCE–100 BCE)

The epic *Ramayana* poem was written by Valmiki, the name adopted by Agni Sharma after being blessed and rechristened by sages. He is revered as the first Hindu poet. The *Ramayana* comprises around 480,000 words and tells the story of Rama, a Hindu deity. The poem refers to over 100 plants, trees and herbs.[3] Herbs, spices, fruits and their sources include ajowan, agarwood, Indian lotus, myrobalan, castor oil plant, neem, Indian jujube, Dragon's Blood, elephant apple, bastard mryobalan, citron, ivy gourd, champak, pomegranate, phalsa, cluster fig, Egyptian balsam, Malabar plum, royal jasmine, saffron crocus, cotton tree, kachnar, karira, camphor tree, wild sugarcane, screw-pine, pithraj tree, Lodh tree, madhuka, mogra, black pepper, Ceylon ironwood, burflower tree, wild Himalayan cherry, white fig, holy basil, charoli, Indian frankincense, field mustard, Indian sandalwood, toddy palm, Himalayan Garcinia, sesame and wax gourd. Many of the plants have value in traditional Ayurvedic medicine.

Hippocrates (460–370 BCE)

Hippocrates is widely recognised today as the 'father of medicine'. He was born on the Aegean island of Kos to a wealthy family, where his father was a physician. He is said to have learned medicine from his father and grandfather and other notable physicians, e.g. Herodicus. He almost certainly studied at the Askleipion (healing temple) of Kos. Askleipions were commonplace in Greece, with several hundred known to have existed – they operated in a similar fashion to the health spas of today, with emphasis on rest, diet and baths. Most of the information we have about Hippocrates himself comes from his earliest biographer, Soranus, a second-century CE Greek physician, with further information from the much later Suidas and Tzetzes.[4]

We know from the above that Hippocrates travelled widely across Greece and that he was sufficiently well regarded for his medical expertise to be sought after by the King of Macedonia (Perdiccas) and the King of Persia (Artaxerxes). Two contemporaries certainly knew of him: Plato referred to him as Hippocrates Asclepiad, using a Greek medical title, and his fame was recognised by Aristotle, who referred to him as 'The Great Hippocrates'. Plato (in Phaedrus) stated a basic principle of Hippocratic medicine was that understanding of the body required understanding of nature as a whole. In fact, Hippocrates is credited with bringing disease out of the shadow of the supernatural and into the light of rational thought, where he regarded it as a natural phenomenon.

The main work that bears his name is the Hippocratic Corpus, a collection of about sixty medical treatises that was certainly the work of several, or even many, different authors, and probably spanning several centuries. The authorship of Hippocrates himself to any of these is unproven, but most scholars agree that a dozen or so of the collection might be ascribed to him.

His approach seems aptly summed up by the following: 'The body's nature is the physician in disease. Nature finds the way for herself, not from thought.'[5]

This is not to say that medicines, drugs, 'recipes', etc., were not used. Where medicines were used, spices and herbs were often part of the prescription. In *Regimen in Acute Diseases*, for example, black hellebore was mixed with cumin, anise, euphorbia, juice of silphium to soften the bowel;[6] in *Epidemics* spodium (burned bone), saffron, stone of a fruit, white lead and myrrh were mixed together for an eye condition;[7] saffron and beans or beans with cumin are used against upset intestines;[8] ground Egyptian nitre, coriander and cumin were used as a pessary to stimulate conception;[9] cumin and egg in broth helped alleviate chest pain;[10] Ethiopian cumin in wine and honey linctus for a breathing problem.[11] Many other examples illustrate the use of spices for medicinal means in the time of Hippocrates; most of these are from plants more or less locally available, and a few are exotics from the Far East, e.g. pepper and castorium solution to relieve toothache,[12] cardamom, cucumber and opium to treat fever an intestinal problem.[13] L. M. V. Totelin listed exotic ingredients of the Hippocratic Corpus, many from the gynaecological treatises, which included amomum, galbanum, sweet flag, cardamom, cassia, cinnamon, safflower, frankincense, spikenard, pepper, sumac, sagapenum, ginger grass, silphium, myrrh, styrax, terebinth (resin from the *Pistacia* tree), saffron and cumin.[14]

Treatment was generally passive, however, with rest and simple treatments typical. Many case histories were accumulated in the Corpus which helped in prognosis of disease. The passive concept is illustrated by the instruction in *Epidemics* I, as good advice today as then: 'Declare the past, diagnose the present, foretell the future; practise these acts. As to diseases, make a habit of two things – to help, or at least, to do no harm.'[15]

Theophrastus (370–285 BCE)

Born in the year of Hippocrates' death, Theophrastus was a Greek scholar who was a student of Plato and Aristotle, and is often regarded as the 'father of botany' because of his pioneering work on plants. Most of what we know about him comes from Diogenes Laertius' *Lives of the Philosophers*, written sometime in the first half of the third century CE. Theophrastus is actually a nickname given to him by Aristotle, meaning 'divine phrase' on account of the skill and rich beauty of his conversation; his formal name was Tyrtamus. After Aristotle's departure, he took over as head of the Lyceum in Athens and its 'Peripatetic School' of philosophers (a large school of some 2,000 students), staying in that position for thirty-six years. (It was called the Peripatetic School because of Aristotle's charming habit of walking while he was giving lectures, presumably in groups smaller than 2,000.) The remains of the Lyceum were discovered as recently as 1996 in a park near the modern Hellenic Parliament building, though it was originally outside of Athens' city wall, and is now open to the public.

Aristotle and Theophrastus were firstly both students of Plato, Aristotle being some fifteen years older – not a huge age difference – and they appear to have been close friends. When Aristotle died, he bequeathed his books and his garden in the grounds of the Lyceum to his old friend. Like his mentor, Theophrastus was a prolific writer – Diogenes credited him with 227 works, most of which have sadly been lost or are only fragmentary. His work covered a very wide variety of subjects – politics, philosophy, botany, mathematics, rhetoric, law, astronomy, logic, geology, history, physics – in other words he was a true polymath. His greatest contributions, however, were in natural history, and the two main botanical works, which are almost complete, are the nine books of *Enquiry into Plants* and the six books of *On the Causes of Plants*.

Apart from being friends with Aristotle and Plato, Theophrastus also lived in the same era as Philip of Macedon and his son, Alexander the Great. Aristotle was appointed tutor to Alexander in 343 BCE and so would have been known to Theophrastus. The significance of these relationships is that when Alexander marched on the East, he took with him trained observers and the results were available to Aristotle and Theophrastus.[16] So, the exotic spices later described by Theophrastus would have been either brought back to Greece, or their descriptions brought back, to be included in his botanical treatises.

As regards the main botanical works, he was the first to attempt a classification of plants, his main groups being trees, shrubs, under-shrubs and herbs. He described about 500 species. That may not sound like many given that there are now estimated to be over 390,000 species known globally, but at that period in history it was a huge undertaking. It also stood the test of time: it was to be another 1,800 years before any significant botanical advances were made. He described many important spices: alexanders, asafoetida, cardamom, cassia, cinnamon, coriander, cumin, dill, fenugreek, frankincense, galingale, ginger grass, juniper, liquorice, mustard, parsley, pepper, saffron, sesame, silphium, spikenard, sumac and tamarind. Of these, several were from the tropical East (cardamom, cassia, cinnamon, galingale, pepper and spikenard) and must have been collected or traded by Alexander's armies or reached Greece via ancient overland trade routes. The descriptions of cinnamon and cassia, for example, are clearly second-hand, with 'various accounts' given of their occurrence, at least one of which he acknowledged as implausible.[17]

Theophrastus lived a long and productive life, finally dying around the age of 85. He is purported to have lamented, 'We die just when we are beginning to live.'[18]

Megasthenes (350–290 BCE)

Megasthenes was a Greek historian, explorer, ambassador and chronicler most famous for his accounts of India in his book *Indika*, of which only fragments found in works by later writers remain. The classic English translation of an earlier compilation of fragments was produced by J. W. McCrindle in the nineteenth century.[19]

Megasthenes was sent by Seleukos Nikator (former general under Alexander and subsequent founder of the Seleucid Empire) on an embassy to the Mauryan King Sandrakottos (Chandragupta). He appears to have been based in Arachosia (an area in the vicinity of modern Kandahar, Afghanistan), from where he made frequent visits to Sandrakottos. He was referred to by Arrian, Pliny and Strabo, though the exact timing of his visits is not clear – they possibly started around 302 BCE. The veracity of his accounts was called into question by Eratosthenes, Strabo and Pliny, but he is now generally regarded as an important and mainly reliable source about India in that era. The most troublesome passages are those that describe certain races, which are plainly absurd, e.g. a race with their feet back-to-front, mouthless peoples who sustain themselves by vapours from roasted meats and fruits, people who have ears that extend to their feet, etc.[20]

His description of the Suppers of the Indians in Fragment XXVIII can surely be interpolated as an early account of rice and curry:

And Megasthenes, in the second book of his Indian History, says – 'Among the Indians at a banquet a table is set before each individual; and it is like a sideboard or beaufet; and on the table is placed a golden dish, in which they throw first of all boiled rice, just as if a person were going to boil groats, and then they add many sorts of meat dressed after the Indian fashion.'[21]

Fragment XLI lists plants that grow in the mountainous land (presumably northern India), including laurel (could include cinnamon, malabathrum and camphor), myrtles (could include Indian bay leaf and myrobalan), box-tree and other evergreens, 'none of which are found beyond the Euphrates'.[22] He described Brahmins, who 'abstained from hot and highly seasoned food'.

In Fragment LVI, several trade emporia are described, e.g. the Cape of Perimula, 'where there is the greatest emporium of trade in India', and Automela (possibly in Gujurat).[23] In this section, Megasthenes, via Pliny, appears to be describing the area around the Gulf of Cambay, which McCrindle notes was the chief seat of Indian trade with the West, which was monopolised by the port of Barygaza.

Eratosthenes (276–194 BCE)

Eratosthenes was a Greek astronomer, geographer and mathematician who was born in Cyrene (in modern Libya). He studied in Athens, where he wrote several poems and historical works, and subsequently moved to Alexandria at the age of 30 to work at the library (the most important such institution of the ancient world) at the invitation of Ptolemy III. He spent the remainder of his life there. After a few years, he was elevated to the position of Chief Librarian. While he was there, he studied and wrote scholarly works in several different fields; all have been lost, but we know of the breadth of his endeavours due to numerous references by succeeding scholars. His three-volume work *Geography* was of huge importance – he perceived the earth to be a globe, devised and used a system of latitudes and meridians to describe it, and calculated the circumference of the earth to be 250,000 stadia (there were 8 stadia to the Roman mile), remarkably close to the actual measurement. Unfortunately, none of his works survived to the present day, but there are over 150 fragments preserved through other authors. In the last years of his life he became blind, which left him unable to study and so depressed him that he ultimately starved himself to death.

Strabo (64 BCE–24 CE)

Strabo, also a Greek geographer, became most famous for his seventeen-volume work *Geographica*. He was born in Amasya (in modern Turkey) to a wealthy and well-connected family. He moved to Rome around the age of 19 or 20 (44 BCE) and studied under Tyrannion, a distinguished geographer, and several other prominent teachers.[24] He also knew Posidonius, another geographer and polymath. He may have stayed in Rome for many years – he was certainly there in 35 BCE and in 31 BCE and visited again in 29 BCE. He travelled widely (for the time): he was in Egypt from 25 to 20 BCE, evidently based in Alexandria; there he sailed up the Nile as far as Philae (Aswan area) and the frontiers of Ethiopia in 25 BCE, then travelled to various locations in Asia Minor, the shores of the Euxine (Black Sea) and Beirut in Syria. His final visit to Rome was around 7 BCE and he may have spent the last twenty-six or twenty-seven years of his life in his native Amasya.

We are mainly interested in Strabo here for his *Geographica*, the greater part of which was probably written before 7 BCE. He probably used his time in Alexandria to research information in the Great Library, one of the most important such institutions of the ancient world. Strabo's world, or rather his view of the world, was substantially narrower than the reality we know today. Africa (largely limited to 'Libya' and adjoining areas) was much smaller, Asia only extended as far as India, and Europe is only recognisable in the Mediterranean area; there was nothing else. Eurasia, and North Africa reduced to a small continent: this was the extent of the Graeco-Roman world. Fifteen of the seventeen books cover specific regions and half of those are focused on Mediterranean countries. He typically describes the places, peoples, products and a little of the history, which often reverts to legend and myth, a good part of it implausible to a twenty-first-century reader. He praises certain earlier geographers, but totally disregards others: 'Still, while many are beneath discussion, such men as Eratosthenes, Posidonius, Hipparchus, Polybius, and others of their stamp, deserve our highest consideration.' However, even these worthies were not exempt from severe criticism.[25]

He draws heavily on Alexander's great expedition to Asia and on the discussion of India, but there is little else. Curiously, there is no mention of black pepper, let alone its provenance, despite his acknowledgement that 120 ships were leaving Myos Hormos annually for India (mainly for the spice trade).[26] Despite this and other shortcomings, his voluminous work is impressive in coverage and provides by far the best understanding of the world in his era.

Aulus Cornelius Celsus (*c.* 25 BCE–*c.* 50 CE)

A near contemporary of Strabo, Celsus was a Roman writer on medicine and was probably himself a physician; however, details of his life are scant. He hails from the time of the early Roman Empire, though his exact dates are uncertain. His famous surviving treatise on medicine, *De Medicina*, is a single volume of an originally much larger work, with eight constituent books. In the later chapters in Book II, he has much to say about food, e.g. those that are hurtful to the stomach, those that heat and cool ('Heat is excited by pepper, salt … garlick, onion, dry figs, salt fish, wine which is the more heating, the stronger it is'), soporifics, diuretics ('The urine is promoted by whatever grows in the garden of a good smell, as smallage, rue, dill, basil, mint, hyssop, anise, coriander, cresses, rocket, fennel'), etc.[27] Book III deals with various remedies for fevers and other ailments and includes many herbal remedies, mainly using locally available medicines, i.e. from within the Mediterranean area. Book IV deals with treatments of illnesses of different parts of the body, again using many herbal remedies. Books V and VI are devoted to pharmacology and contain a vast array of medicines, including many exotics from the Far East – cardamom, nard, costus, cinnamon, cassia, bdellium, sesame, black pepper, long pepper, white pepper, amomum, malabathrum, sweet flag, ginger – as well as the Arabian peninsula and Horn of Africa – frankincense, myrrh, aloe, gum arabic, tragacanth, balsam, opopanax and sandarac. The number and variety of more local herbs and spices is even greater. Poppy tears, i.e. opium, are commonly part of the treatment, a useful drug in an era devoid of painkillers but with much suffering. The overall impression of the works of Celsus is that medicine of the Roman era was more effective and sophisticated than we may care to give credit for, despite a crude level of knowledge of anatomy and physiology compared with today. The huge array of herbal remedies that could be brought to bear was impressive, and in this we can clearly see the early motivation for import and use of exotic spices.

Antonius Castor (First Century CE)

Castor was an eminent Roman botanist who was known for his huge botanical garden. Pliny refers to him several times, and he was one of Pliny's sources on botanical matters. Pliny on Castor:

> Nor is this a kind of knowledge by any means difficult to obtain; at all events, so far as regards myself, with the exception of a very few, it has been my good fortune to examine them all, aided by the scientific researches of Antonius Castor, who in our time enjoyed the highest reputation for an intimate acquaintance with this branch of knowledge. I had the opportunity of visiting his garden, in which, though he had passed his hundredth year, he cultivated vast numbers of plants with the greatest care. Though he had reached this great age, he had never experienced any bodily ailment, and neither his memory nor his natural vigour had been the least impaired by the lapse of time.[28]

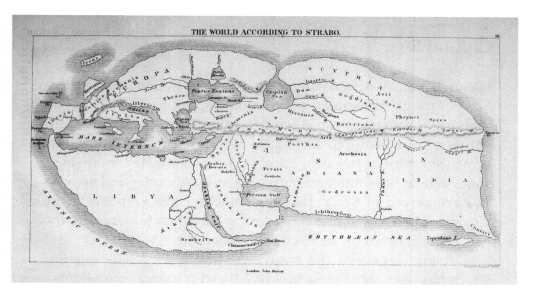

A nineteenth-century reconstruction of Strabo's world map. (Edward Bunbury, 1883) The Mediterranean area and parts of the Middle East are quite recognisable today, but the distortion of the known world is very marked at its peripheries.[29]

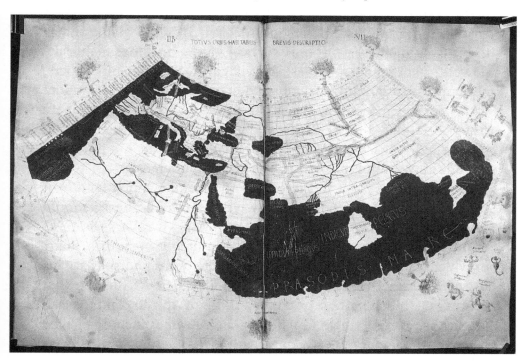

Ptolemy's world map, redrawn in the fifteenth century but based on a late thirteenth-century rediscovery of Ptolemy's work. (British Library Harley MS 7182)

Columella (c. 4–70 CE)

Lucius Junius Moderatus Columella was born in Cádiz in southern Spain to wealthy Roman parents, and grew up to become an authority on agriculture. He apparently spent much time in his youth with a favoured uncle, an expert farmer, in the Baetic province (more or less equivalent to Andalusia). He left Spain at some time in his youth and pursued a military career and appears to have served in Syria. He spent much of his later life in the vicinity of Rome, and may have died at Tarentum (Taranto) in the heel of Italy, based on an inscription found there.[30]

His main legacy is the twelve-volume work *De Re Rustica*, which has been completely preserved, and is a treatise on Roman agriculture. From the point of view of herbs and spices, our main interest is in Books X–XII. Book X, 'On the Culture of Gardens', is a dramatic contrast to the previous nine, which were prose texts describing practical aspects of agriculture, in that it was written in hexameters of verse in the style of Virgil giving praise to his (Columella's) garden. His lyrical garden includes mandrake flowers, giant fennel, poppies, chervil, garlic, wild parsnip, capers, elecampane, mint, dill, rue, mustard, alexanders, onion, *Lepidium*, green parsley, marjoram, sweet cicely, cress, savory, pomegranate tree, coriander, fennel flowers, saffron flowers, sweet cassia, horehound, houseleek, buckthorn, butcher's broom and purslane, in addition to numerous vegetables, fruits and vines.

Book XI deals with the duties of the farmer and calendar of work, and specifies when and how vegetables and herbs should be sown and planted within a garden. Book XII covers the tasks of the farmer's wife and is valuable for a number of recipes, many of which include (mainly) locally available herbs and spices. This is an extremely useful record of Roman cuisine from the first century CE, much more prosaic than those of Apicius, and focused on pickling, preserving and wine-making. Recipes include pickled herbs; oxygal (sour milk seasoned with herbs); lettuce pickled with dill, fennel, rue and leek; pickled purslane and garden samphire; dried figs mixed with parched sesame, Egyptian anise, fennel and cumin seeds; spiced wine using flower-de-luce, fenugreek and sweet rush with boiling of the must, also adding spikenard leaf, dates, costum, cyperus, sweet rush, myrrh, calamus, cassia, amomum, saffron and melilot; preserves for wine; horehound wine; squill wine and squill vinegar; wormwood, hyssop, fennel and pennyroyal wines; squeezed must using rosemary; myrtle wine; pickled elecampane; olives pickled with fennel seeds and mastic seeds; pickled black olives using aniseed, mastic and fennel seed, rue and parsley; a marmalade of olives using fenugreek, cumin, fennel seed and Egyptian aniseed; gleucine oil (made from oil and must) with calamus, sweet-smelling rush, cardamom, palm bark, Egyptian anise and others; prepared mustard; pickled alexanders and skirret roots; spicy salad with garum and vinegar.

Pliny the Elder (23–79 CE)

As well as being one of the greatest natural historians of his era, Gaius Plinius Secundus was also a lawyer, military commander and author. He was born in Como (or possibly Verona) to a wealthy family, and educated as a lawyer in Rome. He joined the army in his early twenties as a junior infantry officer, and later served in Germania under the legatus Pomponius Secundus, the governor of Germania Superior, who became a friend and ally.[31] He was subsequently promoted to command a cavalry battalion and would have fought in military campaigns in the region.

After leaving the army at the age of 29, he returned to Rome and combined a literary career with a return to law. He wrote the twenty-volume *History of the German Wars*, a narrative history of Rome, and a biography of his friend Pomponius, none of which have survived.

After Nero's death in 68 CE, instability in Rome followed in the Year of the Four Emperors (69 CE), the last of these being Vespasian. Pliny had been appointed procurator in Nearer Spain by Nero at some unknown date, but returned to Rome on the death of his brother and adopted his nephew (Pliny the Younger) in 70 CE.

He was known to, and trusted by, Vespasian since the Germanic wars and was appointed to a number of procuratorships. At some stage in the mid-to-late 70s CE, he was given the post of Prefect of the Roman fleet at Misenum in Italy, which set the scene for Pliny's dramatic death.

His sole surviving literary work is the *Natural History*; it is a huge encyclopaedia of the natural sciences written in thirty-seven books and was a tremendous achievement by any standards. The subjects cover astronomy, meteorology, geography, geology, ethnography, anthropology, physiology, zoology, botany, agriculture, pharmacology, medicine, metals, mineralogy and the arts. Books of relevance to spices are Book VI (covering Asia geographically), Books XII and XIII (trees), Book XIX (garden plants), Book XX (remedies from garden plants), Book XXI (flowers), Book XXIII (remedies from cultivated trees) and Book XXIV (remedies from forest trees). *Natural History* was probably started during his period of procuratorships under Vespasian and continued up to his death in 79 CE, the book later published by his nephew. His enormous productivity was enabled by his strong motivation and aided by his ability to work at all hours, and especially through the night; he wasted no time and focused all his efforts on his achievements. His nephew (in an epistle to the Roman senator Baebius Macer) observed that 'he looked upon every moment as lost which was not devoted to study'.

He quoted over 470 earlier or contemporary Greek and Roman authors and authorities. For all that, he was not perfect: errors were frequent, myths were perpetuated, but the work is unrivalled in scope from the era of classical antiquity.

Pliny died at age 56 in suitably dramatic circumstances. He was based at Misenum near Pompeii, where he was in command of the fleet during the cataclysmic eruption of nearby Vesuvius in 79 CE. He sailed to help evacuate his friends but was overwhelmed by a cloud of toxic gases and was asphyxiated.

Pedanius Dioscorides (40–90 CE)

Dioscorides was a medical botanist and physician who served in the Roman army, and is famous for his five-volume book on (mainly) herbal medicine, *De Materia Medica*. He was more or less a contemporary of Pliny, and although it is unknown whether they ever met, it seems plausible that they would have known of each other. Little is known about the man himself, though he wrote the text in Greek and most of his work is on plants that were indigenous to the eastern Mediterranean.[32] He was born in Anabarzos near Tarsus in modern Turkey.

De Materia Medica is organised into five books which are not compatible with modern taxonomical botany. Book I comprises aromatic trees and shrubs, and oils and salves derived from them; Book II animals, animal products, herbs and cereals; Book III roots, seeds and herbs; Book IV further roots and herbs; and Book V vines and their products and minerals. He covers a total of around 600 medicinal plants. Typically, there is a brief botanical description, including any interesting features, aroma, some mention of origin, any adulteration if known, followed by their medical benefits and how to prepare and use them. His influence has been extremely long-lasting: it became the most important pharmacology text for over 1,500 years. It has also been copied, modified, redacted and enhanced innumerable times. The oldest extant complete copy is the 'Vienna Dioscorides', also known as the 'Anicia Juliana Codex', which dates from around 512 CE and was made in Constantinople, the capital of the Eastern Roman Empire. It is beautifully illustrated (Figure 4) and was made as a gift for the Emperor Flavius Olybrius' daughter. Even this early copy was altered from Dioscorides' original.

Spices and culinary herb plants include alexanders, amomum, dill, anise, celery, parsley, wormwood, asafoetida, basil, bay, bdellium, bishop's weed, black mustard, black pepper, borage, box thorn, sweet flag, camphor, caraway, cardamom, cassia, chervil, cinnamon, comfrey, fennel, rosemary, sage, thyme, cumin, coriander, costus, cow parsley, elecampane, fenugreek, ferula, frankincense, ginger, horseradish, hyssop, juniper, laser (silphium), liquorice, long pepper, lovage, lycium, malabathrum, marjoram, mustard, myrobalan, myrrh, nard, spikenard, nigella, nutmeg, oregano, poppy, pennyroyal, rue, saffron, samphire, sesame, styrax, sugar and sumac. While this list is dominated by the plants available within the Roman Empire, there are already numerous exotics from south and Southeast Asia, which reflect increased availability via trade in the first century CE.

Although information about Dioscorides himself is scant, we can get a few clues from his preface to *De Materia Medica*. He dedicated his work to his friend Laecanius Areius, a physician from Tarsus (in modern Turkey), where they both probably studied (or possibly Areius may have been one of Dioscorides' teachers). He emphasised his work as being mainly original.[33] The earliest English translation is that of Goodyer from as late as 1655.[34]

He details the collecting and storing of plant materials and his hands-on approach is apparent. Crateuas the rhizotomist (a physician from the first to second centuries BCE) was given a certain amount of praise, and indeed appears to have been one of Dioscorides' sources, as was Andreas the physician (third century BCE). Along with the praise came criticism – they 'ignored many extremely useful roots and gave meager descriptions of many herbs'. Disoscorides' work was thorough and reliable and stood the test of time. The book was never 'lost'; it has always stayed in circulation. First translations were made to Latin in the sixth century, to Syriac in the ninth century, and Arabic in the tenth century; further translations to Italian, German, Spanish and French were made during the Renaissance, but the Goodyer English translation of 1655 was not published until centuries later. Of great interest is the large number of plant medicines still used in modern pharmacology; it is fair to conclude that *De Materia Medica* is one of the most influential books of all time.[35]

Claudius Ptolemy (100–170 CE)

Ptolemy was a Roman astronomer, geographer and mathematician who lived in Alexandria in Roman Egypt. He is famous for writing numerous scientific treatises, most notably on astronomy (the most important being the *Almagest*), but his work the *Geographia*, an eight-book treatise, is also of huge importance. He produced maps of the known world using geographical coordinates based on latitude measured from the equator (expressed as 'climata'), with thirty-nine parallels from equator to pole, each interval representing fifteen minutes of daylight on the summer solstice. He calculated longitudes from a meridian in the west that passed through the Canary Islands. The *Geographia*, then, is mainly focused on the geometrical representation of geography. His guiding light was his precursor Marinos of Tyre (70–130 CE), and though his treatise was lost, Ptolemy used this as the basis for his work, and improved upon it, at the same time acknowledging the debt owed to Marinos. Ptolemy assumed the world to be a sphere (as had several predecessors) and estimated the circumference as 180,000 stadia – this made a degree of longitude at the equator some 500 stadia instead of the correct 600, i.e. he had underestimated.[36] Ptolemy provided coordinates for 6,345 localities, which could then be placed on a grid to generate his maps; there is clearly excessive distortion in the east–west direction, with the length of the Mediterranean being overestimated in terms of degrees.[37] The world maps were made with two of his three projections, and one is illustrated on p. 31, clearly a huge improvement over Strabo's map. His world maps that would have accompanied the text are lost but were regenerated from his tables by monks during the Middle Ages. Local maps were part of Books VII and VIII. Ptolemy's world maps proved to be the most accurate descriptors of the world until they were superseded in the fifteenth and sixteenth centuries during the Age of Discovery.

Galen (129–216 CE)

Claudius Galenus, usually referred to as Galen, was born in Pergamon (in modern-day western Turkey), to wealthy, if dissimilar, parents. His father was an architect, a just and benevolent man, but he considered his mother a foul-tempered shrew, leading Galen to vow to 'embrace and love the former qualities and to avoid and hate the latter'. His education commenced at Pergamon, itself a noted centre of learning, and he studied the main philosophical disciplines of the era, before commencing medical studies at the age of 17.[38] He continued his medical studies at Smyrna and Alexandria and other locations. His first professional job was working as a surgeon to gladiators at Pergamon, then he subsequently moved to Rome at around the age of 31. In Rome, he rapidly gained a reputation as a brilliant, though outspoken, surgeon, but made enemies in medical circles and withdrew to Pergamon around 168 CE, but returned to Rome within a year.

Galen was nothing if not prolific as a medical author, and may have written as many as 500 works on anatomy, physiology, medicine and philosophy; not all survived, but there is still a huge collection of treatises that remain extant. He undoubtedly benefited from the work of his predecessors, and was notably respectful to Hippocrates, though he was clearly a pioneer in many aspects of anatomy and surgery. It is interesting to reflect that Hippocrates died some 500 years before Galen was born! He accepted and promoted Hippocrates' humoural theory, bloodletting and other areas subsequently found to be plain wrong, but, like Hippocrates, understood the importance of the body's natural ability to heal.

Key texts related to herbal remedies include *On the Powers (and Mixtures) of Simple Remedies*, *On the Composition of Drugs According to Places* and *On the Composition of Drugs According to Kind*. Galen treated imbalances in the four humours or fluids; drugs were composed of animal, vegetable or mineral substances.[39] Great emphasis was placed on authenticity and condition of the substance, e.g. the visual appearance of myrrh and costus, crocus stamens to be bright yellow with a pleasant scent; cinnamon bark should have a pleasant warming fragrance, etc. Galen grouped certain plants by function: major 'opening' roots, e.g. fennel, celery, asparagus, parsley, butcher's broom; 'warm' seeds, e.g. aniseed, cumin, coriander, fennel; 'cold' seeds, e.g. watermelon, cucumber, squash, melon; cordial flowers, e.g. rose, violet, borage. Primary effective qualities were considered to be hot/cold or dry/moist; there were also secondary (e.g. relaxing, astringing, softening, hardening, etc) and tertiary effective qualities (e.g. purgative or promoting sweat, etc.). The first two levels were used to treat the opposite of the particular effective quality. He used various other grading parameters for his prescriptions – some 475 remedies are recorded in his extant works.

Galen's work continued to influence medicine until the seventeenth century or later, even though his anatomical work was rendered incorrect by Renaissance scientists.

Cosmas Indicopleustes (Sixth Century CE)

Cosmas was a Greek merchant famed for his travels to India; in fact, his surname means 'the Indian navigator'. He was probably a native of Alexandria and received an education but was not a scholar. Against the prevailing academic view, he believed the world was flat. He certainly travelled widely – through the Mediterranean, Red Sea, Persian Gulf, west coast of India, and Sri Lanka. He described his adventures in his *Christian Topography*, which was written in the mid-sixth century. His devout Christian views permeate the text, which nonetheless contains an interesting geographic account in the early era of the Eastern Roman Empire. When he had finished with travelling, he returned to Alexandria and became a monk.[40]

The *Christian Topography* is written in twelve books, and we are mainly interested in Books II and XI for his geographic descriptions, the remaining books comprising religious diatribes denouncing the sphericity of the world, describing the size of the sun, and other subjects of a more spiritual nature. In Book II, he describes the Red

Sea, north-eastern Africa, the Arabian peninsula and the passage to India. He writes:

> The region which produces frankincense is situated at the projecting parts of Ethopia, and lies inland, but is washed by the ocean on the other side. Hence the inhabitants of Barbaria, being near at hand, go up into the interior and, engaging in traffic with the natives, bring back from them many kinds of spices, frankincense, cassia, calamus, and many other articles of merchandise ...

His description of Tabropane (Sri Lanka) in Book XI clearly shows that by the sixth century CE it had risen in status to that of a major entrepot: 'The island being, as it is, in a central position, is much frequented by ships from all parts of India and from Persia and Ethiopia, and it likewise sends out many of its own.'

He mentions 'the five marts of Male [the Malabar coast of India] which export pepper', and moving eastwards: 'and then farther away is the clove country, then Tzinista which produces the silk. Beyond this there is no other country, for the ocean surrounds it on the east.' This is important – Indonesia had been identified and China's eastern coast correctly described. Cosmas was one of the few writers on geography in that era who had actually made the journey himself (at least as far as Tabropane) rather than relying on second-hand information.

Paulus of Aegina (625–690 CE)

Paulus was a seventh-century Greek physician about whom very little is known, though he is famous for his extensive treatise *Medical Compendium in Seven Books*.[41] Much of the work refers to that recommended by preceding physicians and scientists, i.e. a compilation of previous observations, though it also contains new ideas, and he appeared to have particular expertise in surgery. For all that, this is an excellent reference book and became understandably popular, particularly in the Arab world (it was translated into Arabic in the ninth century). Book VII deals exclusively with pharmacology. In his 'Simples' chapter he lists some 490 single botanical remedies, as well as mineral and animal remedies; he then describes simple and compound purgatives, antidotes, liniments, ointments and other preparations.

Abu Hanifah Al-Dinawari (c. 820–895 CE)

Abu Hanifah al-Dinawari was a Persian astronomer, botanist, geographer and mathematician born in ninth-century Iran. Although he published many works on a diverse range of subjects, he is most well known for his *Book of Plants*, or *Kitab al-Nabat*. This book originally consisted of six volumes but only three have survived, and one of those is a partial reconstruction; nonetheless, this remaining set documents 482 plants in his alphabetical listing.[42] Al-Dinawari gathered a lot of his own information (e.g. from Bedouins and others) as well as relying on earlier Arabic sources. There are no detailed botanical descriptions, and the writing abounds with poetry, so it is not a conventional botanical treatise in the Western sense, but nonetheless is a valuable step forward. Its main value was that it became the most comprehensive compilation of Arabic plants for many hundreds of years.

Hu Sihui (Fourteenth Century)

Hu Sihui was a nutritionist active in China in the fourteenth century during the Yuan Dynasty. His origin is unclear (possibly Chinese or Mongol), but it is known that he had been appointed to the royal court office in the period 1314–20, ultimately rising to the position of Royal Dietician. He wrote the well-known text *Yinshan Zhengyao*, or *The True Principles of Eating and Drinking*, a work of three chapters containing 219 recipes, of which most, though certainly not all, have some perceived medical or therapeutic value. The work was presented to the emperor in 1330.[43] The first chapter includes a section on 'Rare and Precious Dishes' containing ninety-five recipes.[44] The second chapter includes recipes for various infusions/liquid foods, with notes on their therapeutic value; a section on 'food for immortals', i.e. diets to allow extreme longevity; food for the seasons; the five tastes (moderation is advised here, e.g. too salty a diet should be avoided); and a section on foods as remedies for the sick, among others. The third chapter is an illustrated compilation of different food types, which includes eight seasonings and twenty-eight flavourings. Sabban notes that the most frequently used condiments were scallions, ginger, vinegar, a non-specified amomum, pepper, coriander and tangerine peel, which may be typical of the fourteenth century in China. Cosmopolitan influences were common, e.g. meat coated in asafoetida then browned in 'Arab fat' or mastic soup, also Middle Eastern; foreign words sometimes were used in recipes to add a certain glamour and appeal, and the exoticism of imported spices added to this effect. Asafoetida, used in several dishes, is a popular Indian and West Asian spice. In addition to those listed above, spices included dill, galingale, turmeric, saffron, fagara, black pepper, long pepper, mustard, basil, cinnamon, cardamom, mastic, camphor, fenugreek, sesame and nard. Many of these spices are non-native to China and would have been imported; interestingly, pepper seems to have been used in preference to the native fagara, probably because of its greater pungency. Alkanet and saffron were also used to colour food.

Rembert Dodoens (1517–85) and John Gerard (1545–1612)

Rembert Dodoens was a Flemish botanist and physician. He became a court physician, and in 1582 was appointed Professor of Medicine at the University of Leiden in the Netherlands. He had become interested in plants as a young man and published

De frugum historia in 1552, then his illustrated herbal *Cruydeboeck* in 1554, which had a particular focus on medicinal herbs.[45] It was translated into several languages, including English in 1578 (as *A niewe herball or Historie of plantes* …) and became an 'instant classic' – it was the most translated book after the Bible in that era, such was its popularity.[46]

It had also come to the attention of John Gerard, an English herbalist and barber-surgeon. Gerard lived in Holborn and cared much for his large garden, which became quite well known. He became superintendent of the gardens of William Cecil in 1577, and in 1586 he became curator of the Physic Garden at the College of Physicians. He gradually built up his reputation as a herbalist, and in 1596 produced a *Catalogue of Plants*, a list of over 1,000 rare plants grown in his Holborn garden. About this time, he was also approached by the publisher John Norton to make an English translation of Dodoens' *Stirpium historiae pemptades sex*, which was a 1583 much-revised Latin translation of the *Cruydeboeck*. Gerard, despite his enthusiasm for plants, was not an academic botanist, nor was he Norton's first choice for the translation: this was originally given to Dr Robert Priest, who had since died. Gerard completed the work, and the new book was entitled *Herball, or Generall Historie of Plantes* and was published in 1597.[47] There were several incidences of apparent plagiarism: firstly, the translation seems to be mainly Priest's work, even though Gerard claimed the work as his own; secondly, Matthias de l'Obel, a Flemish botanist, physician and friend, had some of his own work re-used by Gerard; and thirdly, from the German botanist Jacobus Theodorus. Thomas Johnson, an English botanist who revised, amended and expanded the text in his 1633 edition of the *Herball*, wrote a preface which included clarification of some of these misdemeanours.

Most of the major spices could now be found in such botanical literature, though were very resonant of the exotic. About a century after the 'discovery' of chili by Columbus, its origin was still apparently steeped in mystery and called 'Ginnie or Indian Pepper' by Gerard: 'These plants are brought from foreign countries, as Ginnie, India, and those parts, into Spaine and Italy', and:

Ginnie pepper hath the taste of pepper, but not the power or vertue, notwithstanding in Spaine and sundrie parts of the Indies they do use to dresse their meate therewith, as we do with Calecute pepper: but (saith my author) it hath in it a malitious qualitie whereby it is an enimie to the liver & other of the entrails ...

Regardless of the issues about plagiarism (which was rife in this era), the *Herball* became extremely popular and was a hugely important reference for the next two centuries.

Nicholas Culpeper (1616–54)

Culpeper was an English botanist, apothecary and herbalist. He developed an early interest in medicinal herbs under the influence of his grandmother, spending his spare time cataloguing plants. He studied at Cambridge, and in 1640 set up a pharmacy at the Halfway House in Spitalfields, obtaining his herbal medicines from the nearby countryside. He was very busy and treated many patients every day, providing his services free of charge for those who couldn't afford it. He opposed the overpriced practices of physicians of his day and the monopoly exerted by the College of Physicians, believing that medicine should be available to all. As a result, he acquired many enemies, became alienated and was accused of witchcraft.

During the Civil War, he was on the side of the Parliamentarians and served as a battlefield medic. After being seriously wounded (in 1643) he returned to London, and in 1652 published *The English Physitian*, a book of herbal remedies written in the vernacular, subsequently renamed the *Complete Herbal*. It was priced cheaply to make it accessible to the masses and listed several hundred herbs. The herbal makes great reading – there is plenty of earthy humour, mocking the establishment: 'Our physicians must imitate like apes, though they cannot come off half so cleverly.'[48] For each herb he lists the name and alternatives, brief description, place, time, followed by government and virtues. Most of the species are those which would be found in Britain, with a smattering of exotics. The book uses astrology as one of the guiding principles (and so loses modern credibility), but Culpeper's ultimate aim was to break away from tradition and make cheap herbal remedies available to all. This about Gerard (from his 'Epistle to the Reader' preface):

> neither Gerrard nor Parkinson, or any that ever wrote in the like nature, ever gave one wise reason for what they wrote, and so did nothing else but train up young novices in Physic in the School of tradition, and teach them just as a parrot is taught to speak …

The book was a huge success and has not been out of print since the seventeenth century.

Carl Linnaeus (1707–78)

Linnaeus was a Swedish botanist, zoologist and physician who brought biology into the modern age through his system of classification. He studied, first at Lund, then at Uppsala universities, taught botany, and in 1735 travelled to Holland and earned his medical degree (which he had started at Lund). He stayed there for the next three years and published a number of works, including his important *System Naturae*, which introduced his ideas on taxonomy.[49] Linnaeus then returned to Sweden and practised medicine in Stockholm, becoming Professor of Medicine and Botany at Uppsala in 1741.

System Naturae in its first edition comprised only eleven pages, but it was a game-changer; he divided the natural world into Animal, Plant and Mineral Kingdoms, with the Plant Kingdom listing around 6,000 species. The taxonomical hierarchy used five levels – Kingdom, Class, Order, Genus and Species (Family has been subsequently added between Order and Genus) – and each organism was assigned a binomial title, comprising genus and species, written in Latin. The book was expanded, modified and corrected such that twelve editions were eventually published under his authorship, but the 10th edition of 1758 is widely regarded as the most important. The 12th edition had expanded to 2,400 pages.

Other works of botanical importance from Linnaeus include *Biblioteca Botanica* (1735), *Fundamenta Botanica* (1736), *Critica Botanica* (1737), *Genera Plantarum* (1737), *Philosophia Botanica* (1751) and *Species Plantarum* (1753).

Linnaeus' achievements were recognised within his own lifetime, along with his growing international academic reputation; he became the chief physician to the royal family in 1747, rector of Uppsala University in 1750, and was ennobled in 1761.

Meanwhile, since the fifteenth century, a revolution had been ongoing, as European countries strove to push the boundaries of the known world and establish new trade routes, following the fall of the Eastern Roman Empire. This new era would become known as the 'Age of Discovery' … and spices were the key motivator.

2

The Early Spice Trade

A relief from the mortuary temple of Queen Hatshepsut (d. 1458 BCE) at Deir El-Bahari, Egypt, showing the trading expedition to Punt.

Bronze Age

The first long-distance movements of plants and animals date to the third millennium BCE, with East Asian crops moving west along the proto-Silk Road, while wheat and barley travelled east, appearing in East Asia by 2500–2000 BCE.[1] The spice trade itself may have started in the last two millennia BCE (or possibly even earlier), e.g. black peppercorns (from a plant native to India) were identified in the mummy of pharaoh Rameses II (*c.* 1200 BCE). Cumin (and poppy) may have arrived with the Philistines in Israel (twelfth to seventh centuries BCE), though not necessarily by trade. Evidence of the spice trade or movement within the Bronze Age is summarised in Table 2 below:

Table 2 | Evidence for Bronze Age Spice Trade

Evidence	Spice	Age	Comment	Reference
Seeds found in Late Neolithic lakeside settlements in Switzerland	Dill	3400–3050 BCE	Dill non-native, assumed transported from Med area	C. Brombacher, 1997[2]
Decorated incense burners present in royal graves in A-group Nubia	Undefined incense	Late fourth millennium BCE	Presumably imported from Arabia or north-east Africa	N. Boivin & D. Fuller, 2009[3]
Introduction of sesame to Mesopotamia from India	Sesame	2400 BCE?	Evidence supports westward spread from India pre-second millennium BCE	D. Bedigian & J. Harlan, 1986;[4] D. Fuller, 2003,[5] V. Zech-Matterne et al., 2015[6]
Traces of cumin found in residues of vessels in Minoan sites	Cumin	Second millennium BCE		E. Tsafou & J. J. Garcia-Granero, 2021[7]
Inscribed granite blocks at Mit Rahina, Egypt refer to 217 sacks of cinnamon or camphor being carried by ship from the Levant	Cinnamon or Camphor	Nineteenth century BCE	Depends on translation of *ti-Sps* as cinnamon	E. S. Marcus, 2007[8]
Cultivated in Babylon	Turmeric, Cardamom	Eighteenth century BCE	Derived from South and Southeast Asia	F. Rosengarten, 1969[9]

Cloves found at Terqa, Syria	Cloves	1720 BCE	Cloves derived from Southeast Asia	G. Buccellati & M. Kelly Buccellati, 1978;[10] Monica L. Smith, 2019[11]
Described in Ebers Papyrus, Egypt	Cardamom	1550 BCE	Derived from South and Southeast Asia	F. Rosengarten, 1969 (op. cit.)
Obtained on Queen Hatshepsut's expedition to Punt (via either the Nile or Red Sea)	Myrrh, frankincense, (cinnamon)	Sixteenth to fifteenth centuries BCE	Punt location debated – could be part of modern Ethiopia, Somalia, Eritrea or Uganda. 'Cinnamon' translation is debatable	A. B. Edwards, 1891;[12] F. Rosengarten, 1969 (op. cit.); F. Wicker, 1998;[13] J Turner, 2004[14]
Nutmeg remains at Deir El-Bahari in Egypt from 18th dynasty, possibly associated with Queen Hatshepsut's expedition to Punt	Nutmeg	Sixteenth to fourteenth centuries BCE	Nutmeg derived from Indonesia. Equivocal and not substantiated	E. Naville & H. R. Hall, 1913[15]
References to cinnamon in Ancient Egypt, East Africa may be attributed to an active 'Cinnamon Route' in second millennium BCE between Indonesia and Madagascar/Rhapta	Cinnamon (nutmeg, cloves, etc. may have also followed this route)	Mid-second millennium BCE	Cinnamon is native to Southeast Asia and India. Use of double outrigger canoes from Indonesia, early connection to Madagascar supported by various lines of evidence	J. Innes Miller, 1969[16]
Curcuma (Turmeric) protein residues found in dental calculus of individuals in the Levant	Turmeric	Mid-second millennium BCE	Derived from South Asia	Ashley Scott et al., 2020[17]
149 Canaanite amphorae filled with *Pistacia* resin from Ulu Burun shipwreck off south coast of Turkey	*Pistacia* resin (probably for incense), coriander, nigella, sumac, safflower	Fourteenth century BCE	Possible trade route between Syrio-Palestine and Cyprus. Pistacia resin poss origin from north Jordan River valley	C. Glenister, 2008;[18] C. Pulak, 2008[19]
Peppercorns found in nostrils of Rameses II	Black pepper	1213 BCE	Assumed traded from India to Egypt	A. Plu, 1985[20]
Citrus medica seeds found in Hala Sultan Tekke in Cyprus	Citron	Late thirteenth century BCE	Citron originated in Southeast Asia	H. Hjelmqvist 1979[21]
Cinnamaldehyde residues recovered from Phoenician flasks in Israel	Cinnamon	Eleventh to ninth centuries BCE	Suggest trade established between Levant and Asia	D. Namdar et al., 2013[22]
Various occurrences of fenugreek seeds in Bronze Age sites in Bulgaria, India, Pakistan	Fenugreek	Various Bronze Age	Native to East Med. Unclear if traded, grows wild in India and Pakistan	T. Popova, 2016[23]

One of the earliest and most important spices used extensively by modern humans is sesame, though it was particularly valued for its oil. Botanical evidence suggests that sesame (*S. indicum*) was first domesticated in the Indian subcontinent, with the earliest reliably dated specimens dating from 2500 to 2000 BCE at Harappa in the Pakistan Indus Valley and Miri Qalat in south-west Pakistan. The origin has been traced to the domestication of *S. orientale* L. var. *malabaricum*.[24] Numerous other Indian occurrences of sesame have younger dates, e.g. Sanghol in the Indian Punjab (1900–1400 BCE) and Sringaverapura and others in the Ganges basin (1200–800 BCE).[25] Sesame appears to have reached Mesopotamia by 2300 BCE during the era of the Harappan civilisation, with evidence provided by charred seeds from Abu Salabikh, Iraq. Sesame may have reached Egypt at Naqada by the First Intermediate Period (2181–2055 BCE), though pollen was recorded even earlier than this. It has also been found in Tutankhamun's tomb (c. 1325 BCE) and in a storage jar at Deir el Medineh (1200–1000 BCE). Other Middle Eastern Bronze Age occurrences date from 1450 to 1250 BCE. This appears to demonstrate a westward human-driven dispersal of sesame from an origin in the western/north-western part of the Indian subcontinent; it took advantage of existing overland trade between Harappa and Mesopotamia, as well as trade on the Arabian Sea between Mohenjo Daro and Ur.[26] Mesopotamia became a centre of distribution of sesame and sesame oil into the Mediterranean.

More exotic spices were also moving west. Cinnamon is a South Asian spice that has cropped up a few times in archaeological records in Egypt, though inscriptions hinge on the translation of the word *ti-Sps* as 'cinnamon'. A large shipment of 271 sacks of cinnamon (or possibly the related camphor) was recorded on inscribed granite blocks at the Mit Rahina site in Egypt dating back to the nineteenth century BCE. Cinnamon was also inferred from reliefs at the Deir El-Bahari temple near Luxor, Egypt, describing the voyage to the Land of Punt in the sixteenth century BCE. Actual nutmeg remains recovered from this complex could be related to the same journey.[27] Definitive evidence of cinnamon traces was reported from Late Bronze Age Phoenician flasks (eleventh to ninth centuries BCE) at a site in Israel.[28]

Turmeric has also been found – a study of dental calculus from ancient human remains in Meggido (in modern Israel) found evidence for the consumption of turmeric, soybean and banana – certainly proving people in the eastern Mediterranean had access to foods from distant locations, including South Asia, in the mid-second millennium BCE.[29]

Iron Age

Long-distance trade intensified in the Iron Age, with trade developing between Southeast Asia and India, India with the West, and from the end of the period, China with other parts of Asia and the West.[30] Expansion of the Roman, Han and Parthian empires encouraged the new trade links and spices rapidly became available on scales never previously seen. Black pepper, cinnamon, cardamom and spikenard were the most important new imports to Rome, while pepper, sesame, cumin, cinnamon and others reached China from the south and west. Table 3 overleaf shows the greatly increased variety of spices being traded. Figure 5 shows the main early spice trade routes.

Table 3 | Evidence for Iron Age Spice Trade

Evidence	Spice	Age	Comment	Reference
Appearance of sesame in Yemen	Sesame	First half of the first millennium BCE		Boivin & Fuller, 2009 (op. cit.)
C. cassia flower in sacred precinct of Hera at Samos	Cassia	Seventh century BCE	Evidence of Asian spice	D. Kučan, 1995[31]
Sappho Fragment 44 (The marriage of Hector and Andromache) refers to 'mingled scents of myrrh, cinnamon and frankincense'	Myrrh, cinnamon, frankincense	Sixth to seventh centuries BCE	Greek mythologic poem. All these spices are exotic to Greece	www.allpoetry.com/poem/15809044[32]
Various references in Hebrew Bible	Cinnamon, cassia	*c.* mid-first millennium BCE		A. Gilboa & D. Namdar[33]
Chaldaeans burned 1,000 talent weight of frankincense per year on the great altar in a temple in Babylon. Incense burned by Babylonian couples after sexual relations	Frankincense	*c.* 430 BCE	Assumed traded from Arabia to Mesopotamia	Herodotus[34]
Textual	Cassia, myrrh	*c.* 430 BCE	Used in embalming by Egyptians	Herodotus[35]
Scythians filled body cavity with chopped cypress, frankincense, parsleyseed and aniseed during embalming	Frankincense	*c.* 430 BCE	Frankincense imported to Central Asia via proto-Silk Roads	Herodotus[36]
Analysis of residues from Greek amphorae recovered from the sea showed presence of ginger and citrus families among other plants	Zingiberaceae, Rutaceae	Fifth to third centuries BCE	Gingers derived from Asia. Presence in amphorae demonstrates use in trade	B. P. Foley et al., 2011[37]
Hippocrates' documentation and use of multiple non-native spices as medicines	Amomum, cardamom, cassia, cinnamon, Ethiopian cumin, frankincense, galbanum, ginger grass, myrrh, pepper, saffron, styrax, spikenard, sweet flag	460–370 BCE	Substances would have been obtained by trade	Hippocratic Corpus[38]

Theophrastus' documentation of multiple non-native spices	Cassia, cardamom, cinnamon, frankincense, galingale, ginger grass, gum arabic, lime, lyceum, myrrh, pepper, pomegranate, saffron, sesame, spikenard, sweet flag, tamarind, tragacanth	370–285 BCE		Theophrastus[39]
Mentioned by Charaka – early evidence of use in India and in Ramayana	Cloves	Second century BCE (Charaka)	Transported or traded as origin in Moluccas	W. Dymock et al., 1891;[40] R. S. Singh & A. N. Singh, 1983[41]
Textual evidence of cloves' earliest use in China – officers of the court customarily held cloves in mouth before addressing the sovereign	Cloves	c. 266 BCE	Transported or traded as origin in Moluccas	W. Dymock et al., 1891 (op. cit.)
Single sesame seed found in site in southern Thailand	Sesame	200 BCE–20 CE	Possible trade with India	C. C. Costillo et al., 2016[42]
Various occurrences of fenugreek seeds in Iron Age sites in Israel, Jordan, Egypt, Germany	Fenugreek	Various Iron Age	Native to East Med. Unclear if traded	T. Popova, 2016[43]

Trade Routes

The Incense Route

The earliest trade route may have been the so-called Incense Route which linked the Mediterranean region with Saudi Arabia (and across the Red Sea, Egypt) in the first two millennia BCE. Frankincense, myrrh and other aromatics were used in ritual as incense, as perfumes and in medicines in the Mediterranean societies. Resin finds in Egypt date to 2000 BCE at Deir El-Bahari, but use may be much older.[44] The route extended from Sabbatha in the south through capitals of the other kingdoms to Petra, Gaza and the north, and products were carried by caravan, a hard sixty-five-day journey (to Gaza) according to Pliny. The Red Sea was also much utilised in the northward transport of aromatics. Strabo described the rich trade in south Arabian aromatics:

The country of the Sabæi,[Sabaeans] a very populous nation, is contiguous, and is the most fertile of all, producing myrrh, frankincense, and cinnamon. On the coast is found balsamum and another kind of herb of a very fragrant smell, but which is soon dissipated. There are also sweet-smelling palms and the calamus ... The people who live near each other receive, in continued succession, the loads [of perfumes] and deliver them to others, who convey them as far as Syria and Mesopotamia. When the carriers become drowsy by the odour of the aromatics, the drowsiness is removed by the fumes of asphaltus and of goat's beard.[45]

Pliny said that 'the chief productions of Arabia are frankincense and myrrh'.[46] Miller described five species of *Boswellia* (the genus that yields frankincense) native to Arabia, of which one is native to the mainland and four others are native to the island of Socotra.[47] The best frankincense sold for 6 denarii per lb (Pliny) and the finest myrrh up to 50 (200 sesterces) – or fifty days' pay for a first-century CE skilled worker.[48] Miller also described fourteen species of *Commiphora* (myrrh), most of which are native to Africa. The Sabaeans traded for this and exported northwards along the same route. Vast quantities reached the West – in the first century BCE Rome imported 3,000 tons of frankincense and 600 tons of myrrh annually.[49]

In addition to these indigenous aromatics, there would have been imported galbanum, bdellium, mastic, sweet flag, sweet rush, cinnamon, spikenard, styrax and costum, aloe wood and sandalwood, among others recognised by Theophrastus in the fourth century BCE, many of which would have found their way to Arabian ports.

Besides their main uses as incense and perfumes, resins had other ancient uses: in recent years tree resin has been detected in analysis of residues from jars, alongside biomarkers for wine.[50] The oldest jars were from around 5400 BCE and the youngest from the Byzantine era. The jars came from several different locations in the Middle East and Greece, but many were from Ancient Egypt.

In addition to resins, traces of several Mediterranean herbs were also detected, leading to the conclusion that wines were resinated, flavoured and spiced from very early times.

The Levantine–Aegean spice trade was a logical extension of the Incense Route as it delivered aromatics to the Mediterranean customers. Frankincense and myrrh from Arabia or north-east Africa were, naturally, of prime importance.[51] In addition to myrrh, other species/derivatives of *Commiphora* were traded – balm, balsam, bdellium and stakte. The works of Theophrastus and Hippocrates document the end use of many of the products (see Table 3).

The Steppe Route

The Eurasian Steppe is a roughly east–west-oriented zone of rolling grassland extending from Mongolia to Romania. Prehistoric hunter-gatherers were succeeded by herdsman living a life of pastoral nomadism. The steppe naturally became a huge transport route that enabled movement of people, animals, goods and ideas long before the Silk Road became established. It can only be assumed that spices, herbs, medicines and scents also travelled along this route.

Early Indus Valley Routes

Trade routes west would have been via the important city of Mohenjo Daro (about 500km south of Harappa) and then north-west via modern Afghanistan, or south-west inland parallel to the coast via Bampur or the coastal route along the Persian Gulf. G. Algaze described routes through Syro-Mesopotamia in the Classical Age – numerous east–west routes crossed the high plains reaching Antioch and Damascus, and other (more or less north–south) routes closely followed the Tigris and Euphrates.[52] Earlier routes must have followed similar paths.

R. Mookerji thought that seaborne trade between India and Babylon must have been carried on since 3000 BCE, citing Indian teak in the ruins of Ur.[53] Other contemporary academics considered the maritime trade to have been established later. The *Rig-veda*, the oldest Indian Vedic Sanskrit text, probably compiled between 1500 and 1000 BCE or earlier, referred to ships and merchants conducting seaborne trade. Mookerji referred to evidence of very large seagoing ships in the Sanskrit and Pali literature. The Indus River to Persian Gulf route navigability was also demonstrated, first by Scylax, sent by the Persian King Darius I in 515 BCE, then by Alexander the Great, whose army sailed down the Indus under the command of Nearchus and then routed via the Gulf to reach Babylon.[54]

Voyages to the Land of Punt

The Land of Punt was a neighbour of Ancient Egypt whose precise location is unknown but has variously been interpreted to have covered parts of modern Ethiopia, Eritrea, Somalia, Uganda or Saudi Arabia/Yemen. The Egyptian Queen Hatshepsut famously mounted a trading expedition to Punt in 1493 BCE. The expedition used five ships with a complement of around 210 men. The route was probably overland to the Red Sea and then south by ship; distances along the Red Sea would have been in the order of 1,500–2,000km and the hazardous round trip must have taken several months. Frankincense and myrrh, and possibly cinnamon, were among the goods brought back to Egypt. The expedition is described in beautiful narrative reliefs at the temple complex of Deir El-Bahari near Luxor, and includes the following description of preparations for the return journey:

> The loading of the ships very heavily with marvels of the country of Punt; all goodly fragrant woods of God's-Land, heaps of myrrh-resin, with fresh myrrh trees, with ebony and pure ivory, with green gold of Emu, with cinnamon wood, khesyt wood, with ihmut-incense, sonter-incense.[55]

This wasn't the first Egyptian mission to Punt (the oldest known was in the twenty-fifth century BCE – in which the expedition returned with 80,000 measures of myrrh, among other things) but is the best documented and most famous example.[56] There may have been other unrecorded expeditions. The cinnamon (if it was cinnamon – the translation is equivocal) would have come from India or Southeast Asia.

Asia to Madagascar ('The Cinnamon Route')

Various lines of evidence point to the westward migration of Austronesian peoples to Madagascar in the first or second millennium BCE. Miller described the 'Cinnamon Route' as an early Indonesia–Madagascar trade.[57] He referred to Pliny, who scoffed at the prevailing fanciful tales of the origin of cinnamon (e.g. its occurrence in marshes protected by clawed bats and winged serpents) and said that African cinnamon was obtained from others who:

> carry it over vast tracts of sea, upon rafts, which are neither steered by rudder, nor drawn or impelled by oars or sails … in addition to which, they choose the winter season, about the time of the equinox, for their voyage, for then a south easterly wind is blowing; these winds guide them in a straight course from gulf to gulf …[58]

Pliny said that this journey took them to Ocilia (in Yemen) and that the round trip would take five years with many perishing during the journey – naturally, he didn't specify Indonesia as it wasn't known to the West at that time. Miller's view was that the rafts referred to by Pliny were double outrigger Indonesian canoes and Pliny's observations dated this practice to at least the first century CE, though it could have been much earlier (second millennium BCE). Cinnamon would have been transported to Rhapta on the mainland and then northwards by Arab coasting vessels towards the Gulf of Aden, Somalia and the Red Sea, where it would merge into established trade systems.

However, while Pliny (and Miller) described these journeys as trade, the five-year round trip in vessels of very limited capacity, and the enormous danger involved, suggest problems with the concept, with an alternative perhaps being a slow, trickling migration of Indonesian peoples bringing along their valued goods.

The Silk Road

The Silk Road dated from around the second century BCE and was a network of land routes that linked China with the West. The phrase 'Silk Road' wasn't actually coined until the nineteenth century and it remains a somewhat nebulous concept, but one that is grounded in the historic reality of (largely) East–West exchange. It's also a misnomer, as the route is an intricate network of tracks and trails and roads covering an enormous area. From the western side, Alexander the Great extended his empire eastwards by means of military might, invading the Persian Empire in 334 BCE, followed by India in 326 BCE. The Persian Empire at that stage was huge and encompassed Anatolia, Egypt and much of central Asia south of the Caspian. Although Alexander's new empire didn't last long after his death, his legacy was a continuing Greek influence and the Hellenistic Seleucid dynasty, which went on to rule for three centuries in various forms. Eventually, the dynasty was supplanted by the Romans from the West and the Parthians from the East. The Parthian Empire lasted until 224 CE, and was at the centre of the Silk Road.

To the east, the Chinese Han dynasty, which lasted from 206 BCE to 202 CE, was the second Imperial dynasty, and one of great cultural achievement. The Han Chinese had also pushed frontiers far, reaching a province named Xiyu (now Xinjiang).[59] The routes passed through difficult terrain, skirting the Gobi Desert to the south and then to the eastern edge of the Taklamakan Desert, where they passed both north and south and converged again at Kashgar at the western end of the desert, which lay in a strategic location at the junction of the Himalayas, Tien Shan Mountains and Hindu Kush. These routes to the West were physically very challenging, so the hardy twin-humped Bactrian camels were the vehicle of choice for caravans transiting the Silk Road routes.

Although silk was the most valuable Chinese export to the West, many other goods were also traded, as well as food – and spice (small in bulk/weight and therefore easily transportable, but highly valuable). The archaeobotanical evidence for the early movement of spice along the Silk Road routes is modest, though the presence of non-native spices in many countries in the first two millennia BCE is highly suggestive of arrival by trade, or movements of people, and the overland movement of spices would have been a contributor to this. One of the legacies of Alexander's incursions into northern India was to increase botanical knowledge about spices and herbs.[60]

Marine Routes Across the Indian Ocean (Maritime Silk Roads) and Beyond

Seaborne trade goes back to the third millennium BCE involving the Harrapan Trade with Oman, Bahrein and Sumer, though becomes more noticeable after 600 BCE.[61] The good relationship between the huge Mauryan Empire of India (324–187 BCE) and the Seleucids (the Greek-derived state that encompassed much of west Asia) probably led to increasing importance of the north India to Persian Gulf marine route.

Important Gulf ports included El Dur, which has demonstrated commercial contacts involving India, Mesopotamia, Arabia, Persia and the Mediterranean. Nearby Mleiha has a similar heritage.[62] On the Arabian coast, Khor Rori (Sumhuram) in modern Dhofar, Oman, was a key port for the movement of frankincense, and it had been settled for several centuries. Archaeology has shown contacts with India, the Gulf and Mediterranean. Qana in the present Yemen is another ancient port – it was described in the *Periplus Maris Erythraei* (a first-century CE navigational text) as another frankincense hub and there was direct trade with north-west India, at least in the first century CE. The island of Socotra is an important site for aloes, frankincense and Dragon's Blood. Texts and inscriptions have shown the island was visited by sailors of different nationalities between the first century BCE and sixth century CE. In the Red Sea, the port of Adulis may have been active since the second millennium BCE, and later became the main port of the Axumite kingdom. Further north, Berenike was established in the third century BCE by the Ptolemies to gain access to the sea. Nearby Myos Hormos probably had a similar origin; both were to become vital to the Roman spice trade. Indian finds have been made at both of these sites as well as many other places, e.g. Socotra, Khor Rori.[63]

Early trade routes further east probably used Sri Lanka (Tabropane) as a hub, either routing along the east Indian coast or direct through the Malacca Straits and east to the Indonesian archipelago or north to China. Products peculiar to the Moluccas (nutmeg, mace, cloves), for example, would have necessarily needed to use a maritime route for at least part of their journey to the West. Ships from Southeast Asia were sailing to India, Sri Lanka and the East African coast, with exchanges between mainland Southeast Asia and India from at least the fourth century BCE and possibly centuries earlier.[64] Chinese interaction with Indian ports may have developed around the same time but expanded in the first century BCE.[65] More local trade around Southeast Asia and the South China Sea would have been established earlier. The trade between Southeast Asia and southern Chinese ports was known as the 'Nanhai' trade and involved spices, aromatics, woods, pearls, etc., which flourished from the first century CE.

3

Coriander Family (Apiaceae): Ancient Spices of the Middle East and Mediterranean

Coriander fruits, Khan-El-Khalili spice market, Cairo. (Author)

The Apiaceae are a family of aromatic flowering plants with over 400 genera and 3,700 species. The family has global distribution, but the largest number of native genera (including most of the well-known spices) occurs in the temperate Eurasian region. They include numerous well-known herbs and spices, including anise, coriander, cumin, fennel, parsley and others. Carrots and parsnips also fall into this group. The family is also known by its former name of Umbelliferae, based on the common morphology of the flowers, which are arranged in terminal 'umbels', with short flower stalks spreading from a common point, resembling umbrellas or parasols. The group also includes a few highly toxic species, such as hemlock and giant hogweed.

By nature of their general native distribution in the Mediterranean to Middle East/Western Asia region (Figure 2), the Apiaceae spices were among those available at the very start of civilisation (and food production) in the Fertile Crescent. Other centres of origin of food production arose in at least four other areas in the world, but the Fertile Crescent, which saw the earliest domestication around 8500 BCE, is the oldest.[1]

An interesting story illustrating this arose in 2019, when a team of international scholars recreated dishes inscribed in cuneiform writing on clay tablets from Yale University's Babylonian Collection.[2] These could justifiably be labelled the world's oldest recipes. The tablets are all from the Mesopotamian region, covering parts of Iraq, Syria and Turkey, and three date from around 1730 BCE, while a fourth is about a thousand years later. One of the older tablets is mostly intact and contains a list of ingredients that correspond to twenty-five stews and broths; the other two contain a further ten recipes. Four recipes were recreated by repeated experimentation in a modern kitchen: *Pashrutum* (a vegetable soup containing kurrat (spring leek), leek, garlic, coriander, salt and sourdough bread); *Me-e puhadi* (a lamb stew with salt, dried barley cakes, onion, Persian shallot, milk, leek and garlic); *Elamite broth* (a blood-based broth with dill, kurrat, coriander, leek, garlic and sour milk); and *Tuh'u* (a borscht-type dish containing leg meat, salt, beer, onion, rocket, coriander (spice and fresh), Persian shallot, cumin, red beet, leek, garlic and kurrat).

Ajowan (Bishop's Weed)

Trachyspermum ammi is one of several plant species that is informally known as Bishop's Weed, and in Asia as *carom*. It is native to the eastern Mediterranean and is a highly valued spice in North India, Pakistan and North Africa. The plant is an annual herbaceous aromatic with many branched leafy stems and can reach a height of 90cm. The fruits are 2–3mm long, grey-brown coloured, with a ridged surface, resembling caraway and cumin. They have a very pungent aroma and bitter taste, and the odour strongly resembles thyme, due to the presence of thymol. When crushed or ground (or roasted or fried) the fruit has a more intense flavour. Figure 6 shows a comparison of some different coriander family fruits.

The related *Ammi visnaga* (also called Bishop's Weed) was referred to in the first, second and third millennia BCE in Mesopotamia and was used in a similar way to cumin.[3] Ajowan may have arrived in India with the Greeks.[4]

Ajowan seed is used both as a spice and condiment in many countries. It is also used in spice blends – berbere (Ethiopia), panchporan (Bengal) and chat masala (India), among others. As well as being popular in Indian curries, it is often cooked with vegetables and legumes and also added to flatbreads, snacks and pastries; it is also a common ingredient in pickles. Ajowan oleoresins are used in processed foods, snacks and sauces. Fatty oils extracted from ajowan seed have various uses in the pharmaceutical and cosmetic industries, particularly for the scent of soap and deodorant. Thymol isolated from the volatile oil is commonly used as a component in toothpastes, mouthwashes and ointments. It is used as a traditional medicine to treat indigestion, flatulence and other bowel disorders.

Today ajowan is cultivated in the Mediterranean region, south-west Asia (Iran, Iraq, Afghanistan, Pakistan) and especially India, most notably in Rajasthan and Gujurat, although in other states also. India is the largest producer and exporter of ajowan fruit in the world. Saudi Arabia and Pakistan are the largest importers, though the spice is relatively minor in global trade.

Alexanders

Alexanders is a herb related to parsley, also known as horse parsley, but is in fact a different genus, with the Latin name *Smyrnium olusatrum*. It is native to the Mediterranean region, and can reach heights of 1.5m. It produces umbels of tiny yellow-green flowers. It is considered intermediate in flavour between parsley and celery, but with a somewhat bitter aftertaste. It's common in coastal areas and I encountered it along the north Suffolk coast one early April, where it dominated the hedgerows of every field, roadside verge and coastal path, and was widespread for 10 miles or so inland.

Alexanders was known to the ancient Greeks – Theophrastus commenting on its large stalks, thick root and black seeds.[5] It was thought useful to treat those suffering from strangury and stone (being administered in sweet white wine). Pliny also described it under 'Olusatrum'.[6] Both men commented that the juice or gum had the flavour of myrrh, and the genus name is derived from the ancient Greek word for myrrh, *smyrna*. Pliny observed that:

> Olusatrum … is particularly repulsive to scorpions. The seed of it, taken in drink, is a cure for gripings in the stomach and intestinal complaints, and a decoction of the seed, drunk in honied wine, is curative in cases of dysuria. The root of the plant, boiled in wine, expels calculi of the bladder, and is a cure for lumbago and pains in the sides. Taken in drink and applied topically, it is a cure for the bite of a mad dog, and the juice of it, when drunk, is warming for persons benumbed with cold.[7]

Dioscorides also appeared to describe alexanders using the term *Hipposelinon*, which was different to his *Smyrnium* – a source of confusion for later botanists.[8]

Alexanders may have been introduced to Britain by the Romans, but there is presently no firm archaeobotanical evidence for that.

There is a lengthy description of alexanders in John Gerard's 1597 *Herball*:

> the seede is thicke, long, blacke, something bitter, and of an aromaticall or spicie smell: the roote is thicke, blacke without, white within, like to a litle Radish, & is good to be eaten, out of which being broken or cut, there issueth foorth a juice that quickly waxeth thicke, having in it a sharpe bitternesse, like in taste unto Myrhhe ...[9]

Various late sixteenth- to seventeenth-century recipes featured alexanders; there is a recipe under 'sallets for fish daies': 'Alexander buds cut long waies, garnished with welkes'.[10] Alexanders appears with many other herbs in a recipe called Divers Sallets Boyled and in the 1638 *Two Books of Cookerie and Carving*.[11]

A remedy for bladder stones appeared in *The English Huswife*: roots of alexanders, parsley, pellitory and hollyhock were steeped in white wine or chicken broth, strained, then ground sloe kernels were added, and it was then taken as a drink.[12] Chopped alexanders mixed with oatmeal, boiled in milk and then added to beer was used as a topical treatment for the ague. Alexanders, together with other herbs, was used in a remedy for the heart, stomach, spleen, liver, lungs and brain.[13]

In 1660, alexanders appeared in a recipe 'to make a Bisk the best way'; it involves a wide variety of meats boiled in water and stewed in gravy, other meats, herbs and sausages fried in butter, with fried spinach or alexander leaves, eggs, gravy, chestnuts and many other ingredients, all served up ultimately as a thick rich stew, similar to pottage.[14] Also in this book 'ellicksander buds' appear in several salad recipes, including one named 'A grand sallet of Ellicksander-buds':

> Take large ellicksander-buds and boil them in fair water after they be cleansed and washed, but first let the water boil, then put them in, and being boild, drain them ... then have boild capers

and currans and lay them in the midst of a clean scowred dish, the buds parted in two with a sharp knife, and laid round about upright, or one half on one side, and the other against it on the other side, so also carved lemon, scrape on sugar, and serve it with good oyle and wine vinegar.

Alexanders was also employed as a garnish for salmon boiled in wine and water, together with other herbs and berries, in a recipe for fried snails and in one for fried and buttered 'gourds, pumpions, cowcumbers or muskmillions'. It is the key ingredient in Ellicksander Pottage:

Chop ellicksanders and oatmeal together, being picked and washed, then set on a pipkin with fair water, and when it boils put in your herbs, oatmeal and salt, boil it on a soft fire and make it not too thick, being almost boild put in some butter.

Fried alexanders was also featured as a garnish in a 1674 recipe for fried conger and another for fried salmon and one for pickled alexander buds.[15] A recipe for pickled alexander buds (with vinegar, salt and a little stale beer) was also included in a 1661 book, together with one using young alexander leaves in a Spring Pottage and another using buds in 'a Grand Sallet for the Spring'.[16] Young leaves were employed in 'an excellent potage to cleanse the blood'. Parsley, alexanders and sage leaves fried in butter were used as a garnish on a 1677 fried salmon recipe.[17]

The roots of parsley, alexanders, fennel and mallows, together with seeds of parsley, nettles, fennel, caraway, anise and grumel (gromwell), and a handful each of pellitory of the wall, saxifrage, betony, parsley and groundsel were used in a recipe from the same year for 'a metheglin [a flavoured mead] for the collick and stone'; nutmegs, cinnamon, ginger and cloves were also added to what must have been an exotic-tasting drink.[18]

Parsley of Macedonia (another term for alexanders) appears as one of many ingredients in Syrup of Radish (which 'expelleth Gravel and Stone, and scoureth the Kidneys') from the 1690 *The*

Accomplished Ladies Rich Closet of Rarities.[19] It has to be said that this particular book has such obscure and outrageous remedies that they seem to verge on witchcraft rather than herbal or traditional medicine, though syrup of radish seems perfectly innocuous.

As celery rose in popularity in the eighteenth century, so alexanders declined and is now quite rarely used as a culinary herb.

Aniseed

Aniseed is the fruit derived from the flowering plant anise (*Pimpinella anisum*), which is native to the Middle East and eastern Mediterranean. Anise is an annual plant that grows to around 90cm in height. It is mainly used as a sweet and aromatic spice, but also in confections, alcoholic drinks and as a medicine. The 1550 BCE Egyptian 'Ebers Papyrus' lists anise among its herbs and medicines. Herodotus observed that, on the death of a Scythian king, they cleaned out the inside of the belly and 'fill the cavity with a preparation of chopped cypress, frankincense, parsley-seed, and anise-seed, after which they sew up the opening, enclose the body in wax, and, placing it on a wagon, carry it about through all the different tribes'. This was the start of an elaborate and brutal death ritual, which ends up with one of the king's concubines and his servants being killed and placed around the grave.[20]

Anise was listed among the aromatic plants in the scroll of the great library at Nineveh, Assyria (now better known as part of Mosul in Iraq), established by King Ashurbanipal (668–663 BCE). Theophrastus hailed the fragrance of anise.[21] Pliny discussed the medicinal value of anise at length – he claimed the best anise came from Crete and, after that, Egypt.[22] Remedies address a bewildering list of disorders, but at the end of this long list he adds the caveat, 'however, it is injurious to the stomach, except when suffering from flatulency'.

Pliny also referred to its culinary value:

Both green and dried, it is held in high repute, as an ingredient in all seasonings and sauces, and we find it placed beneath the under-crust of bread. Put with bitter-almonds into the cloth strainers for filtering wine, it imparts an agreeable flavour to the wine: it has the effect, also, of sweetening the breath, and removing all bad odours from the mouth, if chewed in the morning with smyrnion [a herb] and a little honey, the mouth being then rinsed with wine.

Dioscorides noted that as well as sweetening the breath it had numerous medicinal qualities, including countering the poison of venomous animals, stopping intestinal discharges and promoting sexual union.[23] The Romans used spiced anise cakes at the end of a ceremonial meal (e.g. weddings) to aid digestion – they were called mustaceoe.[24] Apicius, the possible first-century CE gourmet author of the *De Re Coquinaria* collection of recipes (though they may have originated from as late as the fifth century CE), included it in recipes for laser sauce, in the stuffing of a pig's paunch, and in pig and eel sauces.[25] The Romans probably introduced anise to Britain.[26]

Oribasius, a fourth-century Greek physician, and compiler of the *Medical Collections*, included a recipe for anise wine.[27] In seventh-century Greece a little anise was popular as an additive to bread, along with fennel seed and mastic (a resin from the mastic tree), and these are still in favour with many Aegean bakers.[28] Charlemagne, in the ninth century, ordered anise to be grown on the Imperial farms.[29]

Anise appears in a small number of recipes in *The Forme of Cury* (1390).[30] It wasn't very common in late medieval recipes, occurring in less than 1 per cent of 1,377 recipes in a 2012 study, with a similar frequency for anise in confit.[31] However, royalty was an exception – 28lb of aniseed (at a cost of 9s 4d) were used in the preparation of Richard III's 1483 lavish coronation banquet.

Anise and cumin steeped in wine then dried and powdered were considered a cure for 'wind that is the cause of colic'.[32] Syr Thomas Elyot observed that 'anyseede maketh swete breathe'.[33] Andrew Boorde preferred aniseed comfits to peaches and medlars or other raw fruit at the end of meals.[34] In Gerard's *Herball* of 1597, aniseed, together with monks rhubarb, red madder, liquorice, senna, scabious and agrimony, steeped in 4 gallons of strong ale, makes a drink that 'purifieth the bloud and makes yong wenches look faire and cherry-like'.[35]

Aniseed has long been a popular flavouring in sweet dishes. It appears in recipes in the sixteenth and seventeenth centuries mainly for breads, biscuits, cordials, sweets and medicine.[36] In the seventeenth century, chocolate became a popular drink in Europe and in early recipes aniseed and chili were included.[37]

In 1727, Eliza Smith used aniseed in cordial recipes; similarly, twenty years later Hannah Glasse referred to it in distilled fruit and herb cordials such as black cherry water and 'surfeit water'.[38] Today, anise is also an ingredient in numerous spirits and alcoholic drinks around the world, including pastis and absinthe (France), arak (Middle East), ouzo (Greece), sambuca (Italy), raki (Turkey), chinchon (Spain) and several others.

Anise is one of the ingredients of the Chinese Five Spice mix. The main production today is from southern Europe, the Middle East, North Africa, Pakistan, China, Chile, Mexico and the United States.

Asafoetida

Asafoetida is the dried oleogum from the rootstocks of certain species of *Ferula*. It appears to be in the same genus as the possibly extinct silphium (see below), which was so craved by the Romans. *Ferula asafoetida* is an herbaceous perennial plant native to western and central Asia, primarily Iran and Afghanistan. The most characteristic feature of the spice is the appalling smell, as suggested by the name, and also by some of the informal names, e.g. Devil's Dung, Merde Du Diable, Stinking Gum, etc.

Despite the nauseating smell, asafoetida is extremely popular in Indian food and is a standard component of many curries, and is even used as a condiment. The smell tends to dissipate on cooking, which makes the use somewhat easier to understand. It is said to enhance umami flavours of savoury food.

The *Ferula* plants have massive taproots (like a carrot) which can reach 15cm in diameter at the crown after four to five years. Harvesting takes place in March–April and involves cutting the stem close to the root crown; a milky juice then seeps out of the cut surface. After several days the exudates are scraped off and a fresh slice of the root cut, from which more liquid exudes. This cutting and scraping proceeds for about three months until exudation ceases.

C. K. George lists seventeen commercial species of *Ferula* (there are about sixty species of *Ferula* in total) from Iran, Afghanistan, Kashmir, Punjab, Turkey, North Africa, Syria and Tibet in which the gum (primarily) is used for spice or medicinal purposes.[39] 'Hing' and 'Hingra' are common Asian names to describe the two main varieties, Hing being superior in quality and richer in odour. Hing is derived from *F. asafoetida*, while Hingra is from *F. foetida*.

The armies of Alexander the Great are reputed to have stumbled on asafoetida growing wild, probably during their conquest of Persia, and it was deemed a reasonable substitute for the popular but elusive silphium. Strabo mentioned that in Afghanistan, Alexander's army had to eat raw flesh of the beasts of burden due to the lack of firewood, but silphium (most likely asafoetida) grew in abundance and promoted digestion of the raw food.[40] Dioscorides described the medicinal uses of Narthex (asafoetida): the pith (and seed) taken in a drink could help stomach complaints, while given with wine it was a treatment for snakebites.[41] The gum, called sagapenum, was a painkiller and could also induce miscarriage; it was good to treat venomous bites; if inhaled with vinegar it could treat a blocked womb; and it was also useful as a treatment for cataracts and other eye disorders.

The tenth-century Arabic *Kitab al-Tabikh* contains numerous recipes using asafoetida, with resin, root and leaves all being used.[42] While common in the Middle East, asafoetida has generally been scarce in Europe since the fall of the Roman Empire and appears in very few recipes.

It is not clear when asafoetida first appeared in India (though one may speculate that it could have been associated with Alexander's expedition to the north of the country). Asafoetida is the most common spice referred to in the *Manasolassa*, a part-culinary text written in the twelfth century; it was often used dissolved in water.[43] It has certainly been established in India for a very long time; the sixteenth-century Portuguese naturalist Garcia de Orta said:

> The thing most used throughout India, all parts of it, is that Ass-Fetida, as well as for medicine as in cookery. A great quantity is used, for every Gentio [Hindu] who is able to get the means of buying it will buy it to flavour his food.[44]

Madhur Jaffrey observed that Hindus tend to use asafoetida, while Muslims prefer to use garlic for extra flavouring.[45] Asafoetida is particularly popular with Indian vegetarians because when cooked it exudes an onion-like aroma, a vegetable normally prohibited to Hindu Brahmins and Jains.[46]

Iranians and Afghans eat the stem and leaves as vegetables, and in Iran asafoetida is sometimes rubbed on to warmed plates before putting meat on to them.[47]

Caraway

Caraway (*Carum carvi*) is cultivated throughout most of Europe and is native to Europe and Asia. The plant is biennial, ranges up to 1m in height and has a thick tuberous rootstock. The fruits (commonly referred to as seeds) are about 3–6mm long, ridged, and have a pungent, slightly minty aroma that resembles a mix of anise and cumin with a slightly bitter taste. A slight citrus note is also characteristic. Caraway seeds have been mainly used as a condiment for flavouring food preparations, in certain savoury dishes, in desserts and as an addition to breads. The roots can be used as a vegetable in a similar way to carrot or parsnip.

Caraway was grown on Sumerian field margins in the Ur III period (*c.* 2300 BCE).[48] Caraway, like anise, appears on the Ebers Papyrus and was part of several dubious remedies for ailments including constipation, indigestion, smarting in the anus (used as a suppository with antelope fat), trembling in the fingers, ear discharge, disease of the tongue, and growth in the neck. The spice was well known to the ancient Egyptians: as well as its use as a medicine and a food, it was believed to ward off evil spirits. Archaeobotanical remains recovered from the Urartian site of Ayanis in eastern Turkey (from 685–645 BCE) included caraway fruits (as well as coriander and parsley).[49] It was also very familiar to the ancient Greeks, and Dioscorides described caraway as quite commonplace, good for the stomach and pleasant tasting, with similarities to anise.[50]

Pliny mentioned that caraway was principally employed for culinary purposes (rather than as a medicine). He maintained that the most esteemed variety came from Caria, a region of western Anatolia, and that the name 'careum' was derived from this region in which it was first grown.[51]

Caraway was found in a sackcloth bag from excavations in Roman Colchester from the area of Boudican destruction.[52] Seeds were also found from excavations in the Roman settlement at Oedenburg/Biesheim-Kunheim on the west side of the Rhine, from both the first and second century CE.[53] Caraway occurrences in Roman times are rather limited and localised, mainly being found in modern-day Germany.[54] However, it is listed in Apicius' De Re Coquinaria in numerous recipes, mainly in sauces for birds, boiled and roast meats, wild boar, venison, suckling pig, shellfish, cuttlefish, redfish, moray eel and other fish.[55]

Caraway is well represented in recipes from a thirteenth-century anonymous Andalusian cookbook but is surprisingly rare in English medieval records.[56] In a review of 217 English recipes from the late thirteenth century to late fifteenth century, caraway only appears three times.[57] In a 2012 study it is even less common, occurring in only one of 1,377 recipes.[58] It features in The Forme of Cury in a recipe for Cormarye (pork loin in red wine sauce), alongside coriander and pepper.[59]

Caraway is referred to in the fifteenth century in John Russell's Boke of Nurture as part of a dessert (with apples):

Afftur this, delicatis *mo*.
Blaunderelle, or pepyns, with carawey in confite,
Waffurs to ete / ypocras to drynk with delite.[60]

In *Henry IV Part 2*, Shallow invites Falstaff to try his pippin apples with a dish of caraway seeds.[61] There seems to be a tradition for eating caraway with roast apples, apparently still continued at Trinity College, Cambridge. The seventeenth-century herbalist and apothecary John Parkinson wrote about caraway in his *Paradisi in Sole Paradisus Terrestris*:

> The rootes of Carawayes may be eaten as Carrots, and by reason of the spicie taste doth warme and comfort a cold weake stomacke ... the seede is much used to bee put among baked fruit, or into bread, cakes, &c. to give them a relish ... It is also made into Comfits [seeds coated in sugar].[62]

In the eighteenth century, Hannah Glasse provided several recipes using caraway, mainly cakes, including one for 'carraway cakes'.[63] Traditionally seed cake was baked by farmers' wives to celebrate the end of grain sowing and given to the farm labourers.

It has long been popular in various folk medicines, e.g. it was an old Romany custom to chew caraway seeds to help digestion.[64] S. K. Malhotra provides an extensive list of caraway preparations and their application in medicine.[65]

Caraway seeds are commonly added to rye breads and cheeses in Germany and Holland, to flavour cabbage, sauerkraut, soups and sauces, and are used to flavour the liqueur kümmel and the Scandinavian spirit aquavit. The seeds are often served in a small dish to accompany Munster cheese, but in fact the seeds are a great combination with many cheeses.

The largest producer is the Netherlands, though caraway is cultivated in many countries. Caraway is frequently confused with cumin and has the informal names of *vilayati jeer* (Hindi), *cumin de prés* (France), German cumin, Persian cumin and others.[66]

Black caraway, while also a member of the same genus, is a different species, *Carum bulbocastanum*. However, it is often confused with *Nigella sativa*, or caraway. It is a temperate perennial native to Europe and the Himalayan region. The seeds are used widely in North Indian cuisine.

Celery

Celery is a widely distributed biennial plant native to the lowlands of the Mediterranean region. *Apium graveolens* has long fibrous stalks, which taper and branch into leafy stems. The plant can reach heights exceeding 2m. The small, creamy white flowers occur in dense umbels and the tiny fruits are generally around 1mm long. The fruits are mid to dark brown and ridged, in a similar manner to many of the other Apiaceae species. They have a surprisingly strong, earthy aroma, while the taste is bitter, with a slight burning sensation.

Celery leaves were found on the garland of the second anthropomorphic coffin of Tutankhamun (d. 1325 BCE), there being three coffins, the innermost one made of solid gold. Celery appears in Homer's *Odyssey* (eighth century BCE) as 'selinon'. Celery mericarps from the seventh century BCE were found in the Heraion of Samos in Greece, a huge temple complex dedicated to the goddess Hera. There is doubt as to when cultivation of celery, rather than use of the wild variety, came about, but it was probably sometime in the first millennium BCE. Certainly, the botanist and philosopher Theophrastus (d. 287 BCE) described many of the properties of celery and its cultivation.[67] The wild variety of celery is called 'smallage' and is very leafy, with thin stalks.

Mineralised celery seeds were found (infrequently) in the Cardo V sewer at Herculaneum. The seeds were an important spice in Roman cuisine according to Apicius, and while not to the same degree as the related lovage, they still appeared in a huge variety of recipes. Celery seed was used in spiced salts, though parsley could be substituted, and in a very large variety of sauces, purees, dressings, pickles, marinades, casseroles … and even in a laxative recipe with leeks.

Celery appears in Dioscorides' *De Materia Medica* as selinon, and cultivated versions were used as a medicine to address burning in the stomach, hard swollen breasts, and poisonous animal bites, among numerous other disorders.[68] It could be applied with bread for inflammation of the eyes.

It also appears to be the helioselinon of Pliny, a useful remedy for spider bites. Celery archaeobotanical remains have been found distributed widely across north-west Europe, though, in common with certain other condiments, it has a strong correlation with proximity to Roman military sites and towns and was also found in some more distant rural sites.[69] It also appears to have been introduced to Britain by the Romans (though it is possible that wild celery was already present before their arrival). A 2008 study found forty-nine occurrences of celery from Roman Britain sites.[70] Celery occurrences increased from early to middle Roman times but then decreased by late Roman times, in common with several other introduced species: the strong association with Roman cuisine is the cause of their decline. But despite the decline, by the time the Romans left, it is likely that celery was already part of the horticultural landscape of Britain. It has been found in late Saxon sites at Winchester and was eaten daily according to the monk Aelfric Bata.[71] It was also shown in the plan of the ninth-century monastery kitchen garden of St Gall in Switzerland. The Chinese appear to have used wild celery from at least the fifth century CE and they later developed cultivated varieties; their celery is thinner, juicier and has a stronger flavour than European varieties.[72]

Celery is extremely rare in medieval recipes, despite its evident availability. It is conceivable that it was only eaten raw and in salads.

Giles Rose referred to celery within salads in his delightfully named 1682 book *A perfect School of Instructions for the Officers of the Mouth: shewing the whole art*: 'as for your Sallets of Sellery serve them both boyl'd and raw, as these two former ones, and their Roots in like manner.'[73]

In the mid-nineteenth century, the botanist Dr Antonio Targioni Tozzetti commented that, although celery was known to the ancients, it 'was considered rather as a funereal or ill-omened plant than an article of food', though this seems only partly correct based on the popular usage during the Roman era.[74] It is mentioned only as a medicinal plant by early modern writers; however, it had started to be grown for the table in Tuscany by the sixteenth century.

Smallage appears in a peculiar remedy for the ague in *The Widowes Treasure* (1588):

Take a handfull of smalledge, and a handfull of baye Salte, and a handfull of white frankensence, and *** Plantaine leaves, beate all these finely in a Morter then devide them into foure partes, and lay two partes to your brests, and the other two partes to the bought of your armes. An howre before your fit come, you must have a pinte of Ale sodds to the halfe, and when it riseth, skimme it, then put in a white breade crust, and let it seethe with the Ale, and when your Ague beginneth to come drink it and eat the crust of bread.[75]

Smallage appears in Gerard's late sixteenth-century *Herbal*; the alternative name is water parsley, but this looks very much like celery from drawing and description: 'the stalks be chamfered and divided into branches.'[76] He provides numerous medical uses for the juice, leaves and seed.

Smallage seed is listed in *The English Huswife* of 1615 in a remedy for 'collicke and stone', and smallage occurs in remedies for all manners of swellings and aches, including venomous stings, for toothache, and to dry up any sore.[77] However, celery is absent from the extensive list of herbs and salads and culinary recipes. According to E. L. Sturtevant, the Dutch physician and botanist Rembertus Dodonaeus in his 1616 *Pemptades* commented on the wild plant being transferred to gardens but distinctly said it was not for food use.[78] The French horticulturalist Olivier de Serres referred to a cultivated celery in 1623.[79]

In the 1675 *Accommplish'd Lady's Delight* there is a recipe for syrup of vinegar which uses the roots and greens of smallage, the syrup being a medicine to clear 'Phlegm, or tough Humours'.[80] Smallage and other herbs were also used in a decoction for sore eyes and another one to cure blindness in a man under 50 years of age. The other herbs used were fennel, rue, betony, vervain, agrimony, cinquefoil, pimpernel, eyebright, celandine and sage. They were mixed into a quart of good white wine and then to this was added thirty crushed peppercorns, six spoonfuls of honey and ten spoonfuls of the urine of 'a Man-Child that is wholsom', the whole being boiled, strained and then put into the eyes of the patient with a feather.

The Closet of the Eminently Learned Sir Kenelme Digby Kt opened, first published in 1669, contains a recipe for Smallage-Gruel, which is basically boiled oatmeal, with chopped smallage added, seasoned with salt and optional dash of nutmeg and mace, and butter stirred in after the gruel is removed from the fire.[81]

The Accomplished Ladies Rich Closet of Rarities, from 1691, also used smallage for an eye treatment, syrup of vinegar (again) in a concoction for internal bruising, in a decoction for black jaundice, in a poultice for aches and sprains, and in a recipe to prevent spitting blood, but not in any culinary recipes.[82]

Eliza Smith (1727) gave a recipe for Celery Ragoo:

WASH and make a bunch of celery very clean, cut it in pieces, about two inches long, put it into a stew-pan with just as much water as will cover it, tie three or four blades of mace, two or three cloves, about twenty corns of whole pepper in a muslin rag loose, put it into the stew-pan, a little onion, a little bundle of sweet-herbs; cover it close, and let it stew softly till tender; then take out the spice, onion and sweet-herbs, put in half an ounce of truffles and morels, two spoonfuls of catchup, a gill of red wine, a piece of butter as big as an egg rolled in flour, six farthing French rolls, season with salt to your palate, stir it all together, cover it close, and let it stew till the sauce is thick and good. Take care that the rolls do not break, shake your pan often; when it is enough, dish it up, and garnish with lemon. The yolks of six hard eggs, or more, put in with the rolls, will make it a fine dish. This for a first course. If you would have it white, put in white wine instead of red, and some cream for a second course.

She also provided a recipe for turkey fowl in celery sauce and used celery in a 'hodge podge of beef with savoys', in pease soup (these latter described as French dishes). Hannah Glasse (1747) also used it in numerous recipes. It looks like the late seventeenth century to early eighteenth century was when celery started to become more mainstream as a culinary item.

In 1806, Bernard M'Mahon noted different varieties of celery for American garden use: hollow-stalked, solid-stalked and red solid-stalked (the stalks being deemed the most useful part).[83]

In 1888, Mrs Agnes B. Marshall, a leading Victorian cookery writer (famous among other things for inventing, or at least popularising, the ice cream cone), produced a well-known cookery book, called, unsurprisingly, *Mrs A B Marshall's Cookery Book*.[84] By this time, celery was well established in the kitchen and numerous recipes are included: in celery sauce; chiffonade of chicken à la Princesse; celery sauce with boiled turkey; cucumber and celery salad for plovers eggs à la Charmante; braised celery; celery à la Villeroi; ragout of celery; and celery à la creme.

Celery is cultivated widely in Europe and the USA, primarily as a herb and vegetable. It is also cultivated for seed as a spice, mainly in India, southern France, China and Egypt.[85] Although celery was introduced quite late to India (around 1930), the country is now the largest producer and exporter of celery seed.

Processed products of the seed are the volatile oil (used in food flavourings, perfumery and the pharmaceutical industry), celery oleoresin (food flavourings), seed powder (food flavourings and condiment) and celery salt – mixture of seed or oleoresin or ground stems and finely ground salt. Dehydrated celery stalks and leaves are used for flavouring soups, broths, canned tuna fish, stuffings and stewed tomatoes.[86]

Coriander

Coriander (*Coriandrum sativum*) is a versatile and popular annual herb whose seeds and roots are used as spices, and fresh leaves and stems as seasoning, vegetable and garnish. It is native to southern Europe, North Africa and parts of Asia. In the USA, coriander is called cilantro. The plants reach heights of up to 1.2m and can be either erect and tall with shorter branches or bushy with a weaker main shoot and longer branches. The branches and the main shoot terminate in compound umbels, with each umbel containing numerous white or pale pink flowers. Larger variety fruits (up to 5mm in diameter) are typical of tropical or subtropical climates, while smaller fruits (up to 3mm in diameter) are typical of temperate climates.[87] The mature fruits split into two halves, or mericarps, each containing a single seed. The herbage, seeds and roots all have different flavours. The leaves have a sweet, citrus component. The fruits yield a volatile oil described as warm, spicy-aromatic, sweet and fruity, dominated by linalool, which is largely responsible for the flavour. The roots have a more intense flavour than the leaves or stems. Interestingly, the cooler climate of northern Europe appears to produce more linalool in coriander than the tropical climate of India and similar.

The perception of flavour of coriander is different between differing groups of people: while most find it a very pleasant and attractive addition to food, there is a significant minority who find it tastes soapy. Based on a 2012 article in *Nature*, this may be due to a difference in olfactory receptor genes which influence the sense of smell.[88] In particular, the OR6A2 gene encodes a receptor that is highly sensitive to aldehydes, which contribute to the flavour of coriander. Notwithstanding this divergence of opinion, its popularity goes back a very long way.

The oldest coriander fruits discovered to date are from the Nahal Hemar cave in Israel and date to 6000 BCE.[89] Axel Diederichsen concludes that coriander originated in the Near East based on archaeobotanical research and ancient literature, as well as the distribution of the other species of the tribe Coriandreae.[90] There may be evidence of Egyptian use of coriander as early as the 5th dynasty (2500 BCE).[91] Coriander was recovered from baskets in Tutankhamun's tomb (19th dynasty, *c.* 1325 BCE) among many other well-preserved plant materials.[92] In Mesopotamia, coriander was grown in various cities in the third millennium BCE, including Lagash and Umma. At Lagash, in the Ur III period, it is included in a list of spices and herbs and other foods.[93] At Old Babylonian Ur (*c.* 2000–1600 BCE) coriander was used as part of food offerings at temple sites. It was recorded from the second millennium BCE town of Nuzi, where it was brought into the town from surrounding villages and gardens. Coriander is referred to in the 1550 BCE Ebers Papyrus. Spices used in Mycenaean Greece (1600–1100 BCE) included coriander, fennel and mint, which must have seasoned an otherwise uninteresting cereal diet – we know this from clay tablets written in Linear B script.[94] Coriander was also one of the herbs listed in the seventh-century BCE scroll of the great library at Nineveh, Assyria. The seventh-century BCE list of plants (on a clay tablet) in Merodach-Baladan's garden includes coriander.

Jack Sasson listed condiments and herbs in the court of King Zimri-Lim of Mari (in modern Syria; reigned 1775–1761 BCE) – cumin, black cumin, coriander, saffron, myrtle and scented reed.[95]

A single seed of coriander dated to 540–330 BCE was found at the ancient city of Gordion, Turkey.[96] Coriander and cumin may have been introduced to India via Persia by the second half of the first millennium BCE.[97] Although coriander leaves were used since the Vedic period (1500–500 BCE), the seeds were not used as a spice until the Muslims arrived in India (seventh century CE), possibly explaining the major use of coriander seeds in Mughlai cuisine.[98]

Classical Greek authors wrote about coriander: Aristophanes (446–386 BCE), Theophrastus (371–287 BCE), Hippocrates (460–370 BCE), and Roman authors Pliny and Columella (both first century CE).[99] Coriander seeds were present (among other condiments) at the Roman town of Mons Claudianus in Egypt.[100] They were found in the Cardo V sewer at Herculaneum, the largest sample of Roman shit ever found! The sewer protected its contents from the effects of the 79 CE eruption of Vesuvius.[101] Dioscorides described coriander as cooling and able to reduce infection and inflammation, among other things. Coriander seed taken with wine was thought to both expel worms and create sperm. But too much could dangerously disturb the mind. Apicius listed coriander as one of the most important European spices and Roman demand was very high. It was extensively cultivated in Egypt and elsewhere to meet this pressing demand.

Coriander was present at Silchester, imported before the 43 CE Roman invasion (seeds were found in waterlogged sediments that date from 20 BCE to 20 CE).[102] Coriander was also popular in the post-invasion Roman settlement. Seeds have also been found at several Romano-British forts as well as rural, urban and other sites as part of a diversification of foods in Britain during the Roman period, with as many as fifty new foods introduced during that time.[103] In fact, coriander is characteristic of European Roman settlements but became much less common after the fall of the Roman Empire.[104] It reappears in the medieval period 950–1500 CE, though appears to be a luxury condiment of urban life.

Coriander was referred to in a Chinese book on agriculture from the fifth century CE.[105] Diederichsen notes that the long history of cultivation in India is borne out by the many local names for the plant, as well as Hindi and Sanskrit names, which are often related to each other. Coriander is listed in *De Villis* (c. 771–800 CE), a text related to royal estates during the reign of Charlemagne, and/or the ninth-century Plan of St Gall monastery garden.[106] It was also among the herbs bequeathed by the Bede to his brethren.

However, coriander was an uncommon spice in medieval England. Coriander (and fennel) was found in fourteenth- to fifteenth-century deposits in Winchester.[107]

John Gerard (1597) called coriander 'a very stinking herbe' but highly praised the dried seeds as 'very convenient to sundrie purposes'.

In Hannah Glasse's 1747 recipe for 'Currey the India way' only pepper and coriander seeds and salt are used for seasoning, but by the 4th edition (1751) ginger and turmeric were added.[108]

Coriander seed also appears in 'Cullis the Italian way', pickled pig's feet and ears, dressed calves' liver, baked salmon and seasoning for collar of beef, but generally coriander was used infrequently in her recipes. By contrast, it has in recent times been labelled the favourite fresh herb in Britain, with over 30 million packs sold in 2013, partly due to the popularity of Asian curries, stir fries and the popularisation of Italian cuisine.[109]

India is the world's largest producer of coriander today, with around 750,000 tonnes in 2019–20; it is also the largest consumer. It is grown in many countries, with other large producers including Russia, Italy, Bulgaria, Syria, Morocco, Canada, Argentina, Romania and Iran.

Cumin

Cumin spice is the dried fruit of the herb *Cuminum cyminum*. The cumin plant is a small annual ranging up to 50cm in height, with branching stem and long slender deep green leaves and umbels of small white or pink flowers. The fruits range up to 6mm long and have distinctive longitudinal ridges. The fruit is commonly and wrongly called the seed. It is one of the oldest used spices and has a very distinct earthy aroma and flavour. It has sometimes been somewhat unkindly referred to as 'the sweaty shirt spice'.[110] The taste of the uncooked fruits is quite bitter, with a strong aftertaste. Dry frying before grinding reduces the intensity of the flavour.

The oldest known occurrence of cumin is from the Neolithic of Atlit-Yam in northern Israel, dating from 6900–6300 BCE.[111] But dietary habits must have changed, as it then disappeared from the area. It may have been native to the Mediterranean region and Middle East. Ancient evidence of cumin has also been found in Mesopotamia from 2100 to 1900 BCE and New Kingdom Egypt from 1543 to 1292 BCE. It was grown at Lagash in the late Early Dynastic period in the same field as onions, flax and vegetables, and was used in the Old Babylonian period at Rimah.[112] It was included in the list of spices brought to Nuzi in the middle of the second millennium. A recent study of the bio-archaeology of the Philistine culture in Israel from the twelfth to seventh centuries BCE demonstrates that the invaders didn't only bring themselves but also their plants, specifically sycamore trees, the opium poppy and (once again) cumin.[113] Cumin was listed, among other spices, in cuneiform writing from the seventh-century BCE great library in the ancient Assyrian city of Nineveh.[114] From its origin in the Levant, cumin probably moved eastwards to India via Arab spice traders, and westwards via the Phoenicians.

The Romans regarded cumin as an important seasoning. Apicius refers to it frequently (his third most common spice after pepper and lovage) and it appears in many exotic dishes, e.g. as a cumin sauce for lobsters and shellfish and in sauces for various fish, as a spice in forcemeats, sow's womb sausage, in a laxative broth, in various pumpkin dishes, peeled cucumbers with brains, as an aid to digestion (when mixed with ginger, rue, dates, pepper and honey), as a condiment in a casserole of saltfish, cooked brains, chicken livers, eggs, cheese, herbs, wine and mead, with pears and peaches dishes, fruity ragouts, in a chicken, brain and pea casserole, in sauces for exotic birds such as ostrich, crane and flamingo, in various vegetable dishes and many others. The strong flavour of cumin may have been to counter the tastes and textures of some of the more unusual ingredients; then again, many of these foods would not have been regarded as exotic by the Romans.

Cumin was part of the mid- and late Saxon diets at Hamwic (present-day Southampton) and London.[115] Cumin is listed in *Leechdoms*, a nineteenth-century compilation of Anglo-Saxon texts edited by the wonderfully named Oswald Cockayne, as well as in the early eighth-century *Capitulare de villis*, which described the management of royal estates in Carolingian France.[116] Cumin was also found in the exquisite ninth-century Oseberg Viking ship burial in Norway.

In medieval Europe, cumin was one of the more readily available spices in general use. It may have had some use as a love icon.[117] Ahmin also refers to an Arab tradition of a ground cumin, pepper and honey paste which was considered to have aphrodisiac properties.

In 1158, the Winchester Pipe Rolls – the country's most complete set of manorial accounts – recorded the purchase of cumin (as well as pepper, cinnamon and almonds) specially for the queen.[118] Cumin and other spices were listed in the royal accounts from 1205 to 1207 during the reign of King John. Records from Selby Abbey show that 2lb of cumin was purchased in 1416–17, priced 4d. Cumin appears to have declined in importance in European cuisine after the medieval era.

Medicinal properties of cumin: cumin was associated with women's reproductive health according to the Hippocratic Corpus, a collection of around sixty early ancient Greek medical texts from the fifth century BCE.[119] In the gynaecological treatises, remedies were often applied or administered after a bath and/ or whilst fasting. A hair treatment involved a poultice of cumin or excrement of pigeons, or some herbs and vegetables. Pliny mentioned that cumin was 'much employed in medicine, among the stomachic remedies more particularly' and was usually bruised and taken with bread or drunk in wine and water.[120] Wild cumin was preferred over cultivars for medical uses in general, but both varieties had the effect of producing paleness. This effect was, according to Pliny, used by the students of Marcus Porcius Latro, an eminent Roman rhetorician (d. 4 BCE), in order to imitate the pale complexion of their master. African cumin had the reputation as a remedy against incontinence. If parched and beaten up in vinegar, it was supposedly good for treating liver problems and vertigo, while in sweet wine it helped with urine acridity and problems of the uterus. Parched and beaten up with honey, it was used as an application for swellings of the testes. Among the many other remedies suggested by Pliny, cumin mixed with oil could counter the effects of stings from scorpions, serpents and centipedes. The Greek pharmacologist, physician and botanist Dioscorides had similar views and remedies to Pliny on the medicinal uses of cumin; they were more or less contemporary, both living in the first century CE. Both Pliny and Dioscorides rated Ethiopian cumin very highly, the latter describing cumin as warming, astringent and drying.[121]

One of the less well-known and somewhat gruesome uses of cumin (and certain other spices) was in the preservation of criminals' severed heads. According to Jack Turner, by the fifteenth century in France the severed heads may have been parboiled and seasoned with cheaper aromatics such as cumin, the preserved heads hopefully deterring would-be criminals.[122]

A cautionary story from *The Arabian Nights*, 'The Reeve's Tale', recounts the reluctance of the protagonist to eat a cumin ragout, but if he had to eat it he would need to wash his hands forty times each with soap, potash and galingale.[123] So his hosts brought these materials and he cleaned his hands. As he ate, the group then saw that he had no thumbs, and they pressed him to tell the story. He related how he fell in love with a beautiful girl who worked in the palace of the Chief Consort. After being smuggled into the palace in a chest, he was finally presented to the Lady Zubaydah, who gave them her blessing. A cumin ragout wedding feast was prepared and he ate his fill. He wiped his hands but forgot to wash them. When they brought his bride to the bed chamber, she smelled the ragout on his hands and became angry. After many days she returned and cut off his thumbs and big toes to teach him a lesson. And he swore never to eat cumin ragout again without washing his hands as described. A salutary lesson on the importance of hygiene, the pungency of cumin, and the power of women!

Today, the world's largest cumin producer is India, producing 70 per cent of the world total of 300,000 tons per annum – and it is also the world's largest consumer, using 63 per cent of global production. It is commonly known as *jeera* in South Asia. It is also produced in several Middle Eastern countries, especially Turkey, Iran, Syria and China. Cumin is used as ground (normally dry roasted first) or as whole seed varieties. As well as being used as a spice and condiment, it is also commonly blended in garam masala, curry powder and other spice mixes. It is also a common ingredient in confectionary, bread, sausages, pickles, relishes and other foods.

Cumin is commonly confused with caraway, but, although they belong to the same family and the fruits are of a similar size and shape, they are quite different in flavour and do not share the same genus (caraway is *Carum carvi*). Also, 'black cumin' (*Nigella sativa*) is only a distant relation and not even in the same family.

Dill

Dill (*Anethum graveolens*) is an aromatic annual herb and seed spice. The plant has slender hollow stems, can reach heights of around 1m and has finely divided, thin, wispy leaves. Umbels are large with small white to yellow flowers and yellowish-brown ridged ovoid fruits some 4–5mm long. It is probably native to south-west Asia and the eastern Mediterranean region. Indian dill is considered a sub-species, *Anethum sowa*. The fruits are pungent and aromatic with a slightly bitter aftertaste, with similarities to caraway. The name 'dill' appears to be of Germanic or Scandinavian origin, possibly derived from the Old Norse word 'dilla', meaning 'to soothe', as it was used to ease infants' stomach pains.[124]

Dill was present as a (probably) cultivated plant in Late Neolithic lake settlements in Switzerland (3400–3050 BCE), and was found in the tomb of Amenophis II (d. ?1401 BCE) in Egypt and in seventh-century BCE Samos.[125] Dill-scented oil was burned in Greek homes and the oil was used in making some of their wines.[126] Theophrastus described the fragrant sap of celery, dill, fennel, etc., as well as the roots, stems and seeds.[127] Dioscorides observed that Anethon flowers steeped in oil was a good treatment for soothing and opening female genitals, for coldness and shivers at the start of a fever, warming and countering weariness and for relieving joint pains.[128] The seed and dried filaments in a decoction helped numerous gastric complaints and promoted urine, among other benefits.[129]

Pliny described dill as a carminative; also, the roots could be applied topically in water or wine for defluxions of the eyes, and while the seed could arrest hiccups and dispel indigestion, the plant itself weakened the eyesight and generative powers.[130] Gladiators ate dill as it was thought that the herb would boost their valour.[131] Dill was present in first- to second-century CE deposits from the Roman Mons Porphyrites complex in the Eastern Desert of Egypt.[132] It was introduced to Britain by the Romans.[133]

Dill was well known in Saxon times, is mentioned in *Leechdoms* and, according to the monk Aelfric Bata's *Colloquy*, it was eaten every day, as were chervil, mint and parsley. Ann Hagen commented that dill may have been grown at Dilcar in Cumberland and Dilwick in Bedfordshire.[134] Dill seeds were well represented in mid-ninth- to eleventh-century cesspit deposits in York.[135] Don Patrick O'Meara noted a pre-Conquest distribution for dill archaeobotanical records in northern England, with forty-four out of forty-six samples restricted to this period, and only two (from fourteenth- to fifteenth-century Beverley) occurring later than that.[136] Colin Spencer commented that the white soup called 'dillegrout', traditionally served at coronation feasts since the coronation of William the Conqueror's wife in 1068, was made with dill, and that it became an enduring tradition after William gave to his cook Tezelin the lordship of the Manor of Addington as a reward for creating the soup.[137]

In *The Widowes Treasure* of 1588 there is a remedy 'for a hot burning in the stomacke growen of Choller, which causeth the Fever', which used herbs, including dill, and raisins and prunes seethed in pottage.[138]

John Gerard noted that 'the whole plant is of a strong smell'.[139] He listed the numerous virtues of the tops, seed and plant. A domestic book of 1615 used a small quantity of smallage, dill, aniseeds and burnet, dried and ground to a fine powder, and taken with a good draught of white wine, 'for the difficulty of urine'.[140]

One of dill's most famous uses is that in pickling cucumbers. Pickling of vegetables in general may have started as early as 2400 BCE in Mesopotamia, but the specific use of dill in the process might have originated much later, possibly in the fifteenth century CE.[141] Boiled green fennel or dill was used with verjuice, salt and water to 'preserve cowcumbers all the yeere' in a 1603 cookery book and in similar seventeenth-century recipes.[142] In the *Court & Kitchin of Elizabeth, Commonly called Joan Cromwel* of 1664 there is a pickling recipe that uses caraway, fennel and dill seeds; cloves; mace; ginger; nutmeg; and cinnamon all beaten together.[143] In one recipe, Hannah Woolley in 1670 used dill and bay leaves, together with beaten spices, wine vinegar and salt; another used dill and fennel seeds, pepper, cloves and mace.[144] Despite the wide variety of recipes pickling herbs, vegetables and fruits, dill appears only to be used in the pickling of cucumbers – for example, there are forty-six recipes for pickling in *The English and French Cook* of 1674, but dill only appears in that for cucumbers.[145] Other pickling recipes using dill and/or fennel exist from this period.[146] They were also used by Eliza Smith in 1727 in a similar recipe to pickle cucumbers and she also used dill seeds, along with other spices, in a recipe to pickle walnuts.[147] Large-scale pickling recipes (of a thousand cucumbers) appear in the 1682 *Salt and Fishery: A Discourse thereof*, the first using dill, fennel, a strong brine of refined salt and beer or rape-vinegar, with roach-allom (potassium aluminium sulphate) dissolved therein; the second 'according to the receipt of Mr John Bull' used 6 pennyworth of dill and fennel, 2 pennyworth each of cloves and mace, 1oz of white pepper, 2oz of ginger, 4 gallons of elder vinegar, a handful of walnut leaves and 1 gallon of strong brine, all boiled together and then let stand, then added to the pot with the cucumbers.[148] Perhaps the most famous (and arguably the world's largest) user of dill pickles today is McDonald's, which uses slices of the pickles in its hamburgers.

A 1653 medical text employed dill in several medicines.[149] Dill seed (together with fennel seed, caraway seed, aniseed, liquorice seed, cubebs, nutmeg, mace, galingale, ginger, cloves, cinnamon, coral and amber) was used in a medicine to comfort the stomach. Dill, alongside other herbs, was also used in a curious remedy for the 'numme palsie', which involved putting the herbs mixed with oil of castor, dill and camomile into the belly of a newly killed fox, roasting it and then collecting the oil that drops out to be used as a medicine for all palsies or numbness. Equally or even more bizarre was the remedy for aching joints, back or sciatica, which involved killing a live fox or badger, skinning, cleaning its bowels, breaking its bones to yield the marrow, boiling the carcass in brine, adding leaves of sage, rosemary, dill, oregano, marjoram and juniper berries and then, when well done, straining the whole to make the required liniment. It was also used in another somewhat less messy remedy to bathe aching limbs.

Dill also appeared in *The Compleat Housewife* in a concoction for eye drops 'to strengthen the sight and prevent cataracts'.[150] Dill seeds, with a lesser quantity of fennel seeds, boiled in beer, strained and sweetened with sugar, were given as a drink to children as a remedy for rickets.[151] Dill, mastic, frankincense, cumin seeds and mint were used in a rickets treatment in the 1690 *Accomplished Ladies Rich Closet of Rarities*, and dill seed in a teething treatment.[152]

Dill's modern usage is as a flavouring for breads, sauces, dips, soups (e.g. borscht), pickles, potato dishes and in herb butter; the seeds also enhance the flavour of roasts, stews, soups, pickles and in vegetable and rice dishes, and it has enduring popularity in northern and eastern Europe, Ukraine and Russia. Indian dill seed is used as a spice in various north Indian vegetable dishes. It is popular in Gujarat, where stews of green lentils are prepared with dill weed as the vegetable greens.[153] Dill is also popular in China and several Southeast Asian countries.

Fennel

Fennel (*Foeniculum vulgare*) is a flowering perennial herb, and its seeds provide a popular spice. It grows up to 2.5m tall and has distinctive yellow flowers and feathery leaves. Fennel is a native of the Mediterranean but has spread to many areas. The fruits are oval, pale green to yellowish brown, ridged and about 4–8mm long. The main varieties are sweet fennel (*F. vulgare* var. dulce), also known as French or Roman fennel; and bitter fennel (*F. vulgare* var. Mill). Bitter fennel is the original wild form, with a somewhat bitter-tasting fruit, and this was probably the only type used in the classical world. Sweet fennel appears to have originated in Italy before spreading eastward to India and China.[154] Charlemagne's eighth-century edict (the *Capitulare de villis*) refers to it in a long list of herbs, plants, vegetables and trees intended for the garden. Florence (Italian-type) sweet fennel or Finocchio is the popular vegetable with bulbous hypocotyl.

Fennel appeared in a list of herbs and spices from second-millennium BCE Nuzi, Mesopotamia.[155]

Fennel has lent its name to the site of the Battle of Marathon (490 BCE), where the vastly outnumbered Greeks defeated the Persian invaders, i.e. 'marathon' meant fennel in ancient Greek and so the battle is assumed to have taken place on a field of fennel.

Fennel was the *marathron* of Dioscorides – its medicinal properties when eaten as a herb or with the seed in a decoction of barley assisted lactation, while a drink from decoction of the leaves was good for kidney pains and bladder disorders.[156] The juice from bruised stems and leaves was good for eye disorders affecting vision. It was also effective against snake bites (if taken with wine, assuming that you had a bottle of wine to hand in the wilderness), and the crushed roots mixed with honey and applied as a plaster were a good treatment for dog bites. Pliny noted that when snakes shed their skins they rub themselves on the stalks and sharpen their sight with the juice of the plant, and therefore it was concluded that the juice would be beneficial for human sight also.[157] He continued:

The seed of the cultivated fennel is medicinally employed in wine, for the stings of scorpions and serpents, and the juice of it, injected into the ears, has the effect of destroying small worms that breed there. Fennel is employed as an ingredient in nearly all our seasonings, vinegar sauces more particularly: it is placed also beneath the undercrust of bread. The seed ... is highly esteemed, also, for affections of the lungs and liver. Taken in moderate quantities, it arrests looseness of the bowels, and acts as a diuretic; a decoction of it is good for gripings of the stomach, and taken in drink, it restores the milk. The root, taken in a ptisan, purges the kidneys – an effect which is equally produced by a decoction of the juice or of the seed; the root is good too, boiled in wine, for dropsy and convulsions. The leaves are applied to burning tumours, with vinegar, expel calculi of the bladder, and act as an aphrodisiac.[158]

In addition, it promoted the secretion of seminal fluids when taken as a drink and was extremely beneficial to the generative organs, either as a decoction of the root in wine used as a poultice or used beaten up in oil. It was applied with wax to tumours and bruises, and the root, with wine for the stings of multipedes.

Pliny also described the many uses of a wild, larger variety of fennel (or *Hippomarathron*) which was regarded as more efficacious in every respect than cultivated fennel.

Fennel seeds were found along with others at the Roman town of Mons Claudianus in Egypt, and also at Mons Porphyrites among seven members of the Apiaceae family.[159] Both sites are situated in the Eastern Desert. A small number of fennel seeds were found at the Cardo V sewer at Herculaneum.

Apicius stressed the enormous importance of laser/silphium to the Romans – it's a kind of giant fennel – but fennel itself appears much less frequently in his recipes. It was an ingredient in barley soup, boiled beans or chickpeas with broth, wine, eggs and fresh fennel, in a white sauce for appetisers, in a sauce for broiled mullet, ground fennel seed in a seasoning for roast tenderloins, fennel seed in pottage with brains, in peas or beans *à la vitellius* (with herbs, spices and wine), in sauces for boiled meats, wild boar, venison and veal.

Fennel was certainly used by the Saxons – an old charm to improve low-yielding land, or if sorcery or witchcraft was suspected, included the use of fennel. It is known from late Saxon sites in Winchester and is shown in the physic garden of the St Gall monastery plan (820–830 CE). Wolf Storl documented further examples of the use of fennel to protect against devils, demons and evil spirits, which appears to have been quite widely adopted across medieval Europe.[160]

A 2016 study noted ten records of fennel in medieval cesspit deposits from the north of England (Beverly, Chester, Hull and York), one from the eleventh century, the remainder from the thirteenth to fifteenth centuries, which suggests a largely post-Norman adoption of the herb.[161] The same study reviewed 217 recipes from the thirteenth to fifteenth centuries; generally, the Apiaceae are not well represented in these historic records. Combined, caraway, coriander, cumin, dill and fennel were only present in around 1 per cent of recipes. It appears that fennel was only used as an occasional flavouring.

Two recipes for Cold Brewet appear in the 1390 *Forme of Cury*; one is later repeated in the fifteenth-century manuscript Harley 5401.[162] It was a sauce made from cream of almonds spiced with salt, sugar, ginger, fennel juice and wine. Other recipes using fennel in *The Forme of Cury* are the wonderfully named Eowtes of Flessh, Salat, Fenkel in Soppes, Compost and Erbolates. Compost, in this case, was a highly spiced dish of stewed pickled vegetables and included fennel seed. A contemporary Italian source used fennel flowers in a fennel sauce.[163]

Fennel roots are used in a recipe from 1615 called 'To boyle a capon another way', but it was clearly still not very popular in the English kitchen at this time.[164]

Gerard's *Herball* (1597) differentiates between common fennel and sweet fennel:

The second kind of Fennell is likewise well knowne by the name of sweete Fennell, so called because the seedes thereof are in taste sweete like unto Annise seedes, resembling the common Fennell, saving that the leaves are larger and fatter, or more oileous: the seede greater and whiter, and the whole plant in each respect greater.

The medicinal uses were varied: powdered seed preserved the eyesight; the green leaves eaten or seed made into a beverage and drunk would 'filleth womens brests with milke'; a decoction of fennel when drunk would ease the pain of kidneys, avoid stones and promote urine; roots when boiled in wine and drunk would serve as already mentioned and also guard against dropsy; seeds when drunk would alleviate stomach pain and the desire to vomit and break wind; the herb, seeds and root were all good for lungs, liver and kidneys.

Fennel appears as an ingredient in various cordial waters and health-giving syrups in John Murrell's 1617 book.[165]

Medicinal uses of fennel also appear in Elizabeth Grey's 1653 medical text: fennel juice or steeped in water and wine with other herbs as remedies for eye problems; fennel root in a broth for the weak, and in a medicine to purge and amend the internal organs; young leaves in a syrup to open the liver; and green fennel in a plaster for the head. Fennel seeds were used in numerous recipes: in a 'sovereign water' as a panacea for many conditions; in a drink for 'all kinds of surfets'; in a drink against melancholy and another to promote urine; in two remedies for 'Aqua Composita'; in a powder for sore eyes; in Dr Stephen's Water (a common remedy of the time); in a powder against wind; in an ointment for the spleen; in a remedy for kidney stones and in another one for purging.[166] Oil of fennel was made by placing a quantity between two tiles or iron plates, heating them and pressing out the liquor, which was then a good treatment for tissick (a lung complaint), dry scab, burning and scalding.

Various late seventeenth- and eighteenth-century English cookery books contain recipes using fennel. Young sprouts of fennel are used in a recipe for 'Sallet de Sante', branches of fennel to make white fennel and red fennel syrups, fennel seeds in 'Fennel in Dragee' and green fennel in a seasoned beef broth with venison.[167] Fennel seeds and roots are used in another recipe for Dr Stephen's Water, leaves and roots in a recipe for syrup of vinegar, and fennel tops in one to pickle cucumbers.[168] In *The Whole Duty of a Woman* (1696), as well as use in some homespun remedies, fennel is used in a recipe to souse fish and as garnishes for roast salmon and for turkey.[169] Hannah Glasse seems to have made modest use of fennel – it appears in a recipe to dress mackerel, the seeds in a recipe to make black cherry water, the flowers in a recipe for plague water (in a distillation of a huge number of other roots, flowers and seeds), the seeds in one for 'surfeit water' (a remedy for over-indulgence), fennel flowers in one to make milk water, and one for pickled fennel.[170]

In Europe and North America today, fennel is generally grown for the bulb to be used as a vegetable, but in Asia and the Middle East it is largely grown for the seed. It is cultivated on a large scale in Italy, France, Romania, Russia, Germany, India, Argentina and the USA, as well as in many other countries.

Parsley

Parsley (*Petroselinum crispum*) is an upright branching biennial herb (though generally cultivated as an annual) reaching a height of 80cm with divided, feathery green leaves and yellow-green flowers growing in umbels. It is native to the Mediterranean region. The fruits are ovoid and compressed and split readily into two mericarps, which range up to 2mm long by 1–2mm wide. All parts of the plant are edible, but it is mainly used as a herb and the seeds rarely used as spices. This is curious, as other herbs/spices of the Apiaceae family typically have their seeds widely used for culinary purposes. The flavour of parsley can be described as mildly spicy, slightly bitter, fresh and herb-like; its mild nature enables it to pair easily with other herbs and seasonings. The two most common types of cultivated parsley are the curly and flat-leafed varieties. There is another variety called Hamburg Parsley, or turnip-rooted parsley (*P. crispum* Radicosum group), on account of its thick taproot, which is popular as a vegetable in central and eastern Europe.

The generic term *Petroselinum* means 'rock celery', which emphasises the similarities of the two plants. Even Theophrastus (fourth to third century BCE) recognised the differences between 'mountain celery', i.e. parsley, 'horse celery' or alexanders, and 'marsh celery' or smallage.[171]

Pliny was very enthusiastic about the diverse benefits: 'Parsley is held in universal esteem; for we find sprigs of it swimming in the draughts of milk given us to drink in country-places; and we know that as a seasoning for sauces, it is looked upon with peculiar favour.'[172]

Pliny also listed numerous health benefits attributed to parsley. However, he quoted Dionysius and Chrysippus, who agreed that 'neither kind of parsley should be admitted into the number of our aliments; indeed, they look upon it as nothing less than sacrilege to do so, seeing that parsley is consecrated to the funereal feasts in honour of the dead'. This association with death is long-standing (from the time of Ancient Greece) and has continued throughout history. The mythological killing of the infant Opheltes by a serpent was associated with parsley (or celery), the infant being laid on a bed of it, or the parsley growing from his spilt blood. Either way, Opheltes was later renamed Archemorus, meaning the Beginning of Doom – not a nice name for a child, but establishing the association with death. The Nemean Games were created to commemorate this event. So many legends persisted throughout the following millennia, and in many countries. For example, the slow germination of parsley was ascribed to the seeds having to go to hell and back multiple times. Parsley's association with dubious folklore, superstition and bad luck is also characteristic, tragically exemplified by the case of an Argentinian woman as recently as 2018 who put parsley stems into her vagina to try to induce a miscarriage – she became badly infected and died.

Parsley seeds were used by Apicius in spiced salts, but elsewhere greens were more commonly employed, appearing in recipes for cumin sauce, laser sauce, in Oxygarum (a vinegar and fish pickle digestive), in Lucanian sausages, in a dish of porpoise forcemeats, in sauces for fowl, in a sauce for roast flamingo, and numerous others.

Parsley appears to have been introduced to Britain by the Romans.[173] In the 2008 study referred to previously, parsley was present in Roman sites from almost exclusively major town contexts, especially London and York in England and Xanten in Germany, all important legionary bases, suggestive of a military association.[174] Parsley was absent from early medieval sites, perhaps indicating that it failed to catch on after the Romans left, though by medieval times it had become widespread (in archaeobotanical terms at least).

Chicken with a parsley and bread stuffing is an old Anglo-Saxon dish, and certainly parsley was readily available in that period. It is listed among the plants in the monastery garden of St Gall.

Parsley appears in the fourteenth-century classic *The Vision of Piers Plowman*, in the context of a poor simple farmer, who has no money for luxuries, in a conversation with Hunger:

> And besides I say by my soul I have no salt bacon,
> Nor no little eggs, by Christ, collops for to make.
> But I have parsley and leeks and many cabbages …[175]

Set in a century when half of England's population was wiped out by the Great Famine and the bubonic plague, this austere characterisation still resonates.

In *The Forme of Cury* (1390) it is used as a herb in many dishes, mainly as greens, but root was also used, e.g. in the dish 'compost'. Both parsley and parsley roots are used in several recipes from an 'Anonymous Tuscan Cookbook' (c. 1400).[176] Parsley (assumedly the greens) occurs in numerous recipes in Arundel manuscript 334 dated to *c*. 1425, where it is referred to as 'parsell', 'parcel' or 'parsyly'.

Given the foregoing, the notion of the eighteenth-century Swedish botanist Carl Linnaeus that parsley was introduced to England in 1548 appears flawed – especially so given that the archaeobotanical evidence for parsley supports its establishment in Britain since Roman times.[177]

In *The Good Housewife's Jewel* of 1596 it is again very commonplace, and also in most other contemporary early modern cookery books.[178] Its popularity as a culinary herb never really waned through to the modern era.

Alan Davidson describes it as the most popular herb in European cookery.[179] Well-known examples of modern European usages include persillade, a sauce mixture of parsley, chopped garlic, oil, etc. (France); parsley sauce (UK); gremolata – chopped parsley, lemon zest and garlic (Italy). It is also extremely popular in west Asia and the Middle East: it is an important ingredient of the Lebanese salad dish tabbouleh, commonly included in falafel, the Iranian herb omelette Kookoo Sabzi and many others. In Mexico it is an essential ingredient of salsa verde.

Silphium

Silphium or laser is one of the more mysterious spices/herbs and is likely extinct. It was probably related to the extant *Ferula tingitana* (giant Tangier fennel), which grows in North Africa. It was of great importance to the Romans as they used it as a seasoning, condiment, perfume, medicine, vegetable, preservative and aphrodisiac. It was found in Cyrenaica, Libya, originally settled by the Greeks and annexed by the Romans in 96 BCE. Herodotus mentions it – it was an important part of the ancient commerce of Cyrene: 'The silphium begins to grow in this region, extending from the island of Platea on the one side to the mouth of the Syrtis on the other.'[180]

However, by the late first century CE the herb was gone. It could never be cultivated by the Romans and when it ran out in the wild, that was it. The herb has some similarities with asafoetida (see above, a famously smelly herb), which unscrupulous traders used to adulterate or substitute for silphium; other herbs and substances were also used in adulteration. The Greek author Theophrastus described the plants as having thick roots covered in black bark; they were long with a hollow stalk similar to fennel and golden leaves resembling celery.[181]

Silphium appeared in many of Apicius' recipes, being his fifth most commonly used herb/spice. He used it as a seasoning in sauces and sausages; in dressings for pumpkins, cucumbers and melons; in soups and broths; in lentil dishes, with legumes; in sauces for various birds; in sow's womb (the Romans loved cooking reproductive organs), with pepper and broth for crackling, and trotters, etc.; in meat marinades, roasts and sauces for boiled meats; in a stuffing for pig's stomach, with snails; in sauce for wild boar, venison, beef, lamb and other meats; in stuffing and sauce for suckling pig; in sauce for hare; in a hare blood, liver and lung ragout; in stuffing for dormice; and sauce for fish.

It is possible that silphium could make a comeback, or indeed, it may not even be extinct. The problem is, no one really knows what it looks like.

4

Black Pepper and
the Early Spice Trade:
The First Global Commodity

Piper nigrum peppercorns. (Scot Nelson)

Black pepper (*Piper nigrum*) is a flowering vine native to southern India and its use dates back to the second millennium BCE. The green peppercorns gradually turn red as they ripen on the vine, but black peppers are made by drying the green unripe peppercorns (ideally harvested just as they start to turn orange/red in colour), after brief fermenting. Fresh green peppercorns are commonly used in cooking in some parts of Southeast Asia. White pepper, incidentally, is from the same peppercorns but comprises just the seed of the fully ripe fruit with the dark-coloured skin removed (after soaking for ten days), though the flavour is different, being less complex and less pungent.

Pepper was used in Ancient Egypt for ritual and medicinal purposes. Black peppercorns were found inserted in the nostrils of Rameses II (d. 1213 BCE) as part of the embalming process. Pepper was used in Ancient Greece, but mainly for medicinal reasons. Hippocrates (*c.* 400 BCE) advised on using pepper in several medical preparations. He advised, as a remedy for tetanus, 'Give him pills of pepper and black hellebore [a toxic purgative of the buttercup family], and warm fat bird soup'; pleurisy, 'give him in the fasting state five corns of pepper, silphium juice to the amount of a bean, honey, vinegar and water to drink warm'; and to help breathing and expectoration, 'mix a good pinch of capers, pepper, and a little soda into honey, vinegar and water; administer warm'.[1] It was also employed in a treatment for pneumonia.[2] Hippocrates also used pepper for gynaecological treatments and referred to its Indian origin.[3] L. M. V. Totelin commented that the Greeks learned the word 'peperi' from the Persians, who may have been middlemen in the trade, and may also have learned its usage from them.[4]

Two varieties of pepper were described by Theophrastus (d. *c.* 287 BCE), 'both however are heating' – they were recommended as antidotes for hemlock poisoning.[5] D. R. Bertoni listed other medicinal uses and users in the classical era.[6] A near contemporary, Dilphilius of Siphnos (early third century BCE), may have provided the earliest record of using pepper as a condiment in food – he suggested the use of pepper paired with cumin on scallops to aid digestion.[7] Despite this example, ancient Greek use of pepper seems to have been mainly for medicines rather than the flavouring or seasoning of their food. The other issue must have been the price – as an exotic rarity from the East, it may simply have been too expensive for regular use as a seasoning. That was to change with the Romans.

One of the earliest Roman pepper finds was the fourth- to second-century BCE occurrence in the House of Hercules' Wedding in Pompeii.[8] In the third and second centuries BCE, pepper started to become more widely available, probably via trade with Arabs as Rome expanded its territory. This increased dramatically in the early Imperial era as Egypt and the Red Sea came under Roman control and merchants imported pepper from India. In the late first century BCE, the poet Horace, who lived through the transition from Republic to Empire, made numerous references to the culinary use of pepper.[9] Ovid (d. 18 CE) also wrote about pepper in the context of an aphrodisiac:

> they mingle pepper with the seed of the stinging nettle ... But the Goddess, whom the lofty Eryx receives beneath his shady hill, does not allow us to be impelled in such manner to her delights.[10]

Pepper was the most important seasoning for Romans according to Apicius, the first-century CE gourmet and compiler of recipes – it is used in 76 per cent of nearly 500 dishes described in *De Re Coquinaria* and was used in cooking and as a condiment.[11] Huge quantities were imported from southern India via the Red Sea–Egypt and Persian Gulf routes.[12] The south-west and north-east monsoon winds were exploited to make outbound and return voyages by sea (of course, it wasn't just pepper that was transported and traded but a huge variety of goods, though black pepper was chief among spices and aromatics). Pliny (c. 70 CE) recorded the price of 4 denarii for a Roman pound (about 0.7 of an avoirdupois pound) of black pepper, i.e. not too expensive to preclude use by a wide variety of people, even if not lavishly. Clearly not a big fan, he lamented:

It is quite surprising that the use of pepper has come so much into fashion, seeing that in other substances which we use, it is sometimes their sweetness, and sometimes their appearance that has attracted our notice; whereas pepper has nothing in it that can plead as a recommendation to either fruit or berry, its only desirable quality being a certain pungency; and yet it is for this that we import it all the way from India![13]

Marcus Valerius Martialis, better known as Martial (38–104 CE), was a Roman poet who became famous for his acerbic prose and cutting, often lewd, wit, usually directed at the excesses and foibles of his fellow men and as a general commentary on city life. The subject of pepper did not escape his attention – he quipped on the cost of pepper:

But, ah! my cook will consume a vast heap of pepper, and will have to add Falernian wine to the mysterious sauce. No; return to your master, ruinous wild-boar: my kitchen fire is not for such as you; I hunger for less costly delicacies.[14]

But he recognised its utility in spicing up dull food: 'That insipid beet, the food of artisans, may acquire some flavour, how often must the cook have recourse to wine and pepper!'[15]

The medicinal use of pepper also continued with the Romans, as exemplified by Celsus in the first-century CE *De Medicina*, who used it in various remedies – and he may have been the first to write about pepper's ability to make people sneeze.[16] He also wrote of a cream to treat infections and ease painful joints – it contained 'pepper both round and long', and a bewildering array of other exotic spices. Dioscorides too described it primarily for its medicinal values – well, he was writing a medical text after all – but he did also refer to its pungency and flavour: black pepper was sweeter and sharper than white, more pleasant tasting and more aromatic.[17]

Archaeobotanical evidence from the Roman Empire includes peppercorns found in the Cardo V sewer at Herculaneum, which pre-dates the 79 CE eruption of Vesuvius, and from an early second-century CE septic pit at Roman Mursa, Croatia.[18]

Black peppercorns have also been found in Roman sites in Germany, France and Britain, where waterlogged anaerobic conditions have helped preserve them. The Romans needed this important home comfort in the cold and miserable climates of north-west Europe! The Vindolanda tablets – wafer-thin wooden tablets covered with writing (letters, duty rostas, supply requests, etc.) – reveal much of the everyday life of the soldiers stationed at the northern British fort: Gambax, son of Tappo, had ordered 2 denarii worth of pepper.[19] Anyone who has walked parts of Hadrian's Wall (completed around 128 CE) in the colder months must surely be able to sympathise with the soldiers – around twenty holed up in each of the milecastles, but most in the intervening forts and those to the south; there may have been around 10,000 soldiers garrisoned in total. The wall is elevated, exposed and bone-numbingly cold during the winter months, and soldiers on wall duty must have lived in a perpetual state of discomfort. This could be overplayed – they had shelter, there wasn't much fighting to endure, and they were young and tough, but in any event the presence of small luxuries like pepper to add fire to their diet must have been extremely welcome.

Several lines of evidence point to its common usage, not just by the wealthy. Pepper was exported from the ports of the Malabar coast of south-west India (e.g. from the lost port of Muziris, somewhere near Cochin) as it was grown nearby. A passage from Philostratus' *Life of Apollonius of Tyana*, written in the second or third century CE, described how a tribe of monkeys harvested the inaccessible pepper-bearing trees which grew in precipices, dumping them in clearings around the trees, and that they had learned this by imitating the Indians who picked the fruit from trees lower down.[20] Federico De Romanis reinterprets this rather curious story, with the collectors most probably being local hill people.[21] A postscript to this theme appeared in the BBC news in July 2020 – PETA (People for the Ethical Treatment of Animals) claimed that pig-tailed macaques in Thailand are snatched from the wild and trained to pick up to 1,000 coconuts per day, leading several supermarkets to boycott these products. So maybe Philostratus wasn't mistaken.

Although documentary evidence is scarce, there is a mid-second-century CE description of the cargo for a ship called the *Hermapollon*: De Romanis attempted a reconstruction and interpreted the ship to have a capacity of about 625 tons, of which the black pepper cargo used up 544 tons and that the value of the pepper was around two-thirds of the entire cargo. If this is correct, it emphasises the massive volumes of pepper being imported to Rome. The volume of pepper coming to Rome was so great that warehouses called *Horrea Piperataria* were built to store them.

In 408 CE, in the final century of the western empire, such was the value of pepper that it was used to placate the besieging Visigoth King Alaric and deter him from sacking Rome:

> After long discussions on both sides, it was at length agreed, that the city should give five thousand pounds of gold, and thirty thousand of silver, four thousand silk robes, three thousand scarlet fleeces, and three thousand pounds of pepper.[22]

This was only a temporary respite and Alaric returned to sack the city two years later, and the following decades saw Rome lurch from crisis to crisis before its final collapse.

The Red Sea port of Berenike was abandoned in the sixth century CE and was hidden until the early nineteenth century. Archaeological investigations have identified black peppercorns in their thousands and in over 180 soil samples. Peppercorns have also been found at nearby Myos Hormos.

The Hoxne 'Empress' pepper-pot is part of the Hoxne hoard, the largest Roman treasure ever discovered in Britain, found in 1992 by a metal detectorist searching for a Suffolk tenant farmer's mislaid hammer! The hoard comprises gold and silver coins, silver tableware and jewellery. The Empress pot is a hollow silver vessel designed as a high-status female half-figure with a fourth-century appearance, and was accompanied by three other silver-gilt pepper-pots, all exquisite pieces and on display at the British Museum (Figures 10 and 11). The coins date the hoard to after 407 CE, coinciding with huge instability in Rome and the end of the Roman era in Britain. The pepper-pots emphasise the continued use of exotic spice throughout the empire (among the elite, anyway, and the owners were clearly very wealthy), but the circumstances of the burial can only be guessed at. The dating may suggest a concern of impending catastrophe.

Pepper in Britain After the Romans

The use of pepper in Britain didn't cease with the fall of the Roman Empire, though it was enormously valuable. Spices (at least imported ones) generally seem to have become scarcer in Britain after the Roman era. The Venerable Bede shared his pepper and incense on his deathbed in 735.[23] According to Aldhelm (Anglo-Saxon abbot of Malmesbury Abbey, d. 709), peppered broths were delicacies.[24] By the end of the Anglo-Saxon period, the court and large households seemed to have secured sources of pepper. Pepperers were already organised in the eleventh century and the Guild of Pepperers was founded in London in the twelfth century – it was responsible for overseeing the purity of spices and herbs, weighing, importing and wholesaling. Pepper was imported to Britain in large amounts. P. W. Hammond referred to a Venetian state galley brought into London in 1481 with a cargo of citronade, succade and over 2 tons of pepper.[25] Pepper was sold at about 1*s* per lb throughout the Middle Ages. The household book from 1412–13 of the wealthy Acton Hall in Suffolk provides much detail of the food purchased, stored and consumed.[26] The steward's account of Michaelmas 1419 shows that 3lb of pepper was bought from London at the price of 6*s* 3*d* (expensive!) among numerous other spices. In 1452–53, the Duke of Buckingham bought 316lb of pepper, among other items – a massive amount![27]

The world's largest black pepper producer is now Vietnam, having gone from insignificant production in 1983 to a dominant position at present, with annual production of well over 200,000 tonnes.

This followed the liberalisation of trade relations in 1986 and increased global pepper prices. Indonesia is the second largest producer and India the third.

Spices Imported to Rome from India and the Far East During the Western Roman Empire Era

Although black pepper clearly dominated the Indo-Roman spice trade, it is important to consider the totality of imported spices. J. Innes Miller and E. H. Warmington gave detailed accounts of the spices and their various sources, which in some cases has to be highly interpretive due to the lack of archaeobotanical evidence.[28]

Table 4 | Indo-Roman Spice Trade

SPICE Latin	SPICE English	SOURCE	REFERENCE/COMMENT
Acorus calamus	Sweet Flag	India, Central Asia	Dioscorides stated it was grown in India.[29] Pliny, ditto, also Syria, Arabia.[30] Sweet Flag may or may not have been imported from India. Listed in the Price Edict.
Aquilaria agallocha	Aloe-wood	India	Native to South Asia, referred to in early Tamil texts.[31] Pliny referred to it as 'tarum', coming from the cinnamon country, imported by Nabataeans, while Dioscorides stated it came from India and Arabia.[32] Cosmas I noted (Sri Lanka) received imported Aloe-wood and sent it on to marts such as Malabar.[33]
Cinnamomum malabathrum (*Cinnamomum tamala*)	Malabathrum	India	The *Periplus* (mid-first century CE) records malabathrum being exported from Muziris and Nelkynda (§56) and from the mouth of the Ganges (§63) (latter supplied in part by Chinese tribesmen).[34] C. Ptolemy referred to the area 'beyond Kirrhadia, in which they say the best Malabathrum is produced'.[35] Appears in Price Edict of 301 CE and in Justinian's Digest (as cinnamon leaf).[36]

Cinnamomum verum (Cinnamomum zeylanicum)	Cinnamon	South and Southeast Asia	J. I. Miller opined that some cinnamon bark may have been shipped from Malabar but it would have been minor. Some also may have come from Ceylon after 300 CE. Arab middlemen probably traded it with the West before that. Pliny considered cinnamon to have come from Ethiopia and thence carried on a great sea journey to the Arabian coast (he may have confused Ethiopia with India, or the great sea crossing was to and not from the East African coast).[37] Cinnamon appears in Justinian's Digest.
Cinnamomum cassia	Cassia	China, Southeast Asia	Pliny observed that cassia 'grows not far from the plains where cinnamon is produced' and noted that it was cheaper than cinnamon.[38] Cassia bark appears in Price Edict and Justinian's Digest.
Commiphora mukul	Bdellium	India	Theophrastus referred to bdellium as the 'Indian akantha', which produced a substance resembling myrrh.[39] The Periplus states of the Makran that 'along the coast there is nothing but bdellium' (§37) and that bdellium was exported from Barbarikon (§39) and Barygaza (§49). Pliny stated, 'in the vicinity, too, of India, is Bactriana, in which region we find bdellium'.[40] It also was imported via the overland Silk Road. Quoted in Price Edict.
Curcuma longa	Turmeric	India	Unlikely to have been widely used in Rome. Dioscorides referred to 'another type of cyperus, resembling ginger, which grows in India'.[41] Miller thought it was probably imported as a form of (the very similar) ginger. A. Gismondi et al. found traces of turmeric in dental plaque from remains of a Tuscan woman of late first–early second century CE.[42]
Cymbopogon schoenanthus	Ginger Grass (or Sweet Rush)	India	Cymbopogon is a genus of fragrant grasses some native to South Asia. Theophrastus described it, though located it further west; Pliny also described 'sweet-scented rush'. It may have been the 'nard' mentioned by Arrian during Alexander's return through the deserts of Baluchistan: 'much of it was trampled down by the army, and a sweet perfume was diffused far and wide.'[43] The Phoenicians collected it, but it is unclear if this was a significant import to Rome.

Elettaria cardamomum *Amomum* sp.	Cardamom	India	Listed in the Alexandrian Tariff as amomum and cardamonum – was probably imported in small quantities.[44] Cardamom was found in historic levels in Pattanam, i.e. probable site of Muziris port.[45] Dioscorides and Pliny *may* have described cardamom. Apicius used it, infrequently. Amomum appears in Price Edict. Cardamom was clearly imported from India.
Lycium sp.	Boxthorn	India, Southeast Asia	Recorded in the *Periplus* as being exported from Barbarikon and Barygaza. Listed in Justinian's Digest.
Myristica fragrans	Nutmeg/ Mace	Southeast Asia	Pliny referred to 'comacum' as a kind of cinnamon, a nut whose extract had an agreeable smell – possibly nutmeg – though he said it came from Syria.[46] The *Periplus* records 'macir' or 'macer' exported from Malao on the Red Sea (present Somalia) – possible mace? It became well known in Europe by the sixth century CE.
Nardostachys jatamansi	Spikenard	North India	Theophrastus described the use of spikenard root in perfume preparation. The *Periplus* documented that it was exported from Barbarikon, Barygaza, Muziris, Nelkynda and the mouth of the Ganges. Confusingly, other genera have been labelled nard. Pliny listed twelve varieties.[47] Dioscorides differentiated between Indian and Syrian nard.[48] Indian Spikenard was specified by Apicius. Gangetic nard was one of the known shipments listed in the second century CE Muziris Papyrus. Nard is listed in Justinian's Digest.
Piper nigrum	Black Pepper	South India	Extensive evidence from literature and archaeobotany of the black pepper trade throughout the empire. Described by Hippocrates, Theophrastus, Pliny, Dioscorides, Horace, Cosmas Indicopleustes and others.[49] The *Periplus* records export from Muziris and Nelkynda. White pepper listed in Justinian's Digest.
Piper longum	Long Pepper	South India	Described by Theophrastus.[50] The *Periplus* notes export from Barygaza, reflecting its origin in the northern subcontinent. Pliny differentiated the price of long pepper (more expensive) from white and black.[51] Listed in Justinian's Digest.

Santalam album	Sandalwood	India, Southeast Asia	The *Periplus* (§36) refers to shipment of sandalwood from Barygaza to the Persian Gulf; its source may have been from Indonesia and India.
Saussurea lappa	Costum	North India	Theophrastus described its pungency and heat.[52] Dioscorides listed Arabic, Indian and Syrian varieties.[53] The *Periplus* recorded export from Barbarikon and Barygaza. Listed in Justinian's Digest.
Syzygium aromaticum	Cloves	Molluccas	Cloves described in ancient Indian literature, e.g. the 'Ramayana', 200 BCE or older. Pliny's description of 'caryophyllon' might be cloves (though could be cubeb).[54] Cosmas Indicopleustes, *Christian Topography*, wrote that cloves passed through Kalliena in the sixth century.[55]
Zingiber officinale	Ginger	Southeast Asia	Ginger was described by Dioscorides who wrongly stated it grew in Arabia.[56] Pliny also stated it grew in Arabia and gave its price (6*d* per lb).[57] It may have been re-exported from the Red Sea. Apicius considered it a significant import. Ginger produced by Tabropane (Sri Lanka).[58] Ginger is listed in Diocletian's Price Edict and Justinian's Digest.

The most significant spice imports from the East were black pepper, long pepper, malabathrum and spikenard. While India was the source of many spices, it also acted as an entrepot for spices sourced from further east. In most cases, spices would have been transported on Graeco-Roman ships across the Indian Ocean and along the Red Sea to Myos Hormos and Berenike, and thence to Alexandria. A smaller volume of marine traffic would have routed via the Persian Gulf, while a proportion of the trade would have followed the long-established overland Silk Road routes. The final point is the possibility of Indian ships taking their own trade to markets on the other side of the Indian Ocean, though direct evidence remains scant. It is impossible to quantify the relative importance of the spices other than black pepper, which stands apart in terms of the volume of trade.

Black Pepper and the Indian Ocean Spice Trade in the Roman Era

Rome's transition from republic to empire in the first century BCE immediately followed on from the capture of Egypt. Huge revenues flowed into Rome and the empire looked further to the East: Augustus sent out expeditionary forces and surveyors to investigate the Near East.[59] This period marked a massive expansion of trade with India, via the maritime route across the Arabian Sea and then northwards along the Red Sea. Early trade had been modest and probably via the overland caravan routes and, from Ptolemaic times, by sea via Red Sea ports. The expansion of Roman trade with western India coincided with the *Pax Romana* period of stability that dated from the time of Augustus, and which was to last for around 200 years. As Frankopan noted, trade with India 'did not open up so much as explode'. Young commented that 'The reign of Augustus thus marks the beginning of the large scale "spice trade" in the classical world'.[60]

Within a few years of the capture of Egypt, large numbers of ships were being sent to India from the Red Sea port of Myos Hormos during the period when Aelius Gallus was prefect (26–25 BCE), the other major ports being Berenike and Arsinoe. The geographer Strabo (64 BCE–24 CE) commented that 120 ships sailed to India annually:

> when Gallus was prefect of Egypt, I accompanied him and ascended the Nile as far as Syene and the frontiers of Ethiopia, and I learned that as many as one hundred and twenty vessels were sailing from Myos Hormos to India, whereas formerly, under the Ptolemies, only a very few ventured to undertake the voyage and to carry on traffic in Indian merchandise.[61]

Goods traded were not only those from India, but from many parts of Southeast Asia as well (see Table 4), though it is very unlikely Roman ships ventured beyond India. Black pepper, however, was a particular favourite and was imported in huge quantities.

Large ships are assumed to have been used, as referred to in the *Periplus Maris Erythraei*, a Graeco-Roman navigational digest most likely written in the middle first century CE, dealing with the ports around the Indian Ocean and Red Sea. The author is unknown, but the document is extremely valuable as it is clearly written from first-hand knowledge and specifies the type of goods being traded from individual ports. The issue of cargo was discussed by Federico De Romanis.[62] Based on analysis of the Muziris Papyrus (a second-century CE contract to import pepper and other goods from Muziris on the southern India Malabar coast to Alexandria), De Romanis estimated that the cargo of pepper being brought back from southern India on the *Hermapollon* was likely over 544 tons, and that this represented most of the ship's cargo, the rest being mainly malabathron (Indian bay leaves), with smaller amounts of ivory, tortoiseshell and herbs. The De Romanis estimate of tonnage, the *Periplus* statement of large ships (§56) being employed in this trade and the descriptions of such ships by Philostratus in his (fictional) *Life of Apollonius of Tyana* combine to define the *Hermapollon* and its sister ships as very large by Roman standards.[63] Archaeological evidence for the large merchant ships is scant, but the *Hermapollon* may have been a variant of a 'Corbita'-type sailing ship.

One of the largest Roman shipwrecks ever found in the Mediterranean was described in 2019 – the vessel was found off Kefalonia and was 110ft long, with a well-preserved cargo of amphorae. Other larger ships are known (e.g. *Isis*, *Syracusa*), but for all practical purposes the *Hermapollon* was probably the largest class of merchantman available to the Roman Empire in that era.

The Roman Empire was connected to the Indian Ocean trading sphere through two main routes: the Egypt–Red Sea route and the Persian Gulf–Euphrates route.[64] However, the Red Sea seems to have predominated in the black pepper trade. Alternative viewpoints of the Indian Ocean trade exist also. P. T. Parthasarathi noted that Malabar (present-day Kerala) was known as the 'Spice Garden of India' since time immemorial and its position made it a natural location for commerce and trans-shipment.[65] He takes the view that many of the artefacts and Roman coins found here in abundance were brought here by Arab and Axumite middlemen, who monopolised the spice trade to feed Roman markets, rather than exemplifying direct control by the Romans, though this view is rather controversial. The fact remains that a range of different Roman artefacts have been found in the subcontinent. Around fifty sites have reported Roman amphorae, with Dressel 2–4 types being most common, mostly with estimated ages of first century BCE to first century CE.[66]

The Ptolemies had already constructed ports along the Red Sea coast before the arrival of the Romans, in order to exploit trade with India and Arabia, which was much less than with the Romans.[67] The sea trade was eventually assisted by the monsoons which enabled direct crossings of the Arabian Sea – this was well established by the first century CE (the Greeks being the first to use the monsoons to trade with India), so the Romans would have exploited this from the start after their seizure of Egypt. The first Greek believed to have exploited the monsoons for travel to India was Eudoxus of Cyzicus, recounted in Strabo's *Geography*.[68] Eudoxus had travelled to Egypt and there became acquainted with a shipwrecked Indian mariner who had been found half-dead on the Red Sea coast, or possibly the Gulf of Aden, all his companions having perished from hunger. After learning sufficient Greek to communicate, the sailor agreed to teach the use of the monsoon winds to reach India, thus allowing him to return home. Eudoxus was one of the group appointed by the Egyptian king (Ptolemy VIII, aka 'fatty', a cruel and degenerate leader) to undertake the journey, which took place around 118 BCE. They completed the outward journey successfully. They had taken with them an array of gifts and traded these for aromatics and precious stones, eventually returning safely to Egypt. Ptolemy took possession of these exotic treasures (to the chagrin of Eudoxus, who undoubtedly had felt he had earned his fortune) but died shortly afterwards. His widow, however, decided on another expedition and sent Eudoxus off once more, in 116 BCE, with an even greater stock of merchandise with which to trade. Eudoxus again completed the round trip, despite initially being blown off course southwards somewhere along the coast of Africa. On return, the queen's son had taken power and Eudoxus was once more stripped of his treasure. The unfortunate adventurer made additional expeditions attempting to circumnavigate Africa, on the first of these trips including among the crew an unlikely group of 'singing girls, physicians, and artisans of various kinds'. His companions wearied of the journey and finally ran the ship aground, bringing the journey to an inglorious end. His ultimate fate is unknown, apparently sailing off into the sunset never to be seen again, but his main achievement was significant: to demonstrate the use of the monsoon winds to sail to India and back.

The author of the *Periplus* notes that before the direct routes were exploited (§57): 'The whole ... voyage from Cana and Eudaemon Arabia [Aden] ... used to be performed in small vessels which kept close to shore.'[69] This is evidence that the spice trade was formerly conducted in this laborious manner.

The journey from the Red Sea would have started at either of the two main ports: Berenike or Myos Hormos. The outbound journey to India would have typically started in July to take advantage of the south-west monsoon (Figure 9).[70] Destinations were to the north-west of India (Barbarikon and Barygaza) or to the south-west (Muziris and Nelkynda). The journey took around two months, but there would be two or three months to wait at the destination before the return in order to exploit the north-east monsoon, which didn't begin until late November. The return journey may have commenced in December or January and should have been completed by March, so the round trip might have been around nine months.

Each journey would have been an extremely dangerous venture. Even the relatively straightforward leg down the Red Sea was fraught with danger, with coral reefs and submerged islands, especially in the southern parts, causing many ships to run aground and founder. In addition to the natural hazards, much of the coast was inhabited by unfriendly tribes. The *Periplus* (§20) says this of the Arabian coast south of the Gulf of Aqaba: 'If a vessel is driven from her course upon this shore she is plundered, and if wrecked the crew on escaping to land are reduced to slavery.'

On the southern side of the Red Sea, the *Periplus* author (§4) says of the port of Adulis (probably modern Zula on the present

Eritrean coast) that ships now had to anchor well offshore, because formerly the 'barbarous natives' could attack the previous anchorage at the head of the bay. Further south still, at Avalites (§7) (probably Saylac in modern Somalia), the Berber inhabitants were described as 'very unruly' – no doubt an understatement. Pliny mentioned the piratical Ascitae tribe, who probably operated in the Bab al-Mandab Strait (where the southernmost Red Sea becomes very narrow) using wooden rafts made buoyant with inflated oxen skins, but they were particularly infamous because of their use of poison arrows.[71] The Strait is also known as the Gate of Tears on account of the treacherous currents that have to be negotiated there. When finally out of the Red Sea and into the western Indian Ocean, the south-west monsoon winds would frequently blow Force 7/8 for days on end with large waves battering the ships. Tropical cyclones were rare but possible. At the end of the two-month journey there were coastal hazards to negotiate on approach to several of the main ports ... and then the threat of pirates along the Malabar coast. The Roman ships laden with gold and valuable cargoes for trading would have been very attractive targets. Pliny observed that companies of archers were carried on board for defence against pirates.[72]

The four main Spice Ports (from north to south along the west coast) were Barbarikon, Barygaza, Muziris and Nelkynda. These were the main destinations for ships leaving the Red Sea. A fifth important Spice Port was Ganges, in modern-day West Bengal; spices were probably trans-shipped by local vessels to the western ports for onward export. Figure 13 illustrates the main spice trade routes between India and the Roman Empire in the first two centuries CE.

Barbarikon

Barbarikon (or Barbaricum) was situated near the position of modern Karachi at the mouth of the Indus River. The actual location of the ancient city is uncertain due to the shifting nature of the delta of the lower Indus (the *Periplus* reported that only the central of the seven mouths of the Indus was navigable); it may have been Banbhore, east of Karachi, which dates to the first century BCE. It was one of the most important ports for Indo-Roman trade, and for trade with Arabia and Persia, though trade was effected at the upriver district capital of Minnagar. The Indo-Scythians controlled the region until the late first century CE and later in some areas. The description from the *Periplus* (§38–39):

Beyond this region, the continent making a wide curve from the east across the depths of the bays, there follows the coast district of Scythia, which lies above toward the north; the whole marshy; from which flows down the river Sinthus [=Indus River], the greatest of all the rivers that flow into the Erythraean Sea, bringing down an enormous volume of water; so that a long way out at sea, before reaching this country, the water of the ocean is fresh from it. Now as a sign of approach to this country to those coming from the sea, there are serpents coming forth from the depths to meet you; and a sign of the places just mentioned and in Persia, are those called *graea* [crocodiles]. This river has seven mouths, very shallow and marshy, so that they are not navigable, except the one in the middle; at which by the shore, is the market-town, Barbaricum. Before it there lies a small island, and inland behind it is the metropolis of Scythia, Minnagara; it is subject to Parthian princes who are constantly driving each other out.

The ships lie at anchor at Barbaricum, but all their cargoes are carried up to the metropolis by the river, to the King. There are imported into this market a great deal of thin clothing, and a little spurious; figured linens, topaz, coral [red coral was highly prized by the Indians], storax [a resin used as a perfume and flavouring], frankincense, vessels of glass, silver and gold plate, and a little wine. On the other hand there are exported costus [probably from Kashmir], bdellium, lycium, nard [from the Barbarikon hinterlands], turquoise [from Iran], lapis lazuli [from Afghanistan], Seric skins, cotton cloth, silk yarn [from China], and indigo.

The serpents described in the *Periplus* were quite real: sea-snakes are common today in warm, tropical waters and twenty-six species are known from the Indian coast, mostly venomous.

Barbarikon/Minnagara received goods from the Himalayas and Bactria by caravans following the Silk Roads, and so goods from India, central Asia, Scythia and China were available for trade.[73] Spices, aromatics and plant-based drugs were important components of the trade. Most of the spices were from a local/Himalayan origin, but costus was from Kashmir. When the Han Chinese investigated the Indo-Roman trade they noted that pepper, ginger and black salt were amongst the goods available in the Indus region. Barbarikon mainly traded with the Persian Gulf ports, though as we know from the *Periplus* trade also likely took place with the Red Sea ports.[74] Silk from China may well have travelled down the Indus valley from the main Silk Roads in Central Asia, enabling onward transport from Barbarikon by sea.

Ghosh observed that as Barygaza waxed, the fortunes of Barbarikon waned, which also was partly a function of the increasing importance of the Malabar coast and emergence of direct Red Sea routes.

Barygaza

Barygaza is the Roman name for the port of Bharuch (or Broach), which is situated on the Gulf of Cambay in Gujurat in north-western India. It is situated near the mouth of the Narmada River and because of its position developed as a trading port over several centuries BCE. It is, in fact, the second oldest continuously inhabited city in India, after Varanasi. Barygaza and the approach from the sea is described in detail in the *Periplus*, with obstacles from the narrow gulf, which was difficult to navigate, shoals at the mouth of the river and large tidal range with associated strong currents. The dangers have been illustrated by the discovery of Roman amphorae fragments and the remains of lead anchors on the seabed near the island of Bet Dwarka.[75] Local rowing boats were used to guide the ships through the sandbanks, which can be clearly seen on modern satellite images.

Barygaza may have developed as a Roman trading partner following envoys received by the Emperor Augustus from the ruling Sakas (Indo-Scythians) first in 26 BCE, seeking friendship with the Roman people (Suetonius), and then in 22 BCE. The trade is described thus in the *Periplus* (§49):

There are imported into this market-town, wine, Italian preferred, also Laodicean and Arabian; copper, tin, and lead; coral and topaz; thin clothing and inferior sorts of all kinds; bright-colored girdles a cubit wide; storax, sweet clover, flint glass, realgar [to make paints], antimony, gold and silver coin, on which there is a profit when exchanged for the money of the country; and ointment, but not very costly and not much. And for the King there are brought into those places very costly vessels of silver, singing boys, beautiful maidens for the harem, fine wines, thin clothing of the finest weaves, and the choicest ointments. There are exported from these places spikenard, costus, bdellium, ivory, agate and carnelian, lycium, cotton cloth of all kinds, silk cloth, mallow cloth, yarn, long pepper and such other things as are brought here from the various market-towns.

Costus (Indian Costus or 'putchuk', *Dolomiaea costus*) is a herb related to thistles and the roots were in demand for use in medicines, while bdellium is a resin, also used in medicines. Lycium is a boxthorn shrub whose berries are used as a food, medicine and supplement. Spikenard was a product of Himalayan northern India and Nepal.

Barygaza was a major trading hub, receiving ships from Arabia, East Africa and the Persian Gulf.[76] The port served the inner city of Minnagara (different to the city near Barbarikon), which was located further upstream on the Narmada.

Other Indian Ports Listed in the *Periplus* That May Have Traded in Spices

Eleven ports are listed in the *Periplus* between Barygaza and Muziris, but firm evidence for export of spices from them is scant. The *Periplus* does mention that any Greek ships landing at Calliena would be taken to Barygaza under guard – this surely implies that there were Greek ships landing there, at least on occasion. Based on current cultivation of native spices it is reasonable to expect that ginger and turmeric were grown or at least harvested in the hinterland of this area and may have been available for trade.

Table 5 | Indian Trading Ports Referred to in the *Periplus*

Port in *Periplus*	Modern Location	Product	Comment
Ports between Barygaza and Muziris			
Sopara	Nala Sopara, 25km north of Mumbai	Sandalwood (via coastal commerce)	Dates to sixth century BCE. Trade with Rome, Arabia, Africa, Egypt. Roman amphorae pieces found in 1993. Declined after third century CE.
Kalliena	Kalyan, upstream on Ulhas River from modern Mumbai	Cloves, sandalwood, sesame[77]	Significant city-port. *Periplus* (§52) notes: 'Calliena, which in the time of the elder Saraganus became a lawful Market-town; but since it came into the possession of Sandares the port is much obstructed, and Greek ships landing there may chance to be taken to Barygaza under guard.'
Semylla	Chaul, south of Mumbai	May have received spices from inland sources[78]	
Mangadora	Mandad, *c.* 32km south-south-east of Chaul on Mandad River, a branch of the Rajapuri Creek (wide and deep, protection from monsoons)	Timber	Nearby rock-cut caves at Kuda have Brahmi inscriptions dating to first century CE. Discovery of Roman amphora handle in 2018.

Pala Patma	Dabhol (Debel), *c.* 76km south of Mandad, on the north bank of the Vashishthi River, or Palshet, a further 16km south[79]		Important Muslim trading centre in medieval times, but early history poorly documented.
Meligara	Shirgaon-Ratnagiri, *c.* 225km south of Mumbai – shelter and rivers penetrating interior. Alternatively Jayagada or Rajapur (Schoff)[80]		
Byzantium/ Byzantion	Vijayadurg (Schoff) – at mouth of the Vaghotan River *c.* 48km south of Ratnagiri[81]		
Togarum	Devgad, some 20km further south along the coast on Devgad River estuary. Safe, land-locked natural harbour		
Aurannohoas	Malvan, 35km south of Devgad[82]		
Naura	Mangalore[83]		Important trade port mentioned in *Periplus*.
Tyndis	Ponnani?		Featured on Peutingeriana map (copy of fourth to fifth century CE). *Periplus* (§54) noted that 'Tyndis is of the Kingdom of Cerobothra [the Cheran king]; it is a village in plain sight by the sea'.
Ports beyond Muziris/Nelkynda to the south and east			
Comari	Cape Comorin, the southernmost tip of India		Harbour mentioned in *Periplus*.
Camara	Kaveripattinam (and others), now Poompuhar[84]	Pepper, malabathrum, nard – assumed available in Camara, Poduca and Sopatma due to comment in *Periplus* (§60) that 'there are imported into these places everything made in Damirica'. The Tamil Pattinappalai of the early centuries CE refers to pepper from the west coast, aquila and sandalwood among other products[85]	The excavated site of Puhar or Poompuhar has yielded submerged wharves and pier walls and artefacts dating to several centuries BCE. Former site extensive (30 sq. miles).[86] Identified by Ptolemy as Khaberis.[87] R. Chakravarti stated it received goods from Southeast Asia and West Indian Ocean and was outlet for goods in demand in Med.[88] Casson mentioned in Tamil literature, westerners known.[89]

Arikamedu/ Poduca	(Near) Pondicherry, situated on south-east coast of India	Pepper, malabathrum, nard	Roman trading post, first identified in modern times by L. Faucheux, expanded on by R. E. M. Wheeler.[90] Brick structures, Roman ceramics, amphorae and other items dating from the first century CE, but only four Roman coins. Significance of Roman influence may have been overplayed.[91] Occupied from at least the second century BCE until the seventh or eighth century CE.
Sopatma	Chennai (i.e. Madras as inferred by Schoff)	Pepper, malabathrum, nard	Spices may have been exported via east coast ports to eastern markets, though probably on a smaller scale than that headed west from the Malabar coast.

Muziris

The most important ports dealing with the spice trade (mostly black pepper) in south-west India were Muziris and Nelkynda. Muziris belonged to the Cheran Kingdom, Nelkynda to the neighbouring Pandian Kingdom. Both were mentioned by Pliny:

> To those who are bound for India, Ocelis [an Arabian Red Sea port] is the best place for embarcation. If the wind, called Hippalus, happens to be blowing, it is possible to arrive in forty days at the nearest mart of India, Muziris by name. This, however, is not a very desirable place for disembarcation, on account of the pirates which frequent its vicinity, where they occupy a place called Nitrias; nor, in fact, is it very rich in articles of merchandize. Besides, the road-stead for shipping is a considerable distance from the shore, and the cargoes have to be conveyed in boats, either for loading or discharging ... Another port, and a much more convenient one, is that which lies in the territory of the people called Neacyndi, Barace by name ... The district from which pepper is carried down

to Barace in boats hollowed out of a single tree, is known as Cottonara [possibly Cochin].[92]

Muziris dates from at least the first century BCE and was located (probably) in the area of modern Kodungallur and Pattanam, though the exact location is uncertain and Muziris is regarded as a 'lost city'. Goods were exported to the Arabian coast, Red Sea ports, and probably northwards along the coast to Scythia and the Persian Gulf. Goods traded from here include black pepper, malabathron, spikenard, gemstones, ivory and Chinese silk, though pepper was the main commodity (see below). The goods were purchased with Roman money and several hoards of Roman coins have been found in the area, as well as other evidence of Roman presence. In 2009 a *Hindu Times* article described the discovery of around 500 Roman amphora sherds in the third season of archaeological excavations at Pattanam. Kodungallur and Pattanam are on the north and south sides respectively of the Periyar River; the *Periplus* (§54) described the abundance of Arabian and Greek cargo ships: 'Muziris, of the same Kingdom [as Tyndis], abounds in ships sent there with cargoes from Arabia, and by the Greeks [from Egypt]; it is located on a river, distant from Tyndis by river and sea five hundred stadia, and up the river from the shore twenty stadia' (note: 10 stadia is approximately 1 mile).

The following section (§56) has detail of the trade:

They send large ships to these market-towns [esp. Muziris and Nelkynda] on account of the great quantity and bulk of pepper and malabathrum. There are imported here, in the first place, a great quantity of coin; topaz, thin clothing, not much; figured linens, antimony, coral, crude glass, copper, tin, lead; wine, not much, but as much as at Barygaza; realgar and orpiment; and wheat enough for the sailors, for this is not dealt in by the merchants there. There is exported pepper, which is produced in quantity in only one region near these markets, a district called Cottonara. Besides this there are ex-ported great quantities of fine pearls, ivory, silk cloth, spikenard from the Ganges, malabathrum from the places in the interior, transparent stones of all kinds, diamonds and sapphires, and tortoise-shell; that from Chryse Island, and that taken among the islands along the coast of Damirica [=Limyrike]. They make the voyage to this place in a favorable season who set out from Egypt about the month of July, that is Epiphi.

It is interesting that the peak development of Muziris (second century BCE to fourth century CE) pre-dates but is close to that of the Imperial Roman era, suggesting that its fortunes rose and fell in parallel with those of Rome.

The *Akananuru*, a classical multi-authored Tamil work of poetry mainly from the first to fourth centuries CE, referred to fine ships of the Romans coming with gold to 'the wealthy Musiri town' and departing with pepper.[93] The *Purananuru* (*The Four Hundred Songs of War and Wisdom*) is another ancient anthology (first to fifth centuries CE), which described the busy atmosphere at Muziris when the Romans docked, with sacks of black pepper stacked in (ware)houses and gold being brought ashore in boats.[94]

The *Periplus* (§53) warns of pirates in the coastal area of south-west India, and this hazard is even labelled on the *Tabula Peutingeriana* (see Figure 14, a medieval copy of an original fourth- to fifth-century CE Roman map) in the area near Muziris, as well as by Pliny.

Muziris was also dangerous because of conflict with the neighbouring Pandian kingdom, and Tamil literature describes how it was besieged to destroy its dominant position in trade.

Interestingly, the presence of the 'Templum Augusti' near to Muziris on the *Tabula Peutingeriana* map is highly suggestive of a Roman settlement here, which emphasises the importance to Roman trade.

The Muziris Papyrus

The discovery of the mid-second-century CE Papyrus Vindobonensis G40822, better known as the 'Muziris Papyrus', was a ground-breaking advance in the understanding of the Indo-Roman spice trade. It appeared in the antiquities market in the early 1980s and was acquired by the Austrian National Museum, where it now resides, and has been studied by scholars extensively. It deals with the shipment of goods from Muziris in India – one side of the document (the recto, Figure 15) is an agreement to transport goods from a Red Sea port (almost certainly Myos Hormos or Berenike) across the Egyptian desert to Coptos on the Nile and then downriver to Alexandria;[95] the other side (verso) is a summary of the amounts of the different known cargoes (ivory, *schidai* and nard) and their value for customs duty. The document is fragmentary, but the total weight and monetary value is known, allowing De Romanis to infer the amount and nature of the missing cargo – black pepper and malabathron.[96] The name of the ship carrying the cargo was the *Hermapollon*, a very large ship by the standards of the time. As we will see shortly, the value of the cargo was enormous, and after arrival at port this necessitated carriage through the desert under guard.

Nelkynda

The *Periplus* (§54) stated that 'Nelcynda is distant from Muziris by river and sea about five hundred stadia [50 miles], and is of another Kingdom, the Pandian. This place also is situated on a river, about one hundred and twenty stadia from the sea [i.e. about 12 miles upstream].' As with Muziris, the present position of Nelkynda is uncertain; candidate towns include Kollam, Nakkada, Neendakara, Kannetri, with Kollam (formerly Quilon) favoured by many on account of its long history as a seaport – it had prominence during the Pandyan dynasty (which controlled much of the extreme south of India and Sri Lanka in one form or another from the third century BCE to the fourteenth century CE). Kottayam or nearby Niranam are also possibilities, with Porakad possibly being the ancient coastal Bacare (see below). The problem of identification is compounded by changes in the coastline and inland waterways over the last two millennia. The different possibilities were discussed by Schoff, Ajít Kumar and others. [97]

Further detail about Nelkynda from the *Periplus* (§55) – large vessels were unable to sail upriver to the port and their cargoes had to be transferred upstream on smaller vessels:

> There is another place at the mouth of this river, the village of Bacare; to which ships drop down on the outward voyage from Nelcynda, and anchor in the roadstead to take on their cargoes; because the river is full of shoals and the channels are not clear. The kings of both these market-towns live in the interior. And as a sign to those approaching these places from the sea there are serpents coming forth to meet you, black in color, but shorter, like snakes in the head, and with blood-red eyes.

Supporting evidence for Niranam/Porakad is derived from amphorae sherds found in the vicinity on the banks of the Pamba at Niranam. By the time of Ptolemy's description of Nelkynda and Bacare (second century CE), the towns were then in Aya and Chera hands and their trading status appears to have diminished. The inability of cargo ships to reach Nelkynda from Bacare may have been due to silting up of the river, and reference to Nelkynda is absent in later medieval seafaring accounts.

McLaughlin referred to the ancient Tamil poem *Maturaikkanci*, describing the resplendent coastal city and large ships arriving bearing gold. The pepper was loaded up at the coastal port of Bacare, as mentioned in the *Periplus*. As well as exporting black pepper, Nelkynda was also a centre for the marketing and export of local pearls, much valued by Roman society.

Tabropane (Sri Lanka)

Sri Lanka had been known in the West since the time of Aristotle (384–322 BCE) and Alexander, but the first encounter with the Roman Empire, described by Pliny, relates to a freedman of Roman merchant Annius Plocamus, who was shipwrecked there during the reign of Claudius (41–54 CE). This led to the Lankan king sending a delegation of ambassadors to Rome and the subsequent establishment of trade.

The *Periplus* (§61) records trade in 'pearls, transparent stones, muslins, and tortoise-shell', but didn't mention spices although they were grown and almost certainly traded, though perhaps not extensively in the early centuries CE.

In contrast to southern India, very few early Imperial coins were found in Sri Lanka. Bopearachichi speculated that Sri Lankan products were readily available in southern India, therefore there may have been no need for the Romans to establish direct trade there.[98] However, during the reign of Claudius the situation evolved as described above. The abundance of Roman coinage from the fourth century in Sri Lanka may reflect the activities of Axumite, Himyarite and Persian middlemen, and the move of the seat of Roman power to Byzantium (Constantinople) and a growing importance of foreign trade with Sri Lanka.[99] Ancient Sri Lanka had indigenous products of high export value: gems, pearls, elephants, ivory, tortoise shells, valuable woods, textiles and spices – cloves, cardamom, pepper and cinnamon.[100] D. P. M. Weerakoddy noted that finds of Roman coins have been mainly along the coast, especially on the western and southern shores.[101] The wet zone of the south-west was largely covered with jungle, and produced cash crops such as ginger, turmeric, pepper and (later) cinnamon, but also ivory and precious stones which were important for the island's foreign trade. He logically inferred that ports of the south-west coast must have acted as outlets for the area's products. Various spices, such as cardamom, were exported from early times, but cinnamon came to importance only from the medieval period.[102] Claudius Ptolemy recorded ginger among Tabropane's exports.[103]

Sri Lanka's importance as an Indian Ocean trade hub makes a lot of sense given its geographical position between East and West, ready access to spices and other products from Southeast Asia and India, and its own indigenous high-value products. The trade between Rome/Byzantium and Sri Lanka flourished until the Muslim capture of Alexandria in 641 CE.

The main harbour during the Anuradhapura period (377 BCE to 1017 CE) was Mantai (or Mahathiththa in Sinhalese) on the north-west coast, which existed until the fourteenth century. The port was ideally located for long-distance maritime trade from West and East. The recovery of black pepper remains from around 500 CE suggests it was likely traded from here around that time.[104] Cosmas Indicopleustes, the sixth-century monk, described Tabropane as 'much frequented by ships from all parts of India and from Persia and Ethiopia, and it likewise sends out many of its own' and it was 'a great seat of commerce'.

Ganges

The *Periplus* (§63) refers to a market town on the bank of the Ganges by the same name as the river: 'Through this place are brought malabathrum and Gangetic spikenard and pearls, and muslins of the finest sorts, which are called Gangetic.'

Ranabir Chakravarti suggests that this could be Chandra-ketugarh, a major excavated site in West Bengal, located about 125km upstream (north) from the modern delta shoreline and 35km north-east of Kolkata.[105] Ancient terracotta seals with representations of ships suggest it was a riverine port. The site dates to the Maurya period (200–300 BCE) and it appears to have been continuously occupied until medieval times. Direct evidence for a Roman connection is lacking, but the site appears to have been known to the author of the *Periplus* and spices appear to have been obtained from there indirectly. Chakravarti suggested that commodities may have been carried along the coast to Tamil Nadu and then westwards overland to the Malabar coast via Karur (modern Coimbatore) and then the Palghat Gap. Alternatively, the cargo could have been transported along the coast. The widespread occurrence of (second century BCE to second century CE) Rouletted Ware from sites along the eastern seaboard suggests a well-developed coastal network. The *Periplus* (§60) confirms the plying of large indigenous ships along the east coast: 'those which make the voyage to Chryse and to the Ganges are called *colandia*, and are very large.'

Significance of the East Coast Ports

Pepper and other spices appear to have been available for trade from the east coast ports – but trade with whom? It would make no sense for Roman ships to make the considerable additional journey eastwards from the Malabar coast in order to buy pepper, despite the evidence of the Roman presence at Arikamedu, Alagankulam, etc. So this trade in spices must surely have been with the East. Cai-Zhen Hong noted that in the Qin and Han dynasties several spices were introduced to China from South China, South Asia and Europe.[106]

Epilogue

Many of the Indian west coast ports, and especially those immersed in trade with the Romans, declined after the fall of the Roman Empire in the fifth century CE. In fact, the decline in trade was more gradual and was notable from 250 CE, probably reflecting reduced Roman demand for Indian goods. The huge markets collapsed, leading to economic disaster for the exporters. But life goes on and people adapted to the new circumstances. The east coast of India in particular was relatively unaffected by the fall of Rome and the long-established trade networks continued to operate.

However, although the western Roman Empire fell, finally, in 476 CE, the empire in the east, Byzantium, was to last another thousand years.

Valuation of the Indo-Roman Spice Trade

Chakravarti emphasises Muziris as the main Malabar export port for Gangetic spikenard because of the documentation of the cargo detailed in the mid-second-century CE Muziris Papyrus (valued at 4,500 silver drachmae for each of sixty containers – a huge sum of money), as well as its description in the *Periplus*. However, Nelkynda was also likely to have been involved in the export, also described in the *Periplus*. Gangetic nard was considered the best of all Indian nard. Both ports also exported pepper.

With these large sums of money being spent, it is perhaps unsurprising that there have been more than twenty Roman coin hoards found in southern India. Most of them were found inland and may have been acts of desperation by local merchants in times of crisis. However, the Kottayam hoard, found in 1847 near Nelkynda – the largest hoard yet discovered – may have been hidden by Romans. It contained more than 1,000 documented gold aurei with the youngest coins from the reign of Nero (54–68 CE), but it is thought that the undisturbed hoard may have been in excess of 8,000 coins (the hoard was found by villagers and most of the coins were dispersed and lost). Purchasing power in modern currency might have been around $2 million. The coins were in excellent condition; this from a contemporary, Capt. Drury's (1852), report:

> A most interesting discovery of a large quantity of ancient Roman gold coins has lately been made in the neighbourhood of Cannanore on the Malabar coast, not only remarkable for the numbers found (amounting to some hundreds) but also for their wonderful state of preservation. Many appear almost as fresh as on the day they were struck: the outline of the figures is so sharp and distinct, and the inscriptions so clear and legible. With very few exceptions, they are all of gold, and of the age of Imperial Rome from Augustus downwards, several of them being coeval with the earliest days of the Christian era ...[107]

Some of the coins were in a brass vessel – this, together with the mint condition of the coins and the proximity to the port of Nelkynda, is suggestive of the hoard being buried soon after its arrival in India and possibly representing a typical coin consignment, probably to purchase spices.[108]

McLaughlin added further information regarding expenditure and value. The *Hou Hanshu* (*History of the Later Han*), compiled in the fifth century CE, referred to a Roman profit of ten to one in their dealings with India.[109] Applying this to the cargo value documented in the Muziris Papyrus (9.2 million sesterces pre-tax) fits well with the possible consignment value of 8,000 aurei of the Kottayam hoard, which was equivalent to 800,000 sesterces.

The De Romanis calculation of the *Hermapollon* cargo based on the incomplete Muziris Papyrus assumed (reasonably) that black pepper and malabathron were the main items of the 'unknown cargo', though alternatives are also feasible.[110] He made estimates for the post-tax value of 1,151 talents, 5,852 drachmas, a huge sum.

Correlation of ancient Graeco-Roman currency to modern equivalents is notoriously difficult, but based on rough comparisons (such as purchasing power) the modern value might have been several million US dollars. Though a wild generalisation, it is still useful to put things in rough perspective – and gives an indication of the sort of prize that was being exploited. It seems extremely good business for one shipment, but perhaps not unreasonable given the risks involved.

Annual Indo-Roman Spice Trade

De Romanis doubts that the 120 ships per year sailing from the Red Sea quoted by Strabo were all large ships heading for the Malabar Coast, but a proportion of them would have been, perhaps fewer than twelve.[111] On the other hand, Strabo only mentioned Myos Hormos – what about the other major port, Berenike? Presumably ships were departing there too. As B. Fauconnier commented, the controversy over Strabo's observation led to the so-called 'intensity debate'.[112]

A reality check on all the above is called for. Kerala's black pepper production is currently around 20,000 tons/year, while total production from three southern states is 59,000 tons/year (India's total production). If the *Hermapollon* cargo of (assumed) 544 tons was typical of 120 ships/year, then the historic Roman import in the first century CE (65,280 tons) would have exceeded total modern (2019–20) national production – clearly absurd. The De Romanis estimate of twelve ships/year (6,528 tons) looks possible (a third of current Kerala production).

Following the capture of Egypt in 30 BCE, total Imperial revenues rose to around 420 million sesterces/year, though there was still a deficit. Taxation was one of the big contributors to government revenue, then as now. McLaughlin concluded that based on the fleet of ships quoted by Strabo and the figures from the Muziris Papyrus, the trade could have raised around 1,000 million sesterces of revenue; the quarter tax (25 per cent levied by the Roman state on imports) and surcharge could have raised 275 million sesterces for the government.[113]

Pliny complained about the money flowing out for luxury goods: 'At the very lowest computation, India, the Seres [China], and the Arabian Peninsula, withdraw from our empire one hundred millions of sesterces every year – so dearly do we pay for our luxury and our women.'[114] The money spent in India alone was half that, but he was pragmatic enough to see the value of the enormous profits being made: 'in no year does India drain our empire of less than [usually quoted as] fifty millions of sesterces, giving back her own wares in exchange, which are sold among us at fully one hundred times their prime cost.'[115]

Wilson and Bowman observed that Pliny's figures above could be interpreted as a tenfold increase between India and the Red Sea (where tax would be payable) and a further tenfold increase between the Red Sea and Rome.[116] The quarter tax payable in Egypt on 500 million sesterces would be 125 million sesterces to the government. Pliny had no cause for complaint!

The Red Sea Ports and Onward Shipment to Alexandria

The main Red Sea ports that received, stored and distributed spices from South Asia were Berenike and Myos Hormos, though other ports had long histories and were mentioned in the *Periplus* (§4), e.g. Adulis in modern Eritrea. A. M. Kotarba-Morley listed forty-nine Greco-Roman ports on the Red Sea coast![117] Unlike Alexandria, most were not major urban settlements and existed to service the Indian Ocean trade.

The archaeology of the Red Sea ports appears to show an upswing in activity in the fourth and fifth centuries CE. The late Roman period also saw a preference for use of northerly Red Sea ports over southerly locations, probably a defensive preference, emphasising the key ports closest to the Egyptio-Roman heartlands. According to T. Power, Clysma and Aila (modern Aqaba) became the main Byzantine ports in the sixth century dealing with Indian Ocean trade.[118]

The importance of the trade is highlighted by evidence of Roman soldiers on the Farasan Islands in the southern Red Sea, about 1,000km south of Berenike, referred to in Latin inscriptions from the second century CE.[119] Cobb viewed the peak of Roman Indian Ocean trade in the late first century CE and decline thereafter, for whatever reason.

Berenike

Berenike was established in the third century BCE and was abandoned in the mid-sixth century CE. Its role as a spice trans-shipment port is undisputed. In four seasons of archaeological investigation, almost 1,600 peppercorns were found in the building remains; in addition, large amounts of charred peppercorns were found near the Temple of Serapis and large Indian jars filled with peppercorns in the temple courtyard. The luxury goods, including pepper, were on their way to Alexandria via desert and Nile routes. Residents of Berenike may well have included Indian nationals, based on the presence of ostraka (pottery sherds with writing) with Tamil Brahmi inscriptions and archaeobotanical evidence of rice. In fact, evidence of eleven languages was found on site.[120]

Although black pepper was a common archaeobotanical find at Berenike, there was also a unique discovery of an Indian *dolium* storage jar containing about 7.5kg of black peppercorns recovered from a late first-century BCE or early first-century CE courtyard in the Serapis temple.[121] A total of fifty-four botanical items from Berenike have either been documented in literature or found at Berenike, though hard field evidence for spices from India apart from black pepper is limited to sesame (and coconut).[122] Other spices found (e.g. coriander, fenugreek, cumin and fennel) may have had a different provenance.

The evidence suggests that Berenike enjoyed a peak period of prosperity in the first century CE.[123] In this period, it was a vibrant town in the desert, where the greatest fortunes of the time were made. This was followed by a sharp decline in the second century (though activity continued) and a modest recovery mid-fourth century, before abandonment in the sixth century, after which it was buried under the desert sands.

Myos Hormos

This is situated north of Berenike, also on the western (Egyptian) coast of the Red Sea, 8km north of modern Quseir al-Qadim. It was founded at a similar time to Berenike, and appears to have been abandoned in the early third century CE, possibly a result of the crises that affected Rome around that time. It came in to use again during the medieval era between 1050 and 1500. This is the port described by Strabo, writing in the final years BCE or early years CE, from where 120 ships per year set sail for India. It is also well documented in the *Periplus*. Strabo further mentioned that Myos was linked to the Nile at Coptos by a road across the eastern desert. The Myos archaeological site shows a lot of activity in the late first century BCE and first century CE, including remains of a Roman harbour and artefacts such as Roman rigging material, re-used ships' timbers, coins, etc.[124] Myos may have been the main shipbuilding/repair site on the Egyptian Red Sea coast.

Some eighty-five food plants have been recovered from Quseir/Myos, preserved due to dessication in the extremely arid environment. These include black pepper from the Roman era and cardamom, ginger, turmeric and betel nut from the medieval period.

Onward Shipment to Alexandria

Koptos, situated on the east bank of the Nile, probably dates back to pre-Dynastic times (i.e. before 3100 BCE). It became important due to its strategic position on the Nile and as the starting point for caravans to the Red Sea ports. The road to Myos Hormos exploited Wadi Hammamat – a dry riverbed that connected Koptos with the coast at Myos. The route was protected by the Roman army with forts and caravanserai – with good reason. There was a lot of wealth passing through the route and Koptos. Onward shipment to Alexandria was by boat from Koptos, following the Nile downstream to the Mediterranean.

Alexandria: Spice Entrepot

Alexandria was founded in 331 BCE by Alexander the Great. Its position in the Nile delta enabled it to thrive and in due course it became the second greatest city of the ancient Mediterranean, after Rome. After Alexander it became the capital of the Ptolemies, and it built its wealth on trade. Shortly after the Roman annexation, Alexandria probably had a population of a few hundred thousand and functioned as the granary of Rome, exporting around 83,000 tons of grain/year at the height of the empire.[125] It was also the main emporium for the aromatic and pungent spices of India and elsewhere, before onward distribution to Rome. This, combined with all the other merchant activity, involved a huge number of ships, and the constant coming and going from multiple Mediterranean ports made the wharves and dockyards bustling centres of commerce.

Strabo, noting its good harbours and position on the Nile, described Alexandria as:

> the greatest emporium in the inhabited world ... Large fleets are despatched as far as India and the extremities of Aethiopia, from which the most valuable cargoes are brought to Aegypt, and thence sent forth again to the other regions; so that double duties are collected, on both imports and exports ...[126]

The Emporion was situated near the western end of the Great Harbour – here duties on imports and exports were collected and it served as the market for commodities moving through the port. This was the main market in the empire for spices, perfumes, unguents, medicines and other exotic goods and a large variety of agricultural produce.

The Alexandrian Tariff of Marcus Aurelius (issued 176–180 CE) listed fifty-four commodities subject to import duty at Alexandria en route to Rome. These included spices, e.g. amomum, cardamom and pepper. The list was repeated in the sixth-century CE Justinian's Digest:

> cinnamon; long pepper; white pepper; pentasphaerum leaf; barbary leaf; costum; costamomum; nard; stachys; Tyrian casia; casia-wood; myrrh; amomum; ginger; malabrathrum; Indic spice; galbanurn; asafoetida juice; aloe; lycium; Persian gum; Arabian onyx; cardamonurn; cinnamon-wood; cotton goods; Babylonian hides; Persian hides; ivory; Indian iron; linen; all sorts of gem: pearl, sardonyx, ceraunium, hyacinth stone, emerald, diamond, sapphire, turquoise, beryl, tortoise stone; Indian or Assyrian drugs; raw silk; silk or half-silk clothing; embroidered fine linen; silk thread; Indian eununchs; lions; lionesses; pards; leopards; panthers; purple dye; also: Moroccan wool; dye; Indian hair.

Note that black pepper is exempt from this list, probably due to its continuing popularity.

Alexandria fell firstly to the Persians in 619 CE, though it was recovered ten years later, and finally in 641 CE following a long siege by Ummayad Arabs. Life and commerce were to continue, but the city's golden age had passed. The great lighthouse of Pharos collapsed in the fourteenth century. However, the city continued to exert significant influence during the medieval era, encouraged by the Mamluk sultanate (1250–1517), and spices and other goods re-exported from Egypt brought in considerable wealth.

Other *Piper* Spices

Long Pepper

Long pepper (*Piper longum*) is a flowering vine native to peninsular Southeast Asia, Bangladesh, Assam and southern China. It is also commonly referred to as Indian Long Pepper, or 'pippal' in Sanskrit, and is a separate species from the similar Javanese Long Pepper or Chui Jhal (*Piper chaba*, syn. *P. retrofractum*) and *Piper peepuloides*. The fruit comprises catkin-like cylindrical spikes which range up to 4cm (female) or 7.5cm (male) long, and up to 6mm in diameter. The tiny ovoid fruits are embedded in the spike. The fruits are green initially but turn grey or black on ripening. The female spikes provide the economically useful peppers. The flavour of long pepper is generally described as burning hot and sweet, with a fragrant aroma; the heat sensation tends to linger and it is notably more pungent than black pepper. Interestingly, the roots are also used as a spice, as both fruit and roots contain piperine.

Long pepper was one of the flavourings used in the Vedic era of India (*c.* 1500–500 BCE), alongside black pepper, turmeric, mustard seeds and sesame seeds.[127] The *Sushruta Samhita* is an ancient Sanskrit compilation that appears to have been generated around the mid-first millennium BCE; pippali is referred to several times for its medicinal and culinary benefits – wine with long pepper was paired with venison dishes, for example. Long pepper is mentioned again in the *Arthashastra*, another ancient Sanskrit text compiled between the second century BCE and third century CE.

E. Mcduff speculated that long pepper may have been the first kind of pepper to reach the West, as its origins in the northern

Indian subcontinent were closer to the likely overland trade routes than black pepper, which grew only in southernmost India.[128]

Hippocrates listed pepper among his medicines but didn't directly differentiate between black pepper and long pepper. The pepper referred to in the text is probably *P. longum*, which originated in north-east India.[129] Theophrastus clearly did recognise the difference, though perhaps surprisingly some of the succeeding learned botanists did not. Theophrastus observed:

> Pepper is a fruit, and there are two kinds: one is round like bitter vetch, having a case and flesh like the berries of bay, and it is reddish: the other is elongated and black and has seeds like those of poppy: and this kind is much stronger than the other. Both however are heating ...[130]

Dioscorides appears to describe long pepper, and names it thus, though it is possible he was describing the unripe fruiting spikes of black pepper; he noted the 'stronger biting quality'. The trade of long pepper is documented in the first-century CE *Periplus Maris Erythraei* among the goods obtained by the Romans from Barygaza, but other records of the era are less authoritative.

For example, Pliny makes a confusing description of pepper trees, likening them to junipers, which is not the case. He also incorrectly described seeds being enclosed in pods:

> These pods are picked before they open, and when dried in the sun, make what we call 'long pepper.' But if allowed to ripen, they will open gradually, and when arrived at maturity, discover the white pepper; if left exposed to the heat of the sun, this becomes wrinkled, and changes its colour.[131]

He was clearly on very shaky ground here but was better informed on the market – he claimed the price of long pepper to be 15 denarii per lb, compared to 7 denarii for white pepper and 4 denarii for black.

This raises interesting questions: why did black pepper prevail over long pepper throughout Roman (and later) history, when long pepper is arguably superior (more pungent, more fragrant, sweeter tasting)? Ultimately, the lower price and greater availability of black pepper seem to have been the deciding factors. Matthew Cobb notes that there is no reason to doubt that long pepper was imported to the Roman Empire, or Pliny's record of prices (above) would make no sense; it is also included in the second-century CE Alexandrian Tariff.[132]

Long pepper is again included in the list of dutiable items on entry into Alexandria in the Digest of Justinian of 533 CE, a repeat of the earlier tariff.

Western confusion between long pepper and black pepper persisted through the medieval era, as exemplified in the semi-fictitious mid-fourteenth-century *Travels of Sir John Mandeville*. The author infers that peppers came from the same tree: 'And there is 3 maner of Peper, all upon one Tree; long Peper, blak Peper, and white Peper.'

Long pepper was also used by the Chinese in medieval times: Hu Sihui, the author of *Yinshan Zhengyao* (*The True Principles of Eating and Drinking c.* 1330) referred to spice mixtures or *xi liaowu*, which appear to have included long pepper among numerous other spices, and it is also listed separately. Both long pepper and black pepper appeared to be more highly favoured than the native fagara.[133]

Long pepper was used in late medieval England, but much less frequently than black pepper, recapitulating the situation in Ancient Rome.[134] As in Rome, the price of long pepper was also greater – purchases for the coronation feast of Richard III included 5lb of long pepper for 16s 8d versus 44lb black pepper for £2 18s 4d. This equates to 3s 4d per lb for long pepper and approximately 1s 4d per lb for black pepper, a similar percentage price differential to the time of Pliny!

Long pepper appears in a single recipe (for Hypocras) in *The Forme of Cury* (1390);[135] it also appears in numerous recipes (especially in soups and broths) from *Le Ménagier de Paris* (1393). Long pepper also features as one of several spices in a fifteenth-century Hypocras recipe from John Russell:

> Graynes / gynger, long pepur, & sugre / hoot & moyst in worchynge
> Synamome / Canelle / red wyne / hoot & drye in theire doynge[136]

Long pepper's use in spiced wine seems to have been relatively commonplace. By 1588, long pepper was evidently widely available in England, as Walter Bailey commented that 'Long pepper is to be seene in every shop'.[137]

John Gerard discussed the different kinds of pepper in his 1597 *Herbal*, and correctly differentiated between them.[138] Of long pepper:

> The branches are many and twiggie, whereon doth grow the fruite, consisting of many graines growing upon a slender footestalke, thrust or compact close togither; greene at the first, and afterwarde blackish; in taste sharper and hotter than common blacke Pepper, yet sweeter, and of better taste.

By the seventeenth century, long pepper had once again become extremely scarce in the West, at least in part as chili became rapidly established in Asia as the new hot spice of choice.

Long pepper's usage in the West today is quite infrequent and it is usually only available through speciality spice shops or Indian groceries. It is relatively commonplace as a spice and condiment in South Asia, Indonesia, Malaysia and Thailand, and has an important use in Ayurvedic medicine. According to Manjit Gill, long pepper is good for use in mutton stews, with grilled or roast fish and meats, in smoked foods, in many vegetarian dishes and as an accompaniment to cheese.[139] Ground long pepper is also used in pickles, chutneys and certain breads.[140] It is sometimes used in the *paan* spice mix chewed with areca nuts in betel leaf. Long pepper is also used to some extent in North and East African cuisine, e.g. in the berbere spice mixture.

Cubeb Pepper

Cubeb (*Piper cubeba*) is a close relative of black pepper that was in common use until the end of the seventeenth century. It is also referred to as Java Pepper, as it is native there and in neighbouring Sumatra, or Tailed Pepper on account of the stalks attached to the peppercorns. Figure 7 illustrates dried long pepper, black pepper and cubeb pepper fruits. The plant is a perennial vine, similar to *Piper nigrum*, and thrives in the tropics. It can grow up to 10m in height. Cubeb has a pleasant aromatic odour with a pungent, complex and bitter taste, similar to a mix of allspice and black pepper.

There is doubt over the use of cubeb by the Greeks and Romans – perhaps the similarity to black pepper was too great to separate them into different species at that time. However, it may simply not have been available. Cubeb spread to China in early medieval times.

In India, ancient Sanskrit texts included cubeb in various remedies. Charaka (born between 100 BCE and 200 CE) and Sushruta (born several hundred years BCE) – two of the main contributors to Ayurveda – prescribed cubeb paste as a mouthwash, and dried cubebs internally for oral and dental diseases, loss of voice, halitosis, fevers and coughs. In the fourteenth-century CE *Raja Nirghanta* cubebs appear in the name of kankola. Unani physicians (traditional medicine of Greek origin practised in southern Asia) use a paste of cubeb fruits on male and female genitals to intensify sexual pleasure.[141] The *Arabian Nights* (ninth century CE) refers to cubeb as part of a treatment for infertility.

Cubeb was included among the spices that Bede left to his brethren in 735. We can assume that they weren't using it in the way that the Unani doctors prescribed.

There were fifty-three occurrences of cubeb in 1377 in late medieval English recipes, which demonstrates that it was certainly established even if not used profusely at that time.[142] In medieval Europe, cubeb had the reputation of being able to repel the devil and evil spirits and was used for spells and exorcism.[143] It decreased in availability in Europe from the seventeenth century as black pepper was promoted. It is entirely absent from many eighteenth-century and later cookery books.

John Crawfurd, the British Resident at the court of the Sultan of Java, noted that cubeb was an effective cure for gonorrhoea and that it was already known to the people of Bengal when the English occupied Java (in 1811).[144]

The world cubeb trade today is small, and is used mainly for seasoning, as a botanical in gin, in traditional medicines and in flavouring cigarettes. It is generally unavailable in modern Western supermarkets but can be obtained online via speciality spice sellers.

Less Common Species

Table 6 describes seven less common species of *Piper* that are used in a culinary sense as well as, in most cases, for traditional medicinal purposes.

Table 6 | *Piper* Lesser-Known Species

Ashanti Pepper (*Piper guineense*)	Also known as West African Pepper, African Black Pepper, Guinea Pepper, and False Cubeb, Ashanti is a climbing perennial vine that can grow up to 20m tall by climbing up the bole of trees. Its heart-shaped leaves have a peppery taste and the fruits occur in clusters which are reddish-brown when ripe and black when dry. The plant is native to tropical central and west Africa – it is one of only two *Piper* species native to Africa.[145] Like several other members of the Piperaceae, the plant contains significant piperine content, which imparts its spicy heat, with the fruits containing over 3 per cent.[146] It is used as a traditional medicine in various ways. The fruits act as a spicy flavouring for soups, stews and rice, and the leaves are used to flavour meat and fresh pepper soup as well as being consumed as vegetables.[147]
Kava kava (*Piper methysticum*)	Kava kava is a perennial shrub native to the South Pacific Islands that reaches 3m in height and is characterised by large cordate leaves. The roots of the plant are used to make a psychoactive drink of the same name, which has sedative and euphoric effects. The roots contain compounds such as methysticin, yangonin, dihydromethysticin and dihydrokawain.[148] These are the kavalactones, a class of lactone compounds, which comprise around 15 per cent of dried kava root. Tran Dang Xuan et al. identified eighteen kavalactones.[149] The kavalactone content is greatest in the root and decreases upwards in the stems and leaves. The root is ground or pounded and then mixed with water to produce the drink. The Fijian version is called 'grog'. Kava has a possible origin in Vanuatu and may have spread throughout islands by human transport, with new varieties emerging on different islands; over 100 cultivars are now recognised. The Dutch navigators Le Maire and Schouten noted its presence in the island of Futuna (over 500km north-east of Fiji) in 1616 during their global circumnavigation. *P. wichmanii* (which is very similar to *P. methysticum*) may have been the wild species from which farmers domesticated cultivars of *P. methysticum*.[150] Domestication originated in northern Vanuatu, probably starting around 3,000 years ago, after arrival of the first humans there; cultivars were probably carried from Vanuatu eastwards to Polynesia and westwards to New Guinea and Micronesia.[151] Kava reached the United States from Hawaii. A Sears catalogue from 1915 included an advertisement for kava. It was described as 'the greatest non-alcoholic wine' and 'the finest temperance drink in the world and superior to the highest priced wines on the market. It is exceedingly pleasant to taste, healthful and invigorating … As a wine for the table at meals it has no equal.' That was perhaps a little exaggerated, but there is certainly a growing appeal and kava bars have now become increasingly popular in mainland USA.

Rough-leaved Pepper (*Piper amalago*)	Rough-leaved pepper, also known as pepper elder, is an evergreen shrub native to the Neotropics that commonly grows to heights of 1.5–3m, sometimes greater. The fruit is black and pungent and grows on long spikes; it is very similar to black pepper in flavour and pungency but the fruits are smaller, around the size of mustard seeds.[152] They are used as a hot spice in food and as a condiment. The plant also has medicinal uses, e.g. the leaves are brewed for use as a cough remedy and the root is used to treat snake bites.[153] The leaves are used in Mexico and Brazil to treat a wide range of conditions including heart problems, burns, inflammation and infections, stomach aches and muscle aches, among other conditions.[154] The leaf essential oils were analysed in a recent study and thirty-eight compounds were identified representing just over 90 per cent of the total; major constituents were β-phellandrene (20.42 per cent), spathulenol (10.34 per cent), bicyclogermacrene (8.5 per cent) and α-pinene (7.29 per cent). The main compounds were monoterpenes, sesquiterpenes and oxygenated sesquiterpenes.[155]
African Long Pepper (*Piper capense*)	*Piper capense* is an aromatic shrub or straggling liana native to north-east, central and southern Africa that ranges up to 5m tall or long, with large ovate to elliptical leaves and flowers on long spikes. The fruits are similar to those of Indian long pepper. Local name is 'Timiz'. This is the second of the two species of *Piper* native to Africa. It is a popular spice in Ethiopia because of its availability and lower price than imported Indian long pepper. It is often gathered from the wild but there is competition from baboons, who love the fruits![156] Timiz is used in traditional meat stews, usually together with black pepper, nutmeg, cloves and turmeric. It is also used as a local constituent of berbere, and timiz can be used to spice coffee, tea and butter. The fruits are traditionally used as spices in western Cameroon to make soups called 'Nkui' and 'Nah poh'. The leaves are used as a traditional medicine to treat stomach complaints in São Tomé and Principe and to treat epilepsy in Cameroonian recipes. Many other traditional uses are reported in B. Salehi et al.[157]
Chui Jhal Pepper (*Piper chaba* syn. *retrofractum*)	*Piper chaba*, syn. *Piper retrofractum*, is a perennial flowering vine native to South and Southeast Asia. It is also called Java Long Pepper and, in Thailand, 'dee plee'. Leaves are ovate or lanceolate and typically 10–15cm x 4–6cm. The fruits are developed on long spikes, up to 8.5cm long (male) and 6.5cm long (female); they are red when ripe and turn dark brown or black when dried. They have a pungent, peppery taste and can produce numbness in the mouth – they are used as a spice and in pickles, etc., in a similar manner to Indian long pepper.[158] It is becoming popular in Bangladesh as an intercrop and an article in the *Daily Star* observed that 'every household yard in Chhinai union has a Piper chaba vine'.[159] In Bangladesh, chui jhal is used as a spice in meat, fish and mutton curries amongst other dishes. The chopped stems, roots and skin are used in preference to the fruits and chui jhal is one of the most popular spices in the south-western part of Bangladesh. The roots are more expensive than other parts due to their stronger aroma.[160] Chui jhal also has numerous traditional medicinal uses.[161]

Spiked Pepper (*Piper aduncum*)	Spiked pepper or matico (*Piper aduncum*) is an evergreen shrubby tree native to central and southern America that can reach heights of 7–8m. It has alternate lanceolate leaves that can reach up to 18cm in length set on slightly zig-zag stems and small fruits arranged in long and slender curved spikes. It is grown in numerous tropical regions worldwide and is highly invasive (the most invasive of the *Piper* genus). The entire plant has a peppery aroma and fruits are used as a spice and condiment. The fruits have a certain sweetness when ripe. In addition to its culinary use, it is widely used as a traditional medicine throughout the Amazon; in fact, the name purportedly derives from a wounded Spanish soldier called Matico, who learned from native people to apply leaves to his wounds to staunch the bleeding. It is used as an antiseptic, to stop bleeding, to prevent infection and to speed healing.[162] Leaves are crushed or powdered and sprinkled on to the wound, or it is occasionally used as a poultice. It is also prepared as an infusion to treat inflammation and gastric problems, among other disorders. The invasive nature of the plant has been reviewed by Alfred E. Hartemink on his website, citing the spread in Southeast Asia.[163] It was introduced to the Bogor Botanical Gardens (in Java, Indonesia) in the 1860s; by the late 1920s it had become common in a radius of 50–100km around the Gardens in young secondary vegetation, close to rivers and on steep slopes. It was noted in Jayapura in 1955, Biak in 1960 and Irian Jaya, Malaysia and Borneo in the 1960s. It was also recorded in Singapore and Sumatra. It had become very common in Papua New Guinea by the late 1990s.
Hoja Santa (*Piper auritum*)	Hoja Santa ('sacred leaf' in Spanish) is also known as Mexican Pepper Leaf or the Root Beer Plant, with the Latin name *Piper auritum*. It is a large shrubby plant native to tropical South and Central America. The leaves are large and heart-shaped and are often used in Mexican cuisine, e.g. as a wrapper in tamales or for seafood and meat which is then steamed or baked, the leaf being discarded prior to eating. The leaf helps to season the filling during cooking. It is also an ingredient in the green and yellow seasoning pastes, mole verde and mole amarillo, from Oaxaca.[164] It is also chopped up and added to stews, soups and scrambled eggs. Flavour is a complex mix of sassafras, anise, pepper and liquorice and there is a strong aroma of anise when stems and leaves are crushed; the root beer plant moniker is due to the high concentration of safrole, a phenylpropanoid compound found in sassafras plants.

5

The Ginger Family

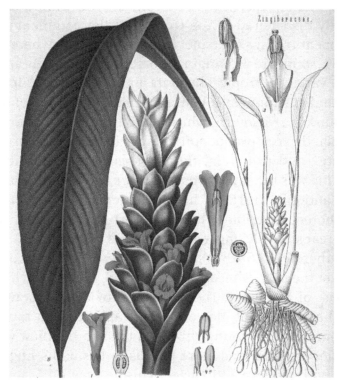

Turmeric (*Curcuma longa*), *Köhler's Medizinal-Pflanzen*, 1883–1914. (Biodiversity Heritage Library)

The Zingiberaceae family includes several commonly used spices – ginger, turmeric, galangal, cardamom, black cardamom, grains of paradise, zedoary – as well as a substantially larger number of lesser-known spices. The largest genus (of the fifty-three genera) is *Alpinia*, with some 244 accepted species, followed by *Etlingera*, *Curcuma*, *Zingiber*, *Globba*, *Renealmia*, *Riedelia*, *Amomum*, *Aframomum* and *Boesenbergia*. Ginger, turmeric, galangal and zedoary are used for their rhizomes, while cardamom and grains of paradise are used for their seeds.

The ginger plant, *Zingiber officinale*, is a slender tropical perennial which grows to a height of around 1m with a rhizome or root stem that bears leafy shoots. Leaves are lanceolate, typically about 15cm long. The inflorescence is a spike with yellowish flowers that have purple edges. The plant is probably native to India and further eastwards to south central China, though is now widely distributed in the tropics. Ridley commented that it doesn't appear to have been met in a wild state anywhere (i.e. it is a cultigen), so its precise original home is not clear.[1] It appears to thrive in a variety of tropical habitats and is widespread in lowland and highland environments. Watt referred to the origin of the word via the Sanskrit *sringavera*, which might imply an Indian origin.[2] In India, the densest production today is in the north-east, Assam, Bengal, etc., and in Kerala, though it is widespread across the country. This was the same over 100 years ago and may have been similar in antiquity. In 1596, the Dutch merchant and explorer Jan van Linschoten, describing the west coast of India, said, 'There is likewise great store of Ginger, as also all the coast [along], but little esteemed there.'[3] He further said, 'Ginger groweth in manie places of India, yet the best, & most caryed abroad, is that which groweth in the coast of Malabar.'[4] The rhizome provides the sought-after spice – it has a pleasant, flowery aroma and pungent taste that is widely admired. The young rhizomes tend to be juicy, while the mature ones are drier and more fibrous. It has had a huge variety of uses in both modern and ancient cuisine.

Turmeric (*Curcuma longa*) is a similar plant to ginger, and its rhizomes are also widely used as a seasoning in cooking. It is also native to India. The plants are perennial herbs reaching up to 1m in height with tufts of lanceloate leaves and colourful inflorescence with pale green bracts on spikes. The rhizome is bright orange-coloured inside and has a warm, bitter, peppery flavour, while the powder has a pleasant, mild, earthy aroma with a bitter aftertaste. It is known colloquially as Indian saffron due to its colouring properties.

Galangal has a bit of an identity crisis. The name is or has been ascribed to three different genera/four different species in the ginger family: greater galangal (*Alpinia galanga*); lesser galangal (*Alpinia officinarum*); Chinese ginger/Chinese keys/lesser galangal (*Boesenbergia rotunda*) with a long history as spice and medicinal plant, especially in Southeast Asia; and black galangal (*Kaempferia galanga*), sometimes confused with lesser galangal.

Galangal is native to tropical Asia and is a perennial plant that grows up to 1–2m in height depending on variety. Leaves are long and blade-like and flowers small and white with red veins. Like ginger, galangal is cultivated for its rhizome, which is most commonly used fresh sliced or dried and powdered. The taste is sharp and peppery with citrus notes. Galangal is commonly used in Southeast Asian cookery, especially in Thai food. Lesser galangal is more pungent than greater galangal.

In addition to the above is the similar zedoary or white turmeric (*Curcuma zedoaria*) and (the unrelated) Cyperus roots (*Cyperus longus*) – the 'English galingale' as described by Culpeper. 'Galingale' was sometimes used archaically as a synonym for galangal. Zedoary is another plant cultivated for its rhizome, though it is infrequently used in the West. It is characterised by large leaf shoots and a flower spike with pale yellow flowers and red and green bracts. The rhizomes are large and fleshy, white to pale orange inside. They are less pungent than ginger or turmeric but have a bitter aftertaste. They are mainly used as spices in India and Southeast Asia.

Cardamom comprises the seeds of *Elettaria cardamomum*, an aromatic perennial herb that can reach heights of almost 4m. The seed pods are pale green coloured and have a characteristic spindle shape with a triangular cross-section. The plant is native to India. In India it thrives at high elevations, between 800 and 1,500m, as an understorey crop, shaded beneath forest trees.[5] Related species (from a different genus) are white cardamom (*Amomum krervanh*) and black cardamom (*Amomum subulatum*), the latter being native to the Himalayan areas of India, Nepal and southern China. Cardamom has a very strong taste and a pungent, resinous aroma, semblent of eucalyptus, menthol and aniseed.

Grains of Paradise (*Aframomum melegueta*), or melegueta pepper, is another ginger family spice. The small red-brown seeds have a mildly fragrant aroma and the taste is hot and peppery, with a slight gingery tang. The reed-like plant is a biennial native to the West African coastal belt from Guinea to Angola, has large blade-like leaves and moderate stems (it can reach 1.5m in height), with purple flowers which develop into pods containing the seeds.

Early Uses of the Ginger Family

Gingers in Asia

Perhaps unsurprisingly, the oldest evidence for the use of ginger family spices has been found in Asia, where it is native. A study of starch grain analysis of dental calculus from cattle teeth at Farmana, India, provided the first direct evidence of cooked ginger and turmeric.[6] This study showed that the Indus Valley Harappan civilisation were eating food flavoured with ginger and turmeric by the second half of the third millennium BCE. They also found remains on human teeth and inside a cooking pot – humans ate the spiced food and cattle ate the leftovers. Analyses also showed other foods were likely present. This suggests, even though chili wasn't available at the time, that this may have been the earliest form of curry anywhere.

In India, turmeric was the most important of the ancient Ayurvedic spices and its use may date back even further – to 4000 BCE or earlier.[7] Furthermore, ginger is mentioned in the *Sushruta Samhita* of c. 800 BCE.[8]

The use of ginger as a medicine was recorded by the legendary Chinese Emperor Shen-Nong (c. 2800 BCE) in his *Shen-Nong Ben Cao Ying*; the original text is lost but later compilations are supposedly based on Shen-Nong's work. The seventh-century CE Tang Herbal includes turmeric as a drug. Confucius (551–479 BCE) considered ginger highly important to diet – 'He never went without ginger at a meal'.[9] J. Innes Miller referred to the practice of ginger being grown in pots in Chinese ships as fresh food (from the Buddhist monk Fa-hsien's *Travels*).[10]

Ptolemy said of Tabropane (Sri Lanka) in the second century CE: 'The country produces rice, honey, ginger, beryl, hyacinth …'[11]

Gingers in the Middle East

Roy Strong refers to Mesopotamian royal banquets in the second millennium BCE in which guests received a phial of oil perfumed with cedar, ginger and myrtle to anoint themselves at the start and finish of the meal.[12] Also, turmeric and cardamom were cultivated as early as the eighteenth century BCE in Babylon and that they must have been introduced from India, where they were indigenous.[13] Both were included in the scroll listing aromatic plants from the great Assyrian library at Nineveh (established by King Ashurbanipal, 668–663 BCE). Some scholars have speculated that the gardens at Nineveh may have been the true Hanging Gardens of Babylon.

Ginger in the Mediterranean

Ancient DNA preserved inside fifth- to third-century BCE Greek amphorae demonstrated the presence of ginger among a range of other foods, proving that it was part of the maritime trade of that era in the Mediterranean region.[14]

Both Pliny and Dioscorides have suggested that ginger was grown in 'Troglodytical Arabia' (i.e. the south-western coast of the Red Sea). This idea has had its supporters, though it seems very unlikely – ginger is a tropical plant.[15] Pliny stated:

> zingiberi, or ginger … is very like it [i.e. black pepper] in taste. For ginger, in fact, grows in Arabia and in Troglodytica, in various cultivated spots, being a small plant with a white root. This plant is apt to decay very speedily, although it is of intense pungency; the price at which it sells is six denarii per pound.[16]

Pliny lamented about the cost of ginger in the same manner that he did with pepper – this implies the popular use was a relatively new 'fad': 'Both pepper and ginger grow wild in their respective countries, and yet here we buy them by weight – just as if they were so much gold or silver.'

Dioscorides commented that it could be mixed and made into a drink, and its pale roots tasted similar to pepper and had a pleasant smell.[17]

The error in reporting the provenance of certain spices was not uncommon, for several reasons: information was second or third hand; the actual source was at the limit or beyond the bounds of the world known to western chroniclers; and middlemen traders persisted in disguising the actual sources in order to protect their monopoly. More importantly, the error proves the route by which ginger was imported from India, i.e. by the Red Sea route certainly and probably also via the Persian Gulf. The absence of ginger from the lists of imported goods in the *Periplus* implies that it was imported by third parties – probably Arab or Persian traders, or by Indians themselves. The same false provenance logic can be applied to amomum and cardamom (Figure 18). Warmington considered that it was imported almost entirely by land routes and that the epithets revealed the routes wherein it was used, hence – Sallust: 'Among the Gorduenians [in Armenia], amomum and other pleasant scents [i.e. scented plants] grow.'[18]

And Pliny observed that 'Amomum is produced, also [i.e. as well as from India], in that part of Armenia which is known as Otene; as, also, in Media and Pontus'.[19] Pliny also commented about cardamom: 'It is gathered in the same manner both in India and Arabia … Cardamom grows also in Media.'[20]

Dioscorides said that amomum came from Armenia, Media and Pontus, while cardamom came from Commagene, Armenia and the Bosphorus, as well as India and Arabia.[21]

Warmington also cited Tyrian (Gallus or Virgil), Babylonian (Galen) and Assyrian (Statius) examples.[22]

These all point strongly to an overland export route via the Silk Roads for amomum and cardamom in the Graeco-Roman era.

But cardamom remains have been found at Pattanam (the site of Muziris on the Malabar coast from where pepper was exported to Rome), which implies that there was at least some export of cardamom to Rome in the early centuries CE along with pepper, i.e. via the Red Sea, even though it wasn't mentioned in the *Periplus*. By the third century CE, the provenance of certain spices would have been better understood.

Ginger was documented in Europe in the first century CE from Roman trade with India.[23] Apicius refers to it in numerous recipes and after pepper it was the most important of the Far Eastern spices.[24] It was an ingredient in spiced salts, in Oxyporum (a digestive), in salad, dishes with peas, suckling pig, stuffed chicken, roast meats and others. Turmeric, however, is unlikely to have been widely used in Ancient Rome.

The ginger family's use as medicines has a long history. Hippocrates listed amomum (probably cardamom) in his medicines.[25] Theophrastus mentioned both amomum and galangal.[26] Celsus used cardamom in several remedies – e.g. for dropsy, and in a remedy for the nerves – but ginger and amomum were employed rarely.[27] Dioscorides noted that ginger, like pepper, was a warming and digestive medicine and was good for the stomach; the root was a treatment against disorders of the eye.[28]

Turmeric appears less frequently in classical literature, though Dioscorides' description of 'Indian cyperus' might have been turmeric – it was similar to ginger and had a bitter taste.[29] However, a recent study by researchers from Tor Vergata University of Rome on the 2,000-year-old remains of teeth and plaque of a young woman from Tuscany who lived with coeliac disease, found that ancient Romans used medicines including roots and herbs only grown in Asia.[30] The chemical residues in her dental plaque pointed to use of medicinal plants such as ginseng and turmeric to treat her condition (which was found by an earlier DNA study). The importance of finding turmeric here proves that there must have been some trade in it between East and West at that time. She was buried with gold, therefore was from a wealthy family, and consequently could afford expensive spices. The Indian author

Susruta II (second century CE) referred to it among an extensive list of plant-based medicines.[31]

By the second century CE, caravans regularly departed the then Chinese capital city of Luoyang with ginger, cassia, cassia leaf and cinnamon.[32] These and other spices were moving along the Silk Road towards the West both during and after the Roman era – in addition to the much larger quantities of spices shipped directly from India to the West via the Red Sea and Persian Gulf. The Alexandrian Tariff of Marcus Aurelius issued between 176 and 180 CE lists fifty-four items subject to import duty, including many botanicals. Diocletian's Maximum Price Edict of 301 CE lists amomum, prepared ginger and dried ginger among the 1,200-plus products, at least showing them to be actively traded items. Justinian's Digest of 533 CE lists fifty-six items subject to *vectigal* (import tax) – in what was essentially a repeat of the Alexandrian Tariff – both included amomum, ginger and cardamom.[33]

Medieval Uses

Ginger was second only to black pepper in terms of volumes imported and consumed by the West during the medieval period. Galangal was also popular, zedoary less so, but turmeric didn't appear (or reappear) until later. It is interesting to see quite heavy medieval use of ginger in European cuisine despite this pre-dating the Western discovery of the southern marine route to Asia. This is likely to be due to Arab traders supplying middlemen in Constantinople, Venice and Alexandria. Just before the discovery of the southern marine route, in November 1496 four ships arrived in Venice from Alexandria carrying over 2 million kg of spices, of which 1,363,934kg were pepper and 288,524kg ginger.[34]

Ginger (raw and preserved) was included in the extensive list of spices Bede left to his fellows and *Leechdoms* includes five references to ginger.[35] In the 960s, Corby Abbey bought 70lb ginger from Cambrai, among other spices.[36] It was certainly well known in England before the Norman conquest.[37]

The eleventh-century physician Constantine the African was a North African who migrated to Italy and became a monk at the abbey at Monte Cassino. He produced several remedies to address flagging sex drive, most of which included ginger and galangal.[38] Ginger's reputation as an aphrodisiac was widespread in the Middle Ages – which may have in part accounted for its popularity! The same appears to be true of ginger in India – van Linschoten described the habit of certain Goan women who 'eate whole handfuls of Cloves, Pepper, Ginger, and a baked kind of meat called Chachunde, which is mixed of all kinds of Spices and hearbes, and such like meates, all to increase their leachery'.[39] Cardamom also has a long history as an aphrodisiac – it appears in the *One Thousand and One Nights* in various places: in Night 250 it is part of a fertility compound for Shams al-Din, who after forty years of marriage was unable to father a child. It comprised cubebs, cinnamon, cloves, cardamom, ginger, white pepper, mountain lizard, frankincense and cumin (and, of course, it worked).

Ginger and cardamom remains were found at the old trading port of Quseir al-Qadim/Myos Hormos on the Red Sea coast of Egypt dating from 1050 to 1500 CE.[40]

Marco Polo noted ginger's presence in China, Malabar and Sumatra, i.e. at that time it was certainly widespread through South and Southeast Asia.[41] He also described turmeric from China, but it was clearly unfamiliar to him: '[it] has all the properties of true Saffron, as well the smell as the colour, and yet it is not really Saffron. It is held in great estimation, and being an ingredient in all their dishes, it bears on that account a high price.'

Colin Spencer notes that ginger was listed in the royal accounts between 1205 and 1207 in the reign of King John, together with numerous other spices, including sugar.[42] This expansion of tastes reflects in part the influence of returning crusaders. The establishment of the London Pepperers' Guild in the late twelfth century and the rise of pepperers, spicers and apothecaries is related. Spencer described several early recipes featuring ginger from the royal household of Edward I (around 1275 CE), e.g. sage sauce comprising ground ginger, cloves, cinnamon, galingale, sage, hard-boiled egg yolk mixed with wine or cider, served with suckling pigs' trotters and other typically rich examples. He also describes a later medieval sauce for meat or fish called 'gravey', which is a puree of almonds and ginger sweetened with sugar. In 1300, the Countess of Pembroke purchased various spices, including ginger, cumin, and sugar at Winchester.[43] In early fourteenth-century France the kitchen of Jeanne d'Evreux (the widow of King Charles le Bel) included, among plentiful other spices, some 23.5lb of ginger.[44] Ginger was then clearly a highly favoured spice in medieval times and it was expensive: the price in England between 1301 and 1304 ranged from 2s 4d to 3s 4d per lb, though Ridley quotes 1s 7d per lb during the thirteenth and fourteenth centuries, i.e. about the price of a sheep.

The early distribution of galangal is not very clear – it appears to have reached Europe from Asia in early medieval times. Galangal appears in *The Forme of Cury* of 1390. It is mainly in powdered form in 'Sawse Madam', an ingredient in Hippocras, in galyntyne sauce and other recipes.[45]

The fourteenth-century Sir John Mandeville, a fanciful pseudonym of an unknown author, described Java and its spices so: 'There growen alle maner of Spicerie, more plentyfous liche than in ony other Contree; as of Gyngevere [ginger], Clowegylofres, [cloves] Canelle [cinnamon], Zedewalle [zedoary], Notemuges and Maces.'[46] Despite the absurdities of much of his writing, in this case he correctly located these spices in Indonesia in an era when that part of the world was virtually unknown to the West, other than from second-hand and unreliable information.

The late fourteenth-century *Ménagier de Paris* was written by an anonymous and probably fictional husband for his younger wife as a household guide for the times, including medieval ideas on marriage and a lot of information on cookery.[47] A small wedding feast is interesting for the volume of spices used, which included 1lb of columbine ginger (i.e. ginger from Kollam, India), ¼lb of mesche ginger (i.e. Mecca ginger, another false provenance), ½lb of ground cinnamon, ¼lb of cloves and seed of garlic, ⅛lb of long pepper, ⅛lb of galingale and ⅛lb of mace. Ginger is amongst the most frequently used spices in the numerous recipes throughout the book.

Ginger appeared in almost 35 per cent of late medieval English recipes in a 2012 study, making it the second most frequently used spice (after saffron).[48] Galangal was fairly popular, appearing in ninety-five recipes (6.9 per cent), cardamom in just one recipe, and turmeric in none, suggesting these latter two were uncommon in England before the fifteenth century. In *The Forme of Cury*, some forty-four of the approximately 200 recipes utilise ginger, e.g. Bruet or Brewet, and Mawmenee (both well-known medieval meat stews), and these examples:

Tostee [Toastie]
Take wyne and hony and found it [mix it] togyder and skym it clene. and seeþ it long, do þerto powdour of gyngur. peper and salt, tost brede and lay the sew þerto. kerue [carve] pecys of gyngur and flour it þerwith and messe it forth.

Peeres [Pears] *In Confyt*
Take peeres and pare hem clene. take gode rede wyne & mulberes oþer saundres and seeþ þe peeres þerin & whan þei buth ysode, take hem up, make a syryp of wyne greke. oþer vernage [a sort of Italian wine] with blaunche powdour oþer white sugur and powdour gyngur & do the peres þerin. seeþ it a lytel & messe it forth.[49]

Ginger also featured in spice mixes, e.g. Blanch powder (white sugar and ginger, possibly with cinnamon), Powder fort (pepper, cloves and ginger) and Powder douce (either powdered galingale or a compound of aromatic spices, e.g. ginger, cinnamon, nutmeg, sugar); they probably varied among cooks.

Galangal appears in the Prologue to *The Canterbury Tales*, published *c.* 1400:

A cook they hadde with hem for the nones
To boille the chiknes with the marybones
And poudre-marchant tart and galyngale
Wel koude he knowe a draughte of London ale.[50]

Dame Alice de Bryene's household used 2½lb ginger in the year 1418–19, but she catered for many people.[51] Hippocras was a spiced wine strained through a filter bag, and popular in that era. This is from a recipe (which includes ginger and grains of paradise) in *The Boke of Nurture* by John Russell (1460–70 CE), set out in a poem:

> Good son, to make ypocras, hit were gret lernynge,
> and for to take the spice therto aftur the proporcionynge,
> Gynger, Synamome / Graynis, Sugur / Turnesole, that is good colourynge;
> For commyn peple / Gynger, Canelle / longe pepur / hony aftur claryfiynge …
> Se that youre gynger be welle y-pared / or hit to powder ye bete,
> and that hit be hard / with-owt worme / bytynge, & good hete ;
> For good gynger colombyne / is best to drynke and ete;
> Gynger valadyne & maydelyn ar not so holsom in mete …
> Graynes of paradise, hoote & moyst they be:
> Sugre of.iij.cute /white / hoot & moyst in his propurte;
> Sugre Candy is best of alle, as y telle the,
> and red wyne is whote & drye to tast, fele, & see.
> Graynes / gynger, longe pepur, & sugre / hoot & moyst in worchynge;
> Synamome / Canelle / red wyne / hoot & drye in theire doynge;
> Turnesole is good & holsom for red wyne colowrynge:
> alle these ingredyentes, they ar for ypocras makynge.[52]

The amount of spices bought by the large aristocratic households could be enormous. In 1452–53 the Duke of Buckingham bought 316lb pepper and 194lb ginger.[53] For the 1483 coronation of Richard III, 26lb of ginger was purchased at a cost of £2 16*s*.[54] Four pounds of galangal was also purchased, at a cost of 13*s* 4*d*, and so was more expensive than ginger. Actually, the cost of ginger varied with quality and it could be similar to the price of pepper, or three times its price.[55] In general, the nominal price of ginger in England appears to increase from the thirteenth century to the late sixteenth century and then fall and stay low until the late eighteenth century, at which point it rises sharply again. The low-price era corresponds with the activities of the English East India Company, to be discussed subsequently, as well as new supplies from the West Indies.

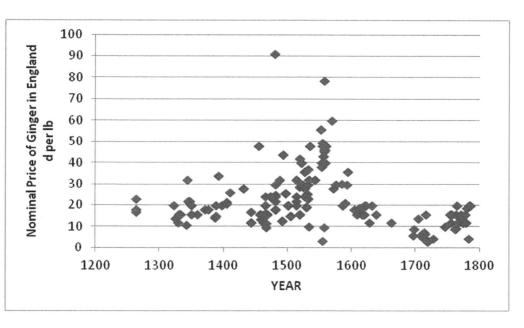

The price of ginger in England between 1264 and 1786. The very low values (below 10d) are mainly wholesale purchases. Note the rapid fall in prices after the sixteenth-century spike related to increased availability and decline of Portuguese monopolies. (Data from J. E. Thorold Rogers, 1866–1902)[56]

Post-Medieval Uses

Stefan Halikowski Smith notes that the Renaissance was the golden age of culinary spices, and that the most startling aspect of late medieval cooking was that it was 'so wildly aromatic and of such strong taste'.[57] Ginger and other exotic spices appear frequently in the 1510 Dutch cookery text *Een notabel boecxken van cokeryen*, which was the earliest printed Dutch cookbook.[58] Ginger was used in a huge range of dishes, from flavouring the earliest waffles to spicing up sausages – for example, this one from Sir Hugh Plat in 1603: 'Take the filets of an hog, chop them verie small with a handful of red sage, season it hote with Ginger and Pepper, and then put it into a great sheepes gut, then let it lie three nights in brine, then boile it and hang it up in a chimney where fire is usually kept.'[59] Crystallised ginger was also a Tudor favourite.[60]

Ginger has always been an important component of Indian cuisine. In 1596, Jan van Linschoten noted that 'the roote is the Ginger, being greene, it is much eaten in India, for sallets, as also sodden in Vineger, which they call Achar ... There is likewise much ginger conserved in Suger [coming out] of Bengala.'[61]

It was exported widely to the Red Sea, Hormuz, Arabia and Persia, but not much to Portugal due to the customs duties imposed, other than on Indian ships. This was a period of decline of the former Portuguese monopoly.

Cardamom, which mainly grew in Malabar, was also popular in India at this time according to Linschoten: 'they put Cardamomum into the pot, it maketh the meate to have as good a savor and a taste as any of the other spices of India.'

It was also valued for its medicinal properties: 'It is very good against a stincking breath and evill humors in the head.' Linschoten also commented on the provenance of galangal – the sweeter-smelling lesser galangal coming from China and the less-attractive greater galangal from Java. In India it was cultivated in gardens and used 'for Sallets and other medicines, specially the midwyves'.

Turmeric was one of the export commodities from Bengal of the English East India Company, though relatively modest – the company's demand in 1657 was only 5 or 10 tons, increasing to 30 tons in 1659.[62] In the early 1680s, the shipments increased to 250 tons for a few years, but it was regarded as a 'dull commodity' by the company directors and reduced again to lower levels. It is strange that turmeric was so late appearing in Europe, compared to the closely related ginger which was widely used over the last two millennia.

Spain was the first European country to use turmeric, introduced by Arabs, and it was certainly known in England by the seventeenth century. Turmeric appears in Hannah Glasse's classic 1747 cookery book, as an ingredient for India Pickle, purple cabbage pickle and milk water.[63] India Pickle evolved into Piccalilli at some time in the eighteenth century – turmeric is always a key ingredient. In Hannah Glasse's 1767 edition it is referred to as paco-lilla, the pickling ingredients of which include 'race-ginger' (i.e. root ginger), salt, long pepper, garlic, mustard seeds, turmeric and white wine vinegar, into which various vegetables and fruits are placed.

Gingerbread appeared in Europe in medieval times and became widely available in Britain during the eighteenth century. Even in the thirteenth century it was quite well known and made a fitting gift for people of high status – in 1284–85 the price ranged from 9d to 2s per lb.[64] Sabina Welserin gave a recipe for Nuremberg gingerbread in her 1553 book of recipes. A simpler recipe for red gingerbread (or leach lumbar) is provided by John Murrel in 1617:

> Grate and dry two stale manchets [medieval wheat yeast bread], either by the fire or in an oven, sift them through a sieue, and put to it Cinamon, Ginger, Sugar, Liquorice, Anis-seed: when you haue mingled all this together, boile a pint of red wine, and put in your mingled bread, and stirre it, that it be as thicke as a Hastie-pudding; then take it out, and coole it, and mould it with Cinamon, Ginger, Liquorice and Anis-seede, and rowle it thinne, and print it with your mould, and dry it in a warme Ouen.[65]

Gingerbread biscuits often appear as gingerbread men, a custom which dates to at least the sixteenth century. The popularity of gingerbread, even in Shakespeare's time, is seen in *Love's Labours Lost* as Costard laments: 'An I had but one penny in the world, thou shoulds't have it to buy gingerbread.'[66] Zara Groundes-Peace observed that gingerbread was welcomed by both noble and peasant and that it was a popular gift at court, in everyday celebrations, and by patrons to workmen.[67] It could be served fresh from the oven or stored for a year. Baking moulds were varied and sometimes elaborate. The use of gingerbread has been taken to extremes over the centuries: around 1400, the Parisian merchant Jacques Duche had a walk-in gingerbread house constructed. The theme continued more recently (2019) at the Fairmont San Francisco – where the chefs baked 8,000 bricks of gingerbread with 3,500lb of icing and nearly a ton of candy in order to construct their particular version of the gingerbread house.[68] Similarly, the world's largest gingerbread pirate ship was on display (for several years in the holiday season) in the lobby at the Ritz-Carlton, Amelia Island, and numerous other establishments continue trying to outdo each other.

The Low Countries have a seasonal treat that is related to gingerbread called *speculaas*. It is widely consumed in early December to celebrate St Nicholas' (Sinterklaas) Day, which falls on 5 or 6 December. They are thin, spiced biscuits typically using ginger, cinnamon, pepper, cardamom, nutmeg, cloves and brown sugar and traditionally made with Frisian flour, though many different varieties exist. The biscuits probably date from the seventeenth century, when these spices became widely available via the Dutch East India Company (VOC).

Ginger was introduced to the Americas and West Indies in the sixteenth century, and in 1547 Jamaica exported over 2 million pounds of ginger to Europe. Jamaica has been a significant producer and exporter since that time.[69] Turmeric was introduced to Jamaica in 1783. Hispaniola also became a significant ginger producer in the sixteenth century, sending 22,000 *quintales* (1 *quintal* = *c*. 46kg) to Seville from 1576 to 1594.[70] Ginger from the West Indies was a lot cheaper than that from India; in 1592, ginger from Santa Domingo was five times less than that from Calicut.[71]

Ginger tea is a modern favourite (use ½oz powdered ginger – or fresh sliced ginger – with 1 pint boiling water, and add small amount of honey to sweeten if required) but similar brews have long been used as a remedy for stomach upsets, nausea and colds. It is widely used in Ayurvedic medicine and traditional medicines elsewhere.

Today the largest producer of ginger is India, followed by China and Nigeria. Other significant producers are Nepal, Indonesia and Thailand. The largest exporter, however, is China. It is sold as fresh young rhizomes, dry mature ones, dried and ground, or preserved. Stem ginger is fresh rhizome that has been peeled, cooked and preserved in sugar syrup. Ginger is a key ingredient of Indian curries and other foods and is used extensively in Asian cuisine. It is also very popular in the West, with the USA being the world's largest importer. It has a long history of use in alcoholic and non-alcoholic beverages – ginger wine, ginger beer, ginger ale, etc., and is also very popular in cakes, puddings, biscuits, pastries, etc.

Turmeric's widespread use includes curry powder (it is usually the major component), chicken stock, sauces, gravies, seasonings, pickles and relishes, soups, beverages and confectionary. Today turmeric is one of *the* trendiest spices: turmeric lattes abound in the smartest cafes frequented by the wellness warriors. However, there are potential downsides with respect to health – the bright yellow colour of turmeric is so appealing that it has been adulterated in Bangladesh, the USA and probably other places by the addition of lead chromate (an industrial paint pigment) in order to enhance and maintain its bright colour.[72]

Turmeric is cultivated most extensively in India, followed by Bangladesh, China, Thailand, Cambodia, Malaysia, Indonesia and the Philippines. India is the largest producer, consumer and exporter.

The Ginger Spice Seeds: Cardamom and Grains of Paradise

Cardamom

Cardamom was used in the preparation of medicines in the early centuries BCE. The fifth-century BCE Ayurveda texts (a Hindu system of medicine) described cardamom as a cure for urinary problems, a means of removing fat from the body and a treatment for piles and jaundice.[73] One of these texts was the Indian Sanskrit *Charaka Samhita* (written between the second century BCE and the second century CE), wherein cardamom was referred to as a component of some medicines.[74]

Cardamom was imported to Rome and Greece in the last few centuries BCE, though, as already shown, the Romans didn't know where it came from. It was only rarely referred to by Apicius. It was listed in the Alexandrian Tariff as 'Antomum' and was probably imported in small quantities and perhaps used more in perfumes than cuisine.[75] There is only a single Indian archaeological record of cardamom – from excavations in early historic Pattanam (Muziris).

Cardamom (or grains of paradise) was listed amongst the spices left by the venerable Bede to his brethren.[76] European spicers of the Middle Ages used cardamom and other spices to flavour drinks, especially after the Crusades, when a greater variety of spices appeared. Nonetheless, it remained scarce in medieval European cuisine relative to many other spices and appears infrequently in recipes of the era.

Guatemala is the biggest commercial producer of cardamom today. It is a common ingredient in Indian cookery – green cardamom is used in traditional Indian sweets and masala chai; black cardamom is sometimes used in garam masala for curries and in basmati rice and other dishes. Cardamom is popular in the Middle East in sweet and savoury dishes and as a flavouring agent in drinks, especially tea and coffee. The cardamom coffee *ghawa* is a traditional beverage in Arab culture and a symbol of hospitality. It is also used in pickling vegetables, with sauerkraut and in vegetable soups. It is also commonly used in baking, e.g. in Danish pastries, gingerbread and coffee cakes.

Cardamom Coffee

<u>Ingredients</u>
Unroasted Arabica coffee beans (or buy roasted, or ground).
4 heaped teaspoons of ground coffee will be sufficient for two cups
1 tablespoon ground cardamom seeds
Sugar to taste
Ground cloves
Water

<u>Method</u>
Roast coffee beans to taste, 165 to 210°C (or use roasted or ground beans).
Grind coffee beans.
Remove the cardamom seeds from the pods and grind finely.
Boil water in a *dallah* (a small saucepan will do), remove from heat and then turn heat down to low/medium.
Add the coffee to the water and return to the stove and let coffee brew for 10 minutes or so (don't bring to the boil again).
Remove the pan from the heat, allow the coffee to settle, then add the ground cardamom (with cloves if desired).
Return coffee to the stove and bring almost to the boil.
Remove and let stand for a few minutes (the grounds will settle at the base of the *dallah*/pan).
Serve directly, or strain and serve.

Serve with dates or sweet pastries. The cardamom takes the edge off the bitterness of the coffee, making a smooth and pleasant drink with a delicious aroma.

The closely related black cardamom has similar-shaped, but larger, pods. The natural aroma is often overpowered by the smell of smoke as wood fires are typically used to dry the pods. Black cardamom is mainly used for savoury dishes in South Asian cuisine and is also used in traditional medicine.

Grains of Paradise

The spice was popular during the Middle Ages and early modern period but has long since fallen out of popularity. Transport to Europe from West Africa was by camel train through the Sahara Desert and thence to Italy, or by ship. It was quite expensive, too – 1s 6d per lb – based on the costs for the 1483 coronation feast of Richard III (more than black pepper). The price in England actually seems to have been quite variable – cheap in the thirteenth century, just 3d or 4d per lb (based on limited data), but becoming expensive in the fourteenth and fifteenth centuries.[77] In the latter part of the fifteenth century, Portuguese traders started to exploit the spice along the West African coast. The sudden abundance led to a steep decline in black pepper prices in Lisbon – and the fall in grains of paradise prices in the late fifteenth century.[78]

Archaeobotanical evidence is scarce; Julian Wiethold described *Aframomum m.* from the fourteenth- to sixteenth-century latrines in Kiel, Germany, and other North German locations.[79] Based on Wiethold's earlier work, Greig reevaluated specimens from a fifteenth-century latrine in Worcester as *Aframomum m.* and also sixteenth-century material from Taunton.[80] Greig notes that grains of paradise have been historically recorded from the thirteenth century, but seem to have gone out of use in the seventeenth century.

After the plant was introduced into South America, it was cultivated in Surinam and Guyana.[81] In the nineteenth century, it was used to adulterate drinks to give the impression of strength, and is now used as a botanical in some gins as well as a spice and condiment. It is also used as a local African folk medicine for various purposes.

The explosion of use of the ginger family spices in medieval times is an interesting phenomenon as it followed on from the collapse of the western Roman Empire. As catastrophic as it was for Rome, trade between the East and West didn't stop, but it certainly changed …

6

The Age of Discovery, Part 1: Nutmeg, Mace, Cloves and Cinnamon

Nutmeg, from *Birds and all Nature*, Chicago, 1899. (Biodiversity Heritage Library)

Nutmeg and Mace

Nutmeg, *Myristica fragrans*, is the fruit of an evergreen tree native to the remote Banda Islands in the Maluku (Molucca) province of Indonesia. Nutmegs are ovoid shaped and around 2–3cm long; mace is the aril, a bright red fleshy covering of the nutmeg, and is itself used as a spice (Figures 20 and 23). The Moluccas were often known as the Spice Islands and the Banda Islands are a group of ten small volcanic islands about 140km south of Seram, which itself is very remote.

The first recorded use of nutmeg as a food is from an archaeological site on Pulau Ai (one of the Banda Islands), where it was found as residue on ceramic potsherds and is thought to be about 3,500 years old.[1] The nutmeg tree grows to around 65ft high and the fruits resemble apricots and are a similar size.

Nutmeg has a pungent fragrance and a slightly sweet taste – the ground-up nut is used as a spice to flavour various dishes: baked foods, puddings, confections, mulled wine, potatoes, meats, vegetables and sauces. In Indonesian cuisine it is used in spicy soups such as soto, sop kambing and bakso, in gravy for meat dishes and in popular sweets like fried bananas.

The Banda Islands were the only source of nutmeg until the late eighteenth century, but it appeared in Europe and the Middle East much earlier than that as a result of Arab traders, who jealously guarded its source. Nutmeg was well known in Europe by the sixth century CE. Spices became expensive in the Dark Ages and even in the fourteenth century, when spices were more readily available, a German price table of 1393 listed a pound of nutmeg as worth seven fat oxen.[2] In England, nutmeg was scarce in the medieval era, though mace was relatively popular based on occurrences in contemporary recipes – but more expensive. Remains of mace were found in the fifteenth-century drains of Paisley Abbey, Scotland; a nutmeg fragment has been found from the medieval hospital at Soutra, Scotland, from the late fifteenth century/early sixteenth century at Bratislava, Slovakia, and from early fourteenth-century Beroun in the Czech Republic.[3] The Portuguese, Dutch and English fought for control of the enormously lucrative trade in Far Eastern spices from the sixteenth to eighteenth centuries, which will be described in the following section.

The nutmeg tree didn't reach the New World until 1773.[4] From the beginning of the eighteenth century, the French had wanted to transplant spice plants to their own territories, and in 1750 a price of 20,000 pieces of silver was offered to bring twenty-five nutmeg plants to the southern Indian port town of Pondicherry (which was under French control). After an unsuccessful attempt in the 1750s, the naturalist Pierre Poivre succeeded in bringing many nutmeg plants to Mauritius in 1770 and 1772. Specimens were sent on to Isle de Cayenne in French Guiana, arriving in 1773. The United States became involved in the spice trade around the end of the eighteenth century and ships sailed from Atlantic coast ports, trading American produce for spices (especially pepper), tea and coffee.

Nutmeg isn't just a spice – it also has hallucinogenic properties, due to a psychoactive substance called myristicin. It was used by Albert Hoffman (predictably, he discovered LSD) and Malcolm X; however, the mild euphoria may be accompanied by nausea, headaches, hallucinations and paranoia, among other unpleasant side effects – so use modestly!

Cloves

Cloves, the flower buds of the evergreen tree *Syzygium aromaticum*, are also native to the Molucca Islands. The trees grow up to 12m in height, have large, simple, lanceolate leaves and clusters of flowers that become crimson red when ripe for harvest (Figure 21). After harvesting, the aromatic flowers are dried under the sun and become dark brown, rather resembling old broken rusty nails (Figure 23).

Cloves *might* have been used as far back as the eighteenth century BCE (based on an unconfirmed report from 1721 BCE in Syria), but they were certainly traded from India to Rome in the first century CE – they were referred to by Pliny as 'caryophyllon' – and they have certainly been growing naturally in the Mollucas for thousands of years.[5] However, the oldest definite archaeological evidence is from a single clove found in Sri Lanka that dates to 900–1100 CE.[6] The value of cloves is illustrated in *Nathaniel's Nutmeg*: David Middleton, captain of the small ship *Consent* on the East India Company's third expedition to the Spice Islands in 1607, chanced upon a passing junk laden with cloves which were for sale. He purchased the whole cargo for £3,000, which was ultimately sold on in London for £36,000.[7] The world's oldest living clove tree is called Afo and is situated on the Moluccan island of Ternate, being reportedly 350–400 years old. Our friend M. Poivre, the naturalist who exported nutmeg to Mauritius in 1770, is also reputed to have stolen clove seedlings from Afo to go along with the nutmeg.

Today, cloves are grown mainly in Indonesia, Madagascar, Zanzibar, Sri Lanka and Brazil. In Indonesia, cloves (*cengkeh*) are used as a flavouring in the popular cigarettes called 'kretek' – the smell is ubiquitous and not unpleasant. In addition to its original function as a spice for both savoury and sweet dishes, it is used in perfumes, cosmetics, toothpaste and medicines, including an analgesic remedy for toothache. It is also a key ingredient in Worcestershire sauce!

Cinnamon

Cinnamon (Figure 23) is the inner bark of the tree *Cinnamomum*, belonging to the Laurels family, and typically grows in tropical or subtropical climates. It is used as a condiment and as a spice in both sweet and savoury dishes, and as a flavouring in some drinks. The organic compound cinnamaldehyde gives cinnamon the sweet taste and pleasant aroma that led to its popularity. Cassia, or Chinese cinnamon (*Cinnamomum cassia*), is a cheaper and more common variety than true cinnamon (*Cinnamomum verum*), and is less delicate, with a thicker bark. Most of the cinnamon sold in supermarkets in the UK and USA is cassia. John Russell compared them in his *Boke of Nurture* (c. 1460–70): 'looke that your stikkes of synamome be thyn, bretille, & fayre in colewre, and in youre mowthe, Fresche, hoot, & swete / that is best & sure, For canelle [cassia] is not so good in this crafte & cure.'[8]

C. verum is native to India, Sri Lanka, Bangladesh and Myanmar. The main producers of cinnamon today are Indonesia, China, Vietnam and Sri Lanka.

Cinnamaldehyde was detected in ten out of twenty-seven Phoenician flasks from archaeological sites in Israel, the flasks dating from the eleventh and ninth centuries BCE.[9] As the plant only grew in South and Southeast Asia at that time, this suggests that trading was established between the Levant and Asia around 3,000 years ago.

The ancient Greeks certainly imported cinnamon, which was one of the medicinal plants that Hippocrates (460–377 BCE) referred to in his treatises.

Herodotus, in the fifth century BCE, described the use of cassia in the ancient Egyptian embalming process for filling the abdominal cavity, together with myrrh 'and every other sort of spicery'. Herodotus also describes Arabia as being the only country that produced cinnamon and cassia. He further described the (rather unlikely) way cinnamon was obtained:

Great birds, they say, bring the sticks which we Greeks, taking the word from the Phoenicians, call cinnamon, and carry them up into the air to make their nests. These are fastened with a sort of mud to a sheer face of rock, where no foot of man is able to climb. So the Arabians, to get the cinnamon, use the following artifice. They cut all the oxen and asses and beasts of burthen that die in their land into large pieces, which they carry with them into those regions, and place near the nests: then they withdraw to a distance, and the old birds, swooping down, seize the pieces of meat and fly with them up to their nests; which, not being able to support the weight, break off and fall to the ground. Hereupon the Arabians return and collect the cinnamon, which is afterwards carried from Arabia into other countries.[10]

Theophrastus differentiated between cinnamon and cassia, proving they were already well known and important in the West by the fourth century BCE. Apicius used malabathrum (leaves of *C. temala*) in laser (or silphium) sauce, in boiled lobster and shellfish dishes. Both cinnamon and cassia are also included in *De Materia Medica* of 50–70 CE.[11]

The cassia used in Egyptian embalming may have been derived from China, where there is record of use in the *Ch'u Ssu* (*Elegies of Ch'u*), written in the fourth century BCE.[12] It was also included in the earlier Chinese herbal of Shennong and others.

For many centuries, Arab merchants maintained a monopoly on oriental spices by feeding disinformation and pretending that cassia and cinnamon came from Africa rather than the Far East, thus discouraging importers from making direct contact with the true sources. Pliny showed as far back as the first century CE that the fanciful stories of Herodotus, etc., were fabrications aimed at keeping prices high, though the disinformation was to continue and even Pliny got it wrong – he believed that cinnamon grew in Ethiopia. Its price was 12 denarii per lb.[13] By the second century CE, the spice route from the Far East to Europe was already established, with caravans regularly leaving the Chinese city of Luoyang laden with ginger, cassia and cinnamon.[14] After the fall of Rome, spices became much more expensive and scarcer. Small volumes of oriental spices were restricted to monasteries and a few merchants.[15]

Ibn Khordadbeh (a ninth-century Persian geographer and official) described the journey of Radhanite Jewish merchants from western Europe to Egypt then to India and China via Arabia in his *Book of Roads and Kingdoms*. They returned to Constantinople with various Eastern products, including cinnamon:

> They transport from the West eunuchs, female slaves, boys, silk, castor, marten and other furs, and swords. They take ship (from France), on the Western Sea, and steer for *Farama* (Pelusium in Egypt's nile delta). There they load their goods on camel-back and go by land to *al-Kolzum* (Suez), in five days journey over a distance of twenty-five parasangs. They embark in the East Sea (Red Sea) and sail from al-Kolzum to al-Jar and al-Jeddah, then they go to Sind, India, and China. On their return

from China they carry back musk, aloes, camphor, cinnamon, and other products of the Eastern countries to al-Kolzum and bring them back to Farama, where they again embark on the Western Sea. Some make sail for Constantinople to sell their goods to the Romans; others go to the palace of the King of the Franks ...[16]

The trade in spices grew rapidly in the second half of the twelfth century (revitalised by the Crusades) and then in 1245 Robert de Montpelier opened London's first pharmacy, selling medicines, spices and confections. In 1250, John Adrian was paid over £54 for dates, gingerbread, cinnamon and other spices – a large sum of money in those times.[17] Alice de Bryene purchased 2lb of cinnamon in 1418, but she was catering for a large household – the price was 19*d* per lb, but from the mid-fifteenth century prices were on an upward trend.[18] Cinnamon (or *cannel* in Latin) appears frequently in *The Forme of Cury* (1390) in both savoury and sweet dishes, and also in the spiced wine hypocras. It became increasingly popular in European medieval and early modern recipes.

Sri Lanka was long considered the source of the very best cinnamon. Jan van Linschoten commented in 1596:

the places where Cinamon groweth, is most and best in the Iland of Seylon, wherein there is whole woods full of [Cinamon trees]: in the coast of Malabar there groweth likewise great store and some woods of Cinamon, but not half so good and lesser trees ... The Cinamon of the Iland of Seylon is the best and finest and is [at the least] three times dearer in the price.[19]

Cinnamon reached the Island of Guadeloupe by 1762 and other Caribbean islands thereafter. By 1800, cinnamon was no longer such an expensive and rare commodity, as it had begun to be cultivated in other parts of the world.

Cinnamon toast and cinnamon rolls are common sweet snacks in Europe and America. It is probably the most common baking spice today.

Cinnamon has historically been used in many kinds of medicine: Dioscorides prescribed cinnamon bark in hot rum for colds and the use of cinnamon or cassia in treating many other complaints, and the Chinese have used it as a cure for flatulence. It was one of several spices used by medieval and early modern physicians to keep plague at bay. Today some believe it has use in lowering blood pressure, alleviating gastro-intestinal problems, helping control diabetes and various other disorders, though this remains unproven.

Malabathrum

Malabathrum is the name for leaves of the aromatic *Cinnamomum malabathrum* or *Cinnamomum tamala* tree, which grow in the eastern Himalayas and Western Ghats of India. Malabathrum was immensely popular with the ancient Romans in order to make a fragrant oil, used in unguent medicines and as a flavouring. Pliny says of this:

> Syria produces the malobathrum also, a tree which bears a folded leaf, with just the colour of a leaf when dried. From this plant an oil is extracted for unguents. Egypt produces it in still greater abundance; but that which is the most esteemed of all comes from India, where it is said to grow in the marshes like the lentil. It has a more powerful odour than saffron, and has a black, rough appearance, with a sort of brackish taste. The white is the least approved of all, and it very soon turns musty when old. In taste it ought to be similar to nard, when placed under the tongue. When made luke-warm in wine, the odour which it emits is superior to any other. The prices at which this drug ranges are something quite marvellous, being from one denarius to four hundred per pound; as for the leaf, it generally sells at sixty denarii per pound.[20]

The fifteenth to seventeenth centuries spanned a period of great geographic discovery by western European nations, as well as a European cultural renaissance. The great maritime discoveries started with a small country lacking in natural resources, but with a significant Atlantic coastline: Portugal.

Portuguese Opening of the European Spice Trade

In the fourteenth century, it was inevitable that Portugal's future would be linked with the sea. King Denis and then his son Afonso IV started to build the Portuguese navy and a commercial fleet that would rapidly develop and lead Portugal to become a major maritime power. Given its position in the extreme west of Europe, Portugal had limited options for growth. It was already trading with north-west Europe, e.g. England, Normandy, Flanders, etc., exporting products such as wine, olive oil, salt, figs, raisins, honey and hides. Trade in the Mediterranean was difficult as those countries had the same products as Portugal or trade was dominated by Venice, Genoa and the Ottomans. Furthermore, the fall of Constantinople to the Ottomans in the mid-fifteenth century resulted in a reduction of trade between Asia and Europe. The only options were to look west into the Atlantic ... or south into Africa. As early as 1415, Portugal seized Ceuta on the North African coast. In 1420, the Atlantic island of Madeira was settled, followed in 1427 by the Azores. Sugarcane became a major industry in the mid-fifteenth century on Madeira. The young Prince Henrique (later known as 'Henry the Navigator') sponsored these adventures, which used manoeuvrable two- or three-masted caravels of less than 100 tons – he would take 20 per cent of any profits. Money, as always, was a key motivator, but he was also driven by religion and zeal for discovery (though he never joined any of the expeditions). The exploration voyages, which all set out from Lagos, pushed further south along the African coast; Cap Blanc was reached in 1441, and then in 1445 the navigator Dinis Dias reached the mouth of the Senegal River.

The big prizes at this time were gold – and slaves, who were sold to Muslim merchants.

In July 1487, Bartolomeo Dias, a Portuguese mariner (and descendant of Dinis Dias), set sail from Lisbon in an attempt to search for the southern tip of Africa and round it, thereby hoping to prove up a new trade route to the East. His fleet comprised two small caravels and a supply ship.[21] They reached Walvis Bay (in modern Namibia) on 8 December. Fierce storms in January forced them further south and they lost sight of land; after several days he turned northwards, and on 3 February reached Mossel Bay in South Africa, about 250km east of the Cape of Good Hope. He continued another 250km east to Algoa Bay, but with a tired and reluctant crew and diminishing supplies he was forced to head back. They finally reached Portugal in December 1488, seeing the Cape for the first time on their way back – Dias named it the Cape of Storms, but it was later changed to the more upbeat term used today. Despite not being able to reach India, as Dias had hoped, this was no mean achievement – the southern tip of Africa had been identified and passed, and the potential route to the East proven. This coast is a horrendously dangerous area where hundreds of ships have foundered in the succeeding centuries, many far more seaworthy than these Portuguese vessels. In a cruel irony, Dias met his own death while captaining a ship caught in a storm near the Cape in May 1500.

It was to be a further ten years from Dias' historic rounding of the Cape before the Portuguese made it to India. The man chosen by King João to lead this attempt (and confirmed by his successor Dom Manuel) was Vasco da Gama, a man trusted by the king as a competent and resourceful mariner. Da Gama's route would be different to that of Dias – he would head out into the mid-South Atlantic from Cape Verde before landfall at St Helena Bay in southern Africa, a journey of ninety-three days in itself. The main sources for the voyage are the anonymous *Roteiro* or *Journal*; letters written by King Manuel and Girolamo Sernigi immediately after the return from India; the *Decades* of João de Barros and the *Chronicle* of King Manuel by Damiao de Goes.[22] There is also the account of Gaspar Correa, a Portuguese historian who lived in India from 1512 to 1529, but whose chronology differs from other reports.[23] The fleet comprised four vessels, the flagship *S. Gabriel*, the *S. Raphael*, captained by Paulo da Gama (Vasco's brother), the *Berrio*, captained by Nicolau Coelho, and an unnamed store ship, and they departed Lisbon in July 1497. The total number of those embarked is unclear, but the number of 170, cited by de Barros, may be close.[24] They resupplied and made repairs at São Thiago, in the Cape Verde Islands, before departing on 3 August. The journey was long but relatively uneventful and they finally sighted land on 4 November (giving rise to celebrations and the firing of cannon) and anchored at St Helena Bay on the 7th. They stayed there eight days, taking in wood and effecting repairs. The inhabitants were evidently ethnic Khoisan with whom the crews had initial friendly contact – though da Gama was later to be wounded by a spear in a minor skirmish. Cinnamon, cloves, pearls and gold were shown to a group of natives who had clearly never seen such items before.

On the 16th they set sail, and then on the 18th they sighted the Cape but were unable to pass until the 22nd because of unfavourable winds. They reached Mossel Bay on the 25th, where they stayed for thirteen days. The store ship was broken up and burned here and stores transferred to the other vessels. Another (peaceful) encounter with Khoisan followed on the 1st. The following day, around 200 people appeared and played music on flutes and danced in a friendly atmosphere. An ox was bought, and later feasted on, 'his meat as toothsome as the beef of Portugal'.

They set sail again on 8 December and marked their progress along this stretch of coast by the pillars erected by Bartolomeo Dias; despite struggling with winds and currents, they soon passed the furthest point that he had reached. On 11 January, short of water, they encountered a small river, the Rio do Cobre, and anchored near the coast in what is now southern Mozambique. They named the country 'Terra da Boa Gente' (Land of Good People, after their friendly reception). Their next stop, on 25 January, at the mouth of a broad river in northern Mozambique (subsequently named Rio dos bons Signaes), was also friendly: 'these people took much delight in us.' One young man was believed to have come from a distant country and was familiar with large ships such as those of the fleet – this was taken as a positive sign by da Gama suggesting proximity to Indian Ocean trading routes. They stayed here for thirty-two days, resupplying and repairing the hulls and mast of the *S. Raphael*, which had cracked in December. Many of the crew fell sick here, evidently from scurvy. On 24 February they set sail, heading north-east, and on 2 March made another approach to land. The leading *Berrio* hit a bank and was damaged but put about and regained deeper water, where they set anchor close to a village on the island of Mozambique. The people were Muslims, dressed in finely embroidered linen or cotton clothes, and appeared friendly. They were merchants and had dealings with Arabs, four of whose vessels were in the port, laden with cloves, pepper, ginger, gold, silver and gemstones. The Arabs confirmed that these goods were plentiful in India, making the crew joyous as it showed them they were closing in on their goal. When Nicolau Coelho had first entered the port, he was hosted and well treated by the local leader, fed and given a jar of bruised dates with cloves and cumin. However, when the inhabitants found out that the arrivals were Christians and not Turks as they first thought, they plotted to capture and kill them. After treachery, threats, adverse winds and skirmishes, they left the area on 29 March, headed north.

On 6 April, the *S. Raphael* ran aground on a sandbank and when the tide fell was left completely high and dry. Fortunately, they were able to refloat the ship at high tide, giving rise to much jubilation, and on the 7th they anchored off Mombasa, staying for six days. They didn't enter the port as they suspected a plot against them, having seen a large armed group approach in a dhow at midnight on their first appearance. The plot to capture the Portuguese ships was later confirmed (by torturing two of the Mozambique natives retained on board) and they departed Mombasa on the 13th, heading north.

The same evening, they anchored off the town of Malindi, about 90 nautical miles from Mombasa. Initial communications were encouraging, and the king sent gifts of cloves, cumin, ginger, nutmeg and pepper. On the 18th, the king's son and da Gama met in one of the boats which came alongside, and the meeting went well. The following days saw musicians playing on the beach and festivities along the harbour; despite invitations to come ashore, da Gama was reluctant to do so, understandably after recent experiences. They came across four Indian vessels in the harbour. Eventually, a Gujurati pilot was sent to them, and after nine days at Malindi they set sail to cross the Indian Ocean for Calicut.

On 18 May, after twenty-three days at sea and sailing before the wind, they sighted land and arrived at Calicut on the 20th. The Portuguese complement of crew included a number of convicts who were brought along for especially risky ventures. One such, Joao Nunez, was sent ashore at Calicut, where he was met by a pair of Tunisians who could speak some Spanish. Their first words were, 'May the Devil take thee! What brought you hither?' They were told that they were in search of Christians and spices. The author of the *Journal* describes Calicut as being inhabited by Christians, but this wasn't the case and probably had more to do with wishful thinking and misinterpretation. The people were judged to be 'well disposed and apparently of mild temper', an assessment which proved premature. Messages were sent to the king (or 'Zamorin') and a meeting arranged which took place on the 28th. Da Gama and thirteen of the crew were received in a friendly manner by the governor and many men, and proceeded to Calicut by road and river. Accompanied by huge crowds, they arrived at the palace. When they finally met the Zamorin he was reclining on a couch chewing betel nut! The following day, they prepared to present their gifts – clothes, material, coral, sugar, oil, honey, etc. – but the courtiers accompanying them laughed at the humble nature of the gifts, saying that 'the poorest merchant from Mecca, or … India, gave more'. Da Gama's muted reception and later ill-treatment was fuelled by scornful Arab merchants and little progress was made.

Apart from some minor trade with locals for cloves, cinnamon and gemstones in the intervening weeks, no real business was done, and in August da Gama sent a message announcing their proposed departure. The Zamorin and Arab traders had proved unfriendly, even hostile, with Diogo Dias temporarily detained following an audience with the Zamorin on 13 August. Da Gama captured eighteen visitors to the ship and held them pending Diogo's return. He set sail on 23 August, with Dias still ashore, and anchored far out at sea. Dias was subsequently returned to the ship on the 27th. On the 29th, da Gama resolved to depart, having proven the existence of spices and precious stones and being unable to do more. They were, however, becalmed, and the next day were approached by seventy boats from Calicut. When in range, da Gama ordered the ships to open fire on them. A thunderstorm approached and carried them out to sea and the pursuers were left behind.

They routed northwards parallel to the coast, and on 20 September they anchored off the Anjediva Islands, around 40 miles south of Goa. They gathered cassia from the islands and took on water; on the 27th, eight vessels were sighted in the distance and the crew fired upon them as they were thought hostile. They stayed until 5 October, having made repairs and gathered more cassia, and established that much of the country was ill-disposed towards them. The return crossing of the Indian Ocean took almost three months (5 October to 2 January) because of poor winds, and many of the crew got sick again with scurvy, with thirty men dying. They routed back via Malindi, but more of the crew died there. They left on the 11th, passed close to Mombasa, and then on the 13th anchored and transferred everything they could from the *S. Raphael*, before abandoning and burning it, as it was impossible to proceed with three ships given the dwindling number of crew. On 3 February they reached Angra de São Bráz in Mossel Bay, where they caught many anchovies, seals and penguins, which they salted for the journey ahead. On the 20th they passed the Cape, though they suffered from the cold winds and were now anxious to return home. They had following winds for the next twenty-seven days and were then close to the Cape Verde Islands.

Details from the *Journal* finished on 25 April in this vicinity. Da Gama and Coelho were separated in a storm, with Coelho continuing onward and arriving at Cascaes near Lisbon on 10 July. Da Gama proceeded to São Thiago – his brother Paulo was dying and he would take him on a caravel to the island of Terceira, where he was to die shortly after arrival there. João de Sa was placed in command of the *S. Gabriel* and proceeded to Lisbon, arriving soon after Coelho. Da Gama's arrival in Lisbon may have been 29 August (it isn't entirely clear) and it was followed some days later by a triumphal, formal entry into the town. Da Gama was to be honoured by King Manuel in various ways – generous pensions, the title Admiral of India, and various territorial titles. He was to make two further voyages to India, one in 1502 and the third and final one in 1524. He died of malaria in Cochin on Christmas Eve of that year.

Subsequent Portuguese Expeditions to India

Following the success of the da Gama expedition, it was followed in March 1500 by the dispatch of a much larger fleet comprising thirteen ships led by Pedro Alvares Cabral.[25] The main goals were to establish trade relations with India and to bring back spices. The expedition would include 1,500 men and would be a much more capable fighting force given the difficulties encountered by da Gama. Two of the ships would be headed for Sofala in Mozambique on a gold expedition, the remainder were all headed for India. Several veterans of da Gama's expedition were included, most notably Nicolau Coelho, Pedro Escobar, João de Sa, Diogo Dias and his brother Bartolomeo Dias. One ship was damaged en route and had to return to Lisbon. After reaching the Cape Verde Islands, they took a south-westerly course which enabled them to benefit from favourable winds and the South Atlantic ocean circulation, though it isn't clear how much knowledge of this system they had at the time. As a consequence of routing further west than da Gama, they sighted land on 22 April – they had discovered Brazil. The navigators calculated that it was east of the Tordesillas Line (a treaty with Spain dividing newly discovered lands between the two countries) and so Cabral claimed the new land for Portugal, naming it 'Terra de Santa Cruz'. The supply ship was sent back to Lisbon on 2 May carrying items traded with local people, and letters to the king announcing the discovery. The remaining eleven ships departed shortly afterwards for the journey to India.

The Cape of Good Hope was reached around the end of May, but severe weather here led to the loss of four ships, a major disaster (this was when Bartolomeo Dias met his end). The surviving ships split into groups; Cabral's three-ship group arrived at Mozambique island on 22 June, and despite the earlier altercations with da Gama, they were received well and allowed to resupply. Three more ships joined shortly afterwards, but that captained by Diogo Dias was missing. Dias had travelled too far east and then continued north past Madagascar, and next saw the African mainland around Mogadishu, far to the north. He stayed separated from the main group and, after a long spell in the Gulf of Aden, returned to Portugal on his own.

The main group, now reduced to only six ships, proceeded to Kilwa and then Malindi before beginning the Indian Ocean crossing on 7 August. They reached Anjediva Island on the 22nd and finally Calicut on 13 September. Cabral released four hostages taken by da Gama, bestowed more lavish gifts than the first trip, entered into talks with the new Zamorin, and successfully negotiated a commercial treaty; all was looking promising and a 'factory' (warehouse) was set up onshore. Aires Correia, the factor for Calicut, started to buy spices for the return journey, but by December had only managed to buy a portion of the spices needed and suspected that the Arab merchants had been closing them out of the market. Cabral complained to the Zamorin, who refused to intervene. Action was needed: he seized an Arab merchant ship and took its cargo of spices, claiming it belonged to Portugal under the terms of the treaty. The Arab merchants went berserk and attacked the Portuguese factory, slaughtering at least fifty-three of the workers, including Correia. There was no assistance from the Zamorin and so the next day Cabral seized further Arab merchant ships' cargoes, burned the ships and killed the crews, before laying down a bombardment of the city, killing hundreds. This was the start of a conflict between Portugal and Calicut that would last intermittently for decades.

On 24 December, Cabral and his ships departed and set sail for Cochin, further south along the Malabar coast. A treaty was quickly signed with Cochin, which was desirous of emerging from under the shadow of its larger neighbour. The spice markets were smaller than those of Calicut, but sufficient to start loading the ships. Invitations were also received from Quilon to the south and Cranganore (close to the site of Ancient Muziris) and Cannanore to the north. Aware that Calicut was mobilising a large armada against him, Cabral made a brief visit to Cannanore and loaded some ginger, before heading back across the Indian Ocean. They lost another ship, which ran aground on the approach to Malindi, but recovered its cargo. The remaining ships reached Mozambique island; from here Cabral dispatched the fastest ship to return to Lisbon on its own with news of the expedition. All five returned safely, between June and July 1501. The third expedition had set sail some two months earlier; the Portuguese India expeditions became an annual event for many years to come.

The third expedition of 1501 comprised four, or possibly five, ships, led by João da Nova, its mission being simply to load up spices from India and return. It was heading for Calicut (the results of the previous expedition being unknown at the point of their departure) with a crew of around 400. They departed in April 1501, passed the Cape in July, and anchored at Mossel Bay, where they found a note left by one of the captains of the second expedition warning about the events at Calicut. They routed, as in previous expeditions, northwards up the East African coast, stopping at Mozambique, Kilwa and Malindi, learning more information about the situation in India along the way. They arrived at Cannanore in November where confusion reigned – the Zamorin of Calicut sent an emissary expressing sadness at the events of the previous year and wished friendship and peace with Portugal. Da Nova was invited to Calicut to collect items left behind and compensation. Da Nova suspected a trick and ignored the offer. Gaspar Correia, however, maintained that he sailed to Calicut and forewarned about the Zamorin's treacherous intentions, seized the cargoes of three ships near the harbour and then destroyed them before heading south again to Cochin.[26] Da Nova had another problem: insufficient silver to pay for the spices he wanted to load. He was ultimately extended credit by the Raja of Cannanore, who allowed him to take the spices he wanted. In mid-December the fleet was ready to depart for home only to find themselves faced by a huge fleet of large and small boats from Calicut. They decided to fight their way through, and a two-day engagement ended on 2 January 1502, with the superior Portuguese weaponry and ships being the deciding factor despite the enemy's far greater numbers; five large Calicut ships and numerous small vessels had been sunk for little damage to the Portuguese. All four ships returned home safely in September 1502, having also discovered the island of St Helena during the journey. They carried 900 quintals of black pepper, 550 quintals of cinnamon and 35 of ginger, in addition to other captured goods. The third expedition was somewhat disappointing given that the ships' holds were not filled.

The fourth expedition of 1502 was commanded by Vasco da Gama – his second voyage to India.[27] This was part commercial, but largely military: to bring Calicut under control, after the disaster of Cabral's second expedition. The fleet comprised twenty ships separated into three squadrons due to the state of readiness at the planned departure date of February 1502. On 29 July, the main force departed Malindi for the Indian Ocean crossing; eighteen ships in total made it across to the Indian coast. In September, the fleet anchored around 75 miles north-west of Calicut. On the 29th, da Gama committed an act of infamy. The *Miri*, a large merchant ship returning from Mecca with pilgrims aboard, was spotted by one of da Gama's fleet and chased down. It was sent to anchor near the flagship, and when da Gama learned that it was based in Calicut, he ordered his men to seize the cargo and burn the vessel with all aboard. Gaspar Correia states that da Gama ignored the appeals of the owner who was on board, saying, 'Alive you shall be burned, because you counselled the King of Calecut to kill and plunder the factor and Portuguese ... for nothing in this world would I desist in giving you a hundred deaths, if I could give you so many.'[28] The ship was burned and sunk by artillery and all aboard killed, though many fought back, and any who escaped were speared by the crews. Several hundred were believed killed.

In mid-October, the fleet reached Cannanore. Negotiations were made for the establishment of a factory and a fixed-price schedule, which according to Correia was accepted by the Raja. On 25 October, the main part of the fleet sailed for Calicut, arriving on the 29th. Despite some conciliatory approaches from the Zamorin, da Gama demanded delivery of the goods taken from the Portuguese factory and all Muslims expelled from Calicut before any discussions could begin. Having received no positive response, the fleet laid down a cruel bombardment of the city on 1 November, continuing for two days. Correia noted that after the bombardment, two large ships and twenty-two smaller vessels were unlucky enough to appear off Calicut. Six of the small vessels were from Cannanore and were excused. The others were plundered and hands, ears and noses of the crew cut off, their teeth knocked out, and they were tied and boats set alight and sent towards the shore. All the body parts were sent in a separate boat with a Brahmin emissary dressed as a friar (who had also been mutilated) and a message to the Zamorin 'to have a curry made to eat of what his friar brought him'. Leaving a blockade in place in Calicut, da Gama headed for Cochin, where a new fixed-price commercial treaty was established, and spices were loaded up.

Meanwhile, the nearby city of Quillon urged da Gama to take spices from themselves also. In early January, an approach was made by a wealthy Brahmin from Calicut acting as ambassador from the Zamorin, who purportedly wanted a permanent treaty with Portugal ... and offered compensation. On 5 January, da Gama took two ships back to Calicut to finalise the treaty, but a trap had been set. He took the large ship *Flor de la Mar* into Calicut harbour, which was temporarily unprotected by the blockade ships, and laid anchor. Negotiations proceeded for three days, but on the early morning of the fourth day they were surrounded by around 100 small armed boats. Unable to bring cannon to bear, the crew tried desperately to keep the swarming vessels away by small arms. The Zamorin's men set a prahu ablaze that was attached to da Gama's large ship, but the crew cut the cables and it drifted free; at the same time, with some difficulty they managed to cut the anchor cables and made their slow escape from the harbour, bringing their cannon to bear as distance grew. Three hostages on board were hanged from the main mast in full view of the city. The fleet returned to Cochin, where there was more disturbing news: an armada comprising the Zamorin's ships and those of privateers from the Red Sea was being assembled at Calicut to chase down the Portuguese; the enemy totalled twenty large ships, many smaller armed vessels and several thousand men. Urged by the Raja to leave for Portugal immediately, da Gama instead prepared for a fight. The fight came in early February near to Calicut, and the Portuguese fleet sank or damaged a large part of the opposition and routed the remainder. Returning to Cannacore, he deposited a small defensive force to protect the factory there, and then in late February set sail for Lisbon with twelve of the ships, leaving five or six caravels under Vincente Sodre to protect Cochin and Cannanore.

Subsequent Armadas

The events of the first few expeditions paved the way for the coming decades: Portugal was to extend its empire and build its commercial power with ruthless violence and extortion. Intermittent wars with Calicut continued for the remainder of the century. A series of coastal fortresses were constructed – initially at Sofala and Kilwa on the East African coast and at Anjediva, Cannanore and Cochin on the Indian coast, later to be followed by many more. Annual armadas continued throughout the sixteenth century and into the first decades of the seventeenth century. However, the Indian population was not easily cowed, particularly where long-established trade relationships with Arab merchants were threatened, as shown by the resistance of Calicut. In 1508, an alliance between the Egyptian Mamluks and Gujaratis attacked a Portuguese squadron at Chaul and Dabul; this alliance was expanded the following year to include the Ottomans and the Zamorin of Calicut, and a vicious naval battle was fought at Diu in

Gujarat, where Portugal prevailed. In an interesting side note, the Muslim force was aided by specialists from the Republic of Venice, which could clearly foresee the threat to its Mediterranean spice distribution monopoly, which depended on Arab-sourced spices.

The Estado da Índia (Portuguese India) was established in 1505, based initially in Cochin, but after 1510 it became headquartered in Goa (which incidentally remained Portuguese until 1961).

Spice imports to Portugal were huge. Annual pepper imports in the period 1503–06 ranged from 10,000 to 26,000 quintals.[29] Official estimates of 'other spices' in that period were only 991 to 6,000 quintals per year. However, Wake estimated that the annual non-pepper spice import for that period was much greater – in the region of 12,000 to 15,000 quintals – the surplus being the private trade conducted by unscrupulous officials. The pepper figures are probably reliable as the crown monopoly was strictly enforced. In this period, these figures probably represented about half of the European spice trade, but a decade later undoubtedly rose to a much greater percentage. Pepper imports rose to a massive 44,000 quintals in 1518.

The Casa da India

The state-run organisation that administered this enormous trade was the Casa da Índia, which was founded in 1500. It looked after Portuguese assets in Africa, India, and subsequently other parts of Asia. It arranged finance for and organised the annual armadas to India and administered the shore bases, warehouses, customs houses, forts and military that became vital to the trade. Its offices in the Ribeira Palace in Lisbon (from 1511) reflected the company's significance. The initial decades were highly lucrative and the objective of maintaining the royal monopoly on spices, precious metals and other valuable commodities was maintained without much difficulty. As the sixteenth century wore on, the cost of maintaining the huge colonial presence grew increasingly burdensome. The Ribeira Palace was destroyed in the devastating earthquake of 1755, but the organisation limped on until its final dissolution in 1833.

Portuguese in Ceylon

Ceylon had been famous for the quality of its cinnamon for well over 1,000 years when the Portuguese arrived in 1505. The viceroy's son, Dom Lourenço, arrived in the vicinity of Galle with a fleet of nine ships – by chance, because they were actually headed for the Red Sea but had encountered adverse winds.[30] The foreigners were cautiously welcomed and Dom Lourenço expressed their interest in a trading relationship. A treaty was agreed with the king (of Kotte, centred around the Colombo area), allowing them to take 400 bahars of cinnamon per year (1 bahar = 550lb/4 quintals) if they would defend the coasts from attack. Actually, in the first few years of the sixteenth century the Portuguese had been able to acquire several hundred quintals of cinnamon per year from the Malabar coast – but only by paying well above market price, which was unsustainable.[31] Large shipments were made from Ceylon; e.g. in 1513 three ships brought 720 quintals into Lisbon port, with similar-sized shipments following in subsequent years. A fort was erected in Colombo in 1518 and Muslim traders were deterred, but the relationship was problematic and subsequently dismantled in 1524. Prices were kept high by a royal monopoly on cinnamon from 1520. In 1521, a bahar of cinnamon cost 3 cruzados, but would be sold at Cochin for 15; in 1525, a bahar could be sold for 195 cruzados in Lisbon! A contract struck in 1533 gave the Portuguese a monopoly over cinnamon purchase, plus an effective tribute of 900 bahars per year free of charge. The cinnamon was transported to Cochin or Goa and thence to Lisbon.

Later attacks on Ceylon from Calicut brought urgent requests for help, and the Portuguese won a decisive victory over the Zamorin's fleet off Ceylon in 1538. In 1540, Miguel Ferreyra wrote to the Viceroy at Goa: 'It was on account of the cinnamon that the Romans and other nations came to Ceilao; I fear, Senhor, that those who have obtained the taste for it will come behind us on its scent.'

The Portuguese lost Kotte city to the neighbouring Sitawaka kingdom in 1565, and their grip on the monopoly weakened. Continued conflict pushed up prices, though supply to Lisbon continued – in fact, it flourished due to a new contract system introduced in 1595. Everyone wanted some of the action, and with the Captain of Colombo being given the sole right to collect and export, numerous exemptions crept in.

In 1600, 4,508 quintals were delivered to Lisbon. Expanding production in Ceylon in the early seventeenth century led to collapse of the market. A strict royal monopoly was enforced from 1614 and annual production was fixed at 1,000 bahars.

Military conflicts with neighbouring kingdoms continued through the first two decades of the seventeenth century, most notably with Kandy, which was brought under control in 1617. After the conquest of Jaffna in the north in 1619, Portuguese control of Ceylon reached its widest extent and a period of relative peace ensued ... until the Dutch appeared on the scene in 1638. The Dutch VOC, intent on controlling the Asian spice trade, saw an opportunity to ally themselves with the kingdom of Kandy, and the combined forces inflicted heavy losses on the Portuguese. Little by little the Portuguese lost ground, Colombo fell in 1656 and two years later they left Ceylon for good. As the Dutch governor would say in the 1670s, cinnamon was 'the bride round whom they all want to dance in Ceylon'.

Portuguese Expansion into Southeast Asia

The expansion into Southeast Asia was a logical one given that many of the spices found in India were imported from further east. The first step was to investigate the Sultanate of Malacca, which had been rumoured to be a huge trading entrepot. Capturing the city would not only enrich Portugal, but it would deny the vital spice trade to the hated Arabs. King Manuel sent an exploratory mission in 1509 led by Admiral Diogo Lopes de Sequeira, which confirmed the wealth of Malacca, but initial contacts soon turned hostile and several of his men were captured. In 1511, Afonso de Albuquerque, the governor of Portuguese India, led a large fleet of eighteen ships and took the city by force. Albuquerque was another brilliant but vicious commander – he was already a veteran of the 1503 and 1506 Indian armadas and led successful ventures against the Arabian coast, and then conquered Goa in 1510 in a bloody engagement. Albuquerque's speech to his men in advance of the attack on Malacca summarised the two main motives:

> The first is the great service which we shall perform to Our Lord in casting the Moors out of this country ... And the other reason is ... because it is the headquarters of all the spiceries and drugs which the Moors carry every year hence to the Straits [of the Red Sea] ... but if we deprive them of this their ancient market there, there does not remain for them a single port ... where they can carry on their trade in these things ... and I hold it as very certain that if we take this trade of Malaca away out of their hands, Cairo and Meca are entirely ruined, and to Venice will no spiceries be conveyed except that which her merchants go and buy in Portugal.[32]

After a difficult battle, Malacca was captured, but Albuquerque hadn't finished there. He had by now learned the approximate location of the 'Spice Islands' and determined to seize them for Portugal. He sent three ships led by Antonió de Abreu, with second-in-command Francisco Serrão captaining another of the ships. Serrão was very close to Ferdinand Magellan (they were possibly cousins) and both had joined the 1506 India expedition and then participated in the conquest of Malacca. While Magellan was to return to Portugal, the new expedition set sail for the East in November 1511. After calling at Java, Serrão's ship was wrecked in a storm, though the crew survived. Meanwhile, Abreu bought a junk to replace the lost ship, but they were forced to wait for favourable winds at Seram before making it to the Banda Islands; after loading up with spices he decided to head back, rather than press on northwards to the Molucca Islands, content with the cargo and information gained. Serrão, however, was shipwrecked a second time on his way back to Malacca in the vicinity of Ambon and again survived. Serrão eventually came to settle in Ternate around May 1512 and became close friend and advisor to the Raja (Ternate and Tidore both saw a chance to ally themselves with the Portuguese in Malacca). In the subsequent years, Serrão sent numerous letters to Magellan, Albuquerque and King Manuel. As a result, the Portuguese sent ships from Malacca to the Spice Islands every year from 1513, with Serrão helping to facilitate the trade.

Serrão died in 1521, but a large fort was built on Ternate in the following year (São João Baptista de Ternate); other small forts were also constructed at various times. However, an increasingly heavy-handed Portuguese presence led to trouble.

Magellan and the First Circumnavigation
Ferdinand Magellan was also Portuguese, but after his plan to reach India by sailing west was rejected by King Manuel I, he fell into the service of King Charles I of Spain in order to reach the Spice Islands by a western route. His expedition of five vessels set sail in 1519, and after a long and arduous voyage discovered the Philippines in 1521 having suffered huge losses from scurvy, hunger, thirst and outbreaks of mutiny, and the loss of one ship and another deserting. Magellan himself was killed by natives on the island of Mactan. The momentous journey was described in great detail by Antonio Pigafetta, an Italian explorer who participated in the voyage as Magellan's assistant.[33] The remaining fleet finally made it to the Moluccas in late 1521, and traded large volumes of cloves in Tidore, but only one ship, the *Victoria*, was seaworthy enough to return home. Despite the huge losses in men (only eighteen survived – which included Pigafetta – from the crews of 230) and materials, they brought back 26 tons of cloves, scores of sacks of nutmegs, mace and cinnamon, and loads of sandalwood, all of which had enormous value.

Conditions Aboard the Ships
Apart from the appalling losses of men to scurvy and other disease, violence and shipwreck, conditions aboard ship were at best unpleasant and at worst a living hell. The French explorer Jean Mocquet related his journey to the East aboard the flagship of a Portuguese fleet headed for Goa in 1608–09:

Amongst us was the greatest disorder and confusion imaginable, because of the peoples vomiting up and down, and making dung upon one another: There was nothing to be heard but lamentations and groans of those who were straightened with thirst, hunger, and sicknesses, and other incommodities, and cursing the time of their embarkment, their fathers and mothers, and themselves ...[34]

He suffered with scurvy also:

I had a fit of Sickness, almost, the whole Voyage; yet this was not all, for I had besides that ... (scurvy) ... which rotted almost all my gumbs, and rendered a sort of a black and putrified blood; My knees were so contracted that I could not bend my limbs; my legs and thighs were as black as members gangreen'd, and was constrained to be continually launcing to get out this black and putrified blood. I launced also my gums, which were black and blue, and surmounting my teeth, going every day out upon the side of the Ship, holding by the cordage, with a little looking glass in my hand to see where to cut: When I had cut away this dead flesh, and drawn away abundance of black blood, I washed my mouth and teeth with urine, but the next morning there was as much; And my ill fortune was, that I could not eat, having more mind to swallow than to chew, upon the account of the great pains which this disease causes. I found no better remedy than the Syrop of Gilli-flowers, and good red wine: Great numbers died every day thereof, and there was nothing to be seen but bodies a flinging over-board.

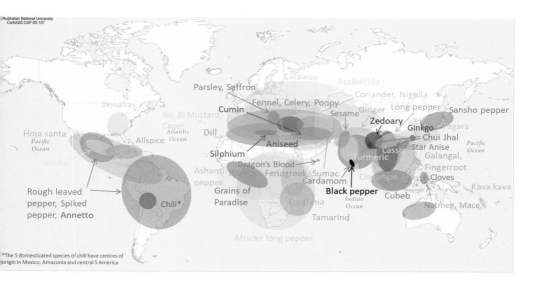

. The global distribution of fifty-five spices in their approximate native locations.

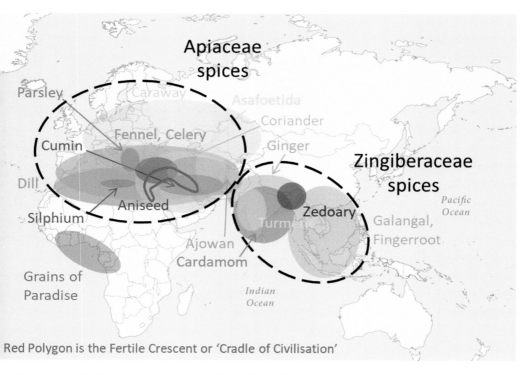

. The native distribution of key spice plants from the coriander (Apiaceae) and ginger Zingiberaceae) families.

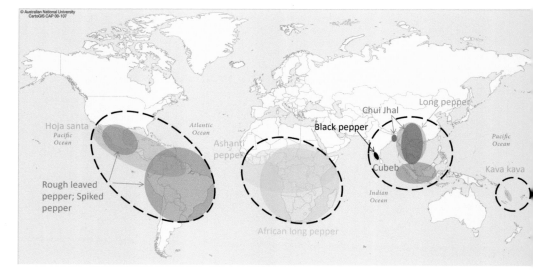

3. The native distribution of key spice plants from the Piperaceae family: note the four centres of origin.

(Basemap reproduced with the permission of CartoGIS Services, Scholarly Information Services, The Australian National University)

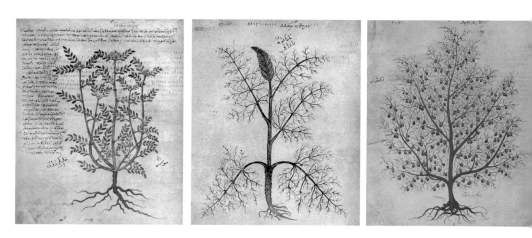

4. Images from a sixth-century CE copy of Dioscorides' *De Materia Medica*.
From left to right: *glykirizon* (liquorice), *marathron* (fennel), *arkeuthis* (juniper). This book was presented to Anicia Juliana in thanks for her funding the construction of a church in Constantinople. (*Codex Aniciae Julianae*, Vienna)

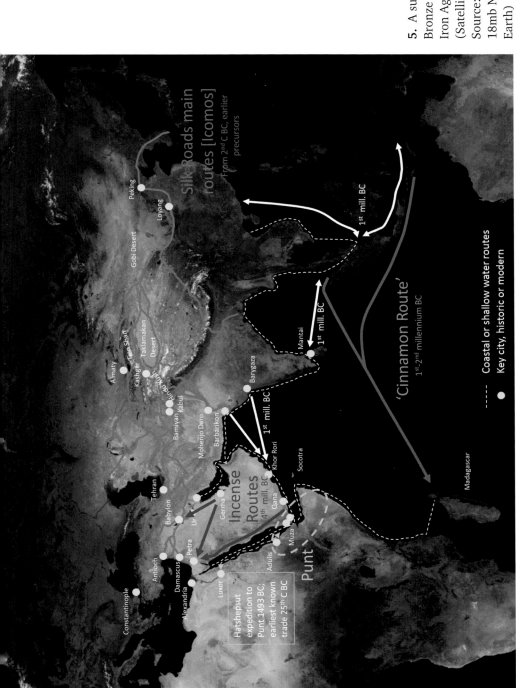

5. A summary of the Bronze Age and Iron Age spice trade. (Satellite Image Source: Blue Marble 18mb NASA Visible Earth)

Constantinople · Antioch · Damascus · Alexandria · Luxor · Babylon · Tehran · Ur · Petra · Gerrha · Adulis · Muza · Qana · Khor Rori · Socotra · Barbarikon · Mohenjo Daro · Kabul · Bamiyan · Kashgar · Almaty · Tien Shan · Taklamakan Desert · Hindu Kush · Barygaza · Mantai · Gobi Desert · Loyang · Peking · Madagascar

Hatshepsut expedition to Punt 1493 BC; earliest known trade 25th C BC

Incense Routes
4th mill. BC

Punt

'Cinnamon Route'
1st–2nd millennium BC

Silk Roads main routes [Icomos]
From 2nd C BC, earlier precursors

1st mill. BC

----- Coastal or shallow water routes
● Key city, historic or modern

Ajowan   Aniseed   Dill

Celery   Fennel   Caraway

6. A comparison of six commonly used spices from the Apiaceae family. (Author)

7. Clockwise from above: dried black pepper fruits; dried long pepper fruits; dried cubeb pepper fruits. (Author)

8. 'Foliage, Flowers, and Fruit of the Pepper Plant' by Marianne North (1830–90). The plant is black pepper – *Piper nigrum* L. (Royal Botanic Gardens, Kew)

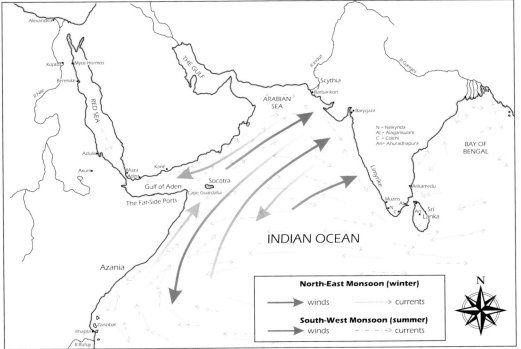

9. The western Indian Ocean, Arabian Sea, Red Sea and Gulf, showing a schematic indication of the monsoon winds and currents. (Courtesy of J. Whitewright, 2018)

10. A pepper-pot depicting
Hercules wrestling a
giant, from the Romano-
British Hoxne hoard,
fifth century CE. (British
Museum

11. The Empress pepper-pot, also
from the Hoxne hoard. (British
Museum)

12. A pepper-pot depicting a slave
in chains from the Chaourse hoard
in northern France, third century CE.
(British Museum)

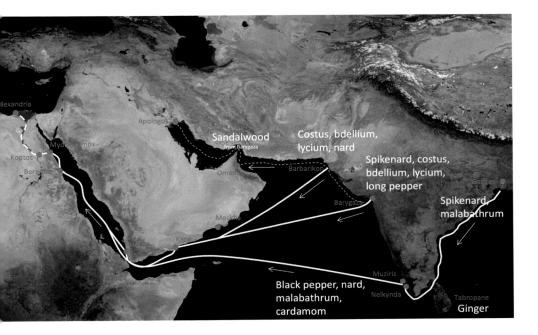

3. Map showing the spice trade routes across the Indian Ocean and Arabian Sea in the first
nd second centuries CE. (Satellite Image Source: Blue Marble 18mb NASA Visible Earth)

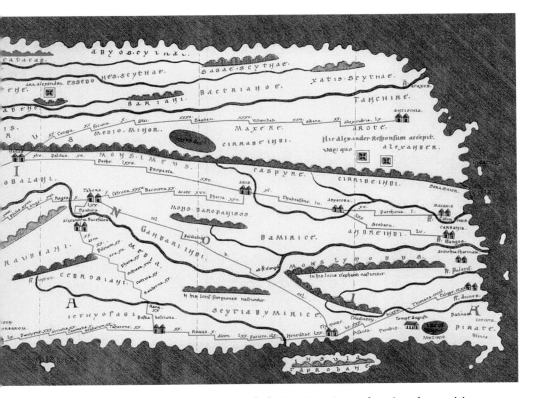

4. A section of the schematic Roman map *Tabula Peutingeriana*, showing the position
f Muziris.

15. The recto of the second-century CE Muziris Papyrus. Note the guard and security needed for this very precious cargo – and the sophisticated style of the almost 2000-year-old contract. (Photograph courtesy of the Austrian National Museum, translation courtesy of D. Rathbone, 2021)

… your other administrators or managers, and on agreement(?) I will hand (the goods) [over(?)] to a trustworthy camel-driver for the arrangement(?) [of the journey up(?)] to Koptos; and I will carry (them) up through the desert under guard and protection [to the] public tax-receiving warehouses at Koptos, and I will place (them) under the [authority] and seal of you or of your administrators or whichever one of them is present, until the loading at the river; and I will load (them) [at the requi]red moment on to a safe river-going ship, and I will carry (them) down to the warehouse for receiving the quarter-tax [at Ale]xandria, and [so too] will place them under the authority and seal of you or your men, with all the expenses from now to collection of the quarter-tax [on my part(?)], and the desert transport charges and the river freight charges and the other incidental outgoings <being up to me(?), and> on terms that if, on occurrence of the time for repayment specified in the contracts of the loan for (the trip to) Muziris, I do not [then] rightly discharge the aforesaid loan in my name, then you and your administrators or managers are to have the option and complete authority, if you so choose, to carry out execution without [notifica]tion or summons to judgement, to possess and own the aforesaid security, and to collect (i.e. deduct) the quarter-tax and transfer the [three] parts which will be left where you choose, and to sell or use them as security [and] to cede them to another person, if you so choose, and to manage the items of the security in whatsoever way you choose, and to buy them for yourself at the price apparent at that moment, and to subtract and reckon in what falls due [for the aforesaid] loan, so the guarantee for what falls due [lies] with you and your administrators or managers, (and) we are free from accusation in every respect, and the surplus or shortfall from the capital [goes] to me the borrower and giver of sec[urity] …

5. Ginger (*Zingiber officinale*) from
ehler's *Medicinal-Pflanzen*, 1887.
iodiversity Heritage Library)

7. Zingiberaceae plants (a–c) and rhizomes (d–g).
a) greater galangal (*A. galanga*); (b) torch ginger flower (*E. elatior*); (c) mioga ginger
Z. mioga); (d) ginger (*Z. officinale*); (e) turmeric (*C. longa*); (f) fingerroot (*B. rotunda*); (g)
reater galangal (*A. galanga*). (Author)

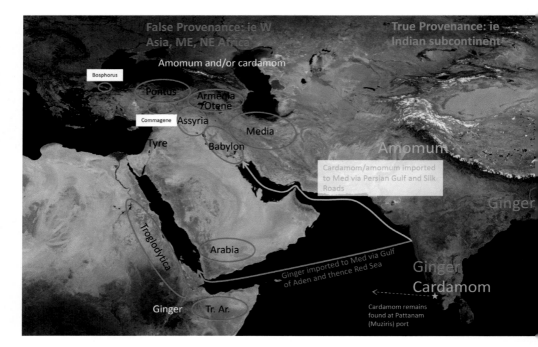

18. A map of the false provenance of the Zingiberaceae family spices before the late second century CE. The locations circled in red are the incorrect reports of provenance provided by ancient writers: these are simply where these spices were brought into contact with the West. Tr. Ar. = Troglodytical Arabia. Plotting these on a map provides an elegant illustration of the main trade routes. (Satellite Image Source: Blue Marble 18mb NASA Visible Earth)

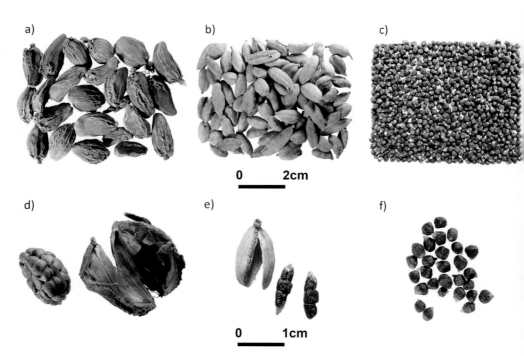

19. Left to right: black cardamom (*Amomum sublatum*), cardamom (*Elettaria cardamomum*) and grains of paradise (*Aframomum melegueta*), with their close-ups below. (Author)

0. 'Foliage, flowers and fruit of the nutmeg ee, and hummingbird, Jamaica', by Iarianne North (1830–90). (Royal Botanic ardens, Kew)

1. Cloves (*Syzygium aromaticum*) from *Birds nd all Nature*, 1899, Chicago. (Biodiversity eritage Library)

2. Hiri Island, as viewed from Ternate in the Molucca (Maluku) Islands of Indonesia. ʿhese were part of the 'Spice Islands' fought over by the Portuguese, Dutch and British. Cloves were the main prize at Ternate. (Author)

23. Cinnamon, nutmeg, mace and cloves: together with black pepper, these were the 'golde[n] spices' sought after by Portuguese, English and Dutch explorers and traders in the fifteenth to seventeenth centuries. (Author)

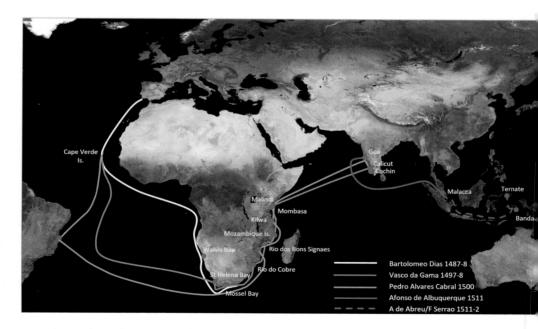

24. The outbound journeys of the major early Portuguese voyages of discovery to the Far East. (Satellite Image Source: Blue Marble 18mb NASA Visible Earth)

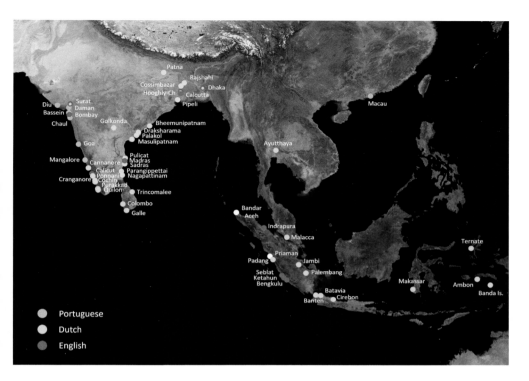

25. Changing fortunes in Asia: Portuguese, Dutch and English trading posts in 1700. (Satellite Image Source: Blue Marble 18mb NASA Visible Earth)

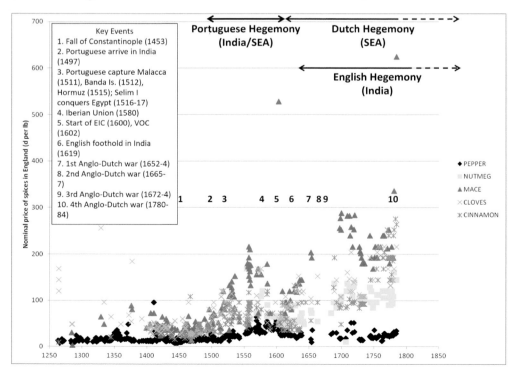

26. The price of Far Eastern spices in England from 1263 to 1786. (Data from J. E. Thorold Rogers, 1866–1902)

27. *Capsicum annuum* from L. Koehler's *Medizinal-Pflanzen*, Vol. 2, 1890. (Biodiversity Heritage Library)

28. Capsicum Diversity: a) *Capsicum chinense* (Hainan yellow lantern) (Anna Frodesiak, CC0-1.0); b) *Capsicum baccatum* (bishop's crown) (Rouibi Dhia Eddine Nadjam , CC-BY-SA-4.0); c) *Capsicum frutescens* (tabasco); d–h) *Capsicum annuum*, various. (Author)

29. Images of *Capsicum* from Fuchs' 1543 translation of *De historia stirpium commentarii insignes*. Left: *C. annuum*; right: possibly *C. chinense*.

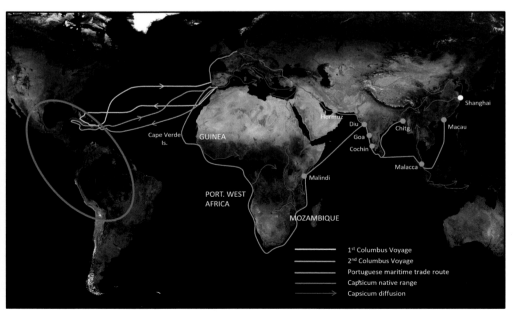

———	1ˢᵗ Columbus Voyage
———	2ⁿᵈ Columbus Voyage
———	Portuguese maritime trade route
———	Capsicum native range
⟶	Capsicum diffusion

30. Conquering the world in 100 years: the global diffusion of *Capsicum*. (Satellite Image Source: Blue Marble 18mb NASA Visible Earth)

31. Design for a Colman's Mustard advert by Alfred Munnings (1858–1959). (© Estate of Sir Alfred Munnings, Dedham, Essex. All rights reserved, DACS 2023)

32. 'Foliage, Flowers, and Seed-vessel of the Opium Poppy' by Marianne North (1830–90). (Royal Botanic Gardens, Kew)

33. 'Harvesting the sugar-cane in Minas Geraes, Brazil' by Marianne North (1830–90). (Royal Botanic Gardens, Kew)

Portugal and Threats to its Brief Era of Dominance in the East

From 1530, a series of disagreements between the *orang Ternate* and the Portuguese led to periodic besieging of the colonial fort, which was relieved in 1536 by an armada arriving from Malacca. Following a period of relative calm under Sultan Hairun, the Portuguese were tolerated, though friendship and loyalty were never close. The Christian proselytising didn't help and Christian communities on nearby Moro (Halmahera) and Bacan were attacked and there were anti-Christian disturbances in Ambon. Things came to a head in 1570 when Captain Diogo Lopes de Mesquita assassinated Hairun, which united the Moluccans against the Portuguese. They were besieged again in their fort for several years, until in 1575 they were finally expelled. But the islanders were nothing if not pragmatic and Portuguese merchants would still be allowed to trade. In the following year, the Portuguese formed an alliance with the rival island of Tidore, which also produced cloves, and a fort was constructed there in 1578 which was occupied until 1605.

About 650km to the south of Tidore, the Portuguese had another problem: the Banda Islands. Although Abreu had landed here in 1512, no permanent settlements had been established in the following years. Instead, the Portuguese sent traders on annual visits to the islands to load up with nutmeg and mace. The annual crop was substantial: 6,000 or 7,000 bahars of nutmeg and 500 or 600 bahars of mace.[35] In 1574, the Bandanese were encouraged by the uprisings in Ternate and eventually became allies with the Sultan of Ternate in preference to the rival Tidore, against the Portuguese.[36]

Meanwhile, the long-established Portuguese presence on Ambon became the centre for Moluccan trading activities following the expulsion from Ternate. It had the benefit of a central position relative to the Banda Islands, which supplied nutmeg and mace, and the northern Moluccas, which supplied cloves. But Ambon too was an insecure foothold, and the Portuguese were prone to attacks from Muslim villagers, part of the issue being stirred by religion.

The Portuguese soldiered on in Ambon until 1605, when they were expelled by the Dutch. The islands continued to supply cloves to the empire but they were now living on borrowed time.

Aftermath
The Portuguese had consolidated their hold on the Spice Islands by brute force, slavery and oppression of the natives. Their monopoly of the spice trade ultimately lasted for a century, when they were kicked out by the equally cruel and oppressive Dutch. It was also an imperfect monopoly – Venice was importing as much pepper from Alexandria in the 1560s as it was in the 1490s.[37] This came about as the Portuguese were unable to maintain a stranglehold on alternative routes – the Red Sea in particular could not be effectively controlled, though they controlled Hormuz from 1615. Overland supplies also continued. However, the proving of the Cape route had an irreversible effect on trade, especially Levantine trade, and the final nail in the coffin was the entry into the scene of the English and Dutch.

England, the East India Company ... and the VOC

The first appearance of the English was in 1580 as part of Francis Drake's west-to-east circumnavigation of the globe. Having departed Plymouth in November 1577 with a fleet of five ships, he routed via the Cape Verde Islands (where he captured a Portuguese merchant vessel) and crossed the Atlantic, eventually reaching the southern Argentine coast.[38] Three ships were abandoned due to loss of men and in one case rotten timbers. After a long winter layover, the remaining ships passed the Strait of Magellan and into the Pacific. Another ship was lost in a violent storm and another returned to England, leaving only Drake's *Pelican* (renamed the *Golden Hind*) to continue. He worked his way up the Pacific coast of South America, attacking and pillaging Spanish settlements and capturing several ships – an extraordinarily aggressive stance from a fleet of one. After following the coast as far north as Oregon, they made the long westward crossing of the Pacific and after several months arrived in the Moluccas. They met with and befriended the Sultan of Ternate. Cloves were certainly loaded up, but part of the cargo (including 3 tons of cloves) had to be jettisoned days later in order to refloat the ship after running aground.

About a month later they reached the island of 'Barateve' (probably in the southern Banda Sea):

> Their fruits are divers likewise and plentiful; as nutmegs, ginger, long pepper, limons, cucumbers, cocoes, figoes, sagu, with divers other sorts whereof we had one in reasonable quantity, in bignesse, forme and huske, much like a bay berry, hard in substance but pleasant in tast … of each of these we received of them, whatsoever we desired for our need.[39]

Drake finally limped back into Plymouth on 26 September 1580, with a cargo of spices and captured Spanish treasure … but only fifty-nine of the original 164 crew. Being the first Englishman to circumnavigate the globe, he was, of course, a hero and was knighted the following year. His subsequent defeat of the Spanish Armada in 1588 undoubtedly raised the profile of the English maritime capabilities and would have stimulated a great deal of confidence amongst the English merchant community.

Partly inspired by Drake's achievements, but also by those of the Portuguese, a fleet of three ships set sail from Plymouth in April 1591 to seek trade and riches in the East Indies. The commander of the fleet was James Lancaster and the journey was to be devilled with misfortune. After reaching a harbour on the western Cape, the *Merchant Royal* was sent back to England carrying crewmen sick with scurvy.[40] Shortly after passing the Cape, another ship, the *Penelope*, was lost with all hands in a ferocious storm. The *Edward Bonaventure* continued northwards along the East African coast, but on reaching the Comoro Islands thirty men were killed by natives while attempting to collect water. They reached Zanzibar and stayed there until February, and then made a slow crossing of the Indian Ocean during which many more men died. They reached Penang and subsequently captured several vessels, mainly Portuguese merchantmen. They landed at the Nicobar Islands, and then made it to Ceylon in November. Lancaster was keen to stay here – 'In this island groweth great store of excellent cinamonn' – but with the remaining crew on the verge of mutiny they set sail for home, short of food and with conditions becoming desperate. They made it to St Helena and then to the West Indies. Helped by a French ship, only twenty-five crew were to survive and return to England in 1594. This first English voyage to the East Indies had been a disaster, but Lancaster wasn't done yet.

Attacks on Portuguese and Spanish ships were proving very lucrative for England's navy. In 1592, Sir Walter Raleigh led a fleet of six ships to the Azores to attack ships returning from the New World and encountered a Portuguese fleet near the island of Flores. He captured the 1,600-ton *Madre de Dios*, which carried a fabulous cargo of jewels, gold and spices – pepper, cloves, cinnamon, nutmeg, mace and ginger – and other valuables. In 1599, a group of London merchants resolved to raise money for a venture to the East Indies and sought the queen's support. She eventually agreed, and in 1600 the 'Governor and Company of Merchants of London trading into the East Indies' was formed and granted a monopoly for English trade in the East.

James Lancaster was one of the directors and he was commissioned to lead the first Company voyage with a fleet of four ships and 480 men, which left Woolwich in February 1601. They routed via the Cape, Madagascar and the Nicobar Islands to Aceh in North Sumatra, which they reached in June 1602. An agreement was reached with the Sultan of Aceh, and after a prolonged stay of some three months, during which they took on a load of pepper, cinnamon and cloves, they sailed for the Malacca Straits.[41] After capturing a Portuguese ship and seizing its contents, they returned to Aceh, before taking their final leave in early November. At this point, one of the ships, the *Ascencion*, was sent home with its cargo of spices. The *Hector* and the *Red Dragon* headed for Banten, a major port in west Java, where they hoped to meet up with the *Susan*, which had been dispatched in advance. They found the

Susan at Priaman on the Sumatran coast, where they had loaded 600 bahars of pepper and 66 bahars of cloves, with the bonus of the pepper being cheaper than at Aceh. The *Susan* was also sent back to England at this point.

On 4 December, the remaining two ships set off for Banten, arriving on the 16th. They established friendly relations with the (10-year-old) Sultan and his court, and stayed there trading for some five weeks, taking away 276 bags of pepper of 62lb weight each. The ships were fully laden by 10 February and prepared to depart. They were to leave behind three factors and eight men to sell their remaining wares and buy goods for the next English fleet. A smaller vessel of 40 tons, laden with commodities, was sent on to the Moluccas to establish a presence there, prepare a factory and acquire spices. The return journey was perilous and they almost lost the *Red Dragon* in bad weather near the Cape, but their luck held and they made it back to England on 11 September 1603. The voyage brought back a total of 1.03 million lb of pepper. In their absence, Elizabeth I had died and James I was the new king – Lancaster was knighted the month following his return.

The second voyage was commanded by Henry Middleton (who had captained the *Susan* in the previous voyage), departing Gravesend in March 1604, the fleet comprising the same four ships as the first voyage.[42] Despite a forced stop at Table Bay in July, as many of the crew were very sick with scurvy, they reached Sumatra in December, which was remarkably good progress. With the crews still extremely sick, they struggled onwards to Banten, arriving on the 22nd. A large fleet of Dutch ships was already there, prescient of things to come, though its captain was friendly. The English contingent who had been left behind by Lancaster were overjoyed at the arrival of the English ships, but on boarding the flagship a party of these men was shocked at the state of the visitors: 'but when we came aboard of our admiral, and saw their weakness, also hearing of the weakness of the other three ships, it grieved us much.'

Middleton and his officers were initially too sick even to go ashore and send their respects to the young Sultan. In early January 1605, it was resolved to send the *Susan* and the *Hector* back to England after loading up with pepper; the *Ascension* and the *Red Dragon* would proceed as per plan to the Moluccas. The latter two departed on the 16th but a different sickness took hold: the 'flux' (dysentery), and reports indicate the severity: 'this night [16th] died Henry Dewbrey of the flux … The seventeenth day died of the flux William Lewed, John Jenkens, and Samuel Porter … this day [20th] died Henry Stiles our master carpenter, and James Varnam, and John Iberson, all of the flux …' and so on.

On 10 February, and after many more deaths, they anchored off Ambon Island. Contact was made with the Ambonese, requesting trade, but this was prohibited – unless permission was granted by the Portuguese occupying the fort in Ambon. The emissaries sent by Middleton were treated kindly and permission granted, but then a curious thing happened. The Dutch fleet (from Banten) had appeared and moored close to the fort, and a Portuguese contingent went aboard the admiral's ship under a flag of truce to ask about their intentions, which, as it turned out, were not peaceable:

> The Dutch general made answer that his coming thither was to have that castle from them, and willed them to deliver him the keys, and they should be kindly dealt withal; which, if they refused to do, he willed them to provide for themselves to defend it, for that he was minded to have it before he departed …

Middleton heard the following day that the fort had fallen and was now in the hands of the Dutch; the Ambonese were unwilling to trade given this new situation. Almost at the point of despair, the decision was made to split up – the *Ascension* was to head for the Banda Islands and the *Dragon* to the north Moluccas. The *Dragon* reached Tidore on 22 March after a long slog, with many more crew dying of the flux. They arrived to the spectacle of the Sultan of Ternate being pursued by seven Tidorean boats with murderous intentions. They rescued the Sultan and were given permission to trade for cloves at Ternate. They also established friendly relations with the Portuguese contingent on Tidore, but on 12 April, in an uncanny repeat of events at Ambon, the Dutch fleet appeared off the island, and on 9 May routed the Portuguese. Middleton had no choice but to leave, more or less empty-handed, and he did so on 18 May, collecting a small shipment of cloves from Makian on his return. He arrived at Banten on 24 July to the unhappy news that twelve of the twenty-four crew left at Banten had died.

The *Ascension*, under Captain Coulthurst, had better luck, arriving at Banda on 20 February 1605. They stayed almost twenty-two weeks, loading up with nutmeg and mace during this period, though details are unclear, and made friendly relations with the Sabandar of Nera, who gifted a bahar of nutmegs to King James. They departed on 21 July and reached Banten on 16 August. The *Ascension* and *Dragon* sailed back to England together. The *Hector* and *Susan* had departed several months in advance, laden with pepper, but with the crews so decimated that they had to hire Chinese and Indians to man the vessels. The *Susan* was lost with all hands off southern Africa, and the *Hector* narrowly escaped a similar fate: with many of its crew dead, only fourteen left alive, it was rescued by the *Dragon*. They arrived back at Plymouth in May 1606.

Middleton's journey had mixed success, but the succeeding voyages of the EIC were all initially focused on the Spice Islands. The Dutch aggression seen in Middleton's encounters became steadily worse, with their increasing belligerence making life difficult for the English. The third voyage (1607–10) used the *Hector* and *Dragon* again, with a third ship, the *Consent*. The *Hector* made history by becoming the first English ship to reach India. It subsequently sailed to the Banda Islands, where nutmeg and mace were purchased, and later picked up 4,900 bags of pepper at Banten on its return journey. The *Dragon* also traded a full load of pepper from Sumatra and Banten; profits of this voyage were 234 per cent of subscribed capital.[43] The fourth voyage (1608–09) comprised only two ships, but both were lost. The fifth voyage (1609–11) used only a single ship, the *Expedition*, which was ultimately successful in taking nutmeg and mace from the Banda Islands despite demands and threats from the Dutch. In a letter to the Company, the commander David Middleton (the younger brother of Sir Henry) summarised:

'I have aboord 139 Tunnes, six Cathayes, 1 quarterne 2 pound of nutmegs; and 622 suckettes of mace, which maketh 36 Tunnes, 15 Cathayes, 1 quarterne, 21 pounds.'[44]

The sixth voyage (1610–13), commanded again by Sir Henry Middleton, comprised three ships: the *Trade's Increase*, *Peppercorn* and *Darling*. The plan was to stop at India en route to the Far East. The ships had a broad remit of goods to bring back to England: indigo, calicos, Ceylon cinnamon, cotton yarn, green ginger, red sandalwood, turbith, opium, benjamin, sal ammoniac, olibanum, lignum aloes, worm seeds, gumlac and Persian silk from India, pepper and gold from Sumatra, and nutmeg and mace from the Banda Islands.[45] They visited Surat but were opposed by the Portuguese and were able to do little trade. Both the *Trade's Increase* and *Darling* were lost on this voyage, and only the *Peppercorn* returned to England laden with pepper – despite this, a healthy profit was made.

The pattern continued over the next decade with mixed success, but generally yielding high profits despite appalling losses in men and ships. The Dutch were better financed, better armed and more ruthless in their dealings in the Far East. The second expedition of 1598 led by Jacob Van Neck showed how it could be done: they took eight ships and returned with a huge volume of pepper, cloves, nutmeg, mace and cinnamon. They had established their United (Dutch) East India Company (*Vereenigde Oostindische Compagnie* or VOC) in 1602 with similar objectives to the British. The VOC was extremely well organised and well equipped, in effect a military-commercial enterprise backed by the Dutch government. It was also the world's first publicly traded company. One of the main objectives was to dominate the Southeast Asian spice trade, which they proceeded to do with ruthless efficiency. The Dutch had already displaced the Portuguese from Ambon in 1605, while in 1603 the newly established VOC had seized the richly laden Portuguese carrack *Santa Catarina* off Singapore and established a trading post at Banten, and subsequently Batavia on Java in 1611. But between 1605 and 1621 the Dutch forced the Portuguese out, giving the Netherlands a monopoly on the trade in nutmeg and cloves.[46]

The British and Dutch clashed in the Banda Islands in 1604 and on numerous subsequent occasions. In 1616, Nathaniel Courthope sailed his ships *Swan* and *Defence* to the island of Run, where he formed an alliance with the islanders and fortified it as a stand against the Dutch. The Dutch finally overran the island and killed Courthope after a 1,540-day siege. The postscript to this was that the Dutch killed or enslaved all the native men on the island and cut down every nutmeg tree to deter future English interest. Events culminated in 1623 with the Amboyna Massacre, when the Dutch arrested, tortured and executed twenty men, including ten English traders. They had been accused of treason and conspiring to seize the Dutch fortress in Ambon and assassinate the governor. They were executed by beheading, and the English leader, Captain Gabriel Towerson, had his head impaled on a pole. The political fallout was immense and indirectly helped lead to the First Anglo-Dutch war of 1652–54.

Nutmeg cultivation was concentrated on Banda Island and Ambon, and in 1651 the Dutch uprooted nutmeg and clove trees on the other islands, as with Run, better to control the monopoly. By 1681, about 75 per cent of the Spice Island clove and nutmeg trees had been destroyed, leading to scarcity of the spice and an increase in prices that benefited the VOC.

According to a letter to the EIC in 1613, the Dutch had twenty-eight factories and fifteen forts in the Far East, compared to the Company's single established factory at Banten.[47] The EIC did establish a factory at Makassar on the south-west coast of Sulawesi in 1613, which was a key entrepot in the region and received a wide range of goods. In addition, it was conveniently close to the Spice Islands, and the EIC could acquire smuggled nutmeg, mace and cloves and avoid Dutch aggression. In December 1632, more than 81,000lb of cloves were shipped to England.[48] Dutch hostility towards Makassar increased from the 1640s, and as a consequence the price of cloves rose dramatically until the mid-1660s, and supply to Makassar all but dried up. The English, hopeful of an upturn in the situation, lingered on in Makassar until 1667, when they were finally expelled by the Dutch, essentially marking the end of Company activity in the eastern archipelago.

By 1700, the Portuguese had lost their hold in the region apart from small enclaves in western India and Macau. The Dutch had usurped their positions in most of Asia and now largely controlled the Asian spice trade. The English would never make major inroads into Southeast Asia other than via a few positions in Sumatra, but they had a solid foothold in India, where they would soon become dominant.

The EIC refocused on developing its tentative foothold in India. Rights had been granted to establish a factory in Surat and other areas in 1612 by the Mughal emperor Jahangir. By 1647, the Company had twenty-three factories in India and had eclipsed the Portuguese – though spices were not the main business here, but silk, calico, indigo and tea, among other commodities. The factories often evolved into forts. Despite several Anglo-Indian wars from the late seventeenth century, the EIC expanded its operations in India and eventually had its own army, which grew dramatically from the mid-eighteenth century. 'Presidencies' were established at Bombay, Madras and Bengal, each administered by a governor.

Spice Prices

The spice prices chart (Figure 26) illustrates several interesting phenomena. Firstly, availability of spices in the Thorold Rogers dataset: cinnamon is scarce before 1430 and nutmeg doesn't appear in these records until 1554.[49] Cloves and mace were available throughout the period, so nutmeg scarcity must be due to lack of popularity in the period up to the 1550s – this is confirmed by extreme scarcity in contemporary English recipes, though several instances are recorded in continental Europe.

Secondly, the relative cost of these spices follows a consistent pattern: black pepper is always more or less affordable and is generally the cheapest of the five under review. Supply was good and, due to EIC authority in India, it was never really constrained. Interestingly, European pepper consumption increased dramatically following the price falls of the early 1600s.[50] Mace is almost always the most expensive of these spices. It is curious to see its widespread use in medieval times (for those who could afford it) – the bitter, pungent and aromatic flavour was popular in savoury dishes. Cloves and cinnamon had broadly similar prices and were available throughout the period. Before 1400, cloves were priced in a similar manner to mace, or were even more expensive.

Thirdly, and most importantly, is the movement of price over time, which was mainly a function of major geopolitical events, starting with the fall of Byzantium. Portuguese control of the spice trade in India and Southeast Asia from the early 1500s corresponded to a large increase in prices compared with the previous century that lasted for about 100 years. Other contributory causes of the price increase were the Portuguese capture of Hormuz in 1515 and the Turkish seizure of Egypt in 1516–17 (resulting in difficulties in transporting spices through the Red Sea route). Portuguese authority declined rapidly with the appearance of the English and the Dutch at the start of the seventeenth century. The monopoly was broken and prices fell sharply, but not for long. The Dutch quickly usurped the Portuguese in most of Southeast Asia and shut the English out from trade in the Moluccas, with the consequence of another sharp rise in prices from a different monopoly.

Aftermath

By the end of the seventeenth century the Dutch had succeeded in dominating the Asian spice trade, not only nutmeg and mace but Indian pepper, ginger and turmeric and cinnamon from Ceylon. Their monopoly lasted until the late eighteenth century; nutmeg, cloves and other spices were smuggled out of the Spice Islands by the French and planted in some of their colonies, and, in 1780, British ships blockaded the Dutch East Indies ports. In the late eighteenth century, the VOC suffered badly because of mismanagement, worsening trade conditions and the Dutch defeat in the Fourth Anglo-Dutch War of 1780–84. It lasted until 1796, when it was nationalised, and then was finally dissolved on the very last day of 1799. The EIC survived a little longer, but after the Indian Rebellion of 1857, the writing was on the wall. In the following year, the Government of India Act was put into effect, and all EIC interests in India were passed to the Crown. The Dutch and English split much of East Asia between them in 1824, and the Dutch stayed in Indonesia until the Second World War. Final EIC dissolution arrived in 1874.

7

The Age of Discovery, Part 2: Chili and the New World Spices

Capsicum annuum from *The Flora Homoeopathica*, London, 1852–53. (Biodiversity Heritage Library)

Chili

There are five domesticated species of the chili plant, which all belong to the genus *Capsicum*. There are also around thirty wild species.[1] The domesticated species are:

C. annuum – the most common chili in the world. These include the characteristic and typically finger-shaped chilis, but have a lot of variability in shape, size and colour. They were first domesticated in Mexico and range from hot to mild.[2]

C. chinense – includes the Scotch Bonnet, Habanero and Carolina Reaper varieties. The fruits are typically globular or cherry-shaped and are super-hot. Domesticated in northern Amazonia.

C. baccatum – includes the Bishop's Crown or Friar's Hat and Ají Amarillo varieties; first domesticated in Bolivia. The chili pods typically hang down and they are very hot.

C. frutescens – includes the Tabasco, Malagueta and Cabe Rawit peppers. They are typically small with elongated conical shape and grow erect on the plant. Domesticated in the Caribbean.

C. pubescens – includes the Rocoto peppers; fruits tend to be globular. It is a long-lived species, and the chilis have a characteristic fruity aroma. Domesticated in the southern Andes.

Capsicum is a member of the Solanaceae family, which includes tomatoes, potatoes and eggplants. Chilis are believed to have first arisen in Bolivia and the various species are all traced to different parts of South America. Wild chili harvesting began about 8,000 years ago and they seem to have been cultivated from around 6,000 years ago.[3] The earliest macro remains of chilis were retrieved from caves in Mexico, being roughly 9,000 to 7,000 years old – this makes them among the oldest spices used by humans.[4] Very early remains (starches) of chili peppers were also recovered from sites in Ecuador in sediment samples, milling stones, and as food residues in sherds of cooking vessels.[5] The sites date to 6,100 years old. Maize and chili often occur together at ancient sites – people have clearly had a taste for the hot stuff for many millennia.

The heat of chilis seems to be quite addictive to a lot of people, myself included. This heat or 'pungency' is recorded in Scoville Heat Units (SHU), and this is based on the amount of capsaicinoids (capsaicin being the most abundant) present. Capsaicinoids are alkaloids which occur in the tissue surrounding the seeds, internal membranes and other parts of the chili. The modern method to measure pungency is 'high performance liquid chromatography' – then multiply capsaicinoids in ppm by 15 to convert to SHU. On the Scoville scale anything above 80,000 SHU is termed 'very highly pungent', but a mere 80,000 score is kids' stuff when you look at the table below. Bear in mind that these are a tiny selection of well-known varieties – there are over 50,000 *Capsicum* cultivars worldwide.

Table 7 | Common Chili Varieties and their Pungency

Name	Species	Scoville Heat Units
Pure capsaicin	N/A	16,000,000
Pepper X	*Capsicum chinense*	2,690,000
Carolina Reaper	*Capsicum chinense*	1,000,000–2,200,000
Trinidad Moruga Scorpion	*Capsicum chinense*	1,000,000–2,000,000+
Chiltepin pepper	*Capsicum annuum* var. *glabriusculum*	465,000–1,628,000
Trinidad Scorpion Butch T	*Capsicum chinense*	1,000,000–1,460,000
Naga Viper	*Capsicum chinense*	1,382,000
Ghost Pepper (Bhut Jolokia)	*C. chinense/C. frutescens* hyb	855,000–1,000,000+
Adjuma pepper	*Capsicum chinense*	100,000–500,000
Habanero	*Capsicum chinense*	100,000–350,000
Scotch Bonnet	*Capsicum chinense*	100,000–350,000
Charleston Hot pepper	*Capsicum annuum*	70,000–100,000
Prik Kee Nu	*Capsicum annuum*	50,000–100,000
Rocoto/Manzano pepper	*Capsicum pubescens*	30,000–100,000
Tabasco pepper	*Capsicum frutescens*	30,000–50,000

Cayenne pepper	*Capsicum annuum*	30,000–50,000
Chile de arbol	*Capsicum annuum*	15,000–30,000
Bishop's Crown/Friar's Hat	*Capsicum baccatum*	10,000–30,000
Serrano pepper	*Capsicum annuum*	10,000–23,000
Jalapeno pepper	*Capsicum annuum*	4,000–8,500
Chipotle pepper (dried Jalapeno)	*Capsicum annuum*	2,500–8,000
Mirasol pepper	*Capsicum annuum*	2,500–5,000
Chilaca/Pasilla pepper	*Capsicum annuum*	1,000–4,000
Poblano pepper	*Capsicum annuum*	1,000–1,500
Mexibell pepper	*Capsicum annuum*	100–1000
Pimento pepper	*Capsicum annuum*	100–500
Pepperoncini	*Capsicum annuum*	100–500
Friggitelli	*Capsicum annuum*	100–500
Banana pepper	*Capsicum annuum*	0–500
Bell pepper	*Capsicum annuum*	0

The world's hottest chili is now (since 2023) Pepper X, with a heat level of 2.69 million SHU. This marvel was created by Smokin' Ed Currie of the appropriately named PuckerButt Pepper Co.[6], displacing his own previous world record holder, the Caroline Reaper. Ed also sells a range of chili sauces with names like Voodoo Prince Death Mamba, Purgatory and The Reaper. However, the world's hottest food additive is 'Blair's 16 Million Reserve', which comprises pure capsaicin crystals, and is essentially inedible. It is only available as a collector's item.

Chilis spread throughout South and Central America – Perry et al. reported a site with chili starch on a groundstone tool, some 5,600 years old, in Panama; in Peru there was cultivation of three domesticated species of chili from 4,000 years BP; in San Salvador from 1,000 years ago; and from a site in Venezuela 450–1,000 years ago. They found the association of chili with maize at every site. Chili plants themselves were spread naturally by birds as they do not have receptors to feel the burn of capsaicin (unlike most mammals, who feel the pain as much as we do).

However, chili didn't spread to Europe until after it was discovered by the Genoese navigator Christopher Columbus in 1492. Columbus was actually searching for a western route to Asia, which was believed to be the source of spices only obtainable at great cost and (it was thought) by the overland Silk Road route. The voyage was financed by Spain after the Portuguese had rejected the idea (this was to be four years after Bartolomeo Dias had rounded the Cape of Good Hope, but still several years before da Gama reached India). Columbus' fleet comprised the *Santa María* (his flagship), the *Niña* and the *Pinta*. The round-trip journey was much shorter than that of da Gama and subsequent expeditions to the East – seven months in this case as opposed to two or three years for the early eastern voyages. Columbus reached San Salvador in the Bahamas a little over two months after departing Spain, and reached the north coast of Cuba about two weeks later.[7] After exploring some of the islands west of San Salvador, they headed south-west for Cuba following native advice, with Columbus confident that it would be rich in gold and spices (he wrongly thought that Cuba might be the island of Cipango, or Japan). Regardless of that, on arrival Columbus was greatly impressed by the natural beauty of Cuba. The indigenous people were shown specimens of cinnamon and pepper, as well as gold and pearls, and they assured the visitors there was plenty in the vicinity. They also encountered Cubans smoking 'half-burned weed' – tobacco. They were to find gold, too, but the Asian spices sought by Columbus would never be found. In fact, he believed for the remainder of his life that the new lands he had discovered were part of Asia. They made their way south-eastwards to the large island, which they were to call *Ila Española* (Hispaniola). The *Santa María* was lost here on Christmas Day 1492 after running aground on a sandbank. They continued eastwards along the coast in the *Niña*, and just before departing for Spain the journal notes: 'There is also plenty of ají [i.e. chili], which is their pepper, which is more valuable than pepper, and all the people eat nothing else, it being very wholesome. Fifty caravels might be annually loaded with it from Española.'

Peter Martyr d'Anghiera, a chronicler in the Spanish court, wrote a letter in 1511 based on the first voyage describing 'rough-coated berries of different colours more pungent to the taste than Caucasian pepper'.[8] Columbus described the indigenous people as 'naked and without arms but hopelessly timid' and scrupulously honest. This observation was sadly prescient, and the subsequent Spanish colonisation of the Americas was terribly brutal. We are indebted to Bartolomé de las Casas, a contemporary writer and priest who arrived in Hispaniola in 1502, for the surviving lengthy abstract of the Columbus journal. Columbus finally reached Spain in March 1493, returning to a hero's welcome.

Columbus' second voyage, in 1493, used a much larger fleet, comprising two carracks and fifteen caravels with around 1,200 men, and their main aim was to spread Christianity. They departed Spain on 25 September and made landfall in Dominica in the southern Leeward Islands on 3 November. They followed the course of the islands towards the north-west, finally reaching Hispaniola. Among other foods, they again encountered the ají peppers. Dr Diego Álvarez Chanca was a physician to the expedition and commented thus in his letter of 1494: 'Their food consists of bread, made of the roots of a vegetable which is between a tree and a vegetable, and the *age* [yam] … they use, to season it, a spice called *ají*, which they also eat with fish, and such birds as they can catch.'[9]

Columbus called this new plant *pimiento* (though the word 'chili' is derived from an Aztec word), associating it with pepper on account of its pungent heat, despite there being no botanical relationship between chili and black pepper.

The second voyage eventually descended into a physical and moral quagmire. Many of the settlers died of illness or malnutrition; officers abused and enslaved the indigenous people; and many of the enslaved natives were shipped back to Spain. The fleet finally returned to Spain in 1496. He was to lead two more voyages, finding the South American mainland at Venezuela and reaching Central America, and had to endure rebellions and imprisonment and other indignities, but he would never find his way westwards to the Spice Islands. He died in 1506.

The *Santa María* at anchor, Andries van Eertvelt, *c.* 1628. Columbus' flagship was lost on Christmas Day 1492 at Hispaniola. (National Maritime Museum, Greenwich, London)

Although Columbus brought the plant back to Spain, it was the Portuguese traders who exported chili to Portuguese Africa, India, Malacca and Indonesia.[10] The chilis were part of a food group, i.e. maize, beans, squash and chili, brought over to Europe by Columbus and the Portuguese. After this initial phase of rediscovery, chili spread to Europe, Africa and Asia very quickly. Initial use in Europe was probably as curiosities within botanical gardens or as ornamental plants, later evolving towards culinary use. Within Spain, Seville was an important starting point for the nurture and expansion of *Capsicum*, and its cultivation was embraced by the Spanish.[11]

The earliest European picture of chili (*C. frutescens*) comes from the *Codex Amphibiorum* of around 1540, held in the Austrian National Library.[12] This, together with the herbal catalogue with *Capsicum* illustrations by the German botanist Leonhart Fuchs in 1543 (Figure 29), proves that peppers were known in central Europe by that time.[13] Both Fuchs and later John Gerard (1597) illustrated rounded, finger- and globular-shaped forms. Gerard described chili as Ginnie or Indian Pepper, suggesting sources from West Africa and from India by the late sixteenth century.[14]

The Portuguese could have obtained their chilis (and associated foods) from the Spanish Main or from Spanish ports. From Portugal the trade went to the Portuguese Atlantic Islands, Angola, Portuguese East Africa and India. They had reached Goa at a very early date; maize was exported from Gujarat in the early 1500s. Shortly after this, the food complex routed to Malacca and Indonesia and to the Bay of Bengal, Burma and China. Diffusion might also have occurred from Africa and India to the Mediterranean and parts of Europe via the Red Sea and/or the Persian Gulf by Turk and Arab traders.[15] Maize was already established with the Ottoman Turks by 1539, and other components of the food group, including chili, also became widespread. Andrews says that the Ottoman Turks were probably more responsible than any other group of people after the Portuguese for distribution of the Meso-American foodstuffs. The Ottomans conquered Hungary in 1526 and laid siege to Vienna; shortly thereafter, peppers were recorded in central Europe. Hungarian pepper was used to make paprika from dried and ground bright red *C. annuum*, a spice now generally associated with Hungary. In the Czech lands of the sixteenth century, peppers were known as 'Turkish Pepper' or 'Indian Pepper'; archaeobotanical remains have been found dating from the sixteenth to eighteenth centuries in Prague and Brno.[16] Chilis reached England by 1548 – and we've never looked back!

M.-C. Daunay et al. documented the variety and changing forms of *Capsicum* illustrations in the sixteenth- and seventeenth-century literature demonstrating that species other than *C. annuum* were present.[17] *C. chinense* and *C. frutescens* were more likely to have been exported before *C. annuum*, as these were the species most likely cultivated in the West Indies in that time.[18] Other authors consider *C. annuum* to have arrived in Europe first – it has certainly been the most successful species – but there probably wasn't much in it as illustrations of all three occur in mid-sixteenth-century European literature. One of the reasons for chili's global conquest is the ease of reproduction – it can self-pollinate and is also adaptable to a wide variety of settings, though it mainly thrives in tropical and subtropical environments.

Chili arrived in China via a southern coastal route, possibly from Zhejiang Province.[19] The first written reference to the plant is in the *Yashangzhai Zunsheng Bajían* of 1591 by Gao Lian. It is also plausible that chili was first introduced by the Portuguese in their Macau colony, which was held from 1557, and only then to Zhejiang via Shanghai and westwards into the interior along the Yangtze River. It may have started to be used for seasoning food in Guizhou Province, still one of the main chili-producing areas today. Chili would also have found its way into China from India via the Indus, and then the overland Silk Road route. Figure 30 illustrates the rapid global diffusion of *Capsicum*.

Curiously, chilis may have had only minor spread to North America from Mexico, etc., and only became established after colonisation by Europeans! Use of slave labour from the early 1600s probably had an impact as the African slaves already used chili.[20]

There is a huge diversity in shapes, sizes and colours of chilis, even among single species.

After the introduction of chili to South Asia it was cultivated rapidly, with the climate being very well suited to this crop. India is now the largest producer and exporter of chilis in the world.[21] Dr Mehta has some good stories about chili folklore and unusual uses: from deterring vampires and werewolves in eastern Europe to marauding wild elephants in Assam. They are often used in hangover cures, have been used in blushers to give cheeks a healthy glow, as a deterrent for children prone to sucking their thumbs and biting their nails and, almost unbelievably (especially to anyone who has inadvertently rubbed their eye after chopping chilis), as eye drops for curing headaches. The main conventional uses of chilis are as a source of pungency, food colourant, flavour and texture. Paprika adds flavour and colour without too much pungency; similarly, bell peppers are used as colourful textured vegetables rather than sources of heat. Common food products include fresh, dried, crushed, powdered, smoked and fermented chili, oleoresin (a viscous liquid extracted from fine powdered chilis), a huge variety of chili sauces and pastes, chili oil, in curry powders and other spice mixes, and in various salsas and seasonings.

Vanilla

Vanilla is the world's most popular flavouring, and after saffron, the second most expensive spice. The plant *Vanilla planifolia* is a member of the orchid family and is native to the Central America region. It is a climbing vine with yellowish, green or white flowers, and the fruits are seed pods typically 15–20cm long. These pods are the much sought-after spice – the curing process that is required to develop the characteristic flavour (by increasing the vanillin concentration) is extremely laborious and takes months, which is a major reason for the high product price. In addition to the curing, the pollination itself is a difficult business. Two other species have less fragrant pods – *V. pompona* and *V. tahitensis* – but they are commercially far less significant. The taste of vanilla is often described as sweet, rich and creamy, with a fragrant aroma. Flavour profiles differ between individual species, varieties and geographic sources.

The earliest vanilla users appear to have been the Totonac and Aztec people of Mexico. The Aztecs had developed an early taste for vanilla before their conquest by the Spanish. Hernán Cortés defeated the Aztecs in 1521, and their king Moctezuma was captured and subsequently killed. Bernal Díaz, one of Cortés' trusted lieutenants, described a feast before Moctezuma's seizure in which a great dinner was followed according to the local custom 'by the frothing jugs of cacao liquor; certainly 2,000 of them'.[22] Chocolate was used as a cold drink by the Aztecs and often flavoured with vanilla, chili and flowers of *Cymbopetalum penduliflorum*, as well as other ingredients.[23]

After the Spanish exposure to vanilla, it quickly became popular – first in Spain, and then throughout Europe. Hugh Morgan was Elizabeth I's apothecary who reportedly introduced vanilla to the queen as a 'sweetmeat'. The seventeenth-century physician Antonio Colmenero de Ledesma provided a recipe for chocolate – cacao mixed with chili, aniseed, *Cymbopetalum*, hoja santa, vanilla, cinnamon, nuts, sugar and achiote for colour – as a spicy and sweet medicinal beverage.[24]

Vanilla's popularity extended to the romantic: the eighteenth-century German physician Bezaar Zimmerman claimed it to be a highly efficient aphrodisiac and claimed that it had helped 342 impotent men become 'astonishing lovers'.[25]

Vanilla was introduced to other suitable tropical environments – Réunion (an island in the Indian Ocean, formerly Île de Bourbon) in 1793, which would overtake Mexico in production by the end of the nineteenth century; Java in 1819; India in 1835; Tahiti in 1848; the Seychelles in 1866; and Madagascar, which is now the world's largest producer.

Early attempts to cultivate vanilla outside of Mexico were unsuccessful, as flowers couldn't be pollinated and therefore the pods wouldn't grow. It was only in the 1830s that it was realised that vanilla flowers were pollinated by local orchid bees and hummingbirds. The solution to this problem came in 1841 when a slave in Réunion, Edmond (12 years old at the time, later 'rewarded' with freedom and the surname Albius), devised a simple but effective technique to hand-pollinate the flowers. He used the sharp tip of a bamboo sliver to place pollen on to the concealed stigma of the flowers; a similar technique is still used today. To complicate matters further, the flowers only last for a day and it takes six to nine months for the fruits to mature. Key vanilla products are pods, powder, vanilla extract (the major commercial product), oleoresin, vanilla sugar and vanilla absolute (used in perfumery products).[26]

Vanilla didn't appear in cookery books until the early nineteenth century, but from that point it became commonplace. *The Virginia Housewife* was the first in the US to provide a recipe for 'Vanilla Cream' (i.e. ice cream):

> Boil a Vanilla bean in a quart of rich milk, until it has imparted the flavour sufficiently then take it out, and mix with the milk, eight eggs, yelks and whites beaten well; let it boil a little longer; make it very sweet, for much of the sugar is lost in the operation of freezing.[27]

The main flavour-producing compound in vanilla is vanillin, a phenolic aldehyde, though many other volatile compounds have been identified. Synthetic vanillin was first created in 1874 by two German scientists – this was an important development given the expense of natural vanilla, but also a serious commercial threat to the newly successful vanilla growers. Synthetic vanillin supply far exceeds that of natural vanillin due to the high global demand which couldn't otherwise be met by natural production. And yet … synthetic vanillin is pure vanillin – it lacks the other complex compounds found for example in natural vanilla extract. True vanilla aficionados demand the natural product and are prepared to pay the price.

Some recent archaeological work has rather turned things upside down regarding the first usage of vanilla. Four Bronze

Age ceramic jugs from a site in Canaan, Israel, were tested using organic residue analysis and significant content of vanillin, and two other components characteristic of vanilla, were found in three of them.[28] These jobs are from around 1650–1550 BCE – how could vanilla have been used here at that time? The source was probably from lesser-known species of vanilla orchids native to East Africa or Asia, that then somehow reached the Levant – it remains an intriguing question.

Allspice (Myrtales)

Allspice is the unripe berry of the tropical tree *Pimenta dioica*, which is native to the Caribbean and Central America. It is also known as Jamaica pepper, myrtle pepper and pimento. On Christopher Columbus' first voyage, in Cuba, he showed specimens of pepper to the natives, who 'said, by signs, that there was plenty in the vicinity'– this could have been allspice.[29] It may have been encountered in Jamaica by Columbus on his second voyage in 1494, and he would certainly have been familiar with it on his fourth voyage in 1503, when he was stranded there for a year. It was introduced to Europe in the early sixteenth century. The Spanish used the term 'pimienta' to describe allspice, based on (loose) physical similarity to the Old World black pepper. Somewhat confusingly, 'pimienta' was also used for capsicum/chili because of its similar pungency to black pepper. The flavour of allspice resembles a mixture of cloves, cinnamon and nutmeg and it is therefore a versatile spice which can be adopted for use in sweet and savoury dishes. M. Preusz et al. referred to two rare finds of ancient allspice in Prague, one from sediment dated from the fifteenth century to 1615, the other from the seventeenth or eighteenth century.[30] A description of allspice occurs in the 1686 botanical work *Historia Plantarum*; however, allspice is absent in early English recipes, cooks tending to continue using nutmeg and cloves, etc.[31] Eliza Smith frequently referred to Jamaica pepper in her 1727 book and Hannah Glasse (1747) used it in a pickling recipe.[32] It started to become more common in cookery books in the late 1700s.[33]

Today, the tree is grown in numerous tropical and subtropical countries. Jamaica is the largest producer and exporter of allspice, with 70 per cent of world trade. While the dried and crushed berries are mainly used to make spice for cooking, it is also used in berry oil production, liqueurs, traditional medicine and in the perfume industry.

8

Sugar

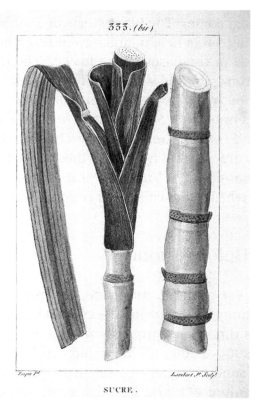

Sugarcane from *Flore Médicale*, 1835.
(Biodiversity Heritage Library)

We tend to associate sugarcane with the Caribbean (because of its long association there with plantations and slavery), but in fact it is indigenous to Asia. *Saccharum officinarum* is native to New Guinea and possibly eastern Indonesia and may have been cultivated for around 10,000 years.[1] It probably developed from an earlier species, *S. robustum*. Almost 80 per cent of the world's sugar comes from *S. officinarum* and its hybrids. It advanced westwards, first through Southeast Asia and then to north-east India around 1000 BCE. Sugarcane spread rapidly through Asia and Africa, eastward through the Pacific, and from India through western Asia and North Africa in early medieval times. Its introduction to the Americas was part of the Columbian Exchange.

The genus *Saccharum* belongs to the Poaceae family, otherwise known as the grasses, with nineteen species, though there are only six species of sugarcane.[2] The plant stems of *S. officinarum* can be very tall, reaching 5m in height, and have marked horizontal joints or nodes formed at the bases of the leaves. The internode areas contain the fibrous pith and sweet sap that the plant is known for.

Wild sugarcane (possibly *Saccharum spontaneum*) is mentioned in the eighth century BCE *Sushruta Samhita*, one of the founder Ayurvedic texts. *S. spontaneum* is native to India and has hybridised with *S. officinarum*. Natural hybrids of these two species may have led to the appearance of *S. barberi* in north India and *S. sinense* in China, both of which were cultivated from prehistoric times.[3]

Sweetness Before Sugar

Long before sugar came on the scene, the main sweetener used was honey. Honey has certainly been collected from the wild since Neolithic times, and probably much earlier. Rock art from Spain dated 8000–2000 BCE depicted wild honey gathering, and beeswax found in pottery vessels from Anatolia dates to the seventh millennium BCE and has also been found at numerous other European Neolithic sites.[4] The oldest evidence of beeswax use is from a sample from the Border Cave of South Africa, which might have been used in an adhesive and is around 40,000 years old.[5] The ancient Egyptians may have been the first to practise beekeeping, with historical evidence dating to *c.* 2400 BCE.[6] Honey was used as food, in medicine and in rituals. Herodotus said that the Babylonians 'bury their dead in honey', possibly meaning embalming.[7] The Greeks and Romans used honey extensively both as medicine and food. Aristotle wrote about honeybees in the fourth century BCE and Pliny made detailed (and sometimes mythical) observations about the natural history of bees and types of honey. He was clearly fond of it, saying that 'it affords us by its flavour a most exquisite pleasure'.[8] He also praises its quality of preventing putrefaction, treating disorders of the throat and tonsils, ailments of the mouth, quinsy and fever; honied wine was used to treat paralysis and honey with rose oil 'as an injection for the ears; it has the effect also of exterminating nits and foul vermin of the head'.[9]

Honey was mixed with water to make hydromel, or with vinegar to make oxymel. They were used in cookery and in medicine. Other mixtures were made combining it with wine, roses, apple juice and sour grapes. Columella, a Roman agriculturist of the first century CE, wrote extensively on beekeeping and honey gathering.[10] References to honey also abound in classical literature. Petronius observed somewhat philosophically: 'Then there's the bee: in my opinion, they're divine insects because they puke honey, though there are folks that claim that they bring it from Jupiter, and that's the reason they sting, too, for wherever you find a sweet, you'll find a bitter too.'[11]

Other sweeteners were dates and mead. Dates, the fruit of the palm *Phoenix dactylifera*, have been cultivated in the Middle East and Indus Valley for thousands of years. Their high natural sugar content (over 60 per cent) gives a lot of sweetness (and energy) in a small package. The oldest evidence of date cultivation is from the Indus Neolithic at Mehrgahr (in modern Pakistan) where dates were used in the period 7000–5500 BCE.[12] Cultivation in the Tigris and Euphrates valleys probably dates to the fourth millennium BCE.[13] Evidence of wild progenitors goes back much further – they would have been part of the Neanderthal diet in the Middle East. Mead is the fermented product of honey mixed with water, and is also ancient, perhaps dating back a few thousand years.

Sugarcane

Cane sugar was (probably) available in the West from the early centuries BCE – as some of the following descriptions attest – but evidently didn't grow there and would have been treated as another spice brought over from the East.

Dioscorides mentions sugar, describing it as a kind of hardened honey found in reeds in India and Arabia, and Pliny made similar comments, adding that it was brittle to the teeth, but only used in medicine.[14] Strabo also made an early reference to sugarcane in India: 'He [Nearchus] says that reeds [sugarcane] yield honey, although there are no bees.'[15] This implies knowledge of sugarcane even if it wasn't cultivated in the West at that time. Eratosthenes (276–194 BCE) wrote about the same sweet reeds. So, a few centuries BCE sugar seems to have been known in the Graeco-Roman world, but not used much (it would have been expensive), and when it was, it seems mainly to have been used as a medicine. Sugar's absence from Diocletian's Price Edict and Justinian's Digest seem to affirm the limited use of the time.

According to G. Watt, sugarcane wasn't known in China until the second century BCE (despite its presence dating back long before that) and a man was sent to Bihar (in north-east India) in the early seventh century to learn the art of refining sugar, which was first developed in India.[16] Watt commented that the ancient Sanskrit name for white sugar is *sarkara*, and that the word *khanda*, which means 'to crush', denotes sugar derived from sugarcane and has been adapted to the modern English 'candy'. Marco Polo noted the production and export of sugar in China in the thirteenth century.[17]

Sugarcane needed to be crushed or ground to extract the juice, which was then boiled to concentrate the sucrose into a raw granular solid. Raw cane sugar is a brownish colour; further refining removed impurities and the black treacly molasses to provide a white crystalline product. Further refining produced an even purer sugar – the market wanted pure and white. Advances in processing were made by mechanisation of the crushing or milling of the cane and by the boiling process.

By the sixth century CE, or possibly earlier, sugarcane had reached Persia. The Byzantine Emperor Heraklios' army found sugar amongst exotic eastern spices in the spoils of their victorious 627 CE Persian campaign. The Muslim conquest of Mesopotamia and then Persia in 642 CE accelerated the introduction of sugar to the West via the conquered lands of the caliphate, including North Africa, Spain and Sicily. Cane was being grown in Egypt by the eighth century. Furthermore, it had spread to Zanzibar by the tenth century.[18] Sugarcane was found in medieval deposits at Quseir al-Qadim on the Red Sea.[19] The Arab appetite and enthusiasm for sugar was phenomenal. In 1040, the Sultan of Cairo used 73 tons of sugar to celebrate the end of Ramadan, and sugar statues, trees and flowers were in abundance.[20]

Sugar is common in European recipes from the thirteenth century. Sugar came from Sicily, Cyprus, Crete and Alexandria, among other places – and was very expensive, usually more so than pepper.[21] One of the earliest recipes is from the Sion Manuscript, of the late thirteenth century, which used sugar as an ingredient in frumenty, a popular porridge dish.[22] It appears in many dishes in *The Forme of Cury* (1390) and by that time was beginning to take the place of honey, though the two were still commonly used together, or as alternatives.[23] It came from the East via Damascus, Aleppo, Genoa and Venice, etc. Sometimes the source of the sugar was specified; in the recipe for Cawdel Ferry (a sweet pudding) 'sugur cypre' is mentioned – sugar had been cultivated in Cyprus since the tenth century CE:

Take flour of Payndemayn [white bread] and gode wyne. and drawe it togydre. Do therto a grete quantite of Sugur cypre. or hony clarified, and do therto safroun. boile it. and whan it is boiled, alye it up with zolkes of ayrenn [egg yolks]. and do therto salt and messe it forth. and lay theron sugur and powdour gyngur.

Sugar and the New World

The Portuguese introduced sugarcane to Madeira shortly after its colonisation in the early 1420s, and it rapidly became the mainstay of the island's economy. By 1500, Madeira was the largest sugar exporter in the world. Processing the sugar was extremely labour intensive and this led the Portuguese to use slave labour alongside paid workers. São Tomé, off Guinea, also became an important producer, again using African slave labour. Sugarcane was introduced to the new Portuguese Brazilian colony in the early sixteenth century, with the first plantation established in 1518.

Sugarcane was also first cultivated in the Canary Islands in the fifteenth century following conquest by the Spanish. Meanwhile, Christopher Columbus had taken sugarcane samples with him, obtained from the Canaries on his second voyage to the Americas in 1493. In his settlement of La Isabella (in the modern Dominican Republic) he reported back to the Spanish king and queen that crops brought along on the journey grew very well in the new land, and this included sugarcane, which rooted and grew well – 'neither is it different with the sugar-canes according to the manner in which some few that were planted have grown'.[24]

From these beginnings the sugarcane industry developed rapidly. It spread through the Caribbean Islands – but the native workers, enslaved by the Spanish, were ill-suited to that kind of work and succumbed to disease, dying at horrific rates. A new labour force was needed, and so the Spanish and Portuguese expanded what they had already started to do, and brought in vast numbers of slaves from Africa. Over a period of 400 years, some 12 million Africans were abducted and enslaved in the Americas.

Hispaniola was the first of the 'sugar islands', followed by Cuba, Jamaica and Puerto Rico in the 1520s.

It wasn't long before the other major colonial powers joined the fray. The Dutch established a colony at Surinam in the seventeenth century and the French in neighbouring Cayenne/French Guiana. Dutch attempts to seize Brazil were finally repulsed by the Portuguese in 1654. The Dutch also established settlements on several Caribbean islands. The French settled Martinique and Guadeloupe in 1635, and later Grenada and Dominica. The British, meanwhile, had settled a number of islands initially to prey on Spanish shipping, later as permanent settlements – St Kitts (1623), Barbados (1627), Nevis (1628), Antigua (1632), Anguilla (1650) and then in 1655, the jewel in the crown, Jamaica. Barbuda (1666), then Montserrat followed and later the Windward Islands, Turks and Caicos, etc. In practice, the European colonial period was extremely complicated, with numerous islands changing hands multiple times due to skirmishes, wars and political machinations. The common factor, however, was sugar, which had become the dominant crop in the seventeenth century, and it was feeding a growing and seemingly insatiable demand in Europe. From the mid-eighteenth century, sugar became Britain's most valuable import and had huge value throughout Europe as it passed from being a luxury item to a necessity.

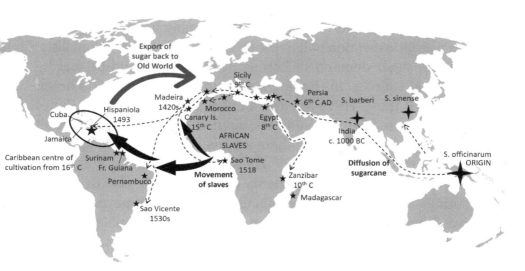

The diffusion of sugarcane through the Old and New Worlds.

In 1807, Britain formally abolished the slave trade (but not slavery); however, the practice continued in the British West Indies until 1834, the French colonies until 1848, and Brazil until 1888. The winding down of the slave trade coincided with the Industrial Revolution, which encouraged better farming methods and improved mills, mechanisation, etc., which had a number of effects. Firstly, the price of sugar came down from 10*d* per lb in the early 1800s to around 2*d* per lb at the end of the nineteenth century. Secondly, the greater availability and lower price meant that a far greater proportion of the population, of all classes, was consuming it. It often accompanied the new imports of tea and coffee, which had also caught on throughout Europe.

Another related product which saw a huge increase in popularity was rum. Despite some evidence of rum usage in ancient times, the rum that we know today originated in the Caribbean in the seventeenth century, when it was discovered that the molasses by-product of sugar refining could be fermented and distilled to produce an alcoholic drink. It quickly became popular in North America, and with the British – especially the Royal Navy, which allowed sailors a daily rum ration (or 'tot'), a practice which continued until 1970.

While sugarcane planting was rapidly developing in the Caribbean, in India, where it had been cultivated for many hundreds of years, there was little mention of it in the literature of the early colonialists. However, sugar demand in Europe at that time could be met by more local sources. In the late sixteenth century, van Linschoten discussed it thus: 'There are also all over India many Sugar Canes in all places, and in great numbers, but not much esteemed of: & all along the coast of Malabare there are many thicke Reeds, specially on the coast of Choramandel.'[25] He went on to describe it as being much used and esteemed in Persia and Arabia. He also described a curious treatment: 'The Indians use it against the payne in their privie members, or such like secret diseases.' It is possible that van Linschoten (and perhaps earlier writers) was confusing his sugarcane with a species of bamboo, some of which have young shoots with sweet interiors; they both belong to the same botanical family.

Gerard was a contemporary of van Linschoten. He observed that 'the Cane itself ... is not hollow as the other Canes or Reedes are; but full, and stuffed with a spungious substance in taste exceeding sweete'.[26] By this time it was growing in many places in Europe – Spain, Portugal, Sardinia, Provence, North Africa, the Canary Islands, Madeira, the East and West Indies, etc. Gerard's attempt to grow it in his London garden failed ('the coldnes of our Clymate made an end of mine'). From the sugar was made 'infinite confections, confectures, sirupes, and such like, as also preserving and conserving of sundrie fruits, herbes and flowres'.

The 'infinite confections' that Gerard mentioned was hardly an understatement. Sugar sculptures, already perfected by the Arabs in medieval times, became a feature of European aristocratic banquets. They appeared at court ceremonies and wedding feasts, e.g. that of Ercole I d'Este, the Duke of Ferrara, in 1473, at which there was a procession of 100 large plates bearing sugar confections such as castles, columns of Hercules, birds, animals, etc.[27] The sculpted objects were known as 'trionfi' (pl.), meaning 'triumphant processions', and later fifteenth- and sixteenth-century Italian examples were increasingly elaborate. They were also popular in other European countries, including England. Elizabeth I was famously fond of sugar, to the extent that she is reputed to have used it to clean her teeth (which unsurprisingly became rotten and black). She would then surely have been impressed by the show put on by Edward Seymour, 1st Earl of Hertford, during her Progress of 1591 at Elvetham in Hampshire, which featured four days of sumptuous entertainment and a banquet with all kinds of sugary delights.

Sugar beet is a cultivar of the common beet, *Beta vulgaris*, that was developed in the eighteenth century. The first factory opened in Poland in 1801 and the new beet spread to other European countries, including France. Napoleon was a firm supporter of its cultivation as it provided an alternative to cane sugar, which was in danger of becoming unavailable due to the English blockades imposed at that time.[28] By the late nineteenth century, sugar beet was being cultivated in America and ultimately thrived, as it did in many temperate climates across the globe. The Nazis were big advocates of the crop as it contributed to their domestic self-sufficiency. Today, sugar beet provides some 20 per cent of global sugar production – the rest is still from cane. Global sugar consumption is enormous – around 176 million tons – with average consumption per person in the order of 24 kg/year (but much higher in some developed countries).[29]

Sugar crystals. (Umberto Salvagnin)

9

Diverse Spices

Khan El-Khallili Spice Market, Cairo, Egypt. (Author)

Pricy Spices

The order Asparagales is one of the larger and most varied groups of flowering plants and includes several flavourings such as onion, garlic, leek, saffron and vanilla. These two latter are the world's most expensive spices.

Saffron is derived from the stigma and styles of crocus flowers (*Crocus sativus*, Iridaceae family). It is the most expensive spice, unsurprisingly, as it takes an awful lot of crocus flowers to produce 1kg of saffron, which is worth about $5,000 or more. The flower has an exquisitely beautiful lilac-to-mauve colour with vivid crimson stigma and styles ('threads'). The taste is delicate and slightly bitter, and it has an earthy or even tea-like aroma. It is also a powerful colourant and is commonly used in rice dishes, soups, cheese and egg dishes, and in many sweets and baked goods.

Saffron-based pigments have been found in Upper Paleolithic cave art from 50,000 years ago in Iraq, though these pigments were derived from wild plants. The saffron crocus has been cultivated for over 3,500 years – its wild precursor may have been *Crocus cartwrightianus*, which originated in Crete or Central Asia.[1] Iran, Greece and Mesopotamia are all possible candidates for its domesticated origin. It was used in the Mesopotamian cities of Mari and Nuzi, probably in the second millennium BCE, and the saffron crocus was documented in a seventh-century BCE Assyrian botanical reference.[2] It was also well known in pre-classical Greece; the first expansive plaster murals at Knossus on Crete date from Middle Minoan II age (starts 1850 BCE) and include the partially extant 'Saffron Gatherer' illustrating the gathering of crocuses by young girls and monkeys.[3] In Egypt, it appeared as a remedy in the 1550 BCE Ebers Papyrus, and Cleopatra used a quarter-cup of saffron in warm baths for its colouring and cosmetic properties; she used it before encounters with men in order to enhance the erotic experience.[4] Its reputation as an aphrodisiac persisted through the Roman era. Ancient Egyptians used it as a panacea for stomach complaints and the Phoenicians also widely traded saffron.

The Greeks and Romans used it mainly as a dye, in medicine and as a perfume, even in powdered form, to impart a pleasant aroma to Roman theatres, but it was also used in cooking. Apicius made use of saffron in spiced salts, sauces for choice cuts/tidbits of meat, for roast boar, and broiled Moray eel; he also used it as an ingredient in spiced wines (common for the period) and in Roman vermouth or absinthe.[5]

Saffron's importance in Europe collapsed in parallel with the fall of the Roman Empire and it only appears to have become popular again in later medieval times, possibly having arrived in Britain (and Europe) with returning Crusaders. An Anglo-Norman recipe (*soutil brouet d'Angleterre*) consists of chestnuts, hard-boiled egg yolks and pork liver ground into a paste and cooked with spices and saffron.[6] It was the most used late medieval spice in England, as it was highly favoured for its flavour and golden yellow colour. The fourteenth-century *cretoyne* was a thick soup or stew made with chicken, milk, breadcrumbs, and egg yolks among other ingredients, and coloured a vivid yellow with saffron.[7] Typical medieval dishes using saffron as a colourant are frumentie and mawmenny. It was also used to endore pie crusts, i.e. paint with a mixture of eggs, ginger and saffron and cook to a golden colour.[8] Fifteenth-century recipes abound with saffron, as in this yummy example from the Harley 5401 manuscript: 'Cenellis. recipe braynes of calvis heds or piges heds and put it on a pan or in a pott; & put therto raw eggs & peper, saferon & vinegre, & stir it wele tyl it be thyk, & serof it forth.'[9]

The price of saffron in medieval times was always high and increased quite steeply over time. In England, the price per lb ranged from a low of around 40*d* in the early 1300s to 384*d* in 1535, this latter being exceptional; nonetheless, prices in the later 1500s were commonly greater than 200*d*.[10] The town of Saffron Walden became a centre for cultivation of the saffron crocus in the fifteenth to seventeenth centuries, for use in condiments, dyes and medicines.

Saffron has long been used as a medicine, e.g. Hippocrates (460–377 BCE). In the first century CE, Celsus used saffron in medicines to treat numerous complaints.[11] Hedodt, a seventeenth-century German physician, said that there was no sickness, from toothache to the plague, that saffron could not eradicate.[12] It was also considered in other European countries to be a remedy for measles, dysentery and jaundice (yellow curing yellow), as illustrated by this remedy from *The English Huswife* of 1615:

> take two-penny worth of the best English Saffron, drie it and grinde it to an exceeding fine powder, then mix it with the pap of a rosted apple, and give it to the diseased party to swallow downe in the manner of a pill; and doe thus divers mornings together, and without doubt it is the most present cure that can be for the same, as hath beene often proved.[13]

The fourteenth-century dietician to the Chinese court, Hu Sihui, said that saffron had the power of banishing sadness and rejoicing the heart.[14] Nicholas Culpeper also praised the virtues of saffron in treating a variety of illnesses (including those of the heart, lungs, epidemical diseases, jaundice and 'hysteric disorders') but warned against using too much: 'However, the use of it ought to be moderate and reasonable; for when the dose is too large, it produces a heaviness of the head and sleepiness; some have fallen into an immoderate convulsive laughter, which ended in death.'[15]

Even as far back as the first century CE, saffron was adulterated with cheaper substitutes. Pliny bemoaned: 'There is nothing so much adulterated as saffron.'[16] It was commonly sold moist to make up the weight with water. Safflower (*Carthamus tinctorius*) is a common substitute and adulterant today.

Azerbaijanis use saffron to colour their 'plov' rice dish and the Spanish to colour paella (though turmeric can also be used); it is also used in some biryanis and risottos. It is an important ingredient of the Provencal bouillabaisse. Iran and Spain are the largest modern-day producers of saffron, though it is cultivated in many other countries.

Sundry Old World Spices

Fenugreek (Fabaceae)

Fenugreek is a distinctive annual plant with an equally distinctive Latin name, *Trigonella foenum-graecum* (meaning 'Greek hay'). It resides in the Fabaceae (bean) family. The plant grows to about 2ft high and has characteristic sets of three oblong leaflets. It is native to the eastern Mediterranean region but is cultivated widely for its seeds and leaves which are used as spices, herbs and in traditional medicines. The seeds are small (about 2–3mm long), pale brown coloured, with a roughly rectangular shape and divided by a furrow and are contained in long thin pods. They have a slightly bitter taste and a pungent aroma.

The oldest known occurrences are from around 6,000 years BP from Tell Halaf in Iraq and *c.* 5450–5650 BP from Ma'di in Egypt.[17] Numerous Bronze and Iron Age examples are known from South Asia, parts of Europe, Egypt and the Levant.[18] Roman period evidence is known from Germany, Egypt and Bulgaria. Fenugreek (*methi* in Hindi) has a long history in the Asian subcontinent and this is still the centre of usage. It occurs in a wild state in areas of the Kashmir and Punjab and in the Upper Gangetic plain.

Classical era authors referring to fenugreek include Theophrastus, Columella, Pliny, Dioscorides, Celsus and Galen. Pliny emphasised use for treating various women's problems, among other disorders. He listed thirty-one remedies, including 'A decoction … of fenugreek seed is a corrective of the rank odours of the armpits'.[19] Fenugreek is mentioned in the Price Edict of Diocletian (310 CE), and also appears in Apicius' *De Re Coquinaria*, where it is treated as a food in its own right rather than a herb or seasoning.

Fenugreek was rarely used in medieval Europe, but in medieval Cairo bad-smelling meat was moistened with pounded fenugreek and boiled in water, which had the effect of 'refreshing' the meat.[20] A more wholesome dish was 'tabikh al-hulba', in which fenugreek seeds were left in a pot over glowing embers overnight, and in the morning were mixed with spices, honey, butter, raisins and figs and cut into two or three parts. But Lewicka points out that use of fenugreek in medieval Arab-Islamic cookery was very rare. Lilia Zaouali refers to the 'jashish' recipe – Andalusian puree of wheat with fenugreek.[21]

Fenugreek's other medical uses are: to reduce fevers; soothe intestinal inflammation; seeds ground to a paste as a poultice for battle wounds; as a treatment for boils and other skin conditions; to assist in labour and to improve lactation; and a cure for baldness. In Turkey it is used as a deodorant and breath freshener, in Albania mixed with lemon and onion juice for head colds and sinusitis, and in Bavaria to dissolve mucus.[22] Avicenna (980–1037 CE), a Persian physician and philosopher, prescribed it for diabetes and blood pressure.[23] John Gerard (1597) listed many medicinal uses for fenugreek.[24] For example, 'the juice of boiled Fenegreeke taken with honie, is good to purge by the stoole all manner of corrupt humours that remaine in the guts'. Nicholas Culpeper noted that the seeds were only used in medicine.[25] According to Pamela Westland, Middle Eastern harem women ate fenugreek seeds as they were the secret to 'rounded plumpness'. In Ethiopia and India, nursing mothers use fenugreek to promote lactation.[26] Modern evidence for the efficacy of these traditional uses of fenugreek is scant!

Modern culinary uses include the leaves, greens or seeds as ingredients in curries, stews, salads and masalas (South Asia), seeds in drinks and in bread (Egypt), and in Turkey and the Middle East as a seasoning. It is also used in chutneys, pickles, confectionary, cakes and syrups. It is a constituent of the North African Berbere mix and (due to its Indian colonial heritage) the French Vadouvan. India is the largest producer, consumer and exporter of fenugreek in the world.[27]

Liquorice (Fabaceae)

Liquorice (*Glycyrrhiza glabra*) is another herbaceous plant in the Fabaceae family and is famous for its sweet flavouring, which is extracted from the root (the generic name *Glycyrrhiza* means 'sweet root'). It is native to southern and eastern Europe, parts of the Middle East and Asia. The distinctive liquorice flavour is due to the presence of anethole (a phenylpropanoid, which is also present in anise, star anise and fennel), while the sweetness is due to the glycoside glycyrrhizin, which is up to fifty times sweeter than sugar.

Liquorice is referred to for its medicinal value in the Chinese *Shennong Ben Cao Ying*, a *materia medica* that probably dates from the third century BCE, though its use probably pre-dates this. Theophrastus referred to liquorice as 'Scythian Root' and commented:

> it is useful against asthma or a dry cough and in general for troubles in the chest: also, administered in honey, for wounds: also it has the property of quenching thirst, if one holds it in the mouth: wherefore they say that the Scythians, with the help of this and mares' milk cheese can go eleven or twelve days without drinking.[28]

It was also known to Pliny, Celsus and others of that era.[29] In Britain, it was one of the many spices reported to have been left by the Bede to his brethren, but it must have been extremely scarce at that time. It may have come to Britain in greater quantities around the time of the Norman conquest, but it is still very rare in medieval recipes, even in Europe. It was generally inexpensive – it sold for 3*d* per lb in 1264, 1½*d* in 1326, and 4*d* in 1360. Pontefract in Yorkshire became a centre for limited liquorice cultivation by local monks, probably from the sixteenth century. Pontefract cakes – small discs of liquorice 'cake' – date from the early seventeenth century and were first used as a medicine. Local apothecary George Dunhill added sugar to the mix, thus creating the eponymous candy still popular today.

A recipe for gingerbread from 1623 includes 'a little Licoras and Aniseeds', but recipes using liquorice were still scarce at this time.[30] In 1727, Eliza Smith used liquorice, but in medicinal compounds (e.g. in cough lozenges, elixirs, a medicine for 'the spotted, and all other malignant fevers', in a medicine to cure stones, and so on) rather than culinary recipes.[31] Compound liquorice powder (a laxative) appeared in the London and Prussian Pharmacopoeia in the seventeenth and eighteenth centuries.[32]

Today, liquorice is chiefly used in confections, particularly in Europe, where it is most popular, but also in China, Turkey and the Middle East.

Tamarind (Fabaceae)

Tamarind (*Tamarindus indicus*) is an evergreen tree belonging to the Fabaceae family, whose fruit is a pod containing the seeds surrounded by a delicious tangy edible pulp. The tree can reach 18m in height and the characteristic leaves are small and oval, arranged in a pinnate pattern. Despite the species name, tamarind is probably native to Africa (or Madagascar) but has spread to many tropical and subtropical environments worldwide. The pods range up to 15cm long and have a hard, cinnamon-coloured shell with a typical arcuate shape, while the fleshy pulp is dark brown and fibrous.

Early evidence of tamarind use was found at the Vadnagar site in Gujrat, India, with seeds apparently representing wild forms in deposits ranging from 100 BCE to 400 CE.[33] However, it is likely that tamarind was introduced to India long before this.

Pliny, describing some trees of India, may have been talking about tamarind in this passage: 'There is another tree ... bearing a still sweeter fruit, though very apt to cause derangement of the bowels. Alexander issued strict orders, forbidding anyone in the expedition to touch this fruit.'[34]

The Arabs considered tamarind an important medicine. Numerous medical authors have commented on its qualities, particularly as a purgative, e.g. Rhases, a ninth- to tenth-century Persian physician, said that 'it extinguishes yellow bile, opens the bowels, removes thirst and vomiting, and strengthens the stomach. Its action is said to be similar to that of prunes.'[35]

Van Linschoten noted that tamarind grew in most parts of India, but especially in Gujrat and the areas north of Goa.[36] He observed that:

> it hath a sowrish and sharp taste, and is the best sauce in all India, like vergis [verjuice] with us, and they never sieth Rice but

they put Tamarinio into it wherewith their composition called Cariil [curry] is made ... yet those that see it drest will have no great desire to eate it, for they crush it through their fingers, whereby it sheweth like rotten Medlers, yet it giveth the Rice & the meate a fine sharp taste.

Van Linschoten also noted its excellent purgative qualities. It was salted and exported to Portugal, Arabia, Persia and elsewhere, and he noted its extensive use in Turkey and Egypt. Sugar conserve was also made from it 'which is verie good'. Export to the Arabian peninsula had probably been carried on since at least the ninth century CE.[37]

Its medicinal use has also persisted through time. Tamarind appeared in a formula for 'Lenitive Electuary' in the first London Pharmacopoeia of 1618, together with prunes, senna, jujubes, violets and liquorice, among others; no doubt it was effective.

The Spanish and Portuguese are believed to have introduced tamarind to the Caribbean, Central and South America in the sixteenth and seventeenth centuries, and it became extremely popular there and is widely used today. Tamarind trees were observed by the naturalist Francisco Hernández de Toledo in the 1570s in Mexico.[38]

India is the main producer of tamarind, though it is grown commercially in many other tropical countries. It is a common ingredient in curries, chutneys and pickles and in many recipes where a souring agent is needed; and also in sauces (including Worcestershire sauce), pastes, jams and syrups. In Thailand, it is a popular snack and is commonly sold candied. It is also made into refreshing soft drinks, e.g. in Egypt and the Middle East.

Mustard (Brassicaceae)
Mustard plants are members of the cabbage family (Brassicaceae) and comprise species of the *Brassica* and *Sinapis* genera. The most common variants are black mustard (*Brassica nigra*), white mustard (*Sinapis alba*) and brown (or Oriental) mustard (*Brassica juncea*). They are probably native to the Mediterranean–Middle

East–West Asia region. They are characterised by yellow flowers, edible leaves, and seeds that are used as spices and to make the common mustard paste. Mustard seeds range up to 2mm in diameter and vary in colour from yellow and brown to black. The name 'mustard' is a contraction of the Latin 'mustum ardens', meaning burning wine. Apart from their use as a spice, mustard plants are widely used as green vegetables, in salads, as an oil seed crop, and as fodder. Seeds and seed oil are important ingredients in Indian cuisine.

The mustards *Brassica/Sinapis* sp. and *Neslia paniculata* were present at a Neolithic site in western Iran (Sheikh-e Abad) where the occupation spanned the agricultural transition (9800–7600 BCE).[39] They could have been used as flavouring and/or for their oil, though there is no evidence for this, and they may only have been crop weeds. A different study looked at phytoliths from the inside of Neolithic cooking pots at three sites around the Danish Straits in Germany and Denmark, dating from around 6,000 years ago.[40] The phytoliths were correlated with modern garlic mustard, *Alliaria petiolata*, one of the mustard family, and their use in cooking pots, which also contained residues of marine animals, proves that it was used as a culinary spice.

Mustard was one of the first cultivated crops in the Near East at the start of the Neolithic agricultural revolution.[41] The earliest Christian and Islamic texts refer to the mustard plant, mainly as a religious symbol; for example, the parable of the mustard seeds is a well-known biblical story.

Mustard was grown by the Indus River Valley civilisation several millennia BCE and seeds were recovered from Harappa and Rodji.[42] It was tentatively identified in Mesopotamia at Umma (third millennium BCE), Lagash (late third millennium), and Ur, Nuzi and Mari (second millennium).[43] If the identification is correct, it was also used to flavour date beer in the Neo-Babylonian (626–539 BCE) period (date beer with mustard … that would be an interesting beverage).

Mustard was referred to in the 1550 BCE Ebers Papyrus from Ancient Egypt and was cultivated in Hellenistic and Roman times.

Black mustard seeds from a building layer (probably from a seed store) in the Roman town of Serdica, Bulgaria, date to the second century CE.[44] Black mustard spread from its origin in Asia Minor and the Middle East to become naturalised in Europe.[45] It became more widespread during medieval times (probably because it was a cheaper alternative to more expensive imported spices). Mustard seed was used extensively in Apicius' *De Re Coquinaria*, appearing in sauces for wild boar, spiced hare, and various birds and fish.

The Romans introduced black and white mustard to England. Mustard seed is mentioned in *Leechdoms* and may have been used as food, flavouring and medicine in Anglo-Saxon times.[46] Prepared mustard appears to have been used as a flavouring with bread or other food, likely to have had the same pasty consistency that mustard has today.

Dijon became a centre for prepared mustard in the thirteenth century. The famous Grey Poupon brand was established in 1877 using white wine in its recipe, replacing the vinegar or verjuice that was previously used. Its only ingredients are mustard seeds, wine and water.

Mustard was popular in medieval England. *The Forme of Cury* (1390) has a recipe for Lumbard Mustard:

Take Mustard seed and waishe it & drye it in an ovene, grynde it drye. farse it thurgh a farse [sieve it]. clarifie hony with wyne & vynegur & stere it wel togedrer and make it thikke ynowz. & whan þou wilt spende þerof make it thynne with wyne.[47]

Lumbard Mustard was also used with wine, honey, vinegar and various spices to make a dish of pickled vegetables called 'Compost' in the same book.

Mustard appeared in a few recipes from *The Viandier of Taillevent* – a fourteenth-century cookbook – such as mustard soup and a sauce that combined it with red wine, sugar and cinnamon powder. Others called for it to be used as a condiment.[48]

Clarissa Dickson Wright referred to a wedding party of forty people which needed 2 quarts of mustard, and a fifteenth-century household that consumed 84lb of mustard seed in a year (presumably a very large household).[49] In 1419, Alice de Bryene purchased seed mustard at 1s per bushel. This seems to have been a favourite spice of Dame Alice – the household ate mustard with almost everything and the seed was ground up with vinegar and honey.

In the *Taylors Feast* of 1638 there is a story of three Highlanders visiting England who, while staying at their inn, had for their dinner powdered beef (salted or preserved beef) and mustard, which they hadn't encountered before:

> one of them demanded what the deele [devil] it was? the Host answered, that it was good sawce for their meate; Sawce said the other? it hath an ill looke, I pray let me see yon eat some first; then the Host took a bit of Beefe, and dipt it in the Mustard, & did eate it: the Highland-man presently took his meate and rowl'd it in the Mustard, and began to chaw, but it was so strong, that it was no sooner in his mouth, but it set him a snuffing and neesing, that he told his friends (Ducan and Donald) that hee was slaine with the grey Grewell in the wee-dish; he bid them draw their Whineards, and sticke the false Lowne, (their Host) hee pray'd them to remember his last love to his wife and Barnes, and withall to have a care for the grey grewell, for the Deele was in't. But after the force of the Mustard was spent, the Gentleman left neesing, all was pacified, mine Host was pardon'd, and Mustard was good sawce for powderd Beefe.[50]

In 1720, a Mrs Clements of Durham originated a process to remove the husks from ground mustard seed, to make a smooth finely milled paste, the first of its kind in England (the brand is still marketed today). A more popular English mustard has an origin in the Norfolk fens at the beginning of the nineteenth century, where Jeremiah Colman milled a blend of brown and white mustard seed to create the very strong and distinctively bright yellow Colman's Mustard. East Anglia is still the main area for mustard growing in the UK. Sadly, the Colman's factory in Norwich closed down in 2020, with Unilever, the brand's owner, moving production to Burton-on-Trent and Germany.

Mustard has long been used as a medicine: Pythagoras hailed it as a treatment for scorpion stings; mustard plasters were used to stimulate blood circulation, treat arthritis and rheumatism; it promotes appetite and has been used as a laxative (helping out at both ends, as it were); it has also been used as a treatment for asthma, to induce vomiting and to treat coughs.[51] It is also popular in Ayurvedic and Yunani medicine. John Gerard in his 1597 *Herbal* recommended mustard seed pounded with vinegar as an excellent sauce to be eaten with fish or flesh and mustard was a good remedy for various ailments.[52] Similarly, Nicholas Culpeper waxed lyrical over the virtues of black mustard for a wide variety of bodily systems – blood, stomach, heart, brain, spleen, bowels, mouth, throat, joints, shoulders, hair, skin and various afflictions thereof![53] Victorian households commonly used mustard baths to relieve and prevent cold symptoms, on the theoretical basis that the heat of the mustard would draw blood away from the congested area.[54] Mustard is cultivated in many countries today, including Canada and the USA, Russia, various European countries, Myanmar, India and Nepal.

Horseradish and Wasabi (Brassicaceae)
Horseradish and wasabi are also members of the Brassica family, the former appealing to Western tastes, the latter to the East, most notably Japan. Horseradish (*Armoracia rusticana*) is grown for its large root which has a sharp pungent taste, best eaten fresh for maximum effect. The leaves are also edible but not so commonly used. It seems to be native to eastern Europe, or possibly Russia. Horseradish sauce is a common European condiment, and in the UK is traditionally served with roast beef, among other dishes.

It has also been used since antiquity, for both medicinal and culinary needs. Both Pliny and Dioscorides referred to horseradish as 'wild radish' or 'Armoracia' and observed that it was diuretic and heating.[55]

Local horseradish was known to be used in mid-fourteenth-century Prague.[56] In 1597, John Gerard observed: 'The roote is long and thicke, white of colour, in taste sharpe, and verie much biting the toong like pepper.'[57] It was mainly planted in gardens (in England) but was also found growing wild. He described its common use by the Germans 'for sauce to eat fish with, and such like meates, as we do with mustarde; but this kinde of sauce doth heate the stomacke better, and causeth better digestion than mustard'.

Horseradish was fairly commonplace in eastern Europe and Germany during the fifteenth and sixteenth centuries and started to appear in English recipes during the seventeenth century, sometimes with fish dishes. It appears in recipes for stewed bream and boiled pike with oysters.[58] Its versatility was shown in recipes for stewed calf's head, boiled haunch of venison, boiled pike, stewed bream, soused ram's head, roast mutton, fricassee of chickens, pigeons and rabbits, fried mushrooms, and fried beans.[59] A simple recipe for horseradish sauce appears in 1669 wherein the horseradish is soaked in water, finely grated then mixed with a little vinegar and sugar.[60] Horseradish was also used in a preparation for mustard in the same text – the blend of mustard and grated horseradish root probably originated in medieval times and is known as Tewkesbury mustard. The roast beef and horseradish sauce combination appears to be an eighteenth-century development. Hannah Glasse said of roast beef: 'Take up your meat, and garnish your dish with nothing but horse-raddish.'[61]

Wasabi belongs to the same family but to an entirely different genus – *Eutrema japonicum* – and has the informal name Japanese horseradish. It is used extensively and almost exclusively in Japanese cuisine, where it is one of the most important flavourings. It has been used in Japan since at least medieval times. Its rhizomes are ground into a paste or powder. The taste develops after mixing with water and is sharp and burning, similar to horseradish, but with sweet and fruity notes. Horseradish is often used as a substitute, especially in the West where fresh wasabi is not usually available. Wasabi's main use is as a condiment for sushi, sashimi, tofu, tempura, etc. and other dishes, but wasabi-flavoured snacks are also quite common now in Japan and elsewhere.

Poppy Seed (Papaveraceae)

The poppy, *Papaver somniferum*, is an annual herb famous for three things: its beautiful flowers, its edible seeds, and the source of opium, the latex being obtained from the seed capsules and processed into heroin or other medicinal alkaloids. The seeds themselves have no narcotic effect. The plant is native to the western Mediterranean area but has been introduced across the globe.

Human use of the poppy is truly ancient, and dates back at least to the Bronze Age, and probably the Neolithic. Sumerian clay tablets dating to the third millennium BCE refer to poppies; it is likely that their knowledge was passed to the Babylonians and ultimately the Egyptians and Persians. Poppy seeds and plants are listed in the 1550 BCE Ebers Papyrus and their use to stop the crying of a child was documented ('It acts at once!').[62]

Poppies were a part of ancient Greek mythology, the plants adorning statues of various deities, e.g. Apollo, Demeter, Pluto and Aphrodite.[63] A Minoan terracotta 'poppy goddess' found on Crete dates from around 1400 to 1100 BCE – various aspects of this find may symbolise the use of opium, not least being that she looks like she's in a state of euphoria. The ancient Greeks used capsules, stems and leaves to produce an extract that was used as a soporific drug. Hippocrates used white poppy as part of a pleurisy treatment, fresh poppies in a consumption treatment and poppy in a typhus treatment.[64] Poppy (or hemlock) also appears to have been used as a means of suicide for the weak and elderly in some areas, and possibly euthanasia.

Pliny mentioned the use of white poppy seed mixed with honey served to the ancients and the continuing use of it sprinkled on bread and bound with egg yolk.[65] Pounded white poppy was taken in wine as a soporific.[66] The milky juice of black poppy was obtained via an incision just beneath the corolla and kneaded into lozenges: 'This juice is possessed not only of certain soporific qualities, but, if taken in too large quantities, is productive of sleep unto death even: the name given to it is "opium".'

Celsus observed that 'Sleep is procured by the poppy, lettuce ... mulberries, and leeks'.[67] He noted that bread laid on with poppies (presumably the seeds) helped reduce fever.[68] White poppies were helpful to promote urine; tears of poppy (i.e. opium) were part of a treatment for disorders of the large intestine, an emollient and an antidote.[69] Poppy tears were used as a treatment for pains in the head, and in another recipe, a handful of wild poppies was boiled in water and the liquor mixed with passum (a raisin wine) and boiled together – 'for they both procure sleep'. Poppy tears appear in cough medicines, medicines for eye disorders, to treat ulcers and scars, ear infections and toothache.[70]

Poppy seeds were referred to as a condiment in the *Excerpts of Apicius* by the fifth-century writer Vinidarius. They also appeared quite frequently in the prolific Cardo V sewer deposits at Herculaneum.[71] However, the second- to third-century writer Athenaeus didn't rate poppy very highly as a food:

And Epicharmus also shows us plainly this ... 'The poppy, fennel, and the rough cactus; now one can eat of the other vegetables when dressed with milk, if he bruises them and serves them up with rich sauce, but by themselves they are not worth much.'[72]

Arabs were responsible for disseminating knowledge of opium's medicinal qualities beyond the West and especially to India and China in medieval times.[73] The existence of the poppy plants there probably extends back long before this, and opium poppies may have been cultivated in China by the seventh century CE. In any event, by the beginning of the sixteenth century India was already exporting opium to China. The nineteenth-century Opium Wars were the result of an extension of this trade, with the British East India Company expanding its (illegal) business to the extent that the Chinese had to react.

In 1596, van Linschoten made a very early account of the habit of opium using in India: 'The Indians use much to eat Amfion [opium] ... He that useth to eate it, must eate it daylie, otherwise he dieth.'[74]

In 1653, Nicholas Culpeper noted that the seeds, ground and mixed with barley water, were good for strangury (painful urination), but lacked any of the qualities of opium, of which he says:

Opium has a faint disagreeable smell, and a bitterish, hot, biting taste; taken in proper doses, it procures sleep, and a short respite from pain, but great caution is required in administering it, for it is a very powerful, and, consequently, a very dangerous medicine in unskilful hands. It relaxes the nerves, abates cramps, and spasmodic complaints; but it increases paralytic disorders, and such as proceed from weakness of the nervous system ... An over-dose causes immoderate mirth or stupidity, redness of the face, swelling of the lips, relaxation of the joints, giddiness of the head, deep sleep, accompanied with turbulent dreams and convulsive starting, cold sweats, and frequently death.[75]

After these scary descriptions, Hannah Glasse's cordial poppy water of 1747 sounds very innocuous:

Take two gallons of very good brandy, and a peck of poppies, and put them together in a wide-mouth'd glass, and let them stand forty-eight hours, and then strain the poppies out; take a pound of raisins of the sun, stone them, and an ounce of coriander seed, and an ounce of sweet fennel seeds, and an ounce of liquorice sliced, bruise them all together, and put them into the brandy, with a pound of good powder sugar, and let them stand four or eight weeks, shaking it every day; and then strain it off, and bottle it close up for use.[76]

Turkey is currently the world's largest producer of poppy seed (while Afghanistan is the largest producer of opium). Poppy seeds are widely used in bakeries, confections and as a spice, e.g. in various curries in Indian food, and to provide texture.

Sesame Seed (Pedaliaceae)

Sesame (*Sesamum indicum*) is a flowering annual plant in the mint family native to northern India. It can grow to about 1m tall and has tubular flowers that can be white, purple or blue. The seeds are small (typically around 3×2mm or less), flat and oval, and occur in a grooved capsule up to 8cm long. The phrase 'Open Sesame!' from the *Arabian Nights* was the magical command used to open the cave in *Ali Baba and the Forty Thieves* – it was based on sesame capsules, which contain about seventy seeds, tending to burst open when ripe. The seeds can occur in many colours but are most commonly creamy white. There are many related species, mostly wild. Sesame seeds have a rich nutty and buttery flavour and are commonly used raw or roasted. After roasting they acquire a golden-brown colour and a mild almond-like flavour. Sesame oil is deep brown, aromatic and nutty and is used both as a cooking oil and flavour enhancer. Its domestication on the Indian subcontinent is proven by DNA analysis, and the data confirm the close relationship between *S. indicum* and its progenitor *S. orientale* var. *malabaricum*.[77]

'A quantity of lumped and burnt' sesame was reported from Harappa in the Indus Valley – probably from 2500 to 2000 BCE.[78] Material from Miri Qalat in Baluchistan dates to the same period. There are numerous other archaeological records of sesame across India from the second and first millennia BCE (see page 50).

It is likely that that sesame arrived in Mesopotamia from trade with the Indus Valley Harappa society, possibly before the end of the third millennium BCE.[79] Charred seeds have been found dating from the third millennium BCE in Abu Salabikh, Iraq.[80] John W. Parry reported that according to translations of tablets in the British Museum, Assyrian gods drank a wine of sesame, perhaps making this the earliest mention of a herb on record.[81] There are several references to sesame seed on sixth-century BCE tablets and sesame seed was highly prized throughout Babylonian history – used in cakes, dainties, wine, medicines and oils.

Sesame may have reached Egypt by the second millennium BCE, though evidence is scant. However, there is also a record of sesame (pollen) from Naqada in Egypt, dating from the Predynastic Period.[82] It was certainly cultivated during the Graeco-Roman period.

Theophrastus refers to sesame and its peculiar seed capsule. He noted that the white seeds are sweeter than the dark. Pliny mentions that the Arabian nomadic tribes extracted oil from sesame, 'like the Indians'.[83] He correctly recognised that India was the source of sesame; there were a few useful medicinal qualities, but 'as an aliment it is injurious to the stomach, and imparts a bad odour to the breath'. Galen, too, appeared to disapprove, at least as a food – being of an oily nature it was heavy on the stomach – though it had merits as an emollient (moisturiser) and was warming.[84] Dioscorides recommended for burns, bites inflammations and the like. Medieval Arabian physicians took a similar view to the Greeks.[85]

A curious story about sesame appears in Herodotus' account of how it helped save 300 boys of Corcyra (Corfu) from castration by the tyrannical Periander of Corinth.[86] Periander had abducted these children and sent them to Alyattes to be made eunuchs, but they stopped en route at Samos, whereupon the Samians, on learning the reason for the journey, had the children seek sanctuary in the Temple of Artemis. The Corinthians were unable to enter the temple and so tried to starve them out. But the Samians invented a festival and:

> Each evening, as night closed in, during the whole time that the boys continued there, choirs of youths and virgins were placed about the temple, carrying in their hands cakes made of sesame and honey, in order that the Corcyraean boys might snatch the cakes, and so get enough to live upon.

This went on so long that the Corinthians tired of waiting, gave up and went away, the boys were saved and returned to their families.

Sesame was certainly used by the Romans – the seed was included in Diocletian's Price Edict of 301 CE and it is recorded as a condiment by Vinidarius, but its main use was almost certainly for the oil. Its export from India in the first century CE is inferred by its listing at the west coast port of Kalliena in the *Periplus*. It was likely introduced to Britain by the Romans (as was poppy seed), but archaeological records are rare.

John Gerard (1597) added little to the Greek and Roman medicinal viewpoint but observed that it 'is a stranger in England'. It certainly never seemed to have been popular in medieval Europe, perhaps apart from Moorish Spain.

Sesame is grown in many tropical and subtropical environments, though it can also handle temperate climates; the largest producers are India, Sudan, China and Myanmar. Most of the production is used for culinary purposes and a large part of that is for sesame oil; the remainder is used in baking and confectionary, a few spice mixes, etc.

Spikenard (Caprifoliaceae)

Spikenard is an oil from the flowering plant *Nardostachys jatamansi*, which belongs to the honeysuckle family and is native to the Himalayan region – and now critically endangered. It is commonly abbreviated as 'nard', which derives from the Latin *nardus*. The oil is obtained from crushing the rhizomes and is highly aromatic; consequently, it has been used in making perfumes and incense. It was also used as a flavouring and was very popular in Ancient Rome. Spikenard is listed in the *Periplus* as an export product from Barbarikon, Barygaza, Muziris and Ganges (town of the same name as the river). Its importance can be seen from the Muziris Papyrus, which records the loading of sixty valuable containers of nard to the ship *Hermapollon*. Nard was very important in Jewish religious ritual of the time; this may also have contributed to its high value.[87] Pliny referred to nard as holding 'the principal place among our unguents' and 'its sweet smell, and the taste more particularly, which parches the mouth, and leaves a pleasant flavour behind it'.[88] He quoted the price of leaf nard as 40–75 denarii per lb, while the spike was 100 denarii per lb. It commonly appeared in medicinal compounds, such as in Celsus' *De Medicina*.

Spikenard essential oil is still used in aromatherapy, perfume and incense, and has a pleasant, intense earthy smell.

Star Anise (Schisandraceae)

The wonderful eight-rayed stars of *Illicium verum* are a visual treat, perhaps one of the most exotic of spices. It is the fruit of a medium-sized evergreen tree that is native to south-eastern China and Vietnam. Each of the star's rays (which are carpels, the female part of the flower) contain a single seed; the fruits are fleshy when fresh but become rusty brown and woody on drying. The flavour is also exotic – an intense, very sweet anise taste and aroma, which is due to the high content of anethole, the same compound found in anise, fennel and liquorice.

It has been cultivated in China since around 2000 BCE but only appeared in Europe in the sixteenth century, reputedly seized with other goods from a Spanish ship in the Philippines by Thomas Cavendish in his first voyage of 1587–88 and brought back to London.[89] Nonetheless, it is infrequent in historic European recipes and appears to be something of a rarity. It was added to fruit syrups and conserves.[90]

In Chinese culture it is sometimes chewed after a meal to aid digestion; the fruit is also used to treat colic and rheumatism.[91] It is an ingredient in Chinese Five Spice mix and is commonly used in marinades, stews, roasts, soups and sauces. It is used in Vietnamese cooking (e.g. in beef pho), a few Indian masalas, some Persian recipes and in certain Malaysian and Thai dishes (e.g. curries and soups). Small quantities are typically employed, due to the intense flavour.

Black Limes and Kaffir Limes (Rutaceae)

Black lime, also called loomi, or dried lime, is a powerful spice which reputedly originated in Oman and is extremely popular in the Middle East. The blackened objects don't look very appealing – like rotten or burnt-out husks – and are very lightweight, all the water of the heavy fresh fruit having been driven out by the drying process. But the taste is concentrated and tangy, acid lime with a smoky acrid aroma.

The limes (*Citrus aurantifolia*) are usually prepared by curing in brine and drying in the sun. They can be used whole or sliced/

broken, but normally they are added as a ground ingredient where a souring agent is needed … and you don't need to use much – a little goes a long way.

Limes are native to Southeast and South Asia and were introduced to other parts of the world via trade. The timing of introduction is unclear; citron (*Citrus medica*) was known to Theophrastus and Pliny, and used by Apicius, but limes were probably not brought to the Mediterranean until medieval times, e.g. lime found in medieval deposits at Quseir al-Qadim (the old Roman port of Myos Hormos on the Red Sea) – on a major trade route from the East – was absent from earlier Roman remains.[92]

Dried limes are also a favourite in Persian cuisine ('limoo amani') and have been cultivated there for many centuries – there are two varieties: almost black, and those of a creamy colour, the latter being generally preferred due to their more delicate flavour.[93]

The distinctive knobbly-skinned Kaffir limes and their leaves (*Citrus hystrix*) are used extensively in Southeast Asian cuisine, e.g. in curry pastes, tom yum, tom kha and other soups and sauces. They are also used in perfumes, cosmetics and medicines.

Szechuan Pepper and Sansho Pepper (Rutaceae)
Szechuan pepper (or Fagara) and Sansho pepper are closely related species of the genus *Zanthoxylum* belonging to the Rutaceae family, which also includes limes and other citrus fruits. Zanthoxylum has about 250 species, but the important ones that produce spices are *Z. bungeanum* and *Z. armatum* (Szechuan pepper) and *Z. piperitum* (Sansho pepper). Despite being named 'pepper', they have no relation to black pepper or chilis.

Szechuan pepper is native to Asia, especially China and the Himalayas. The fruits are small red-brown berries. It has sharp, peppery flavour with a strong citrus tang and a characteristic pungency that has a curious mouth-numbing, tingly effect; all the flavour is in the outer berry husk and not in the seeds contained inside.

It has been used in China since ancient times and is one of the key ingredients of the Chinese Five Spice mix, but never caught on in the West. In fourteenth-century China, the painter Ni Zan referred to fagara as one of the frequently used condiments and it also appeared in the cuisine of the Imperial dietician Hu Sihui, though the latter appeared to rate black pepper above fagara.[94]

Used as a spice, it is typically roasted first to release the strongest flavours, and is used whole, crushed or ground in a variety of roasts, barbecues and stir-fries, and particularly in Szechuan cuisine. It is also used as a dry condiment when ground, sometimes mixed with salt.

Sansho pepper, also called Japanese Prickly Ash, is native to Japan and Korea and is used as a condiment and seasoning (it is an ingredient in Japanese Seven Spice blend), but the leaves and shoots are also used in Japanese cooking, garnishing soups, etc. Both Sansho and Szechuan pepper are used in Himalayan cuisine, especially in curries and pickles.

Amchoor (Anacardiaceae) and Mango Achar/Pickle

Amchoor is the Hindi word for dried green mango powder, which is a spice used in Indian cuisine, primarily as a souring agent, similar in effect to tamarind pulp. It is prepared by peeling, slicing and sun-drying before grinding. A pre-1900 recipe for amchoor appears in an anonymous Indian cookery book and involves peeling and quartering green mangoes, sprinkling with salt, then placing under the sun to dry. After beginning to dry they are then rubbed with dried powdered turmeric, chilis and ground ginger, more salt and then further dried until completely desiccated, bottled and stored for use.

Mangifera indica is a tree native to the north-eastern part of the Indian subcontinent (and perhaps also to Southeast Asia) and has been used here since ancient times – it is closely connected with Sanskrit and early Hindu mythology.[95] The thirteenth- to fourteenth-century Indo-Persian writer Amir Khusrau was lavish in his praise of the fruit. In the late sixteenth century, van Linschoten also sang its praises, both as fresh fruit and pickle: 'they have a verie pleasant taste, better than a peach ... they are gathered when they are greene, and conserved.'[96]

Sumac (Anacardiaceae)

Sumac is one of several plant species belonging to the genus *Rhus* of the Anacardiaceae family. It has a wide range in various tropical and temperate settings, but perhaps the most commonly used species is *R. coriaria*, or Sicilian sumac, which is native to southern Europe and western Asia. Its dried fruit is used as a spice, which has a sharp, fruity but sour taste. It also has a long history in tanning and medicine.

Sumac goes back a long way – both Theophrastus and Pliny observed that the fruit reddens like the grape and that it was used to dye white leather; also that it had medicinal uses – Pliny said the leaves, pounded with honey and applied with vinegar, were good for treating bruises, coeliac (intestinal) affections and ulcers of the rectum.[97] A decoction was good for suppuration of the ears.

Dioscorides hailed its efficacy in a wider range of complaints and also recognised it as a food.

Culpeper (1653) said sumac 'seeds dried, reduced to powder and taken in small doses, stop purgings and hemorrhages, the young shoots have great efficacy in strengthening the stomach and bowels, if taken in a strong infusion'.[98]

The ground spice is used as a condiment for salads, meze, stews, meat and rice dishes, for seasoning kebabs, as an ingredient in the Za'atar spice blend, and also used to make refreshing soft drinks. It is most popular in the Middle East, west Asia and parts of North Africa.

Exotic, Rare and Unusual Spices

There are (very approximately) 400,000 known species of plant worldwide. An unknown but significant number of these might provide rare and exotic spices, because someone, somewhere, will have thought of a way to use parts of a plant to season a food, or add colour, aroma, pungency, sweetness, sourness or bitterness, or to make an incense or perfume, or to use as a medicine.

Ginkgo and juniper are unusual – mainly because they belong to the Gymnosperms, a group of non-flowering plants that date back to the Carboniferous period. Ginkgo itself dates from the Jurassic period – it co-existed with the dinosaurs – and its resilience is legendary, which can lead to a very long life; some individual trees are believed to be over 2,500 years old. Junipers are coniferous trees belonging to the Cypress family, with over fifty species assigned to the genus *Juniperus*. The fleshy seed cones (or 'berries') of some species are used as a spice, most notably *J. communis*. The ancient Greeks may have been the first culture to have used juniper berries, both as medicine and then food. The berries have also been found in ancient Egyptian tombs, and in a bowl next to the coffin of an elderly woman at the Tombos archaeological site in Sudan (which spans the mid-18th dynasty to the 25th dynasty Napatan period, or about 1400–300 BCE) – for use in the afterlife as a scent or a spice.[99]

The lesser-known brethren of the major spice families provide quite a few exotics. The ginger family, or Zingiberaceae, is one of the main contributors to aromatic spices, especially from the East, where there is a high diversity of species and it is a good place to start. The genus *Zingiber* includes common ginger, *Z. officinale*, and the 200 or so other species include a few spice candidates. *Zingiber mioga*, or Japanese ginger, is one, but unlike normal ginger, whose rhizome is the useful part, only the flower buds and shoots are used, as a garnish for miso soup among other things. *Z. zerumbet* is another, also known as 'shampoo ginger' – the stunning conical flower heads become red as they mature and juice from the heads is used to condition hair. Besides this, the rhizomes, leaves and shoots are edible, the rhizomes being somewhat bitter. Even the flower heads themselves are sometimes cooked in stews. *Z. montanum* is cultivated in Southeast Asia and India for medicinal use in stomach disorders, and the rhizome is used as a condiment. Beehive ginger (*Z. spectabile*) is another Southeast Asia native with a beautiful flower spike, and its rhizomes are used as a flavouring.

Alpinia is the largest genus in the ginger family with over 240 species, and quite a few obscure spices. Cardamom ginger (*A. calcarata*) has leaves with an earthy flavour that can be used in a similar way to bay leaves. Native ginger (*A. caerulea*) is indigenous to tropical Australia and Papua New Guinea – young rhizome tips have a gingery flavour and the fruit is also edible. Round Chinese cardamom (*A. globosa*, native to East Asia) has seeds which are used as a condiment.[100] Quite a few species have leaves that are used as food wrappings, e.g. *A. eremochlamys*, *A. nutans* ('cardamom leaf ginger' – the leaves smell like cardamom), *A. nigra*, and *A. zerumbet* ('shell ginger').[101] Others are purely medicinal, e.g. *A. rafflesiana*, but more commonly plants have mixed use – *A. nigra* is a good example, which in addition to its leaves being used as wrappings, young shoots, flowers and rhizomes are eaten raw or cooked, and as a seasoning, while also having traditional medicinal uses.[102] Combined uses are also made from *A. conchigera*, *A. siamensis* and *A. malaccenisis*, the latter's rhizome being used as spice and vegetable and the essential oil in medicine.[103]

The genus *Etlingera* has over 100 species, including a few notable ones used as food, spice or medicine. *E. elatior*, or torch ginger, is a large Southeast Asia native which can reach 6m in height and has a large and beautiful red spike inflorescence, which makes it much in demand for ornamental purposes. The young shoots can be used as a substitute for tamarind and as a condiment in curries; the inflorescence stalks and flowers chopped up are used in Malaysian laksa noodle soups; seeds are eaten raw; fruits are added to stews, etc.; flower buds used in Balinese sambal; the seed pods can be used in Indonesian sayur asam.[104] *E. cevuga*, a Pacific Islands native, has leaves which are used to flavour curries.[105]

Curcuma also has over 120 species, the most famous being turmeric, *C. longa*, and zedoary, *C. zedoaria*. Other edible species include the fascinating mango ginger (*C. amada*), whose freshly cut rhizome has the colour and aroma of mango and a rich taste, commonly used in stir-fries and salads in Southeast Asia and in pickles and chutneys in India; black turmeric (*C. caesia*); wild turmeric (*C. aromatica*); Javanese turmeric (*C. zanthorrhiza*); narrow-leaved turmeric (*C. angustifolia*); and at least seven or eight others.[106] The large bulbous rhizomes of *C. comosa* are a herbal medicine, especially for women's problems, among several other medicinal species of *Curcuma*. *Boesenbergia* has almost

100 species but only one well known as a spice – fingerroot or Chinese keys (*B. rotunda*) on account of its multi-lobed rhizome, which is very popular in Southeast Asia and known as 'krachai' in Thai. *Hedychium* has around eighty species and a few edible ones, including *H. gracile*, *H. coronarium* and *H. spicatum*. Yellow ginger (*H. flavescens*) is much loved for its beautiful yellow flowers and is also used as a medicine and in cosmetics. Other important genera include *Kaempferia* and *Globba*, which both include edible spices.

The genera *Amomum*, *Aframomum*, *Elettaria* and *Renealmia* contain species usually harvested for fruits and seeds as opposed to their rhizomes. The genus *Amomum* has over 100 species including numerous spices – examples are round Siam cardamom (from Thailand), bastard cardamom, Nepal cardamom and round cardamom. Many other species have edible fruits, often used in a similar way to cardamom.

Aframomum has around fifty species, including the most famous spice, Grains of Paradise (*A. melegueta*), and as the name suggests have a range in tropical Africa as well as some islands in the Indian Ocean. The pulpy fruits of *A. alboviolaceum* are edible and have a pleasant sharp taste, similar to *A. angustifolium* from Madagascar (aka Madagascar cardamom). African cardamom (*A. danielli*) or alligator pepper, native to West Africa, has seeds and pods which are used as a highly pungent spice and typically added to soups and rice dishes. The fruit pulp of *A. mala* and *A. albiflorum*, which grow in tropical East Africa, is sweet and acid and eaten as a snack, while the seeds are ground and used as a spice. *A. corrorima* is a ginger from Ethiopia and Eritrea that is harvested for its slightly pungent seeds which are ground up and used as a spice and also as a carminative medicine.

Several species of *Renealmia*, a large South American genus, have fruits and/or rhizomes that are used as foods and medicines, e.g. *R. alpinia*, *R. aromatica*, *R. nicolaioides*.

The pepper (Piperaceae) family is another group of global importance, with 3,600 species divided into only two genera: *Piper* and *Peperomia*. Seven of the lesser-known *Piper* spices are covered in the black pepper chapter, but there are plenty of others in both groups; for example, many of the plants in the *Peperomia* genus have edible spicy aromatic leaves.

The coriander or Apiaceae family is similar in terms of species count – some 3,700. In addition to the major ones already discussed, there are many obscure herbs and spices. Examples are bullwort (*Ammi majus*), great pignut (*Bunium bulbocastanum*), lesser burnet (*Pimpinella saxifrage*), shepherd's needle (*Scandix pecten-venerix*) and spignel (*Meum athamanticum*). Ground elder (*Aegopodium podagraria*) and hogweed (*Heracleum sphondylium*) are hardly exotic or rare but are worth adding to the list because of their interesting history and lack of modern-day usage. Ground elder is native to Europe and western Asia and its leaves have been used as a herb since antiquity. John Gerard noted the leaf's similarity to angelica and its seed to dill; also 'the roote is thicke, knottie, and tuberous, of a good savour, and hot or biting upon the toonge'. Its medicinal qualities were powerful – it 'is not only good against all poison, but also singular against all corrupt and naughtie aire and infection of the pestilence, if it be drunken with wine'. Hogweed is native to Europe and parts of north Africa – all parts of the plant are edible – and has been used for centuries. Gerard called this 'cow parsnep', effective as a medicine for jaundice, epilepsy, and 'them that are short-winded', among other complaints. However, it has a number of toxic hazards. Choru, an Indian spice from *Angelica glauca*, is derived from the thick aromatic root which is used as a flavouring – and the oil derived therefrom is valuable in medicine and aromatherapy, possibly too valuable as the plant is now threatened from unsustainable harvesting.[107]

Australia has some real exotics, some of which were originally used by Aboriginal people, but have now become classed as 'bush tucker' – consider wattleseed, the edible seeds from various species of acacia, which are either eaten raw or roasted and then ground. Anise myrtle (*Syzygium anisatum*) is another, a rainforest tree whose aromatic leaves are semblent of aniseed and are used as flavourings or (now more trendily) in herbal teas. The chemical responsible for the scent is anethole, which gives the anise smell in aniseed, fennel and so on. Akudjura is another, the Australian bush tomato (*Solanum centrale*), known for its strong taste which is a mix of fruity bitterness and caramel![108] Be careful with this one as the unripe fruit is poisonous.

South Asian examples include Kokum (*Garcinia indica*), rare in the West, but quite common in India – the red fleshy outer covering of the fruit is used as a souring agent in a similar fashion to tamarind. Garcinia is quite a large genus which includes mangosteen – *G. indica* even looks like mangosteen. Goraka is a similar spice to *G. gummi-gutta* or Malabar tamarind – the rind of the fruit is used as a condiment in curries, etc., in India and Southeast Asia.[109] Another one is Agyajal (from *Eupatorium* sp.), whose young leaves and twigs are used as a spice in Bangladeshi cuisine.[110] Black stone flower or kalpasi (*Parmotrema perlatum*) is really exotic – it is a lichen that develops a mild, woody aroma when added to food and is used in the Goda Masala spice mix of Maharashtra.[111] Kapok buds are similar to capers and are the dried buds of the silk cotton tree (*Ceiba pentandra*) which are typically roasted and ground with other spices in southern Indian cooking. The flavour resembles a mix of mustard and black pepper.

In China, the delightfully named golden needles are dried lily buds (*Hemerocallis fulva*) with a pleasant fruity aroma that have been used in food and medicine for at least 2,000 years.[112]

Roselle, or *Hibiscus sabdariffa*, is native to West Africa and the dried flowers are used in beverages and marinades.[113] When they are soaked in water they release a sweet but tangy juice that is similar to cranberries. It has a variety of culinary uses, e.g. it can be sprinkled into soups or mixed into bread dough; in Senegal the green leaves are used to add flavour to a well-known fish and rice dish called 'thieboudienne'; it is used in India in chutneys. It was introduced to the West Indies in the sixteenth century and to Asia in the seventeenth century. Grains of Selim are the fruits of the evergreen aromatic tree *Xylopia aethiopica*, which is native to tropical Africa. The fruits consist of linear pods containing the seeds and are used as spice and medicine. The seeds are bitter and pungent while the hull is spicy and resinous. They are typically added to soups and stews, ground up or whole.[114]

Numerous exotics are found in Latin America; however, Annatto (*Bixa orellana*) is only exotic to those outside the continent – the orange-red seeds of the achiote tree are used to colour and season food with its sweet peppery and nutty flavour. Epazote (*Dysphania ambrosioides*), an aromatic leafy herb with a pungent flavour and a mint-anise aroma, is used in Mexican cooking or as a condiment, seasoning or herbal tea, or eaten raw.[115] The fruits of rose pepper (*Schinus molle*) from the Peruvian Andes are dense clusters of small round drupes that ripen to a pink or red colour, which have a mildly piquant sweet flavour.[116]

So, of the 400,000 flowering plants currently known, how many can be used as spices in one form or another? Going back to the first chapter, it comes down to definitions: if one assumes the broadest sense including spices and herbs, culinary and medicinal, aromatics and colourants, then a rough estimate may be in excess of 100,000; more specific estimates are an attractive challenge!

10

Spice Mixes:
Medicinal Compounds, Spiritualism and Eroticism

B lends and mixtures of spices and herbs have been around since pre-medieval times for medicinal, culinary, spiritual and erotic purposes. The oldest mixtures are medical preparations, and herbs and spices feature quite significantly in many of them – concoctions, decoctions (a liquor concentrated by boiling down), tinctures (an extract dissolved in alcohol), electuaries (substances mixed with honey), powders, salves, balsams and liniments and the like. It is quite amazing that many of the medical mixtures described by ancient Greek and Roman physicians featured almost unchanged in the first European national pharmacopoeia of the sixteenth and seventeenth centuries. The list of such preparations runs into the hundreds or thousands, but several are noteworthy for their persistence through time as well as their sometimes bizarre compositions. In the first London Pharmacopoeia of 1618 there were 211 preparations with more than ten ingredients, with the most complex one containing 130 substances! One of these was mithridatium (see overleaf), itself containing fifty substances!

Wootton described the four 'officinal capitals' – ancient drugs that persisted in the medical literature for many centuries or millennia.[1]

Mithridatium was a highly complex poison antidote dating to Mithridates VI of the first century BCE Roman Anatolia. It was much sought after through medieval times. The recipe quoted by Wootton has fifty ingredients.

Venice Treacle (the most famous version was made there from medieval times) or 'Theriac' was an ancient Greek concoction also used as a poison antidote. It was invented by the first-century CE Greek physician Andromachus. Galen paid close attention to *Theriaca Andromachi* (and mithridatium) in his books on antidotes.[2] It contained many herbs and spices and – importantly – the flesh of vipers, on the basis that poison itself (or the animal that produced it) would be the best treatment for poison. Dried scorpion could also be used. Like a good wine, theriac was aged for the best effect. In the sixteenth and seventeenth centuries, English apothecaries started to make it themselves, and a 1612 pamphlet mocked the imported product saying it was 'made only of the rotten garble and refuse outcast of all kinds of spices and drugs, hand over head with a little filthy molasses and tarre to worke it up withal'.[3]

Philonium was invented by Philon of Tarsus in the first century CE and was also quoted by Galen. It was a treatment for colic and included saffron, white pepper, euphorbium (a resin), henbane, pyrethrum, spikenard and opium, mixed with honey. It has persisted through history and was present in the first London Pharmocopoeia of the seventeenth century, and remained in English circulation until 1867 (Wootton), its popularity undoubtedly a result of the opium. Later versions included ginger and caraway seeds.

Diascordium was a product of the sixteenth-century Italian physician Hieronymus Frascatorius, who claimed it as a preventative against plague.[4] The original formula contained cinnamon, true scordium, Cretan dittany, bistort galbanum, gum arabic, storax, opium, sorrel seeds, gentian, Armenian bole, sealed earth, long pepper, ginger, clarified honey and canary (plant). It also evolved into a popular household medicine (on account of the opium) and was used to soothe children in the eighteenth century.

Other long-standing medicines include Elixir Proprietatis, which used saffron, aloes, myrrh ... and sulphuric acid! The latter was later (wisely) replaced by vinegar. Saffron, myrrh and aloes were also sometimes used in Balsam of Sulphur, a treatment for coughs and chest complaints, and required sulphur to be boiled with olive oil or walnut oil. According to Wootton, Hiera Picra may have been the oldest medicine still in existence, a purgative dating back to the first century BCE. The earliest recipe included aloes, mastic, saffron, Indian nard, carpobalsamum and asarum; later versions added or substituted cardamom, cinnamon/canella, ginger, long pepper, various herbs and honey, but aloes were the essential constant. Numerous kinds of hiera are listed by Paulus of Aegina.[5] In the *British Medical Journal* correspondence of 1911, a Dr Dimmock observed that 'the common method of taking it is in gin'.[6]

Laudanum is a tincture of opium used as a painkiller that was invented by the Swiss chemist Paracelsus in the sixteenth century.[7] There were some odd constituents: henbane juice, mummy, salts of pearls and corals, the 'bone of the heart of a stag', bezoar stone, amber, musk, unicorn. Later versions variously included the more conventional saffron, cinnamon, nutmeg or cloves.

Bizarre mixtures of ground-up precious stones, metals and spices were particularly popular in ancient pharmacopoeia. Confection of Hyacinth was a powdered zircon-based astringent remedy, which in addition included a truly fantastic mix of sapphires, emeralds, topaz, pearls, silk, gold and silver leaf, musk, ambergris, myrrh, camphor, coral and some vegetables, made into a cordial with syrup of carnations![8] Alchermes is a liquor that had its origins in eighth-century Italy – its bright red colour comes from cochineal and it is comprised of spirits infused with cloves, cinnamon, nutmeg, vanilla and sugar.

Quack Medicines

Quackery is as old as medicine itself but really took off in the eighteenth century. Quackery was a conscious effort to deceive customers into buying false or ineffective medicines as opposed to plain ignorance or erroneous science. The word was derived from an old Dutch word 'quacksalver' or salve-seller. Americans used the term 'snake oil peddlers' for quacks. One such medicine was Baume de Fioraventi (after the seventeenth-century Italian doctor Leonardo Fioraventi), described by Wootton as a tincture of canella, cloves, nutmegs, ginger, other spices, bay berries, with myrrh, aloes and galbanum, etc., along with ⅙ volume of distilled turpentine. It was supposedly good for kidney disorders, rheumatism and improvement of eyesight, but Fioraventi was a notorious quack who also touted his philosopher's stone or universal panacea.

Dutch Drops or Haarlem Oil dates from 1672 and used the residue of distilled turpentine with oils of amber and cloves. It was used as a general preventive of illness. Godfrey's Cordial of the eighteenth century was a similar general health preparation and comprised tincture of opium with sassafras, ginger, caraway, coriander and anise seeds, Venice Treacle and rectified spirits of wine. Warburg's Tincture was an invention of Dr Carl Warburg of Austria in the mid-nineteenth century – his product developed a reputation for the treatment of fevers. The medicine was a tincture of quinine, camphor and aloes, with saffron, zedoary root and angelica. It became popular in India and there may have been some genuine beneficial effect against malarial fevers given the presence of quinine. Warburg made – and then lost – a large fortune from the drug. James Morison was a Scottish merchant who maintained in 1825 that his vegetable pills – best known as Morison's Pills – could alleviate any conditions. They were made of aloes, rhubarb, cream of tartar, gamboge and myrrh and acted as a laxative; Morison made a lot of money from his pills but was also roundly scorned by many contemporaries. Another famous one from around the same time was Gripe Water, a British invention of 1851 to treat babies' teething pains and colic, that is still in use today, in a modified form. It contained sodium bicarbonate, dill seed oil, sugar, water, and alcohol – which was, of course, the reason for its effectiveness (and therefore popularity with parents). The alcohol content was removed in 1992/93. Ginger and fennel were added to some formulae.

'Indian' (i.e. Native American) medicines became very popular in the USA in the late nineteenth century. Indian Medicine Shows were touring circus-like acts that promoted cure-all Indian liniments or Sagwa, often touted as semi-mystical potions used by the Kickapoo tribe. Native Americans were often employed as part of the shows. Snake oils were popular in the same era and the Texan Stanley Clark termed himself 'The Rattlesnake King', supposedly having learned his arts from Native American medicine men. Snake oil persisted for quite some time, but in 1917, analysis of the medicine found it contained light mineral oil, beef fat oil, capsicum, trace of camphor and turpentine, and Stanley was fined for fraudulent misbranding.[9] Other fraudulent snake oils included Virex, Rattlesnake Bill's Oil and Miller's Oil.

Ayurvedic Medicine

Ayurvedism is an ancient Indian traditional medicine that dates back over 2,700 years and is still widely practised today. It is certainly not quackery, though some conventional medical practitioners today might call it 'pseudoscientific', in the sense of it being contrary to Western medical ideas. The billion or so followers would certainly not describe it like that. Ayurvedic medicine uses complex herbal and mineral compounds and correct physical practices to address imbalances in the three elemental *dosas*. A huge list of around 700 plants appears in the eighth-century BCE *Sushruta Samhita*. Important spices and herbs include turmeric, cardamom, cinnamon, fennel seed, black pepper, asafoetida and ginger, though there are many others. Ayurvedism does not only employ herbal remedies – animal products, minerals, metals and various elixirs are also used.

Ancient Herbalism

Plants have been used as medicines for millennia. Yarrow (*Achillea millefolium* L.) may be one of the oldest botanicals used by humans based on its occurrence, together with five other medicinal plants, in a Neanderthal grave at Shanidar (Iraq) that has been dated to 65,000 years old.[10] Yarrow, like many other plants, has certainly had a very long recorded medicinal use in historical times, being mentioned by Dioscorides and Pliny. Another study showed indications of medicinal plant remains in dental calculus from skeletons found at the El Sidron cave in northern Spain, which were from 47,300 to 50,600 years ago. There was evidence of yarrow and camomile in the calculus of one individual, both of which may have been medicinal.[11]

Herbal medicine was quite widespread in Ancient Egypt and herbal remedies are described in ancient papyri, of which the most important are the Edwin Smith Papyrus, Ebers Papyrus, Kahun Gynaecological Papyrus and Hearst Papyrus. Animal and mineral remedies were equally represented. The Kahun Papyrus dates to around 1825 BCE – references are made to unspecified oils and resins as well as plants such as vitex (in the sage family), white mulberry, onion, cowpea, figs, Egyptian balm, myrrh, etc. In the Hearst Papyrus, about half of the 200 ingredients are plant based; these include gourds and gourd seeds, acacia gum, coriander, cumin, anise, cinnamon, garlic, leek, juniper berries, poppy seeds, frankincense and myrrh.[12] Examples of mixtures include fig, mulberry and anise to cure blood in the mouth; date stones, frankincense and juniper berries to drive out a seizure; and dill in wine as a painkiller.

In general, the ancient Egyptians used a lot of garlic, onion, coriander, cumin, leaves from many plants and trees including willow, sycamore, acacia, etc. Mandrake, cedar oil, henna, aloe and frankincense were among imported plant products used in medicinal treatments.[13] By the time of Hippocrates (460–370 BCE) herbal remedies were already very well established in the eastern Mediterranean.

Modern herbalism tends to use the active ingredients as extracts or synthesised compounds rather than the whole plant, but the variety of substances is enormous, ranging into the thousands.

Magic and Spiritualism

Incenses have been an important part of spiritualism and religion since very ancient times and continue to play an important role in most religions today. They involve the burning of aromatic plant materials (usually gums, resins, woods and oils), which then give off a fragrant odour. The oldest incense burners are those of the Indus civilisation (3300–1300 BCE).[14] Ancient Egyptians also burned incense for mystical/funerary purposes, with evidence dating from the fourth millennium BCE. The main incense sources were frankincense from southern Arabia, aloes wood or agar wood from southern Asia, bdellium (a resin from the tree genus *Commiphora* of India and Africa), sweet flag, cinnamon and cassia, labdanum (a resin from the Mediterranean shrubs *Cistus ladanifer* and *Cistus criticus*), myrrh, storax (resin from the tree genus *Liquidambar*), benzoin (resin from the tree genus *Styrax*), spikenard root and sandalwood.

E. G. Cuthbert F. Atchley noted a description of ceremonies at the Temple of Ra Heliopolis around 730 BCE: 'He made great sacrifice on the sandhill there, before the face of Ra at his rising milch-cows, milk, odorous gums, frankincense, and all precious woods delightful for scent.'[15]

Herodotus described an animal sacrifice in contemporary Egypt, wherein the body was filled with bread, honey, raisins, figs, frankincense, myrrh and other aromatics, before burning.[16] Plutarch stated that Egyptians burnt incense at sunrise, noon and sunset, the latter comprising sixteen ingredients, including odoriferous reeds, bitumen and other scented substances.

Incense was also used in elaborate funeral rites as well as embalming, both for preserving and for the more practical issue of countering smells of decay.

The ancient Babylonians used cedar wood, calamus, *rig-gir* (possibly storax) and other substances. They burned incense for sacrifices, purification rites and magic, e.g. to drive away disease-demons. In the story of Prince Saif el Maluk in the *Thousand and One Nights*, aloes wood and ambergris were burned for three days when the prince fell sick. Another story from the same book relates to the Christian priest Afridun, who referred to a holy incense comprised of the dung of the Chief Patriarch mixed with musk and ambergris, supposedly highly valued by the kings of other Christian countries.

Atchley noted that Hindu incense comprises frankincense, two kinds of rosin (solid substance produced by heating resin), sarsaparilla, zedoary, *Cyperus textilis*, and lime tree root.[17] Benzoin and bdellium resins were also used as traditional Indian incense.

The Jewish 'ketoret' incense is believed to have comprised mastic resin, galbanum, frankincense, myrrh, saffron, agarwood, cassia, cinnamon, costus, spikenard, the gasteropod Operculum, plus ambergris and an unknown herb. Widespread usage dates from the second century BCE, though Jewish incense burning started much earlier than this. Ancient Jewish funerary traditions for nobles involved covering the body with aromatics and diverse spices.

Eroticism was also one of the many uses of incense and fragrant aromatics: in Proverbs 7:17 (written in the mid-first millennium BCE) the wanton woman declares that 'I have perfumed my bed with myrrh, aloes, and cinnamon'. Frequent use at banquets and celebrations emphasises the appreciation of fragrant smells and association with pleasure in very early times. In the *Thousand and One Nights* there are many references to women using exquisite combinations of perfumes of sandal, musk, ambergris, aloes wood and myrrh, among others.

In Greek history there is reference to use of perfumed oils in the later books of the eighth-century BCE *Iliad*.[18] Pythagoras (c. 570–495 BCE) is said to have promoted worship of the gods with incense. Sophocles (c. 497–405 BCE) pointed to the wide use of frankincense in *Aedipus Tyrranus*. The *Orphic Hymns* (second or third century BCE, or possibly early Roman Imperial era) employed different incenses to accompany hymns to specific gods. In 243 BCE, Seleucus II sent 10 talents of frankincense, 1 of myrrh, and 2 minae each of cassia, cinnamon and costum to the Anatolian city of Miletus, presumably for use as incense.[19] Incense was used extensively in the Roman Republic and even more frequently in Imperial times, when there was increased access to exotic aromatics. It was used for spiritual offerings as well as showing respect to people of high status.

Spells and magic were all part of the curative prowess of ancient societies. The *Papyri Graecae Magicae* (PGM) are magical texts written between the second century BCE and the fifth century CE in Graeco-Roman Egypt.[20] A spell to acquire a 'supernatural assistant' required the burning of frankincense and rose oil while incanting the spell. Other plants and plant products used in spells were myrrh, myrtle, storax gum, frankincense, sesame seeds, olive oil, figs, dates, pinecones, barley, wheat, dill, purslane, white hellebore, wormwood, bugloss, etc.

An erotic spell employed manna, storax, opium, myrrh, frankincense, saffron and fig, all mixed together and blended with wine. A restraining rite, that would also induce enmity and sickness in the object, used the bitter aromatics myrrh, bdellium, styrax, aloes and thyme (and river mud!) as a consecration of the written spell, which was then to be thrown into the river. A curious contraceptive involved steeping bitter vetch seeds (the number based on the years of protection required) inside the menses of a woman then giving them to a frog to swallow and the frog was then to be released. A seed of henbane steeped in mare's milk and the nasal mucus of a cow mixed with barley was wrapped up in a fawn leather skin and attached as an amulet on an auspicious day – and ear wax from a mule should also be mixed with the barley. On the other hand, for greater sexual prowess and ability to copulate frequently, a drink of ground-up pine cones mixed with sweet wine and two pepper grains should be taken. Or for an erection – coating the penis with ground pepper and honey was recommended.

One of the most famous texts of the PGM is the *Mithras Liturgy*, which may have been compiled in the fourth century CE. The first part shows the ascent of the soul through seven stages and the second part comprises instructions to enact the liturgy, including use of herbs, plants and spices. Plants and products mentioned include lotometra (related to the lotus), myrrh, kentritis, persea tree, rose oil and verbena.

In medieval Europe, numerous herbs were long associated with magic and mysticism: mandrake roots – which often have human-like shapes and are hallucinogenic; sea holly (*Eryngium*) – an aphrodisiac; absinth (*Artemisia absinthium*) – another hallucinogen; henbane (*Hyoscyamus niger*) – a narcotic and anaesthetic; rosemary; common peony – to protect against evil spirits; and catnip.[21]

Sorcery and medicinal magic were severely impacted after the publication of *Malleus Maleficarum* in 1487, which tended to drive the practice underground.

Spices and Herbs as Aphrodisiacs, Love Potions, etc.

Spices have had a use in romantic life almost as long as they have been used in medicine – and the two were often connected. The use of cyclamen roots (Sowbread) in love potions was cited by Theophrastus and Dioscorides, but also commonly prescribed as a pessary by Hippocrates. Theophrastus also noted its use as a pessary for women but added: 'the root is a good charm for inducing rapid delivery and as a love potion.'[22]

Mandrake has also had a long use in eroticism – the Eryngium of Pliny may well be mandrake, of which he said: 'the root of it ... bears a strong resemblance to the organs of either sex; it is but rarely found, but if a root resembling the male organs should happen to fall in the way of a man, it will ensure him woman's love.'[23]

John Gerard (1597) noted the appearance of the root 'resembling the legs of a man, with other parts of his bodie adjoining thereto, as the privie part', but wrote scathingly about the rumours spread by old wives, etc., such as it only growing under gallows 'where the matter that hath fallen from the dead bodie, hath given it the shape of a man … besides many fables of loving matters, too full of scurrilitie to set foorth in print'.[24]

Gerard also dwells on the orchid varieties he named Dog's Stones, for obvious reasons given their two pronounced subspherical roots. He said that, according to Dioscorides, if men ate the fat root it would cause them to father male children, but if women ate the lesser withered root she would produce female children, with the caveat 'These are some Doctors opinions onely'. Other varieties were Fooles Stones, Goates Stones, Satyrion, Foxes Stones, and so on. *Jacobaea vulgaris* (ragwort), aka 'stinking willy' because of the unpleasant smell of its leaves, has also been identified as satyrion, with supposed aphrodisiac qualities.

Shape of plants, then, is clearly a theme that has influenced the choice of aphrodisiacs, a none-too-subtle aid to the greater population. So, carrots have been an obvious one, but also long pepper and chilis. These latter two add heat or pungency, which would also have been easily understood and appreciated.

Other herbs and spices that have been associated with aphrodisiacs at various times include asafoetida, camphor, cannabis, cinnamon, cubeb, frankincense, galangal, ginger, ginseng, liquorice, myrrh, nutmeg, pepper, poppy, saffron, sage, savory, spurge, tamarind, and tarragon, though this is by no means an exhaustive list.

Many spices, including aromatics and incenses, in the ancient world were outrageously expensive and exotic, which would have added to the mysterious charm of the sweet-smelling substances. Myrrh and frankincense were by far the most important in perfumes and incense.

In medieval Arabic medicine the study of aphrodisiacs bloomed. Constantine the African's work (eleventh century CE) was influential – he wrote *De Coitu*, but the ninth-century Ibn al-Jazzar was probably a major influence.[25] Study didn't rely purely on ancient Greek lore – cosmopolitan views and insights were sought from different cultures, including India.

The *Kama Sutra* is an Indian Sanskrit text on sexuality that almost everybody has heard about. It dates from the last centuries BCE to perhaps the third or fourth century CE. Mood enhancers are commonly mentioned: 'When a lover comes to her abode, a courtesan should give him a mixture of betel leaves and betel nut, garlands of flowers, and perfumed ointments.'[26] Numerous methods of 'subjugating women' are detailed, the following being one of the least bizarre: 'If a man, after anointing his lingam [penis] with a mixture of the powders of the white thorn apple, the long pepper, and the black pepper, and honey, engages in sexual union with a woman, he makes her subject to his will.'[27]

Sexual vigour could be increased by numerous methods, including drinking milk mixed with sugar, *Piper chaba*, liquorice, and the root of the uchchata plant. Alternatively, ghee, honey, sugar, and liquorice in equal quantities, the juice of the fennel plant, and milk mixed together was described as 'nectar-like' and would have the same effect.

The *Ananga-ranga* is another Indian book of sexuality from the fifteenth or sixteenth century CE.[28] There are numerous prescriptions for sexual enhancers, including the following to hasten a woman's orgasm: powdered aniseed mixed with honey to be applied to the penis before congress; pounded tamarind fruit mixed with honey and Sindura (red lead, minium, cinnabar, or red sulphuret of mercury!) applied the same way; and black peppercorns, thornapple seed, long pepper and Lodhora bark (?*Symplocos racemosa*), pounded in white honey.[29] Many other recipes were described – to delay the male's orgasm, aphrodisiacs or medicines to increase sexual vigour, others for erectile disfunction, fertility, enlarging women's breasts, cosmetics for hair and skin, etc. Some of the more well-known ingredients included camphor, costus, *Euphorbia*, liquorice, lotus, myrobalan, orris root and sesame. A whole further chapter is devoted to subduing, fascinating or attracting people, with some extremely bizarre potions and charms.

Musk and ambergris also found their way into the never-ending list of aphrodisiacs, both falling into the strange category of animal-derived spices. Musk is an aromatic substance obtained from the caudal gland of the male musk deer (genus *Moschus*), which is native to western and southern Asia. The musk deer bucks spread the secretions on to shrubs in order to attract females. The paste-like material was formerly used extensively by the perfume industry, but also as a flavouring in medieval and later cookery (in a surprisingly large number of recipes). Musk dries into a dark grainy substance and has a wild rankness about it. Musk and ambergris (another unappetising animal-derived product, this time from the digestive system of the sperm whale) were often used interchangeably in cooking. In the seventeenth century, the French commonly paired musk with ambergris in order to scent pastilles, pralines, marzipans, wines and sweet drinks. Ambergris has a faecal smell when freshly expelled but over a long period of time in the sea it evolves to a sweet and complex aroma. In Egypt and North Africa it is stirred into sweet tea for aphrodisiacal use.[30]

Chocolate is a more conventional excitant (cacao should be considered a spice) and its reputation goes back to the Spanish conquest of Mexico. Francisco Hernández was a physician and naturalist to the king who was sent to the New World in 1570 to look for medicinal plants – he came up with a chocolate recipe that contained vanilla, the leaves or flowers of a *Piper* species and the flower of *Cymbopetalum penduliflorum*, which supposedly had stimulating properties.[31] Regardless of the veracity of this (or any other supposed aphrodisiac), chocolate must surely be the most popular of all modern 'love potions'.

Aphrodisiacs of all kinds have been largely discredited by medicine and trivialised since the late 1800s; however, they endure and continue to fascinate.[32]

Table 8| Culinary Spice Mixes

A selection of some well-known culinary spice mixes from around the world. There is a vast and rapidly growing number of mixtures, blends, pastes, sauces, salsas, broths, chutneys and pickles

Region	Name	Ingredients	Comment
India	Curry powder	Typically contains cumin, turmeric, coriander and ground red chili pepper as a base, but with varying amounts of cinnamon, cloves, cardamom, fenugreek, etc. The 'Hobson-Jobson' dictionary of Anglo-Indian terms of 1886 described curry as 'meat, fish, fruit or vegetables, cooked with a quantity of bruised spices and turmeric'. Chili is an important ingredient, but only became available in India from the early sixteenth century. Cloves are also non-native.	A generic spice mix with widespread European usage dating to colonial era. 'Curry' evolved into a term for any savoury dish with a spicy thick sauce. Hannah Glasse (eighteenth century) gave a recipe 'to make a currey the Indian way'. Indian use of curries originated thousands of years ago (e.g. Megasthenes' description from the fourth century BCE).
North India	Chaat masala[1]	Amchoor (dried mango powder), cumin, coriander, ajowan, ginger, pepper, salt, asafoetida and chili powder.	Added as a garnish to savoury fried snacks (chaat), fruit salads, potatoes and other foods. Sweet, hot and tangy.
North India	Garam masala	Cumin, black and white pepper, cloves, cinnamon, cardamom, mace, coriander, fennel, bay leaves, +/- red chili powder, with many variations. Chili, cloves and mace are non-native and so earlier versions would have been less pungent.	Pungent mix to cope with the cooler climate of the north. Usually ground, often toasted before grinding. Nutmeg, mace and cloves likely used in India from early centuries CE.
North India	Murgh masala	Variations of cumin, coriander, turmeric, ginger, cardamom, cinnamon, curry leaves, pepper, fennel, mace, cloves, pepper, star anise and mustard seeds. Garam masala can be substituted for some of the spices as required.	This is normally used to cook marinated chicken. Turmeric and ginger were used as food flavourings in the Indus Valley as far back as the third millennium BCE.

1 'Masala' means mixture of spices. It is difficult to pinpoint the origin of many of these (there are a lot), though the ingredients have been used in various combinations for hundreds (or even thousands) of years and recorded in Sanskrit texts such as the eleventh-century *Lokopakara* and the twelfth-century *Manasollasa of King Somesvara* and others.

Punjab (North India and Pakistan)	Tandoori masala	Garam masala, ginger, cayenne pepper, garlic and onion, +/- mace, turmeric, coriander seeds, red food colouring.	The meat is usually basted with the masala and yoghurt before cooking in the tandoor. It imparts a characteristic pinkish colour to the meat (usually chicken). Kundan Lal Gujral developed the modern tandoori blend and technique for cooking meat in Peshawar in the 1920s and imported it to India.
Kashmir (North India and Pakistan)	Kashmiri ver (or veri) masala	Dry-roasted whole cumin, coriander, fennel seeds, black pepper, ground ginger, nutmeg, cinnamon, cloves, cardamom, bay leaves, garlic powder and dried red chili, all then ground to a fine powder.	Some versions are made into patties by the addition of a little vegetable oil and then kneaded to shape, leaving a hole in the middle, and then left to dry. Pieces are then broken off for use as needed.
Bengal (India and Bangladesh)	Panch phoron	Whole cumin, fenugreek, nigella, black mustard and fennel seeds in equal proportions.	Often used whole, commonly dry-roasted or fried before use.
Maharashtra (Central India)	Kaala masala	Cumin and coriander seeds, cinnamon, cloves, cardamom, chili, sesame seeds, kalpasi (black stone flower) and coconut.	Dark and pungent.
Karnataka (South India)	Saaru podi/ Rasam powder	Dried red chilis, fenugreek seeds, black pepper, coriander seeds cumin seeds, black mustard seeds, curry leaves and asafoetida.	Ingredients are roasted separately, then ground to a powder. Tamarind pulp is usually added to Saaru curries.
Karnataka (South India)	Vaangi bhath masala powder	Dried red chili, chana dal, urad dal, fenugreek, coriander and poppy seeds, cinnamon, cardamom, cloves and dried coconut, roasted and then ground to a fine powder.	Typically used with an eggplant rice dish.
Karnataka (South India)	Bisi bele bhath powder	As above, with kapok buds.	
Kerala (South India)	Kerala masala	Rice and coconut flakes lightly roasted in vegetable oil, then ground up; then dry roasted pepper, coriander and fenugreek seeds are ground to a powder and mixed with the rice and coconut. These are then mixed with curry powder, ground turmeric, paprika, cayenne and cinnamon.	Typically used with seafood dishes. Van Linschoten (1596) noted of Indian seafood: 'Most of their fish is eaten with rice, that they seeth in broth ... and is somewhat sowre ... but it tasteth well, and is called Carriil.'
Hyderabad (South India)	Potli ka masala	Sandalwood powder, vetiver (khus) root, dried rose petals, cassia buds, cinnamon, coriander seeds, galanga, bay leaf, black cardamom, kapoor kachli (spiked ginger lily), star anise and lichen.	Often used in mild biryanis.

Hyderabad (South India)	Tadka	Cumin and mustard seeds fried in oil or ghee with subsequent addition of fresh chilis, curry leaves, coriander, garlic, powdered turmeric, tomato and onion.	Often used to temper dals or as a finishing touch to curries.
India	Indian pickles (achar)	There are a huge variety of pickles, e.g. mango, mango and ginger, red chili, green chili, madras onions, ginger and tamarind, lime. Chili is generally used and many are very hot.	Van Linschoten observed that pepper was often used for heat in pickles before chilis became widespread, and that mangoes were preserved in sugar, vinegar, oil or salt and could be stuffed with green ginger, garlic or mustard.
Indonesia	Bumbu	Commonly combinations of black pepper, chili powder, turmeric, galangal, ginger, nutmeg, coriander, garlic, plus other spices.	Generic term for dry mixes and pastes.
Indonesia	Sambal	Chilis, tamarind, shallots, brown sugar, lime juice, shrimp paste (terasi).	There are many different varieties, both cooked and raw. Before the widespread use of chili, early hot sauce may have been made using Javanese long pepper.
Malaysia	Sambal belacan	Similar to sambal terasi.	
Philippines	Balado	Stir-fried chili, garlic, shallot and tomato.	
Thailand	Nam prik	Variety of spices but usually includes chilis, garlic and shallots, salt or nam pla (fish sauce); shrimp paste is a common addition.	Many different varieties, often used as dipping sauces.
Thailand	Prik kaeng	Chili, shrimp paste, various spices.	It is a curry paste used in cooking, with many different varieties.
China	Five Spice	Ground Szechuan pepper, cloves, cinnamon/cassia, star anise and fennel seeds.	Used as a seasoning, spice rub and in marinades. Possibly originated as a medicine.
China	Hoisin sauce	Five Spice, soya beans, wheat, sugar, vinegar.	Has a characteristic sweet, tangy flavour.
Japan	Schichimi (Seven Spice)	Sansho (a relative of fagara), chilis, dried and grated orange/ tangerine peel, dried nori/ seaweed flakes, black and white sesame seeds, white poppy seeds.	Ancient blend used to season noodles and soups
Japan	Miso	Soya beans, grains, koji fungus, salt.	A fermented bean paste with ancient origins.
Korea	Toenjang	Soya bean and brine.	

Korea	Gochujang	chili powder, sticky rice, fermented soya bean (meju), barley malt, salt +/- others, all ground and then combined into a red coloured paste	Spicy fermented bean paste.
Middle East	Za'atar	Sesame seeds, sumac, thyme, marjoram, oregano, salt, +/- cumin, coriander, caraway, fennel.	An ancient spice blend used mainly as a condiment but also as a seasoning.
Middle East	Baharat	Black pepper, cardamom, cinnamon/cassia, coriander, cumin, nutmeg, cloves, turmeric and paprika. Local variations use other spices.	
Middle East	Tahini	A creamy paste made from roasted hulled sesame seeds, oil and salt.	An important ingredient of hummus, also used as a dip itself. Tahini-like pastes are probably very old; a recipe appeared in a thirteenth-century Arabic cookbook.
Iran	Advieh	Cumin, cloves, rose petals, cinnamon, cardamom and turmeric.	Analogous to Indian garam masala.
Yemen	Hawaij	Cumin, pepper, turmeric and cardamom.	Used in soups and stews.
Yemen	Hilbeh	Ground fenugreek seeds mixed into a pale green paste with garlic, green chilis, tomatoes, olive oil and lemon juice.	A dipping condiment. Fenugreek has been cultivated for thousands of years.
North Africa	Berbere	Coriander, cumin, ajowan, basil, ginger, black pepper, cardamom, koraima (false cardamom), cloves, cinnamon, fenugreek, chili or paprika and allspice.	A seasoning. Probably ancient, but chili and allspice only available since the sixteenth century.
Morocco	Ras el hanout	Turmeric, saffron, ginger, pepper, cardamom, nutmeg, mace, allspice and salt +/- other exotic spices.	A seasoning.
Maghreb	Harissa	Pounded red chilis, ground coriander, caraway and cumin seeds, garlic and olive oil, sometimes with mint, olives and lemon juice.	Seasoning and condiment. The coastal town of Nabeul has been famous for its harissa since the sixteenth century, when the Spanish introduced chili during their brief occupation.
Egypt	Dukkah	Crushed nuts, pepper, salt, cumin, coriander, sesame and herbs.	The seeds are toasted before crushing; it is normally used as a condiment.

France	Fines herbes	Parsley, chervil, chives and tarragon.	
France	Herbes de Provence	Thyme, rosemary, marjoram, basil, oregano and (sometimes) lavender.	
France	Persillade	Chopped parsley and garlic, sometimes with oil and vinegar.	Added at the end of cooking.
France	Bouquet garni	Typical herbs are parsley, thyme, rosemary, basil, chervil, tarragon, savory, celery, etc.	Herbs tied with string, which are then immersed in stews, soups, casseroles during cooking.
France	Quatre épices	Pepper, cloves, nutmeg and ginger.	Ancient seasoning blend with similarities to French medieval 'poudre fort'.
France	Vadouvan	Cumin, mustard and fenugreek seeds, chopped garlic, onion or shallots, turmeric, curry leaves and salt; oil to form the mix into balls.	Derived from French colonial India (enclaves established from seventeenth century).
France	Tapenade	Caper and olive paste mixed with olive oil; garlic, anchovies, herbs commonly added.	Dip or spread on bread. It has ancient origins: Columella (first century CE) wrote about 'Olivarum conditurae' – mashed ripe olives mixed with spices and salt.
Mediterranean	Seasoned salts	Celery salt, garlic salt, onion salt, Beau Monde seasoning.	
Italy	Pesto	Crushed garlic, basil, pine nuts, salt and Parmesan with olive oil.	Similar to the 'moretum' of Ancient Rome.
Italy	Gremolata	Chopped parsley, garlic and lemon zest.	
Spain (Catalonia)	Romesco	Dried red Romesco chilis, roasted tomatoes, garlic, onions, roasted almonds or hazelnuts, olive oil and salt +/- vinegar, herbs.	Sauce – tomatoes, onion, garlic are roasted in olive oil with boiled chilis, then all pureed.
Spain	Adobo	Paprika, oregano, garlic, salt, vinegar.	Sauce used as marinade or seasoning.
North America	Creole seasoning	A dry mix of paprika, cayenne, pepper, salt, garlic powder, oregano and thyme.	Of New Orleans origin.
North America	Old Bay Seasoning	Paprika, celery salt, crushed red pepper, black pepper, mustard, cardamom, ginger, cloves and bay leaves.	Baltimore origin. Used mainly as a seafood seasoning.

Jamaica	Jerk seasoning	Scotch bonnet chilis, allspice, cloves, nutmeg, spring onions, garlic powder, thyme, brown sugar and salt.	Dry mix but can be made into paste. Developed by fugitive African slaves who fled into the Jamaican bush in the seventeenth century, although nutmeg and cloves are presumably a later addition.
Central America	Recado	Chilis, black pepper, allspice, annatto, cumin, garlic, onions and herbs like coriander and oregano.	Achiote (annatto) pastes probably date from pre-Columbian times.
Argentina	Chimichurri	Paprika, red bell pepper, parsley, garlic, salt, pepper, cumin, sumac, oregano, dried tomato, lemon zest, vinegar and olive oil.	Used to marinate and season meats.
Bolivia	Llajua sauce	Locoto chili (*Capsicum pubescens*), tomatoes, onions and Bolivian coriander.	
Chile	Pebre sauce	Chopped hot ají chilis, coriander, onion, garlic, tomatoes, olive oil.	A dipping condiment.
Colombia	Hogao	Tomato, onion, garlic, coriander mix.	A condiment and seasoning.
Mexico	Salsa verde	Green chilis, tomatillos, garlic.	
Peru	Salsa de ají	Chopped ají limo chilis, sweet yellow chilis, onion, tomatoes, coriander, lemon juice, vinegar.	A hot sauce.

Epilogue

The Influence of Spice on Global Cuisine

Spices have played a huge part in global history and commerce, and it seems reasonable to conclude that they have played a large role in shaping the cuisine of regions and countries. The influences on regional cuisines are extremely varied – availability of ingredients, accessibility to trade, religion, tradition, climate, geography, history, foreign influence/colonialism/conquest and a hundred other factors – but when we try to think what defines Indian food, or Middle Eastern food, or Thai food, for example, then spices surely play a major role. But we need to be more specific and look at this in more detail.

Spices play an important part of defining a cuisine, but they are not the only determinant. The large list of flavouring groups includes herbs, fruits, vegetables, dairy products, flowers, meat, fish, etc. Furthermore, some cuisines employ few or no spices, e.g. Scandinavian and north European, and might be considered bland to some palates, but this is not the same as lacking in flavour, which can be derived from other ingredients. The emerging discipline of 'computational gastronomy' looks at large amounts of data from recipes of various cuisines.[1]

A qualitative attempt to show the prevalence of a broad range of spices and herbs across a range of national cuisines was attempted, though it appears from the outset to be fraught with problems and inconsistencies – national cuisines per se rarely exist other than in a few highly publicised specialist dishes; regional cuisines are more typical, which often or usually don't follow political boundaries; globalisation has blurred lines in the twenty-first century to the extent that foreign foods are often as much appreciated as indigenous ones; spice import data can be misleading, as products are often re-exported; 'exotic' ingredients are available almost anywhere; spice products such as dried, ground, oleoresin or essential oils are often used in medicinal, cosmetic, colouring and food-processing industries in addition to culinary usage; data sources may be unreliable. It is also just a snapshot – it would have been different 100 years ago, vastly different 500 years ago, and 50 years in the future it will be different again.

And yet, despite these and other caveats, patterns do emerge. Asian cuisines show the broadest array of spices and herbs of anywhere in the world. Europe is still dominated by the use of 'herby' flavours, particularly those from the coriander and mint families. The Middle East and North Africa also use a broad range of spices, reflecting more than 2,000 years of interaction with the Indian subcontinent and beyond. Their use is more or less intermediate between Europe and Asia, with plenty of 'Med' herbs and a good variety of Asian spices.

With regard to individual spices, black pepper and garlic are virtually ubiquitous: everybody uses them, everywhere. Chili too, in one form or another, is used almost everywhere, though the intensity of use – and heat – varies dramatically: hot food is still associated with India, the Far East and Latin America. Cinnamon and nutmeg are used widely, though apart from inclusion in popular blends such as various Indian masalas, Baharat, Berbere, Chinese Five Spice and Indonesian bumbus, etc., mainly in sweet dishes. Vanilla, the world's most popular flavour, is also used mainly, but not exclusively, in sweet dishes. Parsley, thyme and oregano are much used, though are relatively uncommon in Asia.

Many spices which were associated with specific geographic regions, around their native locales, are now cultivated in similar climate zones across the world. Examples are nutmeg/mace, cloves, ginger, turmeric, pepper and chilis. Black pepper, originally only produced in south-west India, is grown across South and Southeast Asia, as well as in Central America and Brazil. Cardamom, also native to India, is now grown in Guatemala, Tanzania, El Salvador, Southeast Asia and Papua New Guinea. Ginger and turmeric are other natives of India now cultivated across many tropical regions.

Cloves, native to the Banda Islands of eastern Indonesia, are today produced all over Indonesia as well as in Zanzibar, Madagascar, the Indian subcontinent, Malaysia, China, Brazil, the Caribbean and even Turkey, but the largest user is still Indonesia for flavouring their kretek cigarettes. As with many aromatic spices, the essential oil and oleoresin have widespread uses in sauces, pickles, etc. Coriander, native to the Mediterranean and Middle East, is now produced and consumed globally, with India being the largest producer. India is also the largest producer of cumin, a spice with a similar origin to coriander, now produced and used globally, but especially in India and the Middle East. Parsley is native to the eastern Mediterranean and now has global appeal, though it is not very popular in Asian cuisines. Nonetheless, the greater Mediterranean region is still one of the main areas of cultivation of culinary herbs. Globalisation takes many forms – oregano became a worldwide hit post-Second World War in parallel with increased consumption of pizza![2]

The changing patterns of food and spice use have been driven by mass movement of peoples throughout history, either in peace or in wartime. Examples include Bronze Age Indo-European movements, and the Crusaders returning from their wars in the Middle Ages, bringing home new tastes and stimulating a new demand for spices throughout Europe. The USA and Canada host large immigrant populations (around 40 million in 2020) with the most dominant ethnic types in recent years being Asians and Latin Americans (especially Mexicans); these have had and will continue to have influence on culinary trends in the USA, particularly on demand for spices, given their diverse use of spices and herbs. Spices formerly considered exotic are increasingly regarded as mainstream in many cuisines today – this is not just an American experience. Diaspora from China and the Indian subcontinent have popularised Asian cuisine all over the world via restaurants and Asian supermarkets. The ease of international travel, a trend that exploded in the 1960s with the advent of efficient commercial air transport, has also played a large role in providing access to foreign cultures and cuisines. Air freight, refrigeration and advanced logistics systems have also enabled mass transport of exotic herbs and spices on previously unattainable scales.

So where does all this leave us? Spices have never been more available nor more widely used than they are currently. But we can still see the history of ancient cuisines resonating in the foods of today: Asian cuisine has been defined by the spices native to Asia, especially by the gingers, peppers, laurels and myrtles native to that region. Chili, the American latecomer, increased the pungency still further. European food has been dominated by the herbs and milder spices locally available, spiced up since the Middle Ages by exotic imports from the East. The Middle East, Western Asia and North African cuisines all reflect millennia of trade with India and Southeast Asia but retain the core spices that were available during the birth of civilisation in the Fertile Crescent. The New World countries largely reflect the preferences of the diaspora that have settled there over the last few centuries. Despite the effects of globalisation, regional cuisines remain largely intact. Thai food is still Thai food, the many varieties of Indian, Chinese and Latino foods are unmistakable; Italian and French foods are loved across the world because they are exceptional and unique. The spices and herbs that flavour these cuisines are still mainly those that were available locally during ancient times. The globalisation referred to frequently in this chapter didn't just happen in the late twentieth century, but from continuous trade and successive periods of conquest and migration stretching back thousands of years. The spices and herbs available to the Romans (as seen in the work of Apicius) are astounding even by today's standards, including many Eastern exotics, even though the consumers had no idea where most of them came from. Trade routes were already sophisticated 2,000 years ago and Eastern spices were reaching the Mediterranean 1,000 years before that.

Notes

Introduction

1   M. Van Der Veen in K. B. Metheny & M. C. Beaudry (eds), 2015, *Archaeology of Food: An Encyclopedia*, Rowman & Littlefield.
2   K. Lewis in *Archaeology of Food*.
3   G. Milton, 1999, *Nathaniel's Nutmeg*, Hodder & Stoughton.
4   J.-P. Reduron, 2021, 'Taxonomy, origin and importance of the Apiaceae family' in E. Geoffriau & P. W. Simon (eds), 2021, *Carrots and Related Apiaceae Crops*, CABI Publishing.
5   W. J. Kress & C. D. Specht, 2006, 'The evolutionary and biogeographic origin and diversification of the tropical monocot Order Zingiberales', *Aliso*, vol. 22 pp. 621–32.
6   D. J. Harris et al., 2000, 'Rapid radiation in *Aframomum* (*Zingiberaceae*): evidence from nuclear ribosomal DNA internal transcribed spacer (ITS) sequences', *Edinburgh Journal of Botany*, vol. 57, issue 3 pp. 377–95.
7   J. F. Smith et al., 2008, 'Placing the origin of two species-rich genera in the Late Cretaceous with later species divergence in the Tertiary: a phylogenetic, biogeographic and molecular dating analysis of *Piper* and *Peperomia* (Piperaceae)', *Plant Systematics and Evolution*, vol. 275.

Chapter 1

1   C. P. Bryan, 1930, *The Papyrus Ebers*, G. Bles, London.
2   Kaviraj Kunja Lal Bishagratna (ed.), 1907, *An English translation of the 'Sushruta Samhita' based on original Sanskrit text*, Calcutta.
3   K. M. Balapure, J. K. Maheshwari & R. K. Tandon, 1987, 'Plants of Ramayana', *Ancient Science of Life*, vol. 7, 2; M. Amirthalingam, 2013, 'Plant diversity in the Valmiki Ramayana', *IJEK*, 2, 1.

4 W. H. S. Jones (translator), 1957, *Hippocrates*, Loeb Classical Library
   vol. 1, Introduction, William Heinemann Ltd, London.
5 Hippocrates, *Epidemics* VI, 5, 1.
6 Hippocrates, *Regimen in Acute Diseases*, XXIII.
7 Hippocrates, *Epidemics* II, 5, 22.
8 Ibid. 6, 7.
9 Ibid. 6, 29.
10 Hippocrates, *Epidemics* VII, 2.
11 Ibid. 6.
12 Ibid. 64.
13 Ibid. 118.
14 L. M. V. Totelin, 2006, 'Hippocratic recipes: oral and written
   transmission of pharmacological knowledge in fifth- and fourth-century
   Greece', Doctoral thesis, University of London.
15 Hippocrates, *Epidemics* I, 11.
16 A. Hort, 1916, Theophrastus, *Enquiry into Plants*, English Translation,
   vol. I, Introduction, William Heinemann Ltd, London.
17 Ibid. vol II, Book IX, 5.
18 Ibid.
19 J. W. McCrindle, 1877, *Ancient India as Described by Megasthenes and
   Arrian*, Trubner.
20 Strabo, *c.* 18 CE, *Geographica*, XV, 1.57.
21 Athenaeus, *The Deipnosophists, or Banquet of the Learned of Athenæus*
   IV, 39, C. D. Yonge (translator), 1854, H. G. Bohn, London.
22 Strabo, *c.* 18 CE, *Geographica*, XV, 1, 58–60; W. Falconer (translator),
   1857, *The Geography of Strabo*, vol. 3, H. G. Bohn, London.
23 Pliny, *Natural History*, VI, 21.
24 H. L. Jones (translator), 1917, *The Geography of Strabo*, vol. 1,
   Introduction, William Heinemann Ltd, London.
25 Strabo, *c.* 18 CE, *Geographica*, I, 2.1; H. C. Hamilton (translator), *The
   Geography of Strabo*, vol. 1, H. G. Bohn, London.
26 Strabo, c. 18 CE, *Geographica*, II, 5.12.
27 Celsus, *De Medicina*, II, 27, J. Greive (translator), 1814, Edinburgh;
   Ibid. II, 31.
28 Pliny, *Natural History*, XXV, 5.
29 E. H. Bunbury, 1883, *A history of ancient geography among the Greeks
   and Romans, from the earliest ages till the fall of the Roman Empire*,
   John Murray, London.
30 H. B. Ash (translator), 1960, *Lucius Junius Moderatus Columella on
   Agriculture*, vol. 1, Introduction, William Heinemann, London.
31 J. Bostock & H. T. Riley (translators), 1855, *The Natural History of
   Pliny*, vol. 1, Introduction, H. G. Bohn, London.
32 J. M. Riddle, 1980, *Dioscorides, Catalogus Translationum et
   Commentariorum*, IV, 1–143 Catholic University of America Press.

33 T. A. Osbaldeston & R. P. A. Wood, 2000, Dioscorides, *De Materia Medica*, a new indexed version in modern English, Ibidis.
34 *The Greek Herbal of Dioscorides ... Englished by John Goodyer A. D. 1655*, edited and first printed by R. T. Gunter (1933), Hafner, London and New York.
35 Ibid.
36 J. W. McCrindle, 1885, *Ancient India as Described by Ptolemy*, Trubner.
37 I. Tupikova, 2013, in *Proceedings of the 26th International Cartographic Conference*, Dresden.
38 E. Capps, T. E. Page & W. H. D. House (eds), 1916, Galen, *On the Natural Faculties*, Introduction, W. Heinemann.
39 P. Holmes, 2002, 'Galen of Pergamon: A Sketch of an Original Eclectic and Integrative Practitioner, and His System of Medicine', *Journal of the American Herbalists Guild*.
40 J. W. McCrindle, 1897, *The Christian Topography of Cosmas, an Egyptian Monk*, Hakluyt Society.
41 F. Adams (translator), 1844, *The Seven Books of Paulus Aegineta*, The Sydenham Society, London.
42 C. A. Y. Breslin, 1986, 'Abu Hanifah Al-Dinawari's Book of Plants, an annotated English translation of the extant alphabetical portion', thesis, University of Arizona.
43 P. D. Buell & E. N. Anderson, 2010, *A Soup for the Qan: Chinese dietary medicine of the Mongol eras seen in Hu Sihui's Yinshan Zhengyao*, Brill.
44 F. Sabban, 1985, 'Court cuisine in fourteenth-century imperial China: Some culinary aspects of Hu Sihui's Yinshan Zhengyao', *Food and Foodways: Explorations in the History and Culture of Human Nourishment*, 1:1–2, 161–196, DOI: 10.1080/07409710.1985.9961883.
45 Rembert Dodoens, 1552, *De frugum historia*, Joannis Loëi; Rembert Dodoens, 1554, *Cruydeboeck*, Jan van der Loë.
46 H. Lyte (translator), 1578, *A niewe Herball or Historie of Plantes*, Gerard Dewes, London.
47 J. Gerard, 1597, *The Herball, or Generall Historie of Plantes*, John Norton, London.
48 N. Culpeper, 1653, Angelica, *Complete Herbal*.
49 C. Linnaeus, 1735, *System Naturae sive regna tria naturæ systematice proposita per classes, ordines, genera, & species*, Lugduni Batavorum, Theodorum Haak.

Chapter 2

1 N. Boivin et al., 2015, 'Old World globalization and food exchanges', in *Archaeology of Food*, K. B. Metheny & M. C. Beaudry (eds).
2 C. Brombacher, 1997, 'Archaeobotanical investigations of Late Neolithic lakeshore settlements (Lake Biel, Switzerland)', *Vegetation History and Archaeobotany*, 6.

3   N. Boivin & D. Fuller, 2009, 'Shell Middens, Ships and Seeds: Exploring Coastal Subsistence, Maritime Trade and the Dispersal of Domesticates in and Around the Ancient Arabian Peninsula', *Journal of World Prehistory*, 22.

4   D. Bedigian & J. R. Harlan, 1986, 'Evidence for cultivation of sesame in the ancient world', *Economic Botany*, 40.

5   D. Q. Fuller, 2003, 'Further evidence on the prehistory of sesame', *Asian Agri-History*, vol. 7, 2.

6   V. Zech-Matterne et al., 2015, '*Sesamum indicum* L. (sesame) in 2nd century BC Pompeii, southwest Italy, and a review of early sesame finds in Asia and Europe', *Vegetation History and Archaeobotany*, 24.

7   E. Tsafou & J. J. Garcia-Granero, 2021, 'Beyond staple crops: exploring the use of "invisible" plant ingredients in Minoan cuisine through starch grain analysis on ceramic vessels', *Archaeological and Anthropological Sciences*, 13, 8.

8   E. S. Marcus, 2007, 'Amenemhet II and the sea: maritime aspects of the Mit Rahina (Memphis) inscription', *Egypt and the Levant*, vol. XVII.

9   F. Rosengarten Jr, 1969, *The Book of Spices*, pp.23–96, Jove Publ., Inc., New York.

10 G. Buccellati & M. Kelly-Buccellati, 1978, 'The Terqa Archaeological Project: First Preliminary Report', *Les Annales Archeologiques Arabes Syriennes*, pp. 27–8.

11 M. L. Smith, 2019, 'The Terqa Cloves and the Archaeology of Aroma' in S. Alentini & G. Guarducci (eds), *Between Syria and the Highlands. Studies in Honor of Giorgio Buccellati and Marilyn Kelly-Buccellati, Studies on the Ancient Near East and the Mediterranean* (SANEM 3), Arbor Sapientiae Editore, Roma.

12 A. B. Edwards, 1891, *Pharaohs Fellahs and Explorers*, Harper & Bros, New York.

13 F. D. P. Wicker, 1998, 'The Road to Punt', *The Geographical Journal*, vol. 164, 2.

14 J. Turner, 2004, *Spice: The History of a Temptation*, HarperCollins.

15 E. Naville & H. R. Hall, 1913, 'The XIth Dynasty Temple at Deir El-Bahari Part III', 32nd Memoir of the Egypt Exploration Fund, London.

16 J. Innes Miller, 1969, *The spice trade of the Roman Empire 29 BC to AD 641*, Oxford University Press.

17 A. Scott et al., 2020, 'Exotic foods reveal contact between South Asia and the Near East during the second millennium BCE', www.pnas.org/cgi/doi/10.1073/pnas.2014956117.

18 C. L. Glenister, 2008, 'Profiling Punt: using trade relations to locate "God's Land"', M.Phil. thesis, University of Stellenbosch.

19 C. Pulak, 2008, 'The Uluburun shipwreck and Late Bronze Age trade' in *Beyond Babylon: Art, Trade, and Diplomacy in the Second Millennium BC*, Metropolitan Museum of Art.

20 A. Plu, 1985, 'Bois et graines' in L. Balout & C. Roubet (eds), *La momie de Ramsès II: Contribution scientifique à l'égyptologie*, pp. 166–74, Éditions Recherches sur les Civilisations, Paris.

21 H. Hjelmqvist, 1979, 'Some economics plants and weeds from the Bronze Age of Cyprus' in U. Öbrink (ed.), *Hala Sultan Tekke 5: Studies in Mediterranean Archaeology*, XLV:5, Paul Åströms Förlag, Göteborg.

22 D. Namdar et al., 2013, 'Cinnamaldehyde in early Iron Age Phoenician flasks raises the possibility of Levantine trade with Southeast Asia', *Mediterranean Archaeology and Archaeometry*, 13, 2.

23 T. Popova, 2016, 'New archaeobotanical evidence for *Trigonella foenum-graecum* L. from the 4th century Serdica', *Quaternary International*.

24 D. Bedigian & J. R. Harlan, 1986, op. cit.

25 V. Zech-Matterne et al., 2015, op. cit.

26 D. Bedigian, 2010, 'History of the Cultivation and Use of Sesame' in D. Bedigian (ed.), *Sesame: The genus Sesamum*, CRC Press.

27 E. Naville & H. R. Hall, 1913, op. cit.

28 D. Namdar et al., 2013, op. cit.

29 A. Scott et al., 2020, op. cit.

30 N. Boivin & D. Fuller, 2009, op. cit.

31 D. Kučan, 1995, 'Zur Ernährung und dem Gebrauch von Pflanzen im Heraion von Samos im 7, Jahrhundert v.Chr.' *Jahrbuch des Deutschen Archäologischen Instituts*, 110.

32 www.allpoetry.com/poem/15809044.

33 A. Gilboa & D. Namdar, 2015, 'On the beginnings of South Asian spice trade with the Mediterranean region: a review', *Radiocarbon*, vol. 57, 2.

34 Herodotus, *c.* 430 BCE, *Histories*, I.183; I.198.

35 Ibid. II.86.

36 Ibid. IV.71.

37 B. P. Foley et al., 2011, 'Aspects of ancient Greek trade re-evaluated with amphora DNA evidence', *Journal of Archaeological Science*.

38 Hippocrates, fifth–fourth century BCE, *The Hippocratic Corpus*.

39 Theophrastus, fourth–third century BCE, *Enquiry into Plants*.

40 W. Dymock et al., 1891, *Pharmacographia Indica: A history of the principal drugs of vegetable origin met with in British India*, vol. 2, Kegan Paul, Trench, Trubner & Co., London.

41 R. S. Singh & A. N. Singh, 1983, 'Impact of historical studies on the nomenclature of medicinal and economic plants with particular reference to clove (Lavanga)', *Ancient Science of Life*, 2, 4.

42 C. C. Costillo et al., 2016, 'Rice, beans and trade crops on the early maritime Silk Route in Southeast Asia', *Antiquity*.

43 T. Popova, 2016, op. cit.

44 N. Boivin & D. Fuller, 2009, op. cit.

45 Strabo, *c.* 18 CE, *Geographica*, XVI, 4.19.

46 Pliny, *Natural History*, XII, 30.

47 J. Innes Miller, 1969, op. cit.
48 R. McLaughlin, 2014, *The Roman Empire and the Indian Ocean: The Ancient World Economy and the Kingdoms of Africa, Arabia and India*, Pen & Sword Military.
49 D. O. Pollmer, 2000, 'The spice trade and its importance for European expansion', *Migration & Diffusion*, vol. 1, 4.
50 P. E. McGovern et al., 2009, 'Ancient Egyptian herbal wines', *Proceedings of the National Academy of Sciences*, vol. 106, 18, www.pnas.org.cgi.doi.10.1073.pnas.0811578106.
51 P. G. van Alfen, 2002, 'Pant'Agatha commodities in Levantine–Aegean Trade during the Persian Period, 6–4th c. BC', PhD thesis, University of Texas.
52 G. Algaze, 1993, *The Uruk World System*, University of Chicago Press.
53 R. Mookerji, 1912, *Indian shipping: A history of the sea-borne trade and maritime activity of the Indians from the earliest times*, Longmans, Green and Co.
54 E. J. Chinnock (translator), 1884, *The Anabasis of Alexander or, The History of the Wars and Conquests of Alexander the Great*, Hodder and Stoughton.
55 J. H. Breasted, 1906, *Ancient Records of Egypt*, vol. 2, p. 265, University of Chicago Press.
56 F. D. P. Wicker, 1998, op. cit.
57 J. Innes Miller, 1969, op. cit.
58 Pliny, *Natural History*, XII, 42.
59 P. Frankopan, 2015, *The Silk Roads: A New History of the World*, Bloomsbury.
60 F. Rosengarten Jr, 1969, op. cit.
61 R. Chakravarti, 2012, 'Merchants, Merchandise and Merchantmen in the Western Seaboard of India: A Maritime Profile (c. 500 BCE–1500 CE)' in Om Prakash (ed.), *Trading World of the Indian Ocean, 1500–1800*, New Delhi.
62 E. H. Seland, 2014, 'Archaeology of Trade in the Western Indian Ocean, 300 BC–AD 700', *Journal of Archaeological Research*, 22.
63 R. Gurrukal, 2013, 'Classical Indo-Roman Trade: A Misnomer in Political Economy', *Economic and Political Weekly*, 48 (26).
64 Sing C. Chew, 2016, 'From the *Nanhai* to the Indian Ocean and Beyond: Southeast Asia in the Maritime "Silk" Roads of the Eurasian World Economy 200 BC–AD 500' in Andrey Korotyev, Barry Gills & Chis Chase-Dunn (eds), *Systemic Boundaries: Time Mapping Globalization since the Bronze Age*, Springer, Heidelberg.
65 Kwa Chong Guan, 2016, *The Maritime Silk Road: History of an Idea*, NSC Working Paper No. 23.

Chapter 3

1   J. Diamond, 1997, *Guns, Germs and Steel*, Chatto & Windus.
2   G. Barjamovic et al., 2019, 'Food in Ancient Mesopotamia: Cooking the Yale Babylonian Culinary Recipes' in A. Lassen et al. (eds), 2019, *Ancient Mesopotamia Speaks*, Yale Peabody: New Haven, CT.
3   E. R. Ellison, 1978, 'A study of diet in Mesopotamia (*c.* 3000–600 BC) and associated agricultural techniques and methods of food preparation', PhD thesis, University of London.
4   S. Raghavan, 2007, *Handbook of Spices, Seasonings, and Flavorings*, CRC Press.
5   Theophrastus, fourth–third century BCE, op. cit.
6   Pliny, *Natural History*, XIX, 48.
7   Ibid. XX, 46.
8   Dioscorides, *De Materia Medica*, 3.
9   J. Gerard, 1597, op. cit.
10 Thomas Dawson, 1596, *The Good Huswifes Jewell*.
11 John Murrell, 1615, *A New Book of Cookerie*; John Murrels, 1638, *Two Books of Cookerie and Carving*.
12 Gervase Markeham, 1615, *The English Huswife*.
13 Elizabeth Grey, 1653, *A Choice Manual of Rare and Select Secrets in Physick and Chyrurgery*.
14 Robert May, 1660, *The Accomplisht Cook, or the Art and Mystery of Cooking*.
15 T. P., J. P., R. C., N. B., 1674, *The English and French Cook*.
16 William Rabisha, 1661, *The Whole Body of Cookery Dissected*.
17 Hannah Wooley, 1677, *Compleat Servant-Maid*.
18 Kenelme Digby, 1669, *The Closet of the Eminently Learned Sir Kenelme Digby Kt opened*.
19 John Shirley, 1690, *The Accomplished Ladies Rich Closet of Rarities*.
20 Herodotus, *c.* 430 BCE, *Histories*, IV.71.
21 Theophrastus, fourth–third century BCE, op. cit.
22 Pliny, *Natural History*, XX, 72–3.
23 Dioscorides, *De Materia Medica*, 3.
24 P. Westland, 1987, *The Encyclopedia of Herbs & Spices*, Marshall Cavendish; www.ourherbgarden.com.
25 Apicius, *De Re Coquinaria*.
26 K. Colquhoun, 2007, *Taste: The Story of Britain through its Cooking*, Bloomsbury; M. Van der Veen, A. Livarda & A. Hill, 2008, 'New Plant Foods in Roman Britain: Dispersal and Social Access', *Environmental Archaeology*, vol. 13, 1.
27 Oribasius, *Medical Collections*.
28 A. Dalby, 2003, *Flavours of Byzantium*, Prospect Books.
29 www.ourherbgarden.com.
30 The Master Cooks of Richard II, 1390, *The Forme of Cury*.

31 S. Ims, 2012, 'Spices in Late Medieval England: Uses and Representations', thesis, Monash University.

32 MS 136. 1071, from a fifteenth-century collection called 'A Leechbook', referred to in M. Black, 1992, *The Medieval Cookbook*.

33 Syr Thomas Elyot, 1539, *The Castel of Helth*.

34 Andrew Boorde, 1542, *A Dietary of Health*.

35 J. Gerard, 1597, op. cit.

36 Numerous examples: Thomas Dawson, 1596, op. cit.; Giovanne de Rosselli, 1598, *Epulario or The Italian Banquet*; Sir Hugh Plat, 1603, *Delightes for Ladies, to adorne their Persons, Tables, Closets, and Distillatories*; Gervase Markeham, 1615, op. cit.; John Murrel, 1617, *A Daily Exercise for Ladies and Gentlewomen*; Sir Theodore Mayerne, 1658, *Excellent & Approved Receipts and Experiments in Cookery*; Robert May, 1660, op. cit.; Hannah Woolley, 1675, *The Accomplish'd Lady's Delight*.

37 K. Colquhoun, 2007, op. cit.

38 Eliza Smith, 1727, *The Compleat Housewife*, J. Pemberton, London; Hannah Glasse, 1747, *The Art of Cookery Made Plain and Easy*.

39 C. K. George, 'Asafetida' in K. V. Peter (ed.), 2012, *Handbook of herbs and spices*, vol. 3.

40 Strabo, *c.* 18 CE, *Geographica*, XV, 2.

41 Dioscorides, *De Materia Medica*, 3.

42 Ibn Sayyah al-Warraq, tenth century CE, *Kitab al-Tabikh*.

43 C. Taylor Sen, 2015, *Feasts and Fasts: A History of Food in India*, Reaktion Books.

44 Garcia de Orta, 1563, *Colloquies on the Simples and Drugs of India*.

45 M. Jaffrey, 1985, *A Taste of India*, Pavilion.

46 J. Sahni, 1987, *Classic Indian Vegetarian Cooking*, Dorling Kindersley.

47 S. Raghavan, 2007, op. cit.

48 H. Reculeau, 2017, 'Farming in ancient Mesopotamia', Oriental Institute, *News and Notes*.

49 T. Solmaz and E. Oybak Donmez, 2013, 'Archaeobotanical studies at the Urartian site of Ayanis in Van Province, eastern Turkey', *Turkish Journal of Botany*, 37.

50 Dioscorides, *De Materia Medica*, 3.

51 Pliny, *Natural History*, XIX, 49.

52 www.thecolchesterarchaeologist.co.uk.

53 P. Vandorpe, 2010, 'Plant macro remains from the 1st and 2nd Cent. A.D. in Roman Oedenburg/Biesheim-Kunheim (F). Methodological aspects and insights into local nutrition, agricultural practices, import and the natural environment', PhD thesis.

54 In Kelli C. Rudolph (ed.), 2017, *Taste and the Ancient Senses*.

55 Apicius, *De Re Coquinaria*.

56 www.daviddfriedman.com/Medieval.

57 D. P. O'Meara, 2016, 'An assessment of the cesspit deposits of Northern England: An archaeobotanical perspective', MSc thesis, Durham University.

58 S. Ims, 2012, op. cit.
59 The Master Cooks of Richard II, 1390, op. cit.
60 John Russell, 1460–70, *Boke of Nurture*.
61 William Shakespeare, 1600, *Henry IV Part 2*, Act V Scene 3.
62 John Parkinson, 1629, *Paradisi in Sole Paradisus Terrestris*.
63 Hannah Glasse, 1747, op. cit.
64 P. Westland, 1987, op. cit.
65 S. K. Malhotra, 2012, 'Chapter 15 – Caraway' in *Handbook of herbs and spices*.
66 S. Raghavan, 2007, op. cit.
67 Theophrastus, fourth–third century BCE, op. cit.
68 Dioscorides, *De Materia Medica*, 3.
69 A. Livarda & M. Van der Veen, 2008, 'Social access and dispersal of condiments in North-West Europe from the Roman to the medieval period', *Vegetation History and Archaeobotany*.
70 M. Van der Veen, A. Livarda & A. Hill, 2008, op. cit.
71 A. Hagen, 2006, *Anglo-Saxon Food & Drink*, Anglo-Saxon Books.
72 A. Davidson, 1999, *The Oxford Companion to Food*.
73 Giles Rose, 1682, *A perfect School of Instructions for the Officers of the Mouth: shewing the whole art*.
74 Antonio Targioni Tozzetti, 1850, in 'Historical notes on the introduction of various plants into the agriculture and horticulture of Tuscany', in 1855, *Journal of the Royal Horticultural Society*, London, 9.
75 John Partridge, 1588, *The Widowes Treasure*.
76 J. Gerard, 1597, op. cit.
77 Gervase Markeham, 1615, op. cit.
78 E. L. Sturtevant, 1886, *History of Celery*.
79 Olivier de Serres, 1623, *Théâtre d'agriculture*.
80 Hannah Woolley, 1675, op. cit.
81 Kenelme Digby, 1669, op. cit.
82 John Shirley, 1690, op. cit.
83 Bernard M'Mahon, 1806, *The American Gardener's Calendar*.
84 Agnes B. Marshall, 1888, *Mrs A. B. Marshall's Cookery Book*.
85 S. K. Maholtra, 'Celery' in K. V. Peter (ed.), 2012, *Handbook of herbs and spices*, vol. 3.
86 Ibid.
87 M. M. Sharma & R. K. Sharma, 'Coriander' in K. V. Peter (ed.), 2012, *Handbook of herbs and spices*, vol. 1.
88 E. Callaway, 2012, 'Soapy taste of coriander linked to genetic variants', *Nature*, News.
89 D. Zohary & M. Hopf, 1993, *Domestication of Plants in the Old World* (2nd ed.), p. 188, Clarendon Press, Oxford.
90 A. Diederichsen, 1996, 'Coriander (*Coriandrum sativum* L.): Promoting the conservation and use of underutilized and neglected crops', 3, Institute of Plant Genetics and Crop Plant Research, Gatersleben/International Plant Genetic Resources Institute, Rome.

91 E. N. Sinskaja, 1969, reported in Diederichsen, 1996.
92 R. Germer, 1989, *Die Pflanzenmaterialien aus dem Grab des Tutanchamon*, Gerstenberg Verlag.
93 E. R. Ellison, 1978, op. cit.
94 J. Chadwick, 1972, 'Life in Mycenaean Greece' in *Hunters, Farmers and Civilizations: Old World Archaeology*, Scientific American, W. H. Freeman & Co.
95 J. M. Sasson, 2004, 'The King's Table: Food and Feast in Old Babylonian Mari' in C. Grottanelli and L. Milano (eds), *Food and Identity in the Ancient World*, S.A.R.G.O.N.
96 N. F. Miller in *Archaeology of Food*, K. B. Metheny & M. C. Beaudry (eds), 2015.
97 N. Boivin et al. in *Archaeology of Food*, Ibid.
98 M. M. Sharma and R. K. Sharma, 2012, op. cit.
99 Aristophanes, 424 BCE, *The Knights*; Hippocrates, fifth–fourth century BCE, op. cit.; Columella, *De Re Rustica*, X.
100 L. Moffett in *Archaeology of Food*, K. B. Metheny & M. C. Beaudry (eds), 2015.
101 M. Robinson & E. Rowan, 2015, 'Chapter 10: Roman Food Remains in Archaeology and the Contents of a Roman Sewer at Herculaneum' in J. Wilkins & R. Nadeau (eds), *Companion to Food in the Ancient World*, John Wiley & Sons.
102 L. Lodwick, 2014, 'Agricultural innovations at a Late Iron Age oppidum: Archaeobotanical evidence for flax, food and fodder from Calleva Atrebatum, UK', *Quaternary International*.
103 M. Van der Veen, A. Livarda & A. Hill, 2008, op. cit.
104 A. Livarda & M. Van der Veen, 2008, op. cit.
105 Li, H., 1969, 'The vegetables of ancient China', *Economic Botany*, referred to in Diederichsen, 1996.
106 A. Hagen, 2006, op. cit.
107 F. J. Green, 1979, 'Medieval plant remains: methods and results of archaeobotanical analysis from excavations in southern England with especial reference to Winchester and urban settlements of the 10th–15th centuries', MPhil thesis, University of Southampton.
108 Hannah Glasse, 1747, op. cit.
109 *Daily Mail*, 2 October 2014.
110 www.npr.org/sections/thesalt/2015/03/11/392317352/is-cumin-the-most-globalized-spice-in-the-world.
111 M. E. Kislev, A. Hartmann & E. Galili, 2004, 'Archaeobotanical and archaeoentomological evidence from a well at Atlit-Yam indicates colder, more humid climate on the Israeli coast during the PPNC period', *Journal of Archaeological Science*, 31, 1301–10.
112 E. R. Ellison, 1978, op. cit.
113 S. Frumin et al., 2015, 'Studying Ancient Anthropogenic Impacts on Current Floral Biodiversity in the Southern Levant as reflected by the Philistine Migration', *Nature*.

114 F. Rosengarten Jr, 1969, op. cit.
115 www.wessexarch.co.uk/news/expert-guide-archaeobotanical-evidence-diet-saxon-period.
116 Oswald Cockayne, 1864–66, *Leechdoms, wortcunning, and starcraft of early England. Being a collection of documents, for the most part never before printed, illustrating the history of science in this country before the Norman conquest*; Carolingian Royalty, early eighth century CE, *Capitulare de villis.*
117 Gh. Amin, 'Cumin' in K. V. Peter (ed.), 2012, *Handbook of herbs and spices*, vol. 1.
118 C. Spencer, 2002, *British Food: An extraordinary thousand years of history*, Grub Street.
119 L. M. V. Totelin, 2006, op. cit.
120 Pliny, *Natural History*, XX, 57.
121 Dioscorides, *De Materia Medica*, 3.
122 J. Turner, 2004, op. cit.
123 *One Thousand and One Nights* (or *The Arabian Nights*), various ages, probably from eighth century CE.
124 S. Raghavan, 2007, op. cit.
125 C. Brombacher, 1997, op. cit.; B. Pickersgill, 'Spices' in Sir G. Prance & M. Nesbitt (eds), 2005, *The Cultural History of Plants*, Routledge.
126 *The Herb Society of America's Essential Guide to Dill.*
127 Theophrastus, fourth–third century BCE, op. cit.
128 Dioscorides, *De Materia Medica*, 1.
129 Ibid., 3.
130 Pliny, *Natural History*, XX, 74.
131 *The Herb Society of America's Essential Guide to Dill.*
132 M. Van der Veen & H. Tabinor, 'Food, fodder and fuel at Mons Porphyrites: the botanical evidence' in D. Peacock and V. Maxfield (eds), 2007, *The Roman Imperial Quarries Survey and Excavation at Mons Porphyrites, 1994–1998*, vol. 2.
133 M. Van der Veen, A. Livarda & A. Hill, 2008, op. cit.
134 A. Hagen, 2006, op. cit.
135 A. Hall, 2000, 'A brief history of plant foods in the city of York' in E. White (ed.), *Feeding a city: York: The provision of food from Roman times to the beginning of the twentieth century*, Prospect Books.
136 D. P. O'Meara, 2016, op. cit.
137 C. Spencer, 2002, op. cit.
138 John Partridge, 1588, *The Widowes Treasure.*
139 J. Gerard, 1597, op. cit.
140 Gervase Markeham, 1615, op. cit.
141 www.nyfoodmuseum.org/_ptime.htm.
142 Sir Hugh Plat, 1603, op. cit.; John Murrell, 1615, op. cit.; Robert May, 1660, op. cit; Hannah Woolley, 1664, *Cook's Guide, or Rare Receipts for Cookery.*
143 1664, *Court & Kitchin of Elizabeth, Commonly called Joan Cromwel.*

144 Hannah Woolley, 1670, *The Queen-like Closet, Or Rich Cabinet*.
145 T. P., J. P., R. C., N. B., 1674, op. cit.
146 Hannah Wooley, 1677, op. cit.; Hannah Woolley, 1675, op. cit.
147 Eliza Smith, 1727, op. cit.
148 John Collins, 1682, *Salt and Fishery: a discourse thereof*.
149 Elizabeth Grey, 1653, op. cit.
150 Eliza Smith, 1727, op. cit.
151 Hannah Woolley, 1675, op. cit.
152 John Shirley, 1690, op. cit.
153 J. Sahni, 1987, op. cit.
154 A. Davidson, 1999, op. cit.
155 E. R. Ellison, 1978, op. cit.
156 Dioscorides, *De Materia Medica*, 3.
157 Pliny, *Natural History*, XX, 95.
158 Ibid., 96.
159 M. Van der Veen & H. Tabinor, 2007, op. cit.
160 W. D. Storl, 2016, *A Curious History of Vegetables: Aphrodisiacal and Healing Properties, Folk Tales, Garden Tips, and Recipes*.
161 D. P. O'Meara, 2016, op. cit.
162 The Master Cooks of Richard II, 1390, op. cit.
163 Ariane Helou, trans., c. 1400, *An Anonymous Tuscan Cookery Book*.
164 John Murrell, 1615, op. cit.
165 John Murrell, 1617, op. cit.
166 Elizabeth Grey, 1653, op. cit.
167 Giles Rose, 1682, *A perfect school of Instructions for the Officers of the Mouth: shewing the whole art*.
168 John Shirley, 1690, op. cit.
169 Unknown, 1696, *The whole duty of a woman: or a guide to the female sex*.
170 Hannah Glasse, 1747, op. cit.
171 Theophrastus, fourth–third century BCE, op. cit.
172 Pliny, *Natural History*, XX, 44.
173 M. Van der Veen, A. Livarda & A. Hill, 2008, op. cit.
174 A. Livarda & M. Van der Veen, 2008, op. cit.
175 William Langland, 1380–90?, *The Vision of Piers Plowman*.
176 Ariane Helou, trans., c. 1400, *An Anonymous Tuscan Cookery Book*.
177 Carl Linnaeus, 1753, *Species Plantarum*.
178 Thomas Dawson, 1596, op. cit.
179 A. Davidson, 1999, op. cit.
180 Herodotus, c. 430 BCE, *Histories*, IV, 169
181 'The mystery of the lost Roman herb', BBC Future, www.bbc.com/future/article/20170907-the-mystery-of-the-lost-roman-herb.

Chapter 4

1 Hippocrates, *Diseases* III, 12, 16 (Potter, LCL).
2 Hippocrates, *Regimen in Acute Diseases*, 34.
3 Hippocrates, *Diseases of Women* I.
4 L. M. V. Totelin, 2006, op. cit.
5 Theophrastus, fourth–third century BCE, op. cit., IX, 20.
6 D. R. Bertoni, 2014, 'The Cultivation and Conceptualization of Exotic Plants in the Greek and Roman Worlds', Doctoral dissertation, Harvard University.
7 E. McDuff, 2019, 'The Potentiality of Phytoliths in the Study of Roman Spices: An Investigation into the Nature of Phytoliths in Piper nigrum and Piper longum', MA thesis, Brandeis University.
8 M. Ciaraldi, 2007, 'People and Plants in Ancient Pompeii', *Accordia Specialist Studies*, vol. 12, London.
9 Horace, *Satires* II, 4; II, 8; Horace, 2, *Satire* IV; 2, Epistle 1 to Augustus.
10 Ovid, *Ars Amatoria, or The Art of Love*, 2, H. T. Riley (translator), 1885.
11 Apicius, *De Re Coquinaria*.
12 M. Cobb, 2018, 'Black Pepper Consumption in the Roman Empire', *Journal of the Economic and Social History of the Orient*, 61 (4).
13 Pliny, *Natural History*, XII, 14.
14 Martial, *Epigrams*, 7, 27, 1865, Bohn's Classical Library, Bell & Daldy, London.
15 Martial, *Epigrams*, 13, 13.
16 Celsus, *De Medicina*.
17 Dioscorides, *De Materia Medica*, 2.
18 M. Robinson & E. Rowan, 2015, op. cit.; K. Reed & T. Leleković, 2019, 'First evidence of rice (*Oryza* cf. *sativa* L.) and black pepper (*Piper nigrum*) in Roman Mursa, Croatia', *Archaeological and Anthropological Sciences*, 11.
19 vindolanda.csad.ox.ac.uk/Search/tablet-xml-files/184.xml [Tablet 184].
20 Philostratus, *Life of Apollonius of Tyana*, III, 4.
21 F. De Romanis, 2015, 'Comparative Perspectives on the Pepper Trade' in F. De Romanis & M. Maiuro (eds), 2015, *Across the Ocean: Nine essays on Indo-Mediterranean trade*, Brill.
22 Zosimus, *Historia Nova*, 5.
23 C. Spencer, 2002, op. cit.
24 A. Hagen, 2006, op. cit.
25 P. W. Hammond, 1998, *Food and Feast in Medieval England*, Wrens Park.
26 *The household book of Dame Alice de Bryene, of Acton Hall, Suffolk, Sept 1412–Sept 1413*, Suffolk Institute of Archaeology and Natural History.
27 P. W. Hammond, 1998, op. cit.
28 J. Innes Miller, 1969, op. cit.; E. H. Warmington, 1928, *The commerce between the Roman Empire and India*.
29 Dioscorides, *De Materia Medica*, 1.
30 Pliny, *Natural History*, XII, 48.

31 J. Innes Miller, 1969, op. cit.
32 Pliny, *Natural History*, XII, 44; Dioscorides, *De Materia Medica*, 1.
33 Cosmas Indicopleustes, *The Christian Topography*, Book 11.
34 W. H. Schoff, 1912, *The Periplus of the Erythraean Sea: Travel and Trade in the Indian Ocean by a Merchant of the First Century*, Longmans, Green & Co., New York.
35 C. Ptolemy, *Geography*, VII, 2, 16.
36 Digest of Justinian, Book 39, 7.
37 Pliny, *Natural History*, XII, 42.
38 Pliny, *Natural History*, XII, 43.
39 Theophrastus, fourth–third century BCE, op. cit., IX, 1, 2.
40 Pliny, *Natural History*, XII, 19.
41 Dioscorides, *De Materia Medica*, 1.
42 A. Gismondi, A. D'Agostino, G. Di Marco, C. Martinez-Labarga, V. Leonini, O. Rickards & A. Canini, 2020, 'Back to the roots: dental calculus analysis of the first documented case of coeliac disease', *Archaeological and Anthropological Sciences*, 12, 6.
43 Arrian, *Anabasis Alexandri*, VI, 22.
44 A. Reddy, 2013, 'Looking from Arabia to India: Analysis of the Early Roman "India trade" in the Indian Ocean during the late Pre-Islamic Period (3rd century BC–6th century AD)', PhD thesis, Deccan College Postgraduate and Research Institute.
45 P. J. Cherian, 2011, *Pattanam archaeological site: The wharf context and the maritime exchanges*.
46 Pliny, *Natural History*, XII, 63.
47 Pliny, *Natural History*, XII, 26.
48 Dioscorides, *De Materia Medica*, 1.
49 Theophrastus, fourth–third century BCE, op. cit., IX, 20; Pliny, *Natural History*, XII, 14; Dioscorides, *De Materia Medica*, 2; Horace, 2, *Satire* IV; 2, Epistle 1 to Augustus; Cosmas Indicopleustes, op. cit.
50 Theophrastus, fourth–third century BCE, op. cit., IX, 20.
51 Pliny, *Natural History*, XII, 14.
52 Theophrastus, fourth–third century BCE, op. cit., Odours, 32.
53 Dioscorides, *De Materia Medica*, 1.
54 Pliny, *Natural History*, XII, 15.
55 Cosmas Indicopleustes, op. cit.
56 Dioscorides, *De Materia Medica*, 2.
57 Pliny, *Natural History*, XII, 14.
58 C. Ptolemy, *Geography*, VII, 4, 1.
59 P. Frankopan, 2015, op. cit.
60 G. K. Young, 1988, 'The long-distance "international" trade in the Roman east and its political effects 318 BC–AD 305', PhD thesis, University of Tasmania.
61 Strabo, *c.* 18 CE, *Geographica*, II, 5, 12.
62 F. De Romanis, 2015, op. cit.

63 Philostratus, *Life of Apollonius of Tyana*, Book III, ch. 4.

64 M. Cobb, 2018, op. cit.; G. K. Young, 1988, op. cit.

65 P. T. Parthasarathi, 2015, 'Roman Control and Influence on the Spice Trade Scenario of Indian Ocean World: A Re-Assessment of Evidences', *Heritage: Journal of Multidisciplinary Studies in Archaeology*, 3.

66 M. Cobb, 2015, 'The Chronology of Roman Trade in the Indian Ocean from Augustus to Early Third Century AD', *Journal of the Economic and Social History of the Orient*, 58.

67 G. K. Young, 1988, op. cit.

68 Strabo, c. 18 CE, *Geographica*, II, 3.

69 J. W. McCrindle, 1879, *The Commerce and Navigation of the Erythraean Sea: being a translation of the Periplus Maris Erythraei and Arrian's Account of the Voyage of Nearkhos*, Bombay, Calcutta, London.

70 J. Whitewright, 2018, 'The ships and shipping of Indo-Roman trade', *Journal on Hellenistic and Roman Material Culture*, vol. 6, issue 2.

71 Pliny, *Natural History*, VI, 34.

72 Ibid. VI, 26.

73 R. McLaughlin, 2014, op. cit.

74 S. Ghosh, 2014, 'Barbarikon in the Maritime Trade Network of Early India' in R. Mukherjee (ed.), *Vanguards of Globalization: Port-Cities from the Classical to the Modern*, pp. 59–74, Primus Publications, New Delhi.

75 D. Catsambis, 2012, *The Oxford Handbook of Maritime Archaeology*, pp. 518–19, quoted in R. McLaughlin, 2014, *The Roman Empire and the Indian Ocean*, Pen & Sword.

76 R. McLaughlin, 2014, op. cit.

77 Cosmas Indicopleustes, op. cit.

78 R. McLaughlin, 2014, op. cit.

79 D. Dayalan, 2018, 'Ancient seaports on the western coast of India – the hub of maritime silk route network', *Acta Via Serica*, vol. 3, 2; R. Nanji & V. D. Gogte, 2005, *A search for the Early Historic ports on the west coast of India*.

80 K. F. Dalal, E. Emanuel Mayer, R. G. Raghavan, R. Mitra-Dalat, S. Kale & A. Shinde, 2018, 'The Hippocampus of Kuda: A Mediterranean motif which validates the identification of the Indo-Roman port of Mandagora', *Journal of Indian Ocean Archaeology*, Nos 13–14.

81 D. Dayalan, 2018, op. cit.

82 Ibid.

83 Ibid.

84 A. C. Burnell, *Ind. Ant.*, vol. VII, p.40.

85 D. Dayalan, 2019, 'Ancient seaports on the eastern coast of India – the hub of the maritime silk route network', *Acta Via Serica*, vol. 4, 1.

86 Sundaresh & P. Gudigar, 1992, 'Kaveripattinam: an ancient port' in Baiderbettu Upendra Nayak et al. (eds), *New Trends in Indian Art and Archaeology*.

87 C. Ptolemy, *Geography*, VII, 1, 13.

88 R. Chakravarti, 2012, op. cit.
89 L. Casson, 1989, *The Periplus Maris Erythraei*, Princeton University Press.
90 L. Faucheux, 1945, *Une vieille cisé indienne pres de Pondichéry*, Virampatnam, Pondicherry; R. E. M. Wheeler et al., 1946, 'Arikamedu: an Indo-Roman trading station on the east coast of India', *Ancient India*, 2.
91 V. Begley, 1983, 'New investigations at the port of Arikamedu', *Journal of Roman Archaeology*, 6.
92 Pliny, *Natural History*, VI, 26.
93 *The Akananuru*, 149.
94 R. McLaughlin, 2014, op. cit.
95 D. Rathbone, 2021, 'Too much pepper? F. De Romanis, *The Indo-Roman Pepper Trade and the Muziris Papyrus*, Oxford (2020)', *Topoi*, vol. 24, 439–65.
96 F. De Romanis, 2015, op. cit.
97 W. H. Schoff, 1912, *The Periplus of the Erythraean Sea*, Longmans, Green, and Co.; A. Kumar, 2008, 'A probe to locate Kerala's early historic trade emporium of Nelcynda', *Journal of Indian Ocean Archaeology*, 5.
98 O. Bopearachichi, 2014, *Maritime Trade and Cultural Exchanges in the Indian Ocean: India and Sri Lanka*, IGNC.
99 E. H. Warmington, 1928, op. cit.
100 D. S. A. Munasinghe & D. C. V. Fernando, *Trading Relationships between Ancient Sri Lanka and Ancient Greece and Rome*, Oracle.
101 D. P. M. Weerakoddy, 1995, 'Roman coins of Sri Lanka: some observations', *The Sri Lanka Journal of the Humanities*, vol. 21, 1&2.
102 J. M. Sudharmawathei, 2017, 'Foreign trade relations in Sri Lanka in the ancient period: with special reference to the period from 6th century BC to 16th century AD', *Humanities and Social Sciences Review*, 7, 2.
103 C. Ptolemy, *Geography*, VII, 4, 1.
104 E. Kingwell-Banham et al., 2018, 'Spice and rice: pepper, cloves and everyday cereal foods at the ancient port of Mantai, Sri Lanka', *Antiquity*, 92, 366.
105 R. Chakravarti, 2012, op. cit.
106 Cai-Zhen Hong, 2016, 'A Study of Spice Trade from the Quanzhou Maritime Silk Road in Song and Yuan Dynasties', 2nd Annual International Conference on Social Science and Contemporary Humanity Development, Atlantis.
107 Capt. Drury, 1851, 'Remarks on some lately-discovered Roman Gold Coins', *Journal of the Asiatic Society of Bengal*, XX, V.
108 R. McLaughlin, 2014, op. cit.
109 Ibid.
110 F. De Romanis, 2012, 'Playing Sudoku on the Verso of the "Muziris Papyrus": Pepper, Malabathron and Tortoise Shell in the Cargo of the *Hermapollon*', *Journal of Ancient Indian History*, 27.

111 F. De Romanis, 2015, op. cit.
112 B. Fauconnier, 2012, 'Graeco-Roman merchants in the Indian Ocean: Revealing a multicultural trade', *Topoi Orient-Occident*, Suppl. 11.
113 R. McLaughlin, 2014, op. cit.
114 Pliny, *Natural History*, XII, 41.
115 Pliny, *Natural History*, VI, 26.
116 A. Wilson & A. Bowman (eds), 2017, *Trade, Commerce, and the State in the Roman World*, Oxford University Press.
117 A. M. Kotarba-Morley, 2019, 'Ancient Ports of Trade on the Red Sea Coasts – The "Parameters of Attractiveness" of Site Locations and Human Adaptations to Fluctuating Land- and Sea-Scapes. Case Study *Berenike Troglodytica*, Southeastern Egypt' in Najeeb M. A. Rasul & I. C. F. Stewart (eds), *Geological Setting, Palaeoenvironment and Archaeology of the Red Sea*, Springer.
118 T. Power, 2013, *The Red Sea from Byzantium to the Caliphate AD 500–1000*, American University in Cairo Press.
119 M. Cobb, 2015, op. cit.
120 pcma.uw.edu.pl/en/2019/04/17/berenike-2/.
121 A. Reddy, 2013, op. cit.
122 W. Z. Wendrich et al., 2003, 'Berenike Crossroads: The integration of information', *Journal of the Economic and Social History of the Orient*, 46, 1.
123 M. Cobb, 2015, op. cit.
124 J. Whitewright, 2007, 'Roman Rigging Material from the Red Sea Port of Myos Hormos', *The International Journal of Nautical Archaeology*, 36.2.
125 C. Haas, 1997, *Alexandria in Late Antiquity: Topography and Social Conflict*, John Hopkins University Press.
126 Strabo, *c.*18 CE, *Geographica*, XVII, 1.13
127 C. Taylor Sen, 2015, op. cit.; P. N. Ravindran, 2009, spicesbuds. blogspot.com/2009/05/spices-in-ancient-india.html.
128 E. McDuff, 2019, op. cit.
129 L. M. V. Totelin, 2006, op. cit.
130 Theophrastus, fourth–third century BCE, op. cit., IX, 20.
131 Pliny, *Natural History*, XII, 14.
132 M. Cobb, 2018, op. cit.
133 F. Sabban, 1985, op. cit.
134 S. Ims, 2012, op. cit.
135 The Master Cooks of Richard II, 1390, op. cit.
136 John Russell, 1460–70, op. cit.
137 Walter Bailey, 1588, *A short discourse on the three kinds of pepper in common use and certaine special medicines made of the same, tending to the preseruation of health.*
138 J. Gerard, 1597, op. cit.
139 M. Gill, 2016, 'Spices', *Indian Horizons*, vol. 63, 3.

140 J. Sahni, 1987, op. cit.
141 Dr Q. Z. Ahmad, A. U. Rahman & Tajuddin, 2017, 'Ethnobotany and therapeutic potential of kabab chini (*Piper cubeba*)', World Journal of Pharmacy and Pharmaceutical Sciences.
142 S. Ims, 2012, op. cit.
143 P. N. Ravindran, 2017, *The Encyclopedia of Herbs and Spices*.
144 John Crawfurd, 1820, *History of the Indian Archipelago*, vol. 1, Archibald Constable & Co., Edinburgh.

Table 6

145 J. F. Smith et al., 2008, op. cit.
146 I. Y. Attah, 2012, 'Characterisation and HPLC quantification of piperine in various parts of Piper Guineense', MPhil thesis, Kwame Nkrumah University, Ghana.
147 E. Besong et al., 2016, 'A Review of Piper guineense (African Black Pepper)', *Human Journals*, vol. 6, 1.
148 U. C. Srivastava & K. V. Sají, 'Under-exploited species of Piperaceae and their uses' in K. S. Krishnamurthy et al., 2008, *Piperaceae Crops – Technologies and Future Perspectives, National Seminar on Plperaceae – Harnessing Agro-technologies for Accelerated Production of Economically Important Piper Species*, Indian Institute of Spices Research, Calicut.
149 Tran Dang Xuan et al., 2008, 'Efficacy of extracting solvents to chemical components of kava (Piper methysticum) roots', *Journal of Natural Medicines*, 62.
150 V. Lebot & J. Levesque, 1989, 'The origin and distribution of kava (*Piper methysticum*, Forst. F., Piperaceae): a phytochemical approach', *Allertonia*, vol. 5, 2.
151 V. Lebot & P. Simeoni, 2004, 'Is the Quality of Kava (*Piper methysticum* Forst. f.) Responsible for Different Geographical Patterns?', *Ethnobotany Research & Applications*, 2, 19–28.
152 J. Lindley, 1838, *Flora medica*.
153 tropical.theferns.info/viewtropical.php?id=Piper+amalago.
154 B. Salehi et al., 2019, '*Piper* Species: A Comprehensive Review on Their Phytochemistry, Biological Activities and Applications', *Molecules*, 24, 7.
155 A. Baptista et al., 2019, 'Antimicrobial activity of the essential oil of *Piper amalago* L. (Piperaceae) collected in coastal Ecuador', *Pharmacology* online, vol. 3.
156 M. Avril, 2008, 'A study case on Timiz (Piper Capense)'.
157 B. Salehi et al., 2019, op. cit.
158 U. C. Srivastava & K. V. Sají, 'Under-exploited species of Piperaceae and their uses' in K. S. Krishnamurthy et al., 2008, op. cit.
159 'Piper chaba vines lucrative for Kurigram farmers', *The Daily Star*, 4 August 2017.
160 Local spice consumption can save foreign currency, www.newagebd.net, 25 December 2019.

161 B. Salehi et al., 2019, op. cit.
162 www.rain-tree.com.
163 alfredhartemink.nl.
164 M. Vann, 2012, 'Hoja Santa: a story of the sacred Mexican root beer leaf pepper plant', www.austinchronicle.com/daily/food/2012-08-24/hoja-santa/.

Chapter 5

1   H. N. Ridley, 1912, *Spices*, Macmillan & Co. Ltd, London.
2   G. Watt, 1908, *The commercial products of India*, John Murray, London.
3   A. C. Burnell, 1885, *The voyage of John Huyghen van Linschoten to the East Indies*, vol. 1, ch. 10, The Hakluyt Society, London.
4   P. A. Tiele, 1885, *The voyage of John Huyghen van Linschoten to the East Indies*, vol. 2, ch. 64, The Hakluyt Society, London.
5   K. P. Nair, 2020, *The Geography of Cardamom (Elettaria cardamomum M) The Queen of Spices*, vol. 2, Springer.
6   A. Kashyap, 2015 in K. B. Metheny & M. C. Beaudry (eds), *Archaeology of Food: An Encyclopedia*, Rowman & Littlefield; A. Kashyap & S. Weber, 2010, 'Harappan plant use revealed by starch grains from Farmana, India', *Antiquity*, 84, 326.
7   K. P. Prabhakaran Nair, 2013, *The Agronomy and Economy of Turmeric and Ginger*, Elsevier.
8   Sushruta, c. eighth century BCE, *Sushruta Samhita*, Ch. 46.
9   L. A. Lyall (translator), 1909, *The Sayings of Confucius*, Book X, 8, Longmans, Green & Co.
10 J. Innes Miller, 1969, op. cit.
11 C. Ptolemy, *Geography*, VII, 4, 1.
12 R. Strong, 2002, *Feast: A History of Grand Eating*, Jonathan Cape, London.
13 F. Rosengarten Jr, 1969, op. cit.
14 B. P. Foley et al., 2011, op. cit.
15 J. Innes Miller, 1969, op. cit.; M. Khvostov, 1907, *Researches into the history of oriental commerce in Graeco-Roman Egypt*, Kazan University.
16 Pliny, *Natural History*, XII, 14.
17 Dioscorides, *De Materia Medica*, 2.
18 E. H. Warmington, 1928, op. cit.; Sallust, *Histories*, Book IV, 72, B. Maurenbrecher (ed.), 1891 (in Latin).
19 Pliny, *Natural History*, XII, 28.
20 Ibid. XII, 29.
21 Dioscorides, *De Materia Medica*, 1.
22 E. H. Warmington, 1928, op. cit., p. 185.
23 S. Santos Braga, 2019, 'Ginger: Panacea or Consumer's Hype?', *Applied Science*, 9, 1570.
24 Apicius, *De Re Coquinaria*.
25 Hippocrates, *Epidemics* VII, 118.

26 Theophrastus, fourth–third century BCE, op. cit.
27 Celsus, *De Medicina*, III, 21; Ibid. vol. 24.
28 Dioscorides, *De Materia Medica*, 2.
29 Ibid. 1.
30 A. Gismondi et al., 2020, op. cit.
31 F. Rosengarten Jr, 1969, op. cit.
32 R. Tannahill, 1973, *Food in History*.
33 Digest of Justinian, 39, 16.7.
34 K. S. Mathew, 1983, *Portuguese trade with India in the sixteenth century*, New Delhi.
35 A. Hagen, 2006, op. cit.
36 C. Spencer, 2002, op. cit.
37 H. N. Ridley, 1912, op. cit.
38 J. Turner, 2004, op. cit.
39 A. C. Burnell, 1885, op. cit., ch. 31.
40 M. Van Der Veen, 2015, op. cit.
41 H. N. Ridley, 1912, op. cit.
42 C. Spencer, 2002, op. cit.
43 F. J. Green, 1979, op. cit.
44 W. E. Mead, 1931, *The English Medieval Feast*, George Allen & Unwin Ltd.
45 The Master Cooks of Richard II, 1390, op. cit.
46 J. O. Halliwell (ed.), 1883, *The voiage and travaile of Sir John Maundeville, kt., which treateth of the way to Hierusalem; and of marvayles of Inde, with other ilands and countryes*, rKeprinted from 1725 edition, Reeves and Turner, London.
47 Anon., 1393, *Le Ménagier de Paris*, Jerome Pichon (ed.), 1846, La Société des Bibliophiles François.
48 S. Ims, 2012, op. cit.
49 The Master Cooks of Richard II, 1390, op. cit.
50 Geoffrey Chaucer, c. 1400, *The Canterbury Tales*, General Prologue.
51 *The household book of Dame Alice de Bryene*, op. cit.
52 John Russell, 1460–70, op. cit.
53 P. W. Hammond, 1998, op. cit.
54 S. Ims, 2012, op. cit.
55 P. Freedman, 2005, 'Spices and Late-Medieval European Ideas of Scarcity and Value', *Speculum*, vol. 80, 4.
56 J. E. Thorold Rogers, 1866–1902, *A history of agriculture and prices in England*, vols 1–7, Oxford.
57 S. Halikowski Smith, 2001, 'Portugal and the European spice trade, 1480–1580', PhD thesis, European University Institute.
58 Thomas Vander Noot, c. 1510, *Een notabel boecxken van cokeryen*.
59 Sir Hugh Plat, 1603, op. cit.
60 K. Colquhoun, 2007, op. cit.
61 P. A. Tiele, 1885, op. cit., ch. 64.

62 S. Chaudhuri, 1969, 'Trade and Commercial Organisation in Bengal, with special reference to the English East India Company, 1650–1720', PhD thesis, University of London.
63 Hannah Glasse, 1747, op. cit.
64 J. E. Thorold Rogers, 1866, *A history of agriculture and prices in England*, vol. 1, Oxford.
65 John Murrel, 1617, op. cit.
66 William Shakespeare, 1598, *Love's Labours Lost*, Act V, Scene I.
67 Z. Groundes-Peace, 1971, *Mrs Groundes-Peace's Old Cookery Notebook*, David & Charles.
68 16 December 2019, abc7news.com.
69 H. N. Ridley, 1912, op. cit.
70 Juan José Ponce Vázquez, 2020, *Islanders and Empire: Smuggling and Political Defiance in Hispaniola, 1580–1690*, Cambridge University Press.
71 S. Halikowski Smith, 2001, op. cit.
72 daily.jstor.org/plant-of-the-month-turmeric.
73 P. Westland, 1987, op. cit.
74 www.indianmirror.com/ayurveda/indian-spices/cardamom.html.
75 A. Reddy, 2013, op. cit.
76 A. Hagen, 2006, op. cit.
77 J. E. Thorold Rogers, 1882, *A history of agriculture and prices in England*, vol. 4, Oxford.
78 F. Rosengarten Jr, 1969, op. cit.
79 J. Wiethold, 2007, *Exotische Gewurze aus archaologischen Ausgrabungen als Quellen zur mittelalterlichen und fruhneuzeitlichen Ernahrungsgeschichte.*
80 James Greig, 1996, 'Archaeobotanical and historical records compared – a new look at the taphonomy of edible and other useful plants from the 11th to the 18th centuries AD', *Circaea: The Journal of the Association for Environmental Archaeology*, 12 (2).
81 A. C. Zeven & J. M. J. De Wet, 1975, *Dictionary of cultivated plants and their regions of diversity.*

Chapter 6

1 P. Lape et al., 2018, 'New Data from an Open Neolithic Site in Eastern Indonesia', *Asian Perspectives*, 57, 2.
2 F. Rosengarten Jr, 1969, op. cit.
3 C. Dickson, 1996, 'Food, medicinal and other plants from the 15th century drains of Paisley Abbey, Scotland', *Vegetation History and Archaeobotany*, 5, 1–2; E. Hajnalova, 1985, 'New palaeobotanical finds from Medieval towns in Slovakia', *Slovenská Archeológia*, 33/2.
4 T. J. Zumbroich, 2005, 'The introduction of nutmeg (*Myristica Fragrans* Houtt.) and cinnamon (*Cinnamomum Verum* J.Presl) to America', *Acta Botanica Venezuelica*, 28, 1.
5 M. L. Smith, 2019, op. cit.; Pliny, *Natural History*, XII, 15.

6   E. Kingwell-Banham et al., 2018, op. cit.
7   G. Milton, 1999, op. cit.
8   John Russell, 1460–70, op. cit.
9   D. Namdar et al., 2013, op. cit.
10 Herodotus, c. 430 BCE, *Histories*, III, 111.
11 Dioscorides, *De Materia Medica*, 1.
12 F. Rosengarten Jr, 1969, op. cit.
13 Pliny, *Natural History*, XII, 42.
14 A. Hagen, 2006, op. cit.
15 F. Rosengarten Jr, 1969, op. cit.
16 J. Jacobs, 1919, 'Jewish contributions to civilization: an estimate', *The Jewish Publication Society of America*.
17 C. Spencer, 2002, op. cit.
18 *The household book of Dame Alice de Bryene*, op. cit.
19 P. A. Tiele, 1885, op. cit., ch. 63.
20 Pliny, *Natural History*, XII, 59.
21 E. G. Ravenstein, 1900, 'The Voyages of Diogo Cão and Bartholomeu Dias, 1482–88', *The Geographical Journal*, vol. 16, 6.
22 E. G. Ravenstein (ed.), 1898, *A Journal of the First Voyage of Vasco da Gama, 1497–1499*, The Hakluyt Society, London; João de Barros, 1552–63, *Décadas da Ásia: Dos feitos, que os Portuguezes fizeram no descubrimento, e conquista, dos mares, e terras do Oriente.*
23 H. E. J. Stanley (ed.), 1869, *The Three Voyages of Vasco da Gama and his Viceroyalty, from the Lendas da India of Gaspar Correa*, The Hakluyt Society, London.
24 E. G. Ravenstein (ed.), 1898, op. cit.
25 W. B. Greenlee (translator), 1938, *The Voyage of Pedro Alvares Cabral to Brazil and India*, The Hakluyt Society, London.
26 G. Correa, 1550s, 'Lendas da India', Academia Real das Sciencias de Lisboa, 1858–66.
27 H. E. J. Stanley (ed.), 1869, op. cit.
28 Ibid.
29 C. Wake, 1979, 'The changing pattern of Europe's pepper and spice imports, ca 1400–1700', *Journal of European Economic History*, vol. 8, 2.
30 P. E. Pieris, 1920, *Ceylon and the Portuguese, 1505–1658*, American Ceylon Mission Press.
31 C. R. de Silva, 1973, 'Trade in Ceylon cinnamon in the sixteenth century', *The Ceylon Journal of Historical and Social Studies*, vol. III, New Series, No. 2.
32 W. D. G. Birch (ed.), 1880, *The commentaries of the great Afonso DAlboquerque*, translated from the Portuguese edition of 1774, The Hakluyt Society, London.
33 H. E. J. Stanley, 1874, *The first voyage around the world, by Magellan*, The Hakluyt Society, London.

34 N. Pullen (translator), 1696, *Travels and voyages into Africa, Asia, and America, the East and West-Indies, Syria, Jerusalem, and the Holy-land performed by Mr. John Mocquet*, London.
35 J. Villiers, 1981, 'Trade and Society in the Banda Islands in the Sixteenth Century', *Modern Asian Studies*, vol. 15, 4.
36 M. Lobato, 1995, 'The Moluccan Archipelago and Eastern Indonesia in the Second Half of the 16th Century in the Light of Portuguese and Spanish Accounts', The Portuguese and the Pacific, International Colloquium at Santa Barbara.
37 F. C. Lane, 1940, 'The Mediterranean Spice Trade: Further Evidence of its Revival in the Sixteenth Century', *The American Historical Review*, vol. 45, 3.
38 F. Pretty, *Sir Francis Drake's Famous Voyage Round the World*.
39 Francis Fletcher (From notes of), 1652, *The World Encompassed by Sir Francis Drake*, Nicholas Bourne, London.
40 C. R. Markham (ed.), 1877, *The voyages of Sir James Lancaster to the East Indies, Narrative of the first voyage by Henry May*, The Hakluyt Society, London.
41 C. R. Markham (ed.), 1877, Ibid., 'The first voyage made to East India by Master James Lancaster', the Hakluyt Society, London.
42 B. Corney (ed.), 1855, *The Voyage of Sir Henry Middleton to Bantam and the Maluco Islands*, The Hakluyt Society, London.
43 F. C. Danvers (ed.), 1896, *Letters received by the East India Company*, vol. 1, Sampson, Low, Martson & Co., London.
44 S. Purchas, 1625, *Purchas his Pilgrimes*, vol. 3, James MacLehose and sons, Glasgow, 1905.
45 C. R. Markham (ed.), 1877, op. cit., *Commission Issued to Sir Henry Middleton*, The Hakluyt Society, London.
46 F. Rosengarten Jr, 1969, op. cit.
47 F. C. Danvers (ed.), 1896, op. cit., Document 119.
48 J. Villiers, 1990, 'One of the Especiallest Flowers in our Garden: The English Factory at Makassar, 1613–1667' in *Archipel*, vol. 39.
49 J. E. Thorold Rogers, 1866–1902, op. cit.
50 C. Wake, 1979, op. cit.

Chapter 7

1 H. K. M. Padilha & R. L. Barbieri, 2016, 'Plant breeding of chili peppers (Capsicum, Solanaceae) – A review', *Australian Journal of Basic and Applied Sciences*, 10 (15).
2 L. Perry et al., 2007, 'Starch Fossils and the Domestication and Dispersal of Chili Peppers (*Capsicum* spp L.) in the Americas', *Science*, 315.
3 L. Perry, 2015, in K. B. Metheny & M. C. Beaudry (eds), *Archaeology of Food*, Rowman & Littlefield.
4 K. H. Kraft et al., 2014, 'Multiple lines of evidence for the origin of domesticated chili pepper, *Capsicum annuum*, in Mexico', *Proceedings of the National Academy of Sciences*, 111, 17.

5   L. Perry et al., 2007, op. cit.
6   puckerbuttpeppercompany.com.
7   C. R. Markham (translator), 1893, *The Journal of Christopher Columbus (during his first voyage, 1492–93)*, The Hakluyt Society, London.
8   F. A. MacNutt (translator), 1912, *The Eight Decades of Peter Martyr D'Anghera*, vol. 1, First Decade Book 1, p.65, G. P. Putnam's Sons.
9   R. H. Major (translator), 1870, 'Letter of Dr Chanca on the second voyage of Columbus', *Select Letters of Christopher Columbus*, The Hakluyt Society, London.
10 J. Andrews, 1993, 'Diffusion of Mesoamerican Food Complex to Southeastern Europe', *Geographical Review*, vol. 83, 2.
11 S. Halikowski Smith, 2015, 'In the shadow of a pepper-centric historiography: Understanding the global diffusion of capsicums in the sixteenth and seventeenth centuries', *Journal of Ethnopharmacology* (2015), dx.doi.org/10.1016/j.jep.2014.10.048i.
12 M. Christine Daunay, H. Laterrot & J. Janick, 2008, 'Iconography and History of Solanaceae: Antiquity to the 17th century' in J. Janick (ed.), *Horticultural Reviews*, vol. 34.
13 L. Fuchs, 1543, *New kreuterbuch* (De historia stirpium 1542).
14 J. Gerard, 1597, op. cit.
15 J. Andrews, 1993, op. cit.
16 M. Preusz et al., 2015, 'Exotic Spices in Flux: Archaeobotanical Material from Medieval and Early Modern Sites of the Czech Lands (Czech Republic)', *IANSA*, vol. 1, 2.
17 M. Christine Daunay, H. Laterrot & J. Janick, 2008, op. cit.
18 E. Katz, 2009, 'Chili Pepper, from Mexico to Europe: Food, Imaginary and Cultural Identity' in *Food, Imaginaries and Cultural Frontiers: Essays in Honour of Helen Macbeth*, University of Guadalajara.
19 'The History of Chili Peppers in China', storymaps.arcgis.com/stories.
20 J. Ettenberg, 2019, 'A brief history of chili peppers', www.legalnomads.com/history-chili-peppers.
21 I. Mehta, 2017, 'Chillies – The Prime Spice – A History', *IOSR-Journal of Humanities and Social Science*.
22 J. I. Lockhart (translator), 1844, *The Memoirs of the Conquistador Bernal Díaz Del Castillo*, J. Hatchard & Son, London.
23 S. D. & M. D. Coe, 1996, *The True History of Chocolate*, Thames & Hudson.
24 Antonio Colmenero de Ledesma, 1631, *Curioso tratado de la naturalez y calidad del Chocolate*, Madrid.
25 J. O. Swahn, 1997, *The Lore of Spices*, Barnes & Noble.
26 C. C. de Guzman & R. R. Zara, 2012, 'Vanilla' in K. V. Peter (ed.), *Handbook of herbs and spices*, vol. 1, Woodhead Publishing Ltd.
27 M. Randolph, 1836, *The Virginia Housewife*, John Plaskitt, Baltimore, Internet Archive.
28 V. Linares et al., 2019, 'First evidence for vanillin in the old world: Its use as mortuary offering in Middle Bronze Canaan', *Journal of Archaeological Science*, Reports 25.

29 C. R. Markham (translator), 1893, op. cit.
30 M. Preusz et al., 2015, op. cit.
31 J. Ray, 1686, *Historia Plantarum*, London.
32 Eliza Smith, 1727, op. cit.; Hannah Glasse, 1747, op. cit.
33 E. Kay, 2014, *Dining with the Georgians*, Amberley.

Chapter 8

1   R. P. Woodward, 'Sucrose' in K. B. Metheny & M. C. Beaudry (eds), 2015, *Archaeology of Food*, Rowman & Littlefield.
2   Plants of the World Online, Kew.
3   A. H. Paterson, P. H. Moore & T. L. Tew, 'The Gene Pool of *Saccharum* Species and their improvement' in A. H. Paterson (ed.), 2013, *Genomics of the Saccharinae*, Springer.
4   M. Dams & L. Dams, 1977, 'Spanish rock art depicting honey gathering during the Mesolithic', *Nature*, 268; M. Roffet-Salque et al., 2015, 'Widespread exploitation of the honeybee by early Neolithic farmers', Open Research Exeter, *Nature*.
5   F. d'Errico et al., 2012, 'Early evidence of San material culture represented by organic artifacts from Border Cave, South Africa', *Proceedings of the National Academy of Sciences*, vol. 109, 33.
6   M. B. Hammad, 2018, 'Bees and Beekeeping in Ancient Egypt', *Journal of Association of Arab Universities for Tourism and Hospitality*.
7   Herodotus, *c.* 430 BCE, *Histories*, I, 198.
8   Pliny, *Natural History*, XI, 12
9   Ibid. XXII, 50
10 Columella, *De Re Rustica*.
11 Petronius, 54–68 CE, *Satyricon*, Ch. 56.
12 Wu Mingren, 2019, 'A Treasure in Ruins: Ancient Mehrgarh Lost to Thieves and Violence', www.ancient-origins.net.
13 M. Gros-Balthazard & J. M. Flowers, 2021, 'A Brief History of the Origin of Domesticated Date Palms' in J. M. Al-Khayri et al. (eds), *The Date Palm Genome*, vol. 1, Compendium of Plant Genomes, Springer, doi. org/10.1007/978-3-030-73746-7_3.
14 Dioscorides, *De Materia Medica*, 2; Pliny, *Natural History*, XII, 17.
15 Strabo, *c.* 18 CE, *Geographica*, XV, 1.20.
16 G. Watt, 1908, op. cit.
17 E. Rhys (ed.), 1908, *The Travels of Marco Polo*, J. M. Dent & Sons Ltd.
18 R. C. Power et al., 2019, 'Asian Crop Dispersal in Africa and Late Holocene Human Adaptation to Tropical Environments', *Journal of World Prehistory*, 32.
19 M. Van Der Veen, 'Quseir Al-Qadim (Egypt)' in K. B. Metheny & M. C. Beaudry (eds), 2015, *Archaeology of Food*.
20 J. O. Swahn, 1997, op. cit.
21 J. E. Thorold Rogers, 1866, op. cit.
22 B. K. Wheaton, 1983, *Savouring the Past*, Chatto & Windus.

23 The Master Cooks of Richard II, 1390, op. cit.
24 J. B. Thacher, 1903, *The De Torres Memorandum, Christopher Columbus, His Life, His Work, His Remains*, G. P. Putnam's Sons.
25 P. A. Tiele, 1885, op. cit., ch. 58.
26 J. Gerard, 1597, op. cit.
27 R. Strong, 2002, op. cit.
28 E. Abbott, 2009, *Sugar*, Duckworth Overlook.
29 OECD-FAO Agricultural Outlook 2020–2029.

Chapter 9

1 A. Rubio-Moraga, et al., 2009, 'Saffron is a monomorphic species as revealed by RAPD, ISSR and microsatellite analyses', BMC Research Notes, 2:189, www.biomedcentral.com/1756-0500/2/189.
2 E. R. Ellison, 1978, op. cit.
3 C. M. Hogan, 2007, *Knossos Fieldnotes*, The Modern Antiquarian.
4 P. Willard, 2002, *Secrets of Saffron: The Vagabond Life of the World's Most Seductive Spice*, Souvenir Press.
5 Apicius, *De Re Coquinaria*.
6 A. Hagen, 2006, op. cit.
7 B. L. Evans, 1995, 'Cretoyne, Cretonée' in Mary-Jo Arn (ed.), *Medieval Food and Drink*, ACTA vol. XXI.
8 P. W. Hammond, 1998, op. cit.
9 C. B. Hieatt, 1996, 'The Middle English culinary recipes in MS. Harley 5401: an edition and commentary', *Medium Ævum*, 65.
10 J. E. Thorold Rogers, 1866–1902, op. cit.
11 Celsus, *De Medicina*, Books III, IV, V, VI.
12 P. Westland, 1987, op. cit.
13 Gervase Markeham, 1615, op. cit.
14 F. Sabban, 1985, op. cit.
15 N. Culpeper, 1653, *Complete Herbal*.
16 Pliny, *Natural History*, Book XXI, 17.
17 T. Popova, 2016, op. cit.
18 Ibid.; A. K. Pokharia et al., 2011, 'Archaeobotany and archaeology at Kanmer, a Harappan site in Kachchh, Gujarat: evidence for adaptation in response to climatic variability', *Current Science*, vol. 100, 12.
19 Pliny, *Natural History*, XXIV, 120.
20 P. B. Lewicka, 2011, *Food and Foodways of Medieval Cairenes: Aspects of Life in an Islamic Metropolis of the Eastern Mediterranean*, Brill.
21 L. Zaouali, 2007, *Medieval Cuisine of the Islamic World: A Concise History with 174 Recipes*, University of California Press.
22 P. Westland, 1987, op. cit.
23 C. Ulbright, 2010, *Natural Standard Herb and Supplement Guide: an Evidence-based Reference*.
24 J. Gerard, 1597, op. cit.
25 N. Culpeper, 1653, *Complete Herbal*.

26 S. Raghaven, 2007, op. cit.
27 R. K. Kakani & M. M. Anwer, 'Chapter 16, Fenugreek' in K. V. Peter (ed.), 2012, *Handbook of herbs and spices*, vol. 1, Wiley.
28 Theophrastus, fourth–third century BCE, op. cit., Book IX, 13.
29 Pliny, *Natural History*, XXII, 11.
30 G. Markham, 1623, *Country Contentments*.
31 Eliza Smith, 1727, op. cit.
32 A. C. Wootton, 1910, *Chronicles of Pharmacy*, vol. 2, Macmillan and Co. Ltd, London.
33 A. K. Pokharia et al., 2021, 'Rice, beans and pulses at Vadnagar: an early historical site with a Buddhist monastery in Gujarat, western India', Geobios (2021), doi.org/10.1016/j.geobios.2020.12.002.
34 Pliny, *Natural History*, XII, 12.
35 F. Adams, 1847, *The Seven Books of Paulus Aegineta*, vol. 3, The Sydenham Society.
36 P. A. Tiele, 1885, op. cit., ch. 81.
37 O. B. Frenkel, 2017, 'Transplantation of Asian spices in the Spanish empire 1518–1640: entrepreneurship, empiricism, and the crown', PhD thesis, McGill University.
38 Ibid.
39 J. Whitlam et al., 2018, 'Pre-agricultural plant management in the uplands of the central Zagros: the archaeobotanical evidence from Sheikh-e Abad', *Vegetation History and Archaeobotany*, 27(6).
40 H. Saul et al., 2013, 'Phytoliths in Pottery Reveal the Use of Spice in European Prehistoric Cuisine', *Plos One*.
41 A. Mikic, 2015, 'Reminiscences of the cultivated plants early days as treasured by ancient religious traditions: the mustard crop (Brassica spp. and Sinapis spp.) in earliest Christian and Islamic texts', *Genetic Resources and Crop Evolution*, 63.
42 S. Weber, 1999, 'Seeds of urbanism: palaeoethnobotany and the Indus civilisation', *Antiquity*, 73, 813–26.
43 E. R. Ellison, 1978, op. cit.
44 T. Popova, 2016, op. cit.
45 A. Livarda & M. Van der Veen, 2008, op. cit.
46 A. Hagen, 2006, op. cit.
47 The Master Cooks of Richard II, 1390, op. cit.
48 G. Tirel, fourteenth century, 'The Viandier of Taillevent'.
49 C. D. Wright, 2011, *A History of English Food*, Random House.
50 J. Taylor, 1638, *Taylors Feast*.
51 P. Westland, 1987, op. cit.; J. Thomas et al., 2012, 'Mustard' in K. V. Peter (ed.), *Handbook of herbs and spices*, vol. 1, Woodhead.
52 J. Gerard, 1597, op. cit.
53 N. Culpeper, 1653, *Complete Herbal*.
54 P. Westland, 1987, op. cit.
55 Pliny, *Natural History*, XX, 12.

56 M. Preusz et al., 2015, op. cit.

57 J. Gerard, 1597, op. cit.

58 T. Mayerne, 1658, *Archimagirus Anglo-Gallicus*; T. P., J. P., R. C., N. B., 1674, *The English and French Cook*; Hannah Woolley, 1670, op. cit.

59 J. Cooper, 1654, *The Art of Cookery Refin'd and Augmented*.

60 Kenelme Digby, 1669, op. cit.

61 Hannah Glasse, 1747, op. cit.

62 C. P. Bryan, 1930, op. cit.

63 P. G. Kritikos & S. P. Papadaki, 1967, 'The history of the poppy and of opium and their expansion in antiquity in the Eastern Mediterranean', *Bulletin of Narcotics*, 19, 3.

64 Hippocrates, *Diseases* III, Ch. 16; Hippocrates, *Internal Affections* Ch. 12; Ibid. Ch. 40.

65 Pliny, *Natural History*, XIX Ch. 53.

66 Ibid. XX Ch. 76.

67 Celsus, *De Medicina*, II, 32.

68 Ibid. III, 10.

69 Ibid. IV, 10; IV, 14; V, 15; V, 23.

70 Ibid. VI, 6; VI, 7; VI, 9.

71 M. Robinson & E. Rowan, 2015, op. cit.

72 Athenaeus, op. cit., *Epitome* II Ch. 83.

73 G. Watt, 1908, op. cit.

74 P. A. Tiele, 1885, op. cit., Ch. 78.

75 N. Culpeper, 1653, *Complete Herbal*.

76 Hannah Glasse, 1747, op. cit.

77 D. Bedigian, 2010, op. cit.

78 M. S. Vats, 1940, 'Excavations at Harappa', Manager of Publications, Government of India, Delhi; D. Q. Fuller, 2003, op. cit.

79 Ibid.

80 M. P. Charles, 1993, 'Botanical remains' in A. Green (ed.), *Abu Salabikh Excavations: The 6G Ash-Tip and its Contents: Cultic and Administrative Discard from the Temple?* vol. 4. British School of Archaeology in Iraq, London.

81 J. W. Parry, 1955, 'The story of spices', *Economic Botany*, vol. 9, 2.

82 A. Emery-Barbier, 1990, 'L'homme et l'environnement en Egypte durant la periode pre-dynastique' in S. Bottema, G. Entjes-Nieborg & W. Van Zeist (eds), *Man's role in the shaping of the Eastern Mediterranean Landscape*, Balkema, Rotterdam.

83 Pliny, *Natural History*, VI Ch. 32.

84 Ibid. XVIII Ch. 22; XXII Ch. 64.

85 F. Adams (translator), 1847, op. cit.

86 Herodotus, c. 430 BCE, *Histories*, III, 48.

87 R. Chakravarti, 2012, op. cit.

88 Pliny, *Natural History*, XII Ch. 26.

89 Kew Online, Plants of the World.

90 J. Mulherin, 1988, *Spices & Natural Flavourings*, Ward Lock.

91 P. Westland, 1987, op. cit.
92 M. Van Der Veen, 'Quseir Al-Qadim (Egypt)' in K. B. Metheny & M. C. Beaudry (eds), 2015, *Archaeology of Food*.
93 M. Shaida, 2000, *The Legendary Cuisine of Persia*, Grub Street.
94 F. Sabban, 1985, op. cit.
95 G. Watt, 1908, op. cit.
96 P. A. Tiele, 1885, op. cit., Ch. 51.
97 Theophrastus, fourth–third century BCE, op. cit., Book III, 18, 5; Pliny, *Natural History*, XIII, 13.
98 N. Culpeper, 1653, *Complete Herbal*.
99 www.tombos.org.
100 Useful Tropical Plants, tropical.theferns.info.
101 R. Pitopang et al., 2019, 'Diversity of Zingiberaceae and traditional uses by three indigenous groups at Lore Lindu National Park, Central Sulawesi, Indonesia', IOP Conf. Series: *Journal of Physics*: Conf. Series 1242; www.perennialsolutions.org/hardy-gingers-for-the-food-forest-understory; R. Teschke & Tran Dang Xuan, 2018, 'Viewpoint: A Contributory Role of Shell Ginger (*Alpinia zerumbet*) for Human Longevity in Okinawa, Japan?', *Nutrients*, 10, 2.
102 www.indiabiodiversity.org.
103 Useful Tropical Plants, op. cit.
104 Mansfeld's world database of agricultural and horticultural crops.
105 Useful Tropical Plants, op. cit.
106 P. N. Ravindra, G. S. Pillai & M. Divakaran, 2014, 'Other herbs and spices: mango ginger to wasabi' in *Handbook of herbs and spices*, pub. online, ncbi. nlm.nih.gov; K. Anoop, 2015, 'Curcuma aromatica Salisb: a multifaceted spice', *International Journal of Phytopharmacy Research*, vol. 6, 1.
107 J. S. Butola & R. K. Vashistha, 2013, 'An overview on conservation and utilisation of *Angelica glauca* Edgew. In three Himalayan states of India', *Medicinal Plants*, 5, 3.
108 www.theepicentre.com/spice/bush-tomato_akudjura.
109 V. Anju & K. B. Rameshkumar, 2017, 'Phytochemicals and bioactivities of *Garcinia gummi-gutta* (L.) N. Robson – A review', *Diversity of Garcinia species in the Western Ghats: Phytochemical Perspective*.
110 newagebd.net.
111 Sanchari Pal, 2016, 'Food secrets: 14 unusual Indian spices you're probably not using but definitely should try', thebetterindia.com.
112 www.thespruceeats.com/dried-lily-buds-695013.
113 www.thespicehouse.com.
114 A. O. Tairu et al., 1999, 'Identification of the Key Aroma Compounds in Dried Fruits of Xylopia aethiopica' in J. Janick (ed.), *Perspectives on New Crops and New Uses*, ASHS Press, Alexandria, VA.
115 J. E. Laferrière, 1990, 'Nutritional and pharmacological properties of yerbaníz, epazote, and Mountain Pima oregano', *Seedhead News* No. 29. *Native Seeds*.
116 J. O. Swahn, 1997, op. cit.

Chapter 10

1   A. C. Wootton, 1910, op. cit.
2   J. R. Coxe, 1846, *The Writings of Hippocrates and Galen*, Lindsay and Blakiston, Philadelphia.
3   A. C. Wootton, 1910, op. cit.
4   Hieronymus Frascatorius, 1546, *De Contagione et Contagiosis Morbis*.
5   F. Adams, 1847, op. cit. Book VII, 8.
6   *British Medical Journal* Correspondence, 19 August 1911.
7   A. C. Wootton, 1910, op. cit.
8   Ibid.
9   M. Jaafar, R. Vafamansouri, M. Tareen, D. Kamel, V. C. Ayroso, F. Tareen and A. I. Spielman, 2021, 'Quackery, Claims and Cures: Elixirs of the Past – Snake Oil and Indian Liniment', www.researchgate.net/publication/353417368.
10   W. L. Applequist & D. E. Moerman, 2011, 'Yarrow (*Achillea millefolium* L.): A Neglected Panacea? A Review of Ethnobotany, Bioactivity, and Biomedical Research', *Economic Botany*, 65, 2.
11   K. Hardy et al., 2012, 'Neanderthal medics? Evidence for food, cooking, and medicinal plants entrapped in dental calculus', *Naturwissenschaften*, DOI 10.1007/s00114-012-0942-0, Springer-Verlag.
12   C. D. Leake, 1952, *The Old Egyptian Medical Papyri*, University of Kansas Press.
13   N. H. Aboelsoud, 2010, 'Herbal medicine in ancient Egypt', *Journal of Medicinal Plants Research*, vol. 4 (2).
14   N. Boivin & D. Fuller, 2009, op. cit.
15   E. G. Cuthbert F. Atchley, 1909, *A History of the Use of Incense in Divine Worship*, Longmans, Green & Co.
16   Herodotus, *c.* 430 BCE, *Histories*, II, 40.
17   E. G. Cuthbert F. Atchley, 1909, op. cit.
18   Homer, eighth century BCE, *The Iliad*, Book XIV.
19   E. G. Cuthbert F. Atchley, 1909, op. cit.
20   *Papyri Graecae Magicae*, Internet Archive.
21   '7 "magic potions" grown by medieval monks', English Heritage blog (english-heritage.org.uk).
22   Theophrastus, fourth–third century BCE, op. cit. IX, 9, 3.
23   Pliny, *Natural History*, XXII, 9.
24   J. Gerard, 1597, op. cit.
25   A. M. Downham Moore & R. Pithavadian, 2021, 'Aphrodisiacs in the global history of medical thought', *Journal of Global History*, 16, 1.
26   R. Burton (translator), 1883, *The Kama Sutra of Vatsyayana*, VI, Ch. 1.
27   Ibid. VII Ch. 1.
28   F. F. Arbuthnot & R. Burton (translators), 1885, *Ananga-Ranga*, Kama Shastra Society of London and Benares, Cosmopoli.

29 Ibid. Ch. VI.
30 'The Origin of Ambergris' (uchicago.edu).
31 S. D. & M. D. Coe, 1996, op. cit.
32 A. M. Downham Moore & R. Pithavadian, 2021, op. cit.

Chapter 11

1 cosylab.iiitd.edu.in/recipedb; cosylab.iiitd.edu.in/flavordb;
    S. E. Ahnert, 2013, 'Network analysis and data mining in food science:
    the emergence of computational gastronomy', *Flavour*, 2:4; A. Jain,
    N. K. Rakhi, G. Bagler, 2015, *Analysis of Food Pairing in Regional
    Cuisines of India*, Plos One, doi.org/10.1371/journal.pone.0139539.
2 S. E. Kintzios, 'Oregano' in *Handbook of herbs and spices*, vol. 2.

Bibliography

Adams, F., (translator), 1844, *The Seven Books of Paulus Aegineta*, The Sydenham Society, London

Apicius, *De Re Coquinaria*

Andrews, J., 1993, 'Diffusion of Mesoamerican Food Complex to Southeastern Europe', *Geographical Review*, vol. 83, No. 2

Arbuthnot, F. F. & Burton, R., (translators), 1885, *Ananga-Ranga*, Kama Shastra Society of London and Benares, Cosmopoli

Atchley, E. G. Cuthbert F., 1909, *A History of the Use of Incense in Divine Worship*, Longmans, Green & Co.

Barjamovic, G. et al., 2019, 'Food in Ancient Mesopotamia: Cooking the Yale Babylonian Culinary Recipes' in A. Lassen et al. (eds), 2019, *Ancient Mesopotamia Speaks*, Yale Peabody: New Haven, CT

Bedigian, D., 2010, 'History of the Cultivation and Use of Sesame', in D. Bedigian (ed.), *Sesame: The genus Sesamum*, CRC Press

Bedigian, D. & Harlan, J. R., 1986, 'Evidence for cultivation of sesame in the ancient world', *Economic Botany*, 40

Birch, W. D. G. (ed.), 1880, *The commentaries of the great Afonso DAlboquerque*, translated from the Portuguese edition of 1774, The Hakluyt Society, London

Boivin, N. & Fuller, D., 2009, 'Shell Middens, Ships and Seeds: Exploring Coastal Subsistence, Maritime Trade and the Dispersal of Domesticates in and Around the Ancient Arabian Peninsula', *Journal of World Prehistory*, 22

Breasted, J. H., 1906, *Ancient Records of Egypt*, vol. 2, p.265, University of Chicago Press

Bryan, C. P., 1930, *The Papyrus Ebers*, G. Bles, London

Burnell, A. C., 1885, *The voyage of John Huyghen van Linschoten to the East Indies*, vol. 1, The Hakluyt Society, London

Burton, R. (translator), 1883, *The Kama Sutra of Vatsyayana*, VI, Ch. 1

Casson, L., 1989, *The Periplus Maris Erythraei*, Princeton University Press

Celsus, *De Medicina*

Chakravarti, R., 2012, 'Merchants, Merchandise and Merchantmen in the Western Seaboard of India: A Maritime Profile (*c.* 500 BCE–1500 CE)' in Prakash, Om (ed.), *Trading World of the Indian Ocean, 1500–1800*, New Delhi

Chinnock, E. J. (translator), 1884, *The Anabasis of Alexander or, The History of the Wars and Conquests of Alexander the Great*, Hodder and Stoughton

Cobb, M., 2018, 'Black Pepper Consumption in the Roman Empire', *Journal of the Economic and Social History of the Orient*, 61 (4)

Coe, S. D. & M. D., 1996, *The True History of Chocolate*, Thames & Hudson

Colquhoun, K., 2007, *Taste: The Story of Britain through its Cooking*, Bloomsbury

Columella, *De Re Rustica*, X

Corney, B. (ed.), 1855, *The Voyage of Sir Henry Middleton to Bantam and the Maluco Islands*, The Hakluyt Society, London

Culpeper, N., 1653, *Complete Herbal*

Danvers, F. C. (ed.), 1896, *Letters received by the East India Company*, vol. 1, Sampson, Low, Martson & Co., London

Daunay, M. Christine, Laterrot, H. & Janick, J., 2008, 'Iconography and History of Solanaceae: Antiquity to the 17th Century' in Janick, J. (ed.), *Horticultural Reviews*, vol. 34

Davidson, A., 1999, *The Oxford Companion to Food*

Dawson, Thomas, 1596, *The Good Huswifes Jewell*

Dayalan, D., 2018, 'Ancient seaports on the western coast of India: the hub of maritime silk route network', *Acta Via Serica*, vol. 3, 2

De Romanis, F., 2012, 'Playing Sudoku on the Verso of the "Muziris Papyrus": Pepper, Malabathron and Tortoise Shell in the Cargo of the *Hermapollon*', *Journal of Ancient Indian History*, 27

De Romanis, F., 2015, 'Comparitive Perspectives on the Pepper Trade' in De Romanis, F. & Maiuro. M. (eds), 2015, *Across the Ocean: Nine essays on Indo-Mediterranean trade*, Brill

Diamond, J., 1997, *Guns, Germs and Steel*, Chatto & Windus

Digby, Kenelme, 1669, *The Closet of the Eminently Learned Sir Kenelme Digby Kt opened*

Digest of Justinian, Book 39, 7

Dioscorides, *De Materia Medica*

Downham Moore, A. M. & Pithavadian, R., 2021, 'Aphrodisiacs in the global history of medical thought', *Journal of Global History*, 16, 1

Edwards, A. B., 1891, *Pharaohs Fellahs and Explorers*, Harper & Bros, New York

Ellison, E. R., 1978, 'A study of diet in Mesopotamia (*c.* 3000–600 BC) and associated agricultural techniques and methods of food preparation', PhD thesis, University of London

Fletcher, Francis (From notes of), 1652, *The World Encompassed by Sir Francis Drake*, Nicholas Bourne, London

Foley, B. P. et al., 2011, 'Aspects of ancient Greek trade re-evaluated with amphora DNA evidence', *Journal of Archaeological Science*

Frankopan, P., 2015, *The Silk Roads: A New History of the World*, Bloomsbury

Fuchs, L., 1543, *New kreuterbuch* (De historia stirpium 1542)

Fuller, D. Q., 2003, 'Further evidence on the prehistory of sesame', *Asian Agri-History*, vol. 7, 2

Gerard, J., 1597, *The Herball, or Generall Historie of Plantes*, John Norton, London

Gilboa, A. & Namdar, D., 2015, 'On the beginnings of South Asian spice trade with the Mediterranean region: a review', *Radiocarbon*, vol. 57, 2

Glasse, Hannah, 1747, *The Art of Cookery Made Plain and Easy*

Glenister, C. L., 2008, 'Profiling Punt: using trade relations to locate "God's Land"', M.Phil. thesis, University of Stellenbosch

Greenlee, W. B. (translator), 1938, *The Voyage of Pedro Alvares Cabral to Brazil and India*, The Hakluyt Society, London

Grey, Elizabeth, 1653, *A Choice Manual of Rare and Select Secrets in Physick and Chyrurgery*

Hagen, A., 2006, *Anglo-Saxon Food & Drink*, Anglo-Saxon Books

Hammond, P. W., 1998, *Food and Feast in Medieval England*, Wrens Park

Herodotus, c. 430 BCE, *Histories*

Hippocrates, fifth–fourth century BCE, *The Hippocratic Corpus*

The household book of Dame Alice de Bryene, of Acton Hall, Suffolk, Sept 1412–Sept 1413, Suffolk Institute of Archaeology and Natural History

Ims, S., 2012, 'Spices in Late Medieval England Uses and Representations', thesis, Monash University

Kraft, K. H. et al., 2014, 'Multiple lines of evidence for the origin of domesticated chili pepper, *Capsicum annuum*, in Mexico', *Proceedings of the National Academy of Sciences*, 111, 17

Kwa Chong Guan, 2016, *The Maritime Silk Road: History of an Idea*, NSC Working Paper No. 23

Lane, F. C., 1940, 'The Mediterranean Spice Trade: Further Evidence of its Revival in the Sixteenth Century', *The American Historical Review*, vol. 45, 3

Leake, C. D., 1952, *The Old Egyptian Medical Papyri*, University of Kansas Press

Livarda, A. & Van der Veen, M., 2008, 'Social access and dispersal of condiments in North-West Europe from the Roman to the medieval period', *Vegetation History & Archaeobotany*

Lobato, M., 1995, 'The Moluccan Archipelago and Eastern Indonesia in the Second Half of the 16th century in the Light of Portuguese and Spanish Accounts', The Portuguese and the Pacific, International Colloquium at Santa Barbara

Lockhart, J. I. (translator), 1844, *The Memoirs of the Conquistador Bernal Díaz Del Castillo*, J. Hatchard & Son, London

MacNutt, F. A. (translator), 1912, *The Eight Decades of Peter Martyr D'Anghera*, vol. 1, G. P. Putnam's Sons

Major, R. H. (translator), 1870, 'Letter of Dr Chanca on the second voyage of Columbus', *Select Letters of Christopher Columbus*, The Hakluyt Society, London

Markeham, Gervase, 1615, *The English Huswife*

Markham, C. R. (ed.), 1877, *The Voyages of Sir James Lancaster to the East Indies*, The Hakluyt Society, London

Markham, C. R. (translator), 1893, *The Journal of Christopher Columbus (during his first voyage, 1492–93)*, The Hakluyt Society, London

Martial, *Epigrams*

The Master Cooks of Richard II, 1390, *The Forme of Cury*

May, Robert, 1660, *The Accomplisht Cook, or the Art and Mystery of Cooking*

McCrindle, J. W., 1877, *Ancient India as Described by Megasthenes and Arrian*, Trubner

McCrindle, J. W., 1885, *Ancient India as Described by Ptolemy*, Trubner

McCrindle, J. W., 1897, *The Christian Topography of Cosmas, an Egyptian Monk*, Hakluyt Society

McLaughlin, R., 2014, *The Roman Empire and the Indian Ocean: The Ancient World Economy and the Kingdoms of Africa, Arabia and India*, Pen & Sword Military

Miller, J. Innes, 1969, *The spice trade of the Roman Empire 29 BC to AD 641*, Oxford University Press

Murrell, John, 1615, *A New Book of Cookerie*

Murrel, John, 1617, *A Daily Exercise for Ladies and Gentlewomen*

'The mystery of the lost Roman herb', BBC Future, www.bbc.com/future/article/20170907-the-mystery-of-the-lost-roman-herb

Namdar, D. et al., 2013, 'Cinnamaldehyde in early Iron Age Phoenician flasks raises the possibility of Levantine trade with Southeast Asia', *Mediterranean Archaeology and Archaeometry*, 13, 2

Naville, E. & Hall, H. R., 1913, 'The XIth Dynasty Temple at Deir El-Bahari Part III', 32nd Memoir of the Egypt Exploration Fund, London

O'Meara, D. P., 2016, 'An assessment of the cesspit deposits of Northern England: An archaeobotanical perspective', MSc thesis, Durham University

One Thousand and One Nights (or *The Arabian Nights*), various ages, probably from eighth century CE

Osbaldeston, T. A. and Wood, R. P. A., 2000, Dioscorides, *De Materia Medica*, a new indexed version in modern English, Ibidis

The *Periplus Maris Erythraei*

Perry, L. et al., 2007, 'Starch Fossils and the Domestication and Dispersal of Chili Peppers (*Capsicum* spp L.) in the Americas', *Science*, 315

Peter, K. V. (ed.), 2001–06, *Handbook of Herbs and Spices*, vols 1–3, Woodhead Publishing Ltd

Plat, Sir Hugh, 1603, *Delightes for Ladies, to adorne their Persons, Tables, Closets, and Distillatories*

Pliny, *Natural History*

Popova, T., 2016, 'New archaeobotanical evidence for *Trigonella foenum-graecum* L. from the 4th century Serdica', *Quaternary International*

Pretty, F., *Sir Francis Drake's Famous Voyage Round the World*

Ptolemy, C., *Geography*

Pullen, N. (translator), 1696, *Travels and voyages into Africa, Asia, and America, the East and West-Indies, Syria, Jerusalem, and the Holy-land performed by Mr John Mocquet*, London

Raghavan, S., 2007, *Handbook of Spices, Seasonings, and Flavorings*, CRC Press

Ravenstein, E. G. (ed.), 1898, *A Journal of the First Voyage of Vasco da Gama, 1497–1499*, The Hakluyt Society, London

Ravenstein, E. G., 1900, 'The Voyages of Diogo Cão and Bartholomeu Dias, 1482–88', *The Geographical Journal*, vol. 16, 6

Reddy, A., 2013, 'Looking from Arabia to India: Analysis of the Early Roman 'India trade' in the Indian Ocean during the late Pre-Islamic Period (3rd century BC – 6th century AD)', PhD thesis, Deccan College Postgraduate and Research Institute

Robinson, M. & Rowan, E., 2015, 'Chapter 10: Roman Food Remains in Archaeology and the Contents of a Roman Sewer at Herculaneum' in Wilkins, J. & Nadeau, R. (eds), *Companion to Food in the Ancient World*, John Wiley & Sons

Rosengarten, F. Jr, 1969, *The Book of Spices*, pp. 23–96, Jove Publ., Inc., New York

Russell, John, 1460–70, *Boke of Nurture*

Sabban, F., 1985, 'Court cuisine in fourteenth-century imperial China: Some culinary aspects of Hu Sihui's Yinshan Zhengyao', *Food and Foodways: Explorations in the History and Culture of Human Nourishment*, 1:1–2, 161–96, DOI: 10.1080/07409710.1985.9961883

Schoff, W. H., 1912, *The Periplus of the Erythraean Sea*, Longmans, Green, and Co.

Scott, A. et al., 2020, 'Exotic foods reveal contact between South Asia and the Near East during the second millennium BCE', www.pnas.org/cgi/doi/10.1073/pnas.2014956117

Shirley, John, 1690, *The Accomplished Ladies Rich Closet of Rarities*

Sing C. Chew, 2016, 'From the *Nanhai* to the Indian Ocean and Beyond: Southeast Asia in the Maritime "Silk" Roads of the Eurasian World Economy 200 BC–AD 500' in Korotyev, Andrey, Gills, Barry & Chase-Dunn, Chis (eds), *Systemic Boundaries: Time Mapping Globalization since the Bronze Age*, Heidelberg, Springer

Smith, Eliza, 1727, *The Compleat Housewife*, J. Pemberton, London

Smith, J. F. et al., 2008, 'Placing the origin of two species-rich genera in the Late Cretaceous with later species divergence in the Tertiary: a phylogenetic, biogeographic and molecular dating analysis of *Piper* and *Peperomia* (Piperaceae)', *Plant Systematics and Evolution*, 275

Smith, S. Halikowski, 2001, 'Portugal and the European spice trade, 1480–1580', PhD thesis, European University Institute

Smith, S. Halikowski, 2015, 'In the shadow of a pepper-centric historiography: Understanding the global diffusion of capsicums in the sixteenth and seventeenth centuries', *Journal of Ethnopharmacology*, dx.doi.org/10.1016/j.jep.2014.10.048i

Spencer, C., 2002, *British Food: An extraordinary thousand years of history*, Grub Street

Stanley, H. E. J. (ed.), 1869, *The Three Voyages of Vasco da Gama and his Viceroyalty, from the Lendas da India of Gaspar Correa*, The Hakluyt Society, London

Stanley, H. E. J., 1874, *The first voyage around the world, by Magellan*, The Hakluyt Society, London

Strabo, c. 18 CE, *Geographica*

Sushruta, c. eighth century BCE, *Sushruta Samhita*

Swahn, J. O., 1997, *The Lore of Spices*, Barnes & Noble

Theophrastus, fourth–third century BCE, *Enquiry into Plants*

Thorold Rogers, J. E., 1866–1902, *A history of agriculture and prices in England*, vols 1–7, Oxford

Tiele, P. A., 1885, *The voyage of John Huyghen van Linschoten to the East Indies*, vol. 2, The Hakluyt Society, London

Totelin, L. M. V., 2006, 'Hippocratic recipes: oral and written transmission of pharmacological knowledge in fifth- and fourth-century Greece', Doctoral thesis, University of London

Turner, J., 2004, *Spice: The History of a Temptation*, HarperCollins

Van der Veen, M., Livarda, A. & Hill, A., 2008, 'New Plant Foods in Roman Britain: Dispersal and Social Access', *Environmental Archaeology*, vol. 13, 1

Wake, C., 1979, 'The changing pattern of Europe's pepper and spice imports, ca 1400–1700', *Journal of European Economic History*, vol. 8, 2

Warmington, E. H., 1928, *The commerce between the Roman Empire and India*

Watt, G., 1908, *The commercial products of India*, John Murray, London

Westland, P., 1987, *The Encyclopedia of Herbs & Spices*, Marshall Cavendish

Whitewright, J., 2007, 'Roman Rigging Material from the Red Sea Port of Myos Hormos', *The International Journal of Nautical Archaeology*, 36.2

Wicker, F. D. P., 1998, 'The Road to Punt', *The Geographical Journal*, vol. 164, 2

Woolley, Hannah, 1675, *The Accomplish'd Lady's Delight*

Wootton, A. C., 1910, *Chronicles of Pharmacy*, Macmillan and Co. Ltd, London

Young, G. K., 1988, 'The long-distance "international" trade in the Roman east and its political effects 318 BC–AD 305', PhD thesis, University of Tasmania

Zech-Matterne, V. et al., 2015, '*Sesamum indicum* L. (sesame) in 2nd century BC Pompeii, southwest Italy, and a review of early sesame finds in Asia and Europe', *Vegetation History and Archaeobotany*, 24

Zosimus, *Historia Nova*, 5

Index

Bede 81, 105, 139, 152, 162, 235
beehive ginger 253
benzoin 265–6
berbere 63, 138, 142, 234, 275, 280
Berenike 59, 104, 109–10, 113, 123, 129, 131–2
betel nut (areca) 133, 138, 179, 270
black galangal 147
black hellebore 23, 100
black lime 16, 249–50
black pepper 7, 9, 14, 21, 22–5, 29, 35, 40, 42, 44, 48–9, 51–3, 72, 77, 81, 83–4, 88, 97, 99–143, 149–53, 155–6, 158, 160, 164, 169, 178–9, 184, 187, 194, 196–200, 202–3, 209–10, 217, 223, 242, 250–1, 255, 257, 260, 263, 267, 269–70, 272–7, 280, 282
black stone flower 257, 273
black turmeric 254
borage 9, 35, 39
Bryene, Dame Alice de 156, 173, 240
Byzantium 119, 125–7, 203

Cabral, Pedro Alvares 181–4
cacao 16, 215, 271
calamus 33, 40, 54, 106, 266
Calicut 160, 179–80, 182–6, 188
camphor 14, 22, 27, 35, 42, 48, 50, 173, 261–3, 269–70
candlenut 16
Cannanore 128, 183–6
caper 14, 32, 65, 100, 257, 276
capsaicin 207–8
Capsicum 14–15, 18, 205–8, 212–13, 217, 263, 277
caraway 15, 20, 35, 63, 66, 71–4, 86, 88, 92, 260, 262, 275
cardamom 14, 23–5, 29, 33, 35, 42, 48–9, 51–3, 108, 125, 133–4, 146–53, 155, 158, 160–4, 254–5, 261, 263, 272–3, 275–6, 281
cardamom leaf ginger 254
Caribbean 13, 173, 206, 217, 220, 224–6, 237, 281
Casa da India 187

cassia 14, 21, 24–5, 29, 32–3, 35, 40, 52–3, 107, 134, 152, 170–2, 174, 180, 265–7, 273–5
Castor, Antonius 30
celeriac 11
celery 11, 15, 35, 39, 64, 67, 74–8, 86, 94–5, 97, 276
Celsus, Aulus Cornelius 29, 30, 102, 151, 232–3, 235, 244, 248
Ceylon 22, 107, 188–9, 196, 200, 203
charoli 16, 22
chat masala, chaat masala 63, 272
chenpi 16
chervil 32, 35, 87, 276
chili 8, 14, 18, 43, 69, 138, 148, 205–10, 212–15, 217, 250–1, 269, 272–7, 280, 282
Chinese keys 15, 147, 255
choru 256
chui jhal pepper 15, 135, 142
cinnamon 14, 24–5, 27, 29, 35, 39, 42, 48–54, 56–7, 66, 84, 88, 106–8, 125, 134, 152–5, 160, 167, 170–4, 177, 179, 184, 188–9, 191, 196, 200, 202–3, 209, 215, 217, 239, 260–1, 263–7, 269, 272–5, 280
Cinnamon Route 49, 57
citron 22, 49, 250
cloves 8, 14, 49, 53, 60, 66, 77, 88, 109, 118, 125, 142, 153–5, 160, 163, 167, 169–70, 177–9, 191, 193–203, 217, 261–2, 272–7, 280–1
cochineal 261
Coelho, Nicolau 177–8, 180–1
Columbus, Christopher 8, 43, 209–12, 217, 224
Columella 32, 80, 221, 233, 276
comfrey 35
Constantine the African 153, 269
coriander 10, 12, 14, 20–1, 23, 25, 29, 32, 35, 39, 42, 49, 61–3, 72, 79–82, 92, 132, 245, 256, 262, 264, 272–5, 277, 280–1
Cosmas Indicopleustes 39–40, 106, 108–9, 126
costum 33, 54, 109, 134, 267

The destination for history
www.thehistorypress.co.uk